D0826427

WELCOME no.1 | TOMO TAKEUCHI
to the BALLROOM

WITHDRAWN

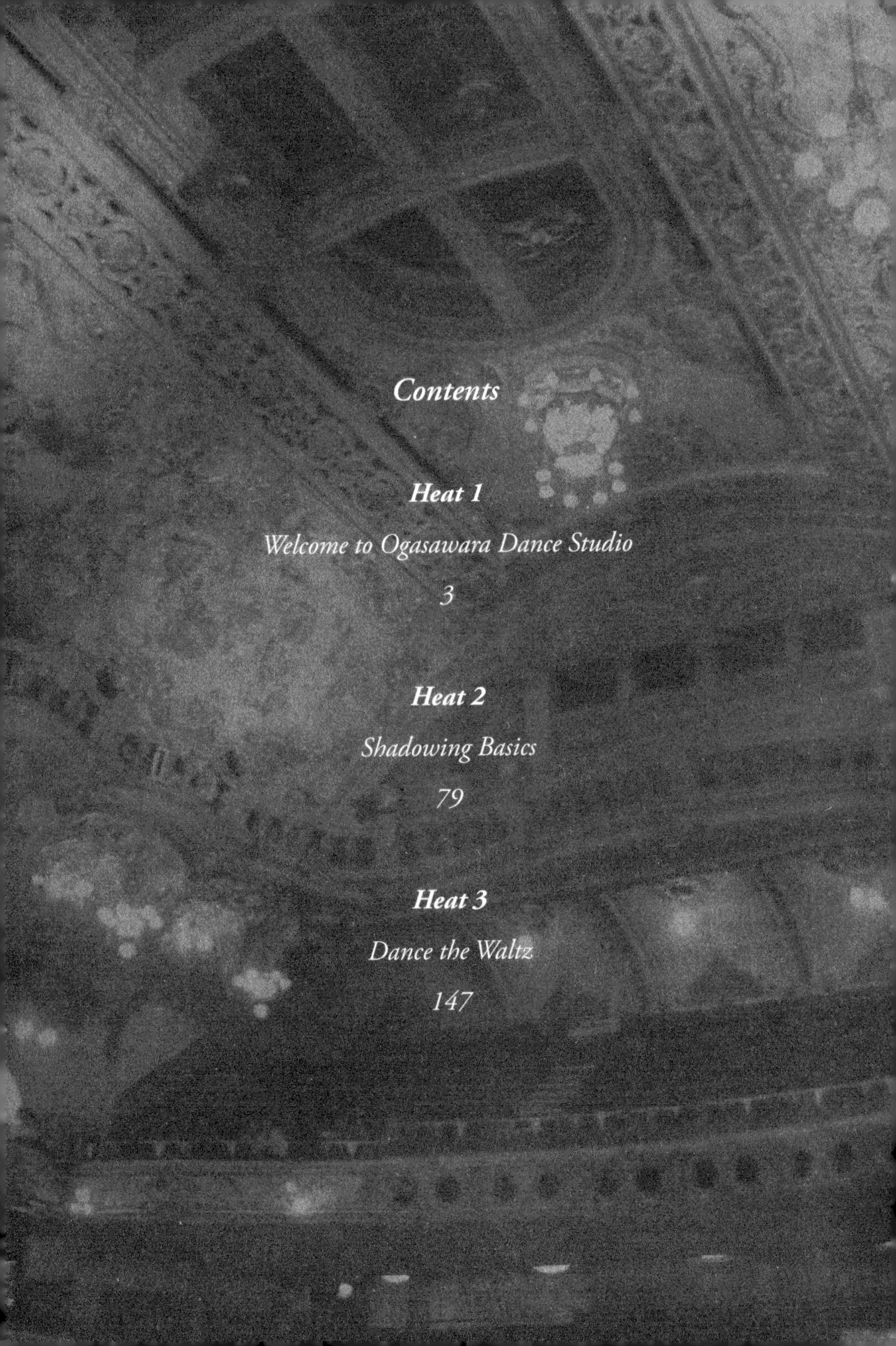

Contents

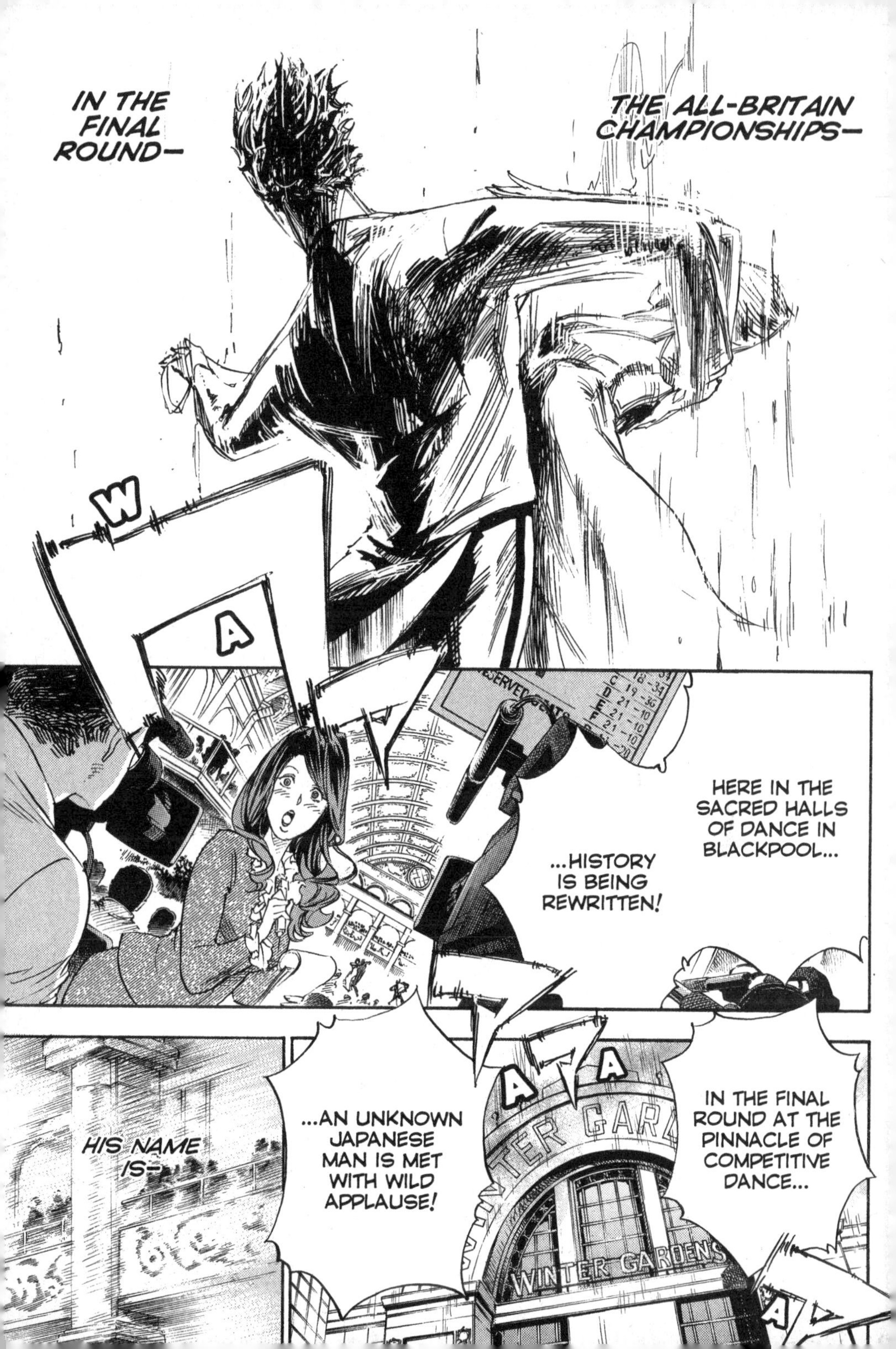
THE ALL-BRITAIN CHAMPIONSHIPS—
IN THE FINAL ROUND—
W
A
HERE IN THE SACRED HALLS OF DANCE IN BLACKPOOL...
...HISTORY IS BEING REWRITTEN!
A
A
IN THE FINAL ROUND AT THE PINNACLE OF COMPETITIVE DANCE...
WINTER GARDENS
A
...AN UNKNOWN JAPANESE MAN IS MET WITH WILD APPLAUSE!
HIS NAME IS—

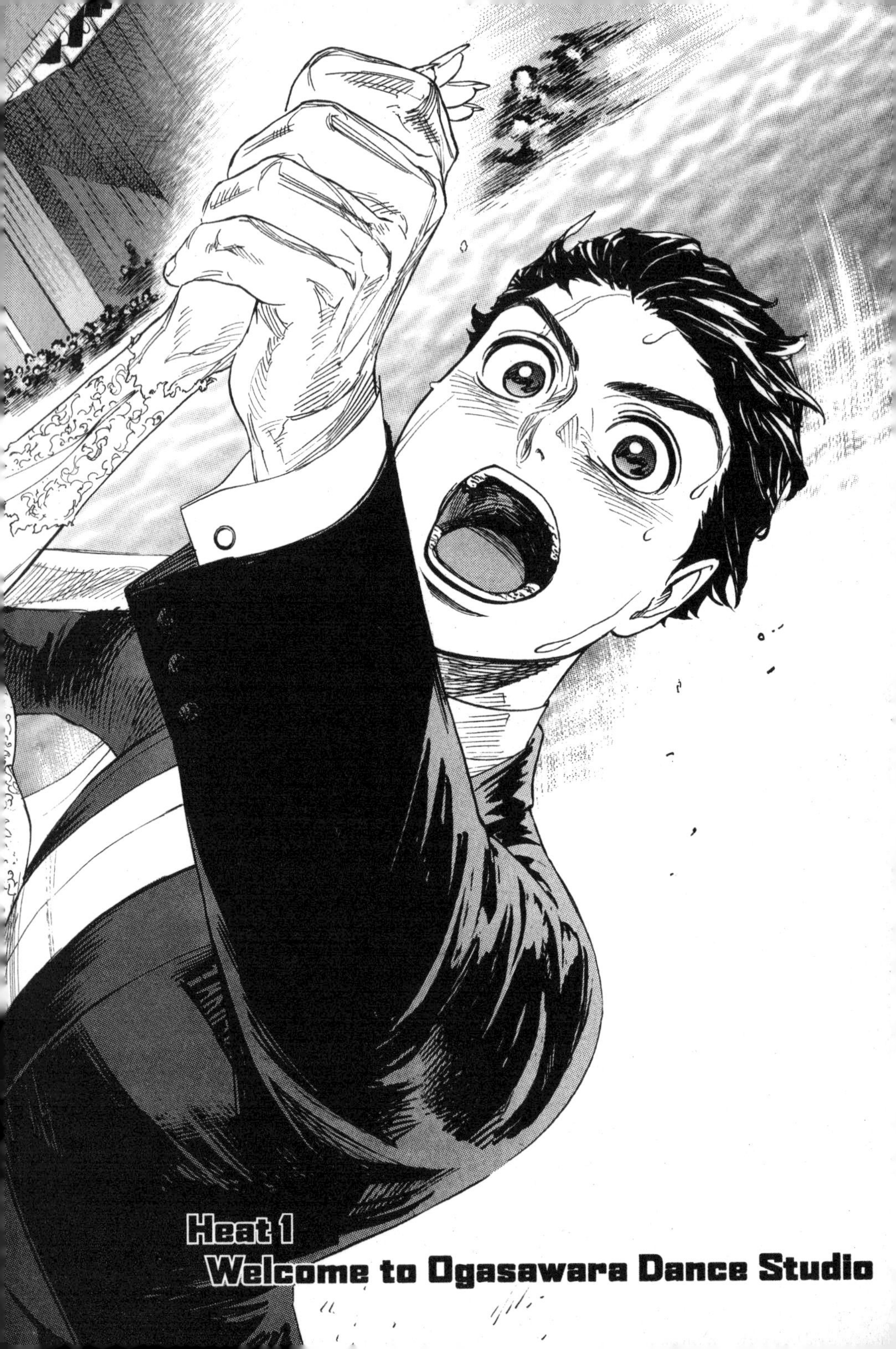

Heat 1
Welcome to Ogasawara Dance Studio

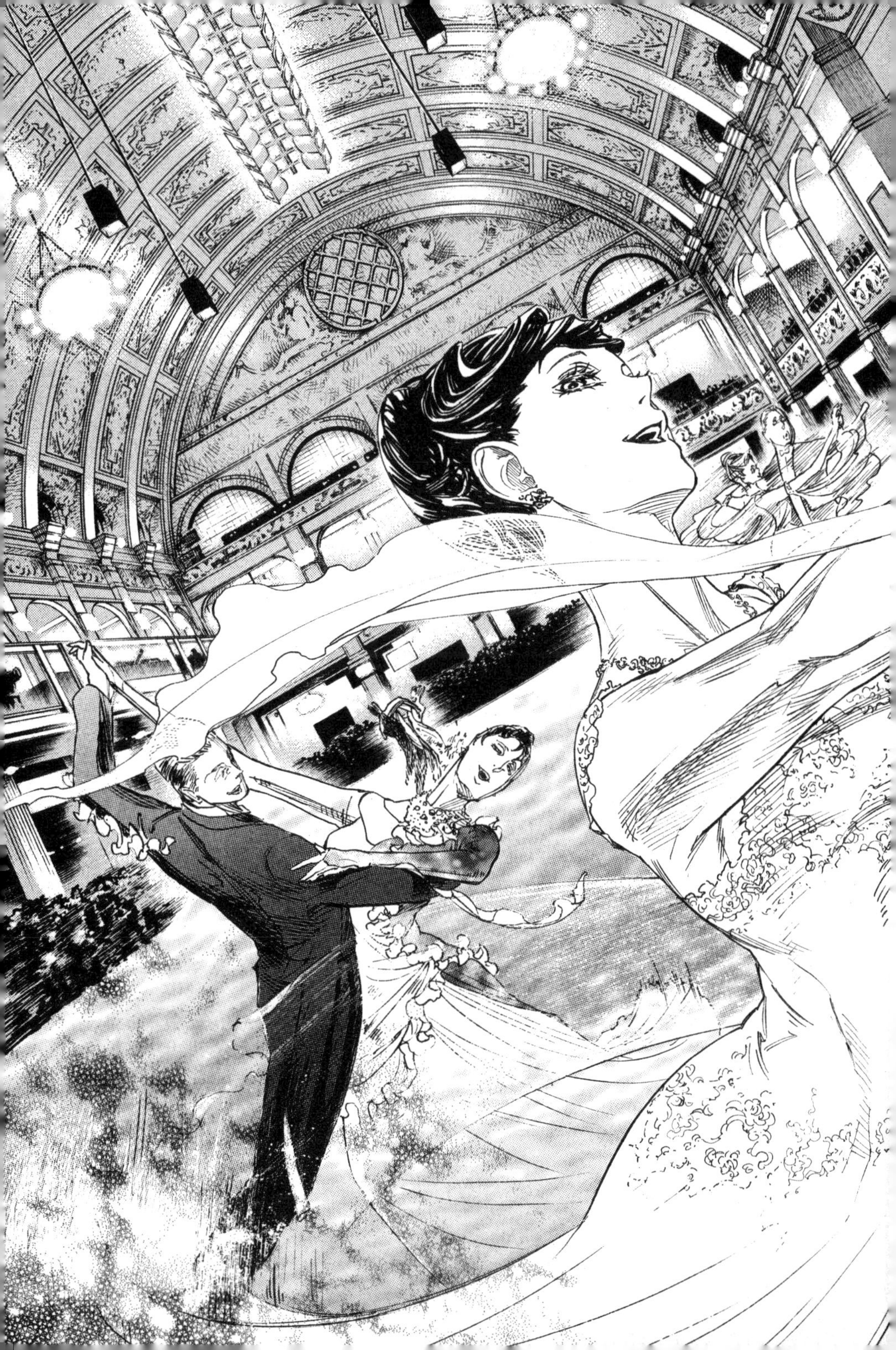

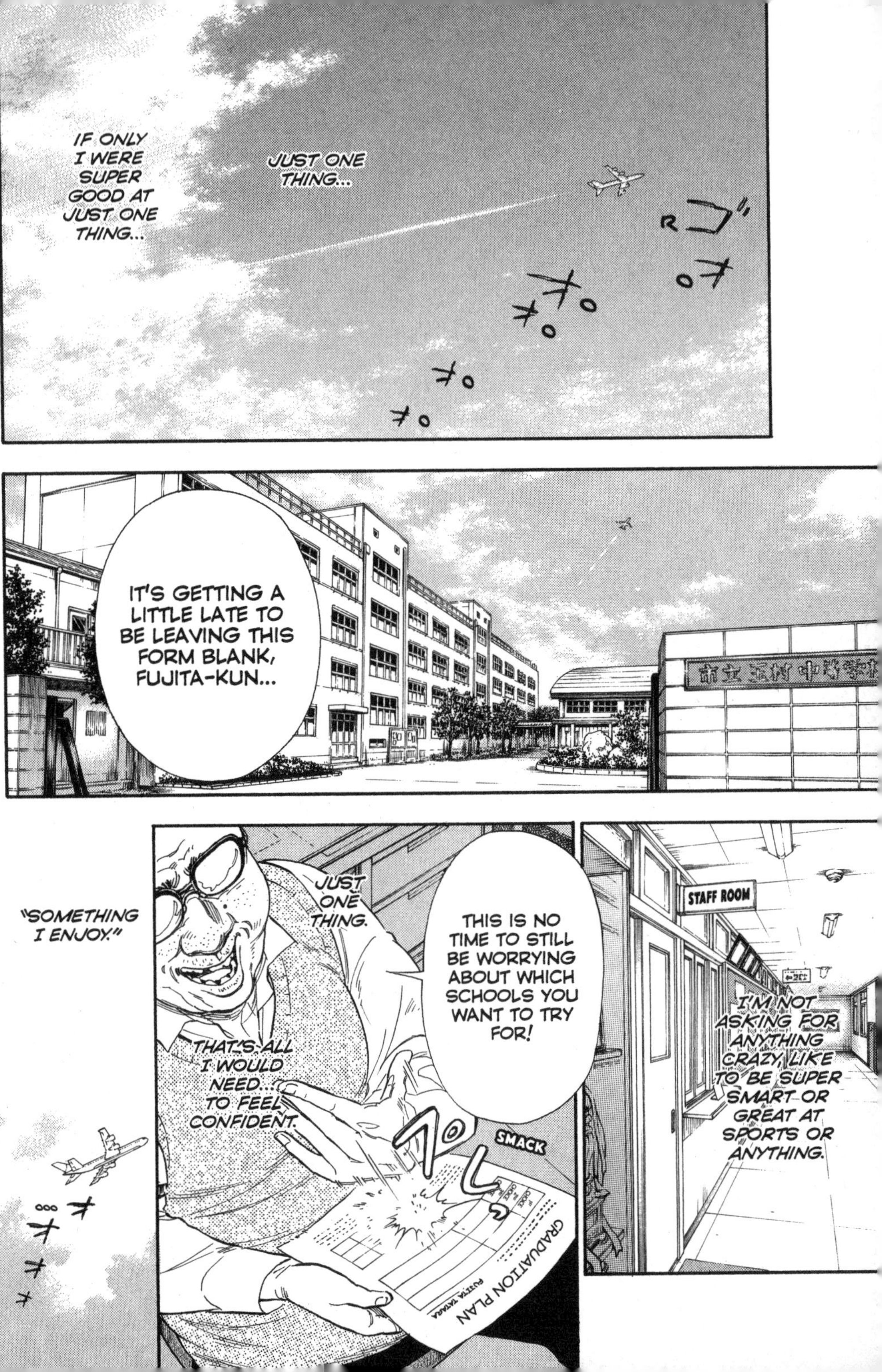
IF ONLY I WERE SUPER GOOD AT JUST ONE THING...
JUST ONE THING...
IT'S GETTING A LITTLE LATE TO BE LEAVING THIS FORM BLANK, FUJITA-KUN...
STAFF ROOM
I'M NOT ASKING FOR ANYTHING CRAZY, LIKE TO BE SUPER SMART OR GREAT AT SPORTS OR ANYTHING.
THIS IS NO TIME TO STILL BE WORRYING ABOUT WHICH SCHOOLS YOU WANT TO TRY FOR!
JUST ONE THING.
"SOMETHING I ENJOY."
THAT'S ALL I WOULD NEED... TO FEEL CONFIDENT.
SMACK
GRADUATION PLAN

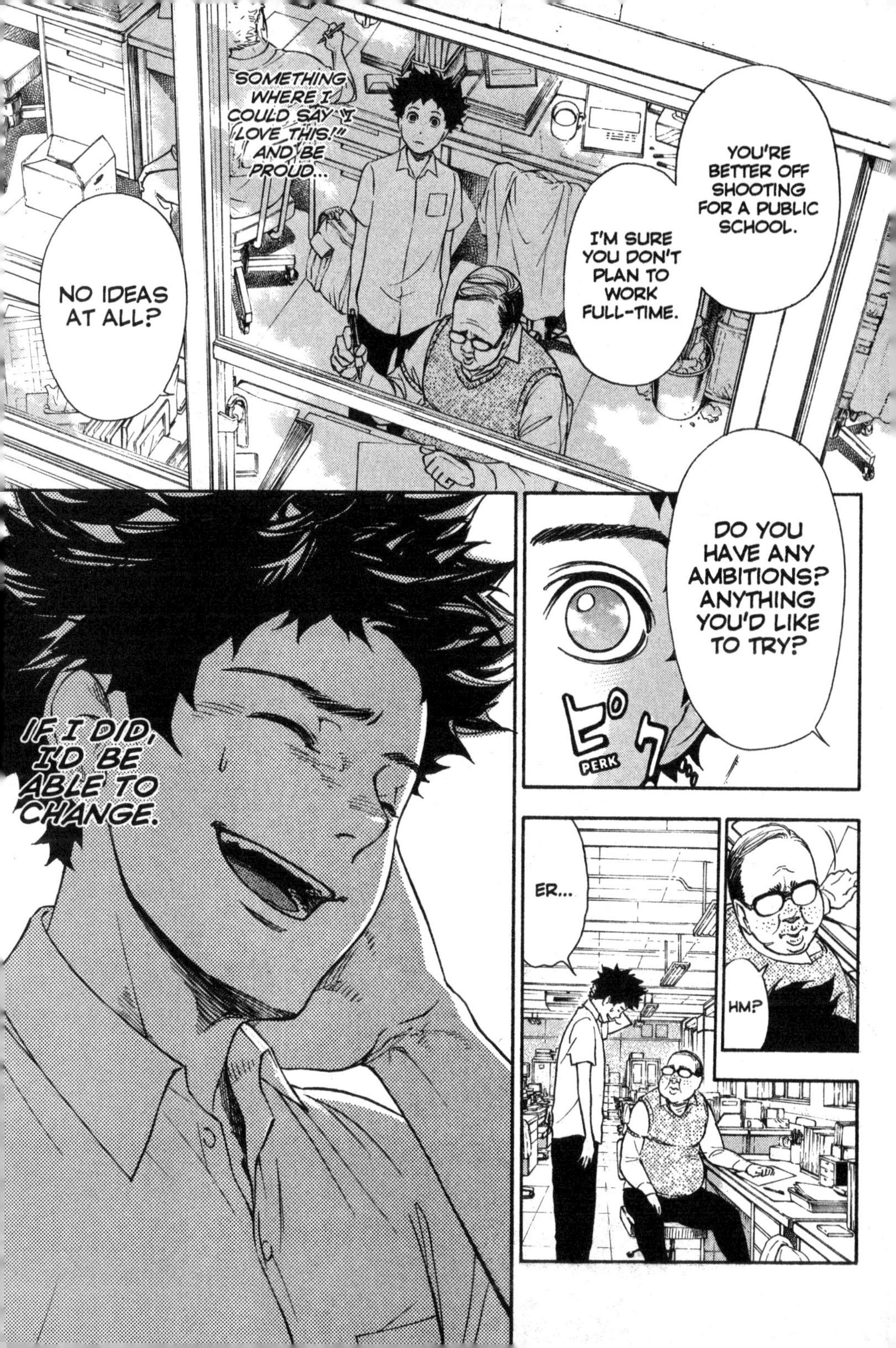
YOU'RE BETTER OFF SHOOTING FOR A PUBLIC SCHOOL.
I'M SURE YOU DON'T PLAN TO WORK FULL-TIME.
SOMETHING WHERE I COULD SAY "I LOVE THIS!" AND BE PROUD...
NO IDEAS AT ALL?
DO YOU HAVE ANY AMBITIONS? ANYTHING YOU'D LIKE TO TRY?
ピク
PERK
HM?
ER...
IF I DID, I'D BE ABLE TO CHANGE.

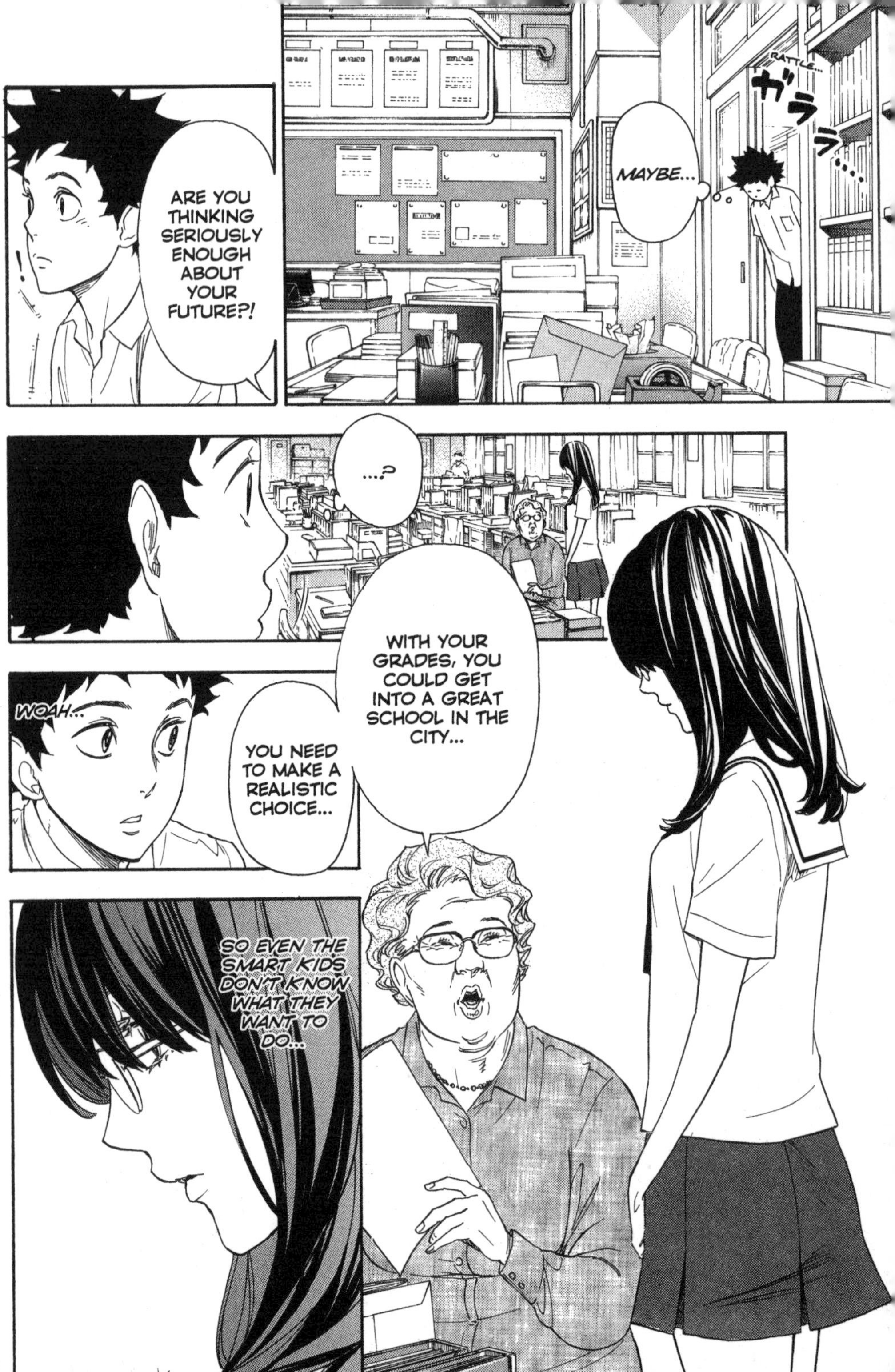
RATTLE...
ガラ ラ...
MAYBE...
ARE YOU THINKING SERIOUSLY ENOUGH ABOUT YOUR FUTURE?!
...?
WITH YOUR GRADES, YOU COULD GET INTO A GREAT SCHOOL IN THE CITY...
YOU NEED TO MAKE A REALISTIC CHOICE...
WOAH...
SO EVEN THE SMART KIDS DON'T KNOW WHAT THEY WANT TO DO...

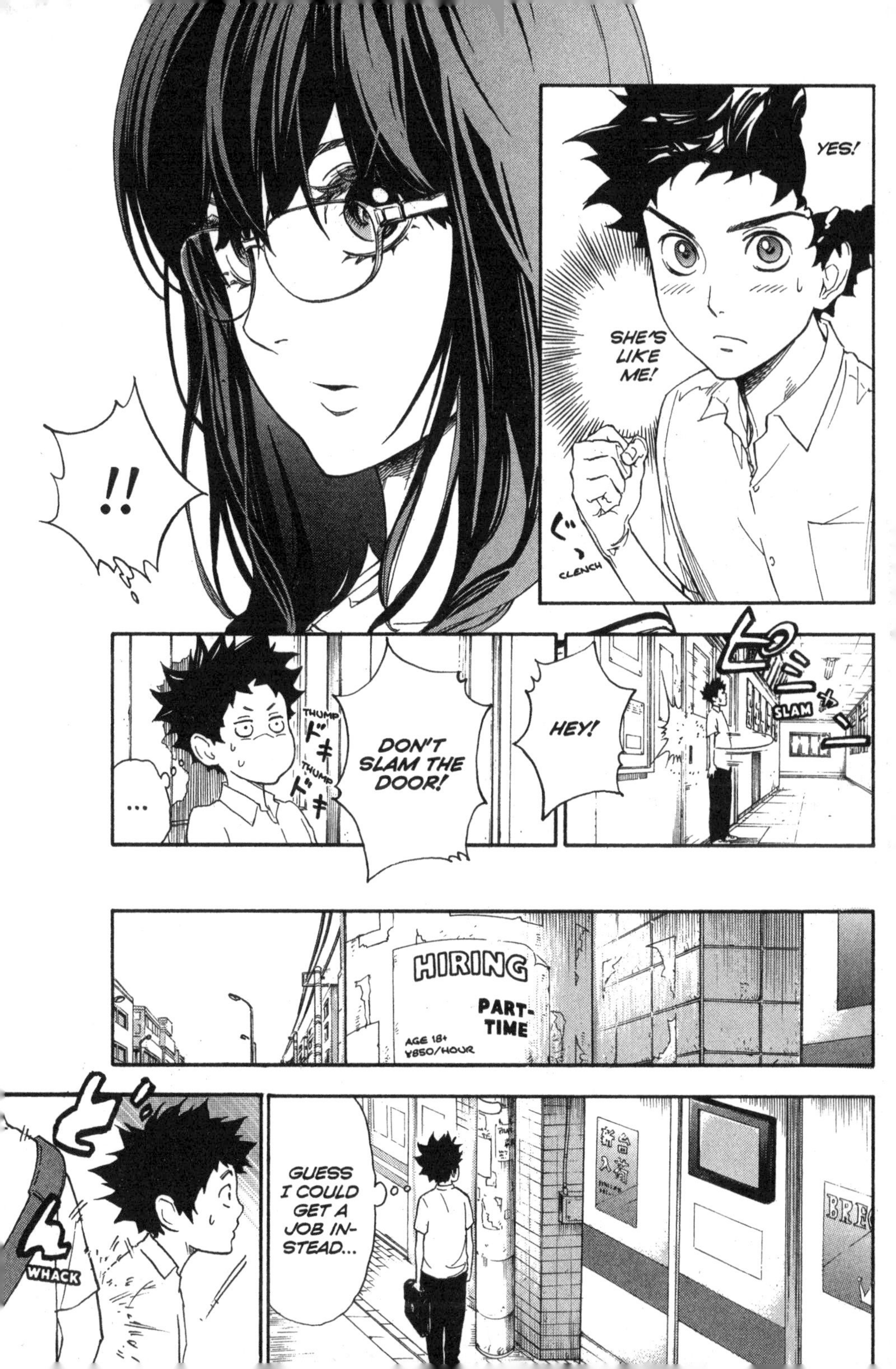
YES!
SHE'S LIKE ME!
CLENCH
!!
SLAM
HEY!
DON'T SLAM THE DOOR!
THUMP
THUMP
...
HIRING
PART-TIME
AGE 18+
¥850/HOUR
GUESS I COULD GET A JOB IN-STEAD...
WHACK

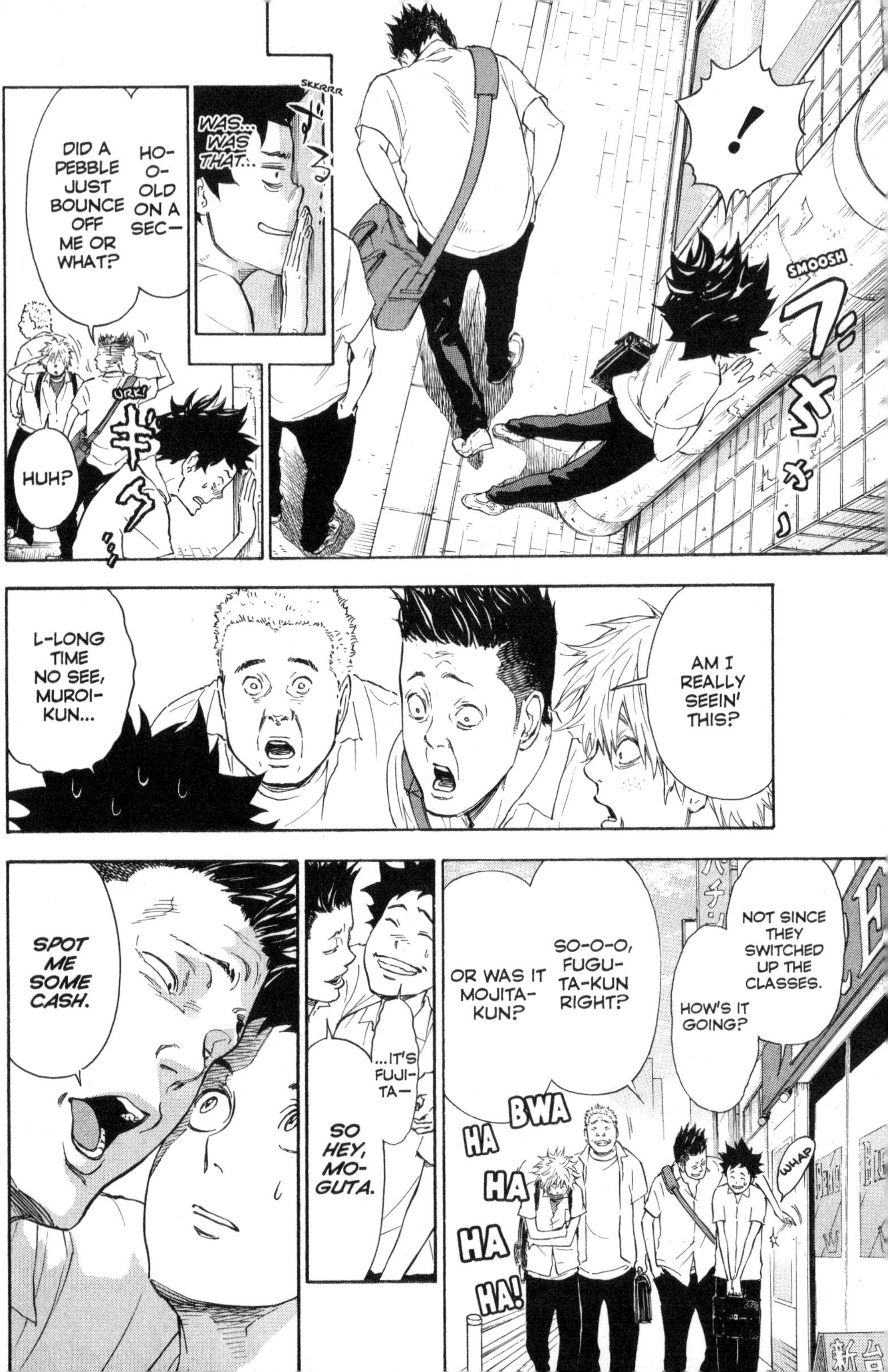
!
SMOOSH
SKKRRR
WAS... WAS THAT...
HO-O-OLD ON A SEC—
DID A PEBBLE JUST BOUNCE OFF ME OR WHAT?
URK!
HUH?
AM I REALLY SEEIN' THIS?
L-LONG TIME NO SEE, MUROI-KUN...
NOT SINCE THEY SWITCHED UP THE CLASSES.
HOW'S IT GOING?
SO-O-O, FUGUTA-KUN RIGHT?
OR WAS IT MOJITA-KUN?
BWA HA HA HA HA!
WHAP
...IT'S FUJITA—
SO HEY, MOGUTA.
SPOT ME SOME CASH.

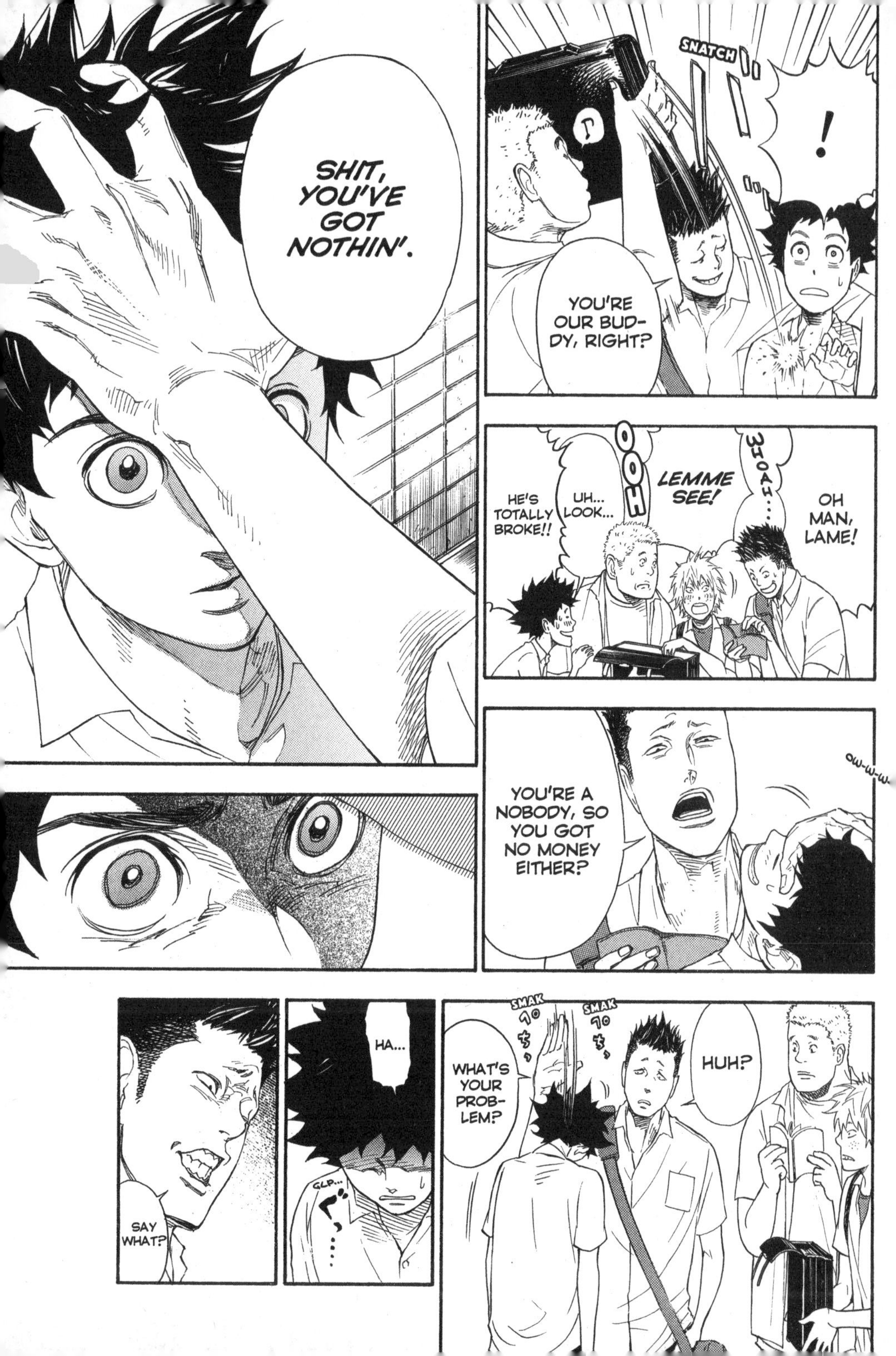
SNATCH
!
YOU'RE OUR BUDDY, RIGHT?
WHOAH...
OH MAN, LAME!
LEMME SEE!
OOH
UH... LOOK...
HE'S TOTALLY BROKE!!
OW-W-W.
YOU'RE A NOBODY, SO YOU GOT NO MONEY EITHER?
SHIT, YOU'VE GOT NOTHIN'.
HUH?
SMAK
SMAK
WHAT'S YOUR PROB-LEM?
HA...
GLP...
SAY WHAT?

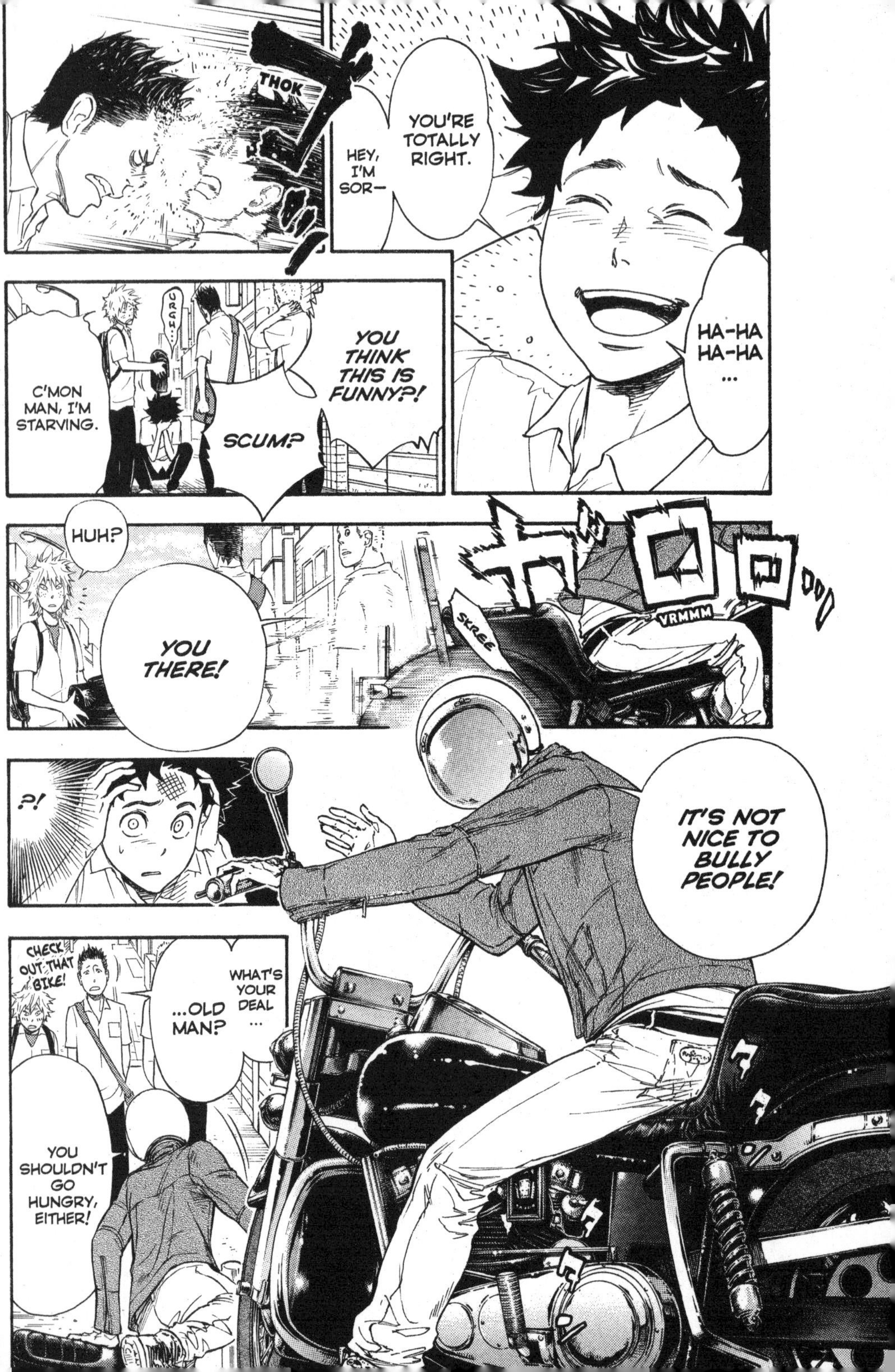
YOU'RE TOTALLY RIGHT.
HEY, I'M SOR—
HA-HA HA-HA ...
THOK
URGH...
YOU THINK THIS IS FUNNY?!
SCUM?
C'MON MAN, I'M STARVING.
VRMMM
SKREE
HUH?
YOU THERE!
IT'S NOT NICE TO BULLY PEOPLE!
?!
WHAT'S YOUR DEAL ...
...OLD MAN?
CHECK OUT THAT BIKE!
YOU SHOULDN'T GO HUNGRY, EITHER!

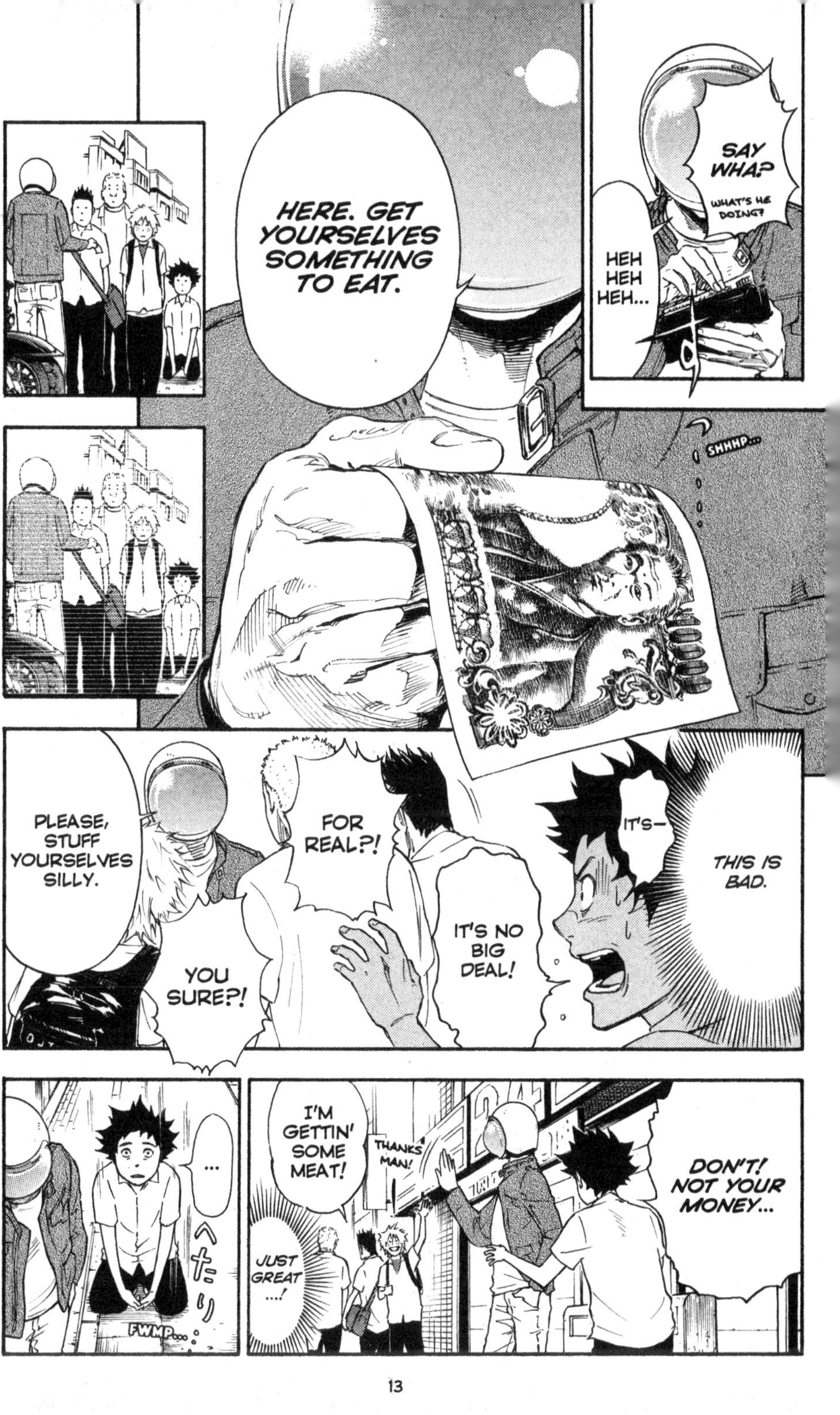

SAY WHA?
WHAT'S HE DOING?
HEH HEH HEH...
HERE. GET YOURSELVES SOMETHING TO EAT.
SHHHP...
IT'S—
THIS IS BAD.
IT'S NO BIG DEAL!
FOR REAL?!
YOU SURE?!
PLEASE, STUFF YOURSELVES SILLY.
DON'T! NOT YOUR MONEY...
THANKS MAN!
I'M GETTIN' SOME MEAT!
JUST GREAT...!
...
へたり
FWMP...

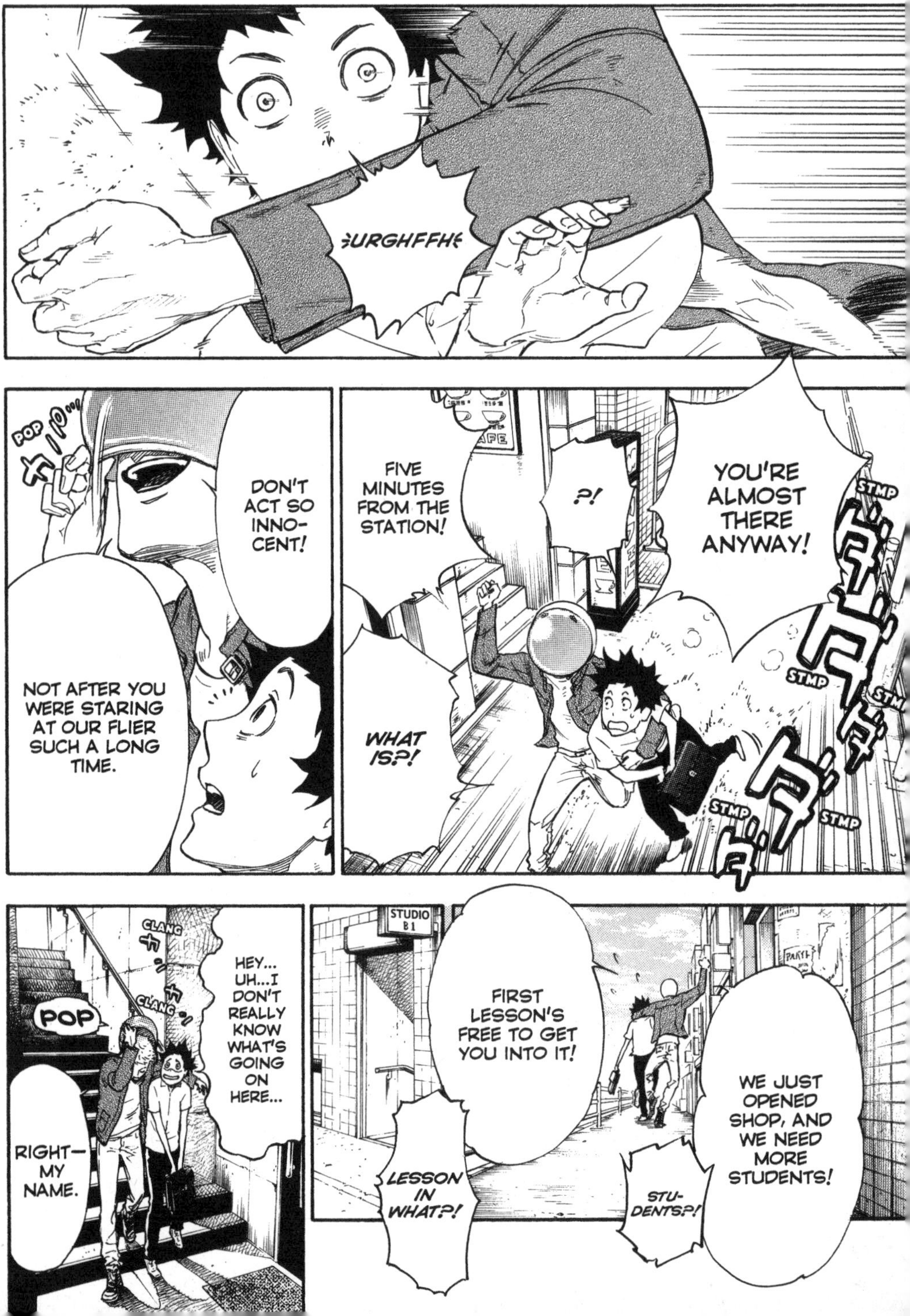
URGHFFH
STMP
YOU'RE ALMOST THERE ANYWAY!
?!
FIVE MINUTES FROM THE STATION!
STMP
STMP
STMP
STMP
WHAT IS?!
DON'T ACT SO INNO-CENT!
POP
NOT AFTER YOU WERE STARING AT OUR FLIER SUCH A LONG TIME.
STUDIO B1
WE JUST OPENED SHOP, AND WE NEED MORE STUDENTS!
FIRST LESSON'S FREE TO GET YOU INTO IT!
STU-DENTS?!
LESSON IN WHAT?!
HEY... UH...I DON'T REALLY KNOW WHAT'S GOING ON HERE...
CLANG
CLANG
POP
RIGHT—MY NAME.

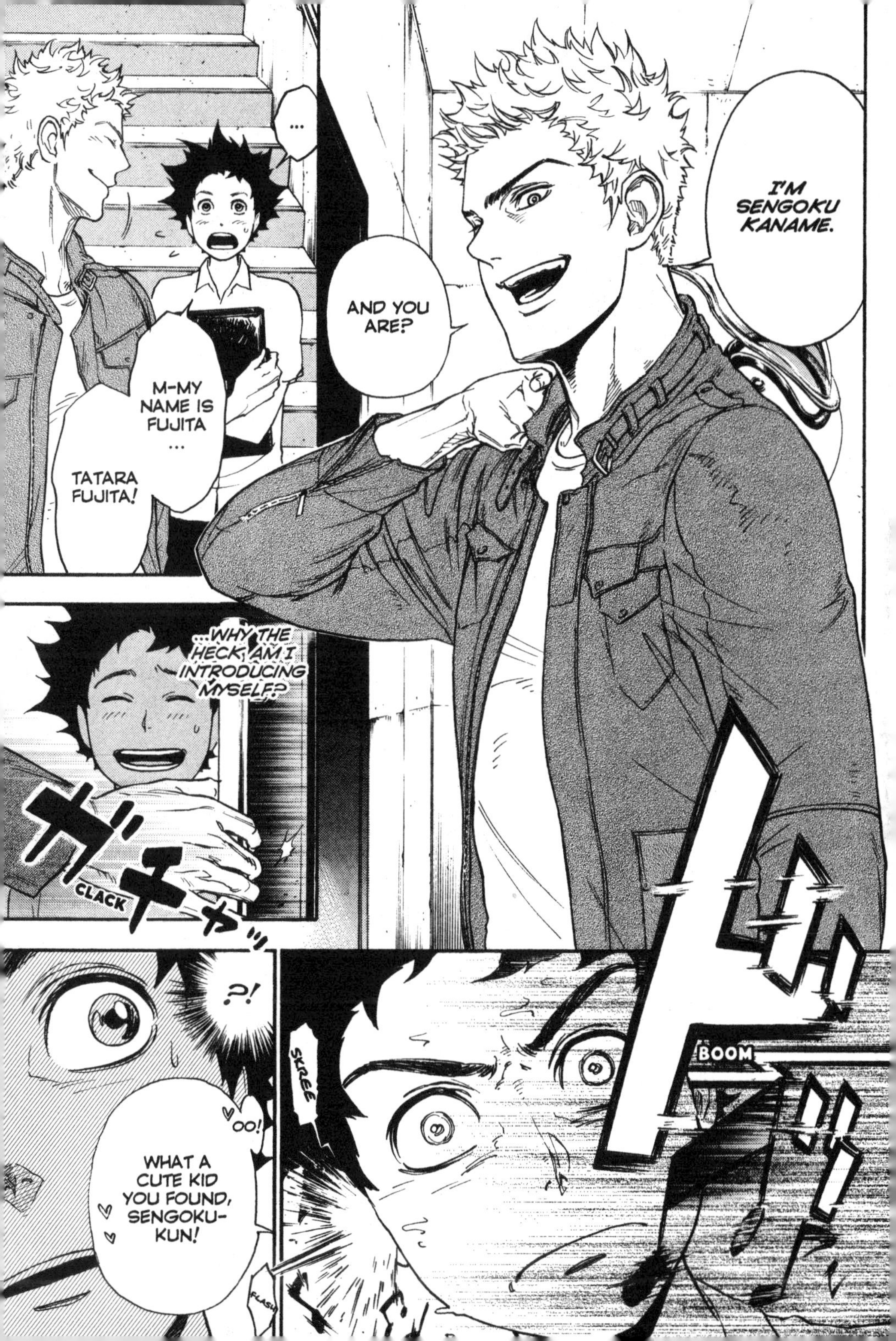
I'M SENGOKU KANAME.
AND YOU ARE?
...
M-MY NAME IS FUJITA ...
TATARA FUJITA!
...WHY THE HECK AM I INTRODUCING MYSELF?
CLACK
BOOM
SKREE
?!
OO!
WHAT A CUTE KID YOU FOUND, SENGOKU-KUN!
FLASH

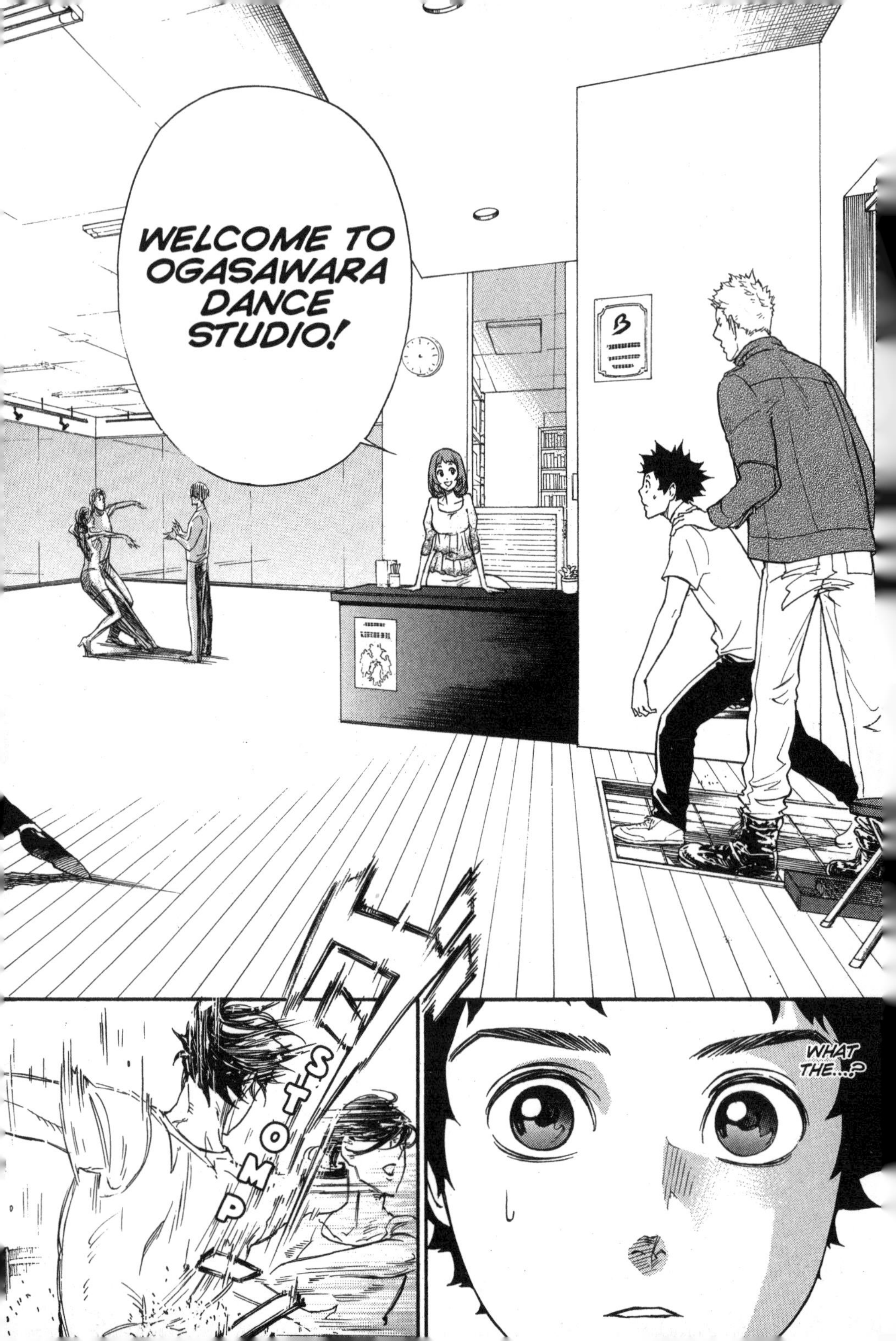
WELCOME TO OGASAWARA DANCE STUDIO!
WHAT THE...?
STOMP

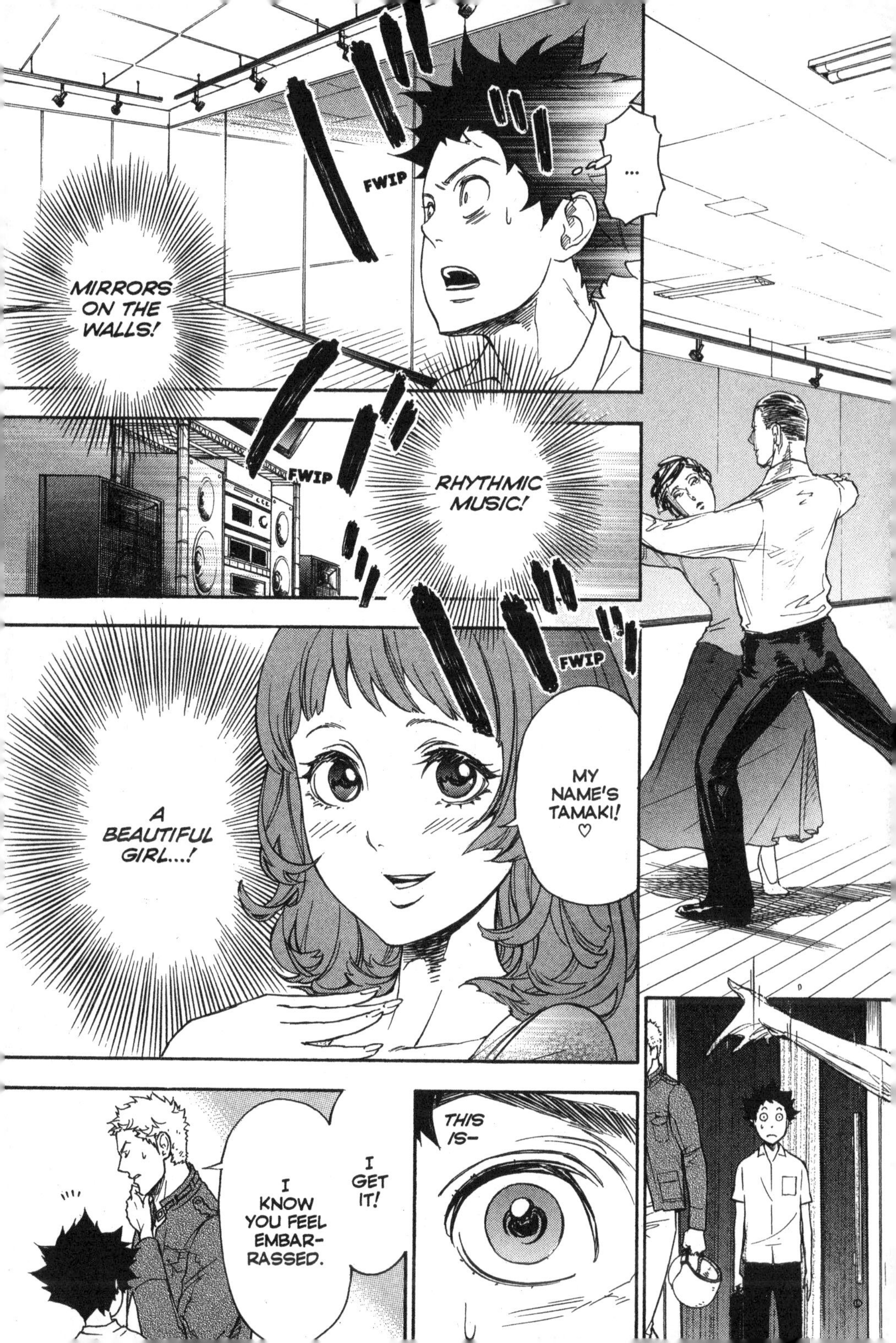
...
FWIP
MIRRORS ON THE WALLS!
FWIP
RHYTHMIC MUSIC!
FWIP
MY NAME'S TAMAKI! ♡
A BEAUTIFUL GIRL...!
THIS IS-
I GET IT!
I KNOW YOU FEEL EMBARRASSED.

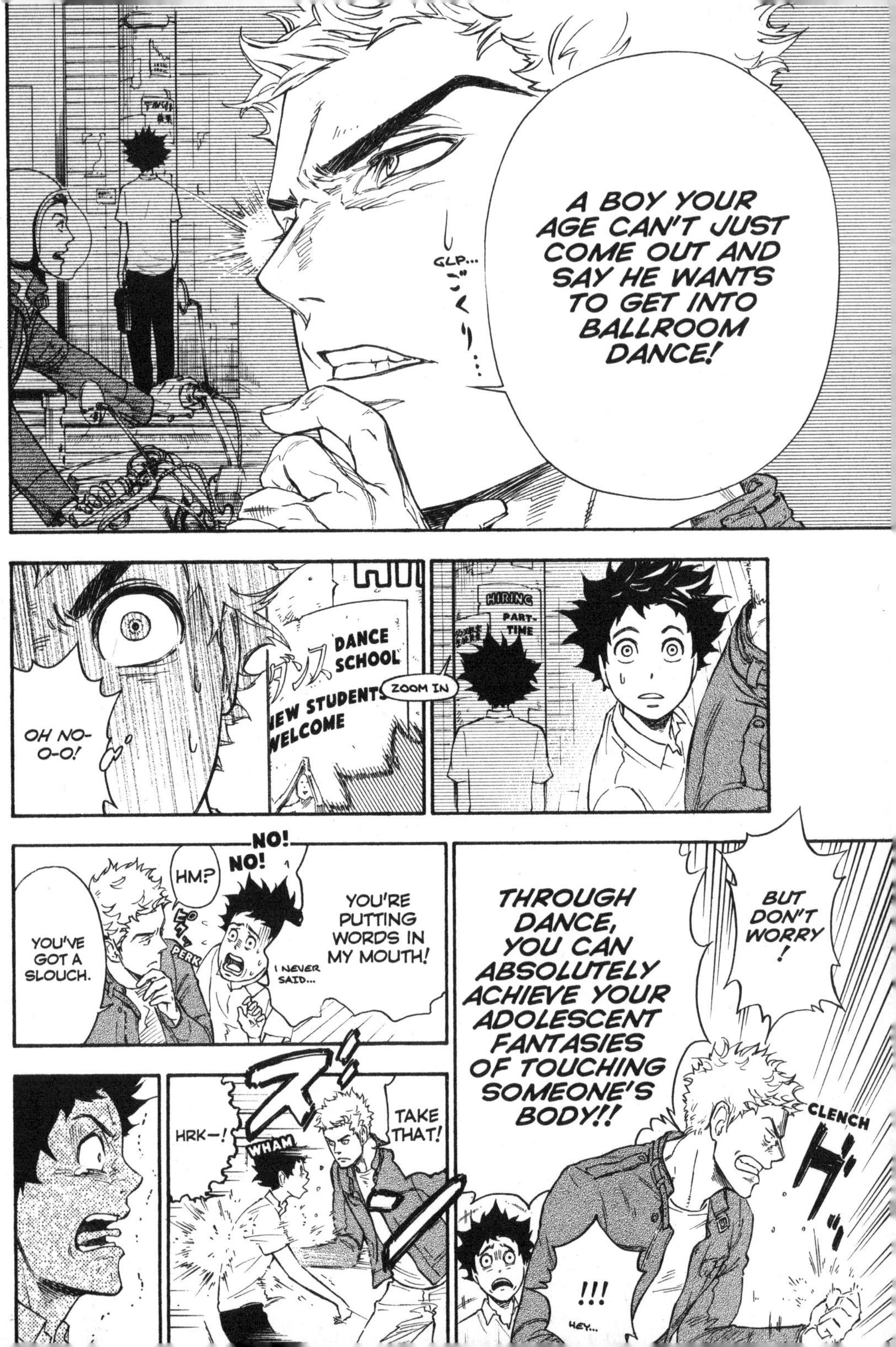
A BOY YOUR AGE CAN'T JUST COME OUT AND SAY HE WANTS TO GET INTO BALLROOM DANCE!
GLP...
HIRING
PART-TIME
ZOOM IN
DANCE SCHOOL
NEW STUDENTS WELCOME
OH NO-O-O!
BUT DON'T WORRY!
THROUGH DANCE, YOU CAN ABSOLUTELY ACHIEVE YOUR ADOLESCENT FANTASIES OF TOUCHING SOMEONE'S BODY!!
CLENCH
!!!
HEY...
NO! NO!
YOU'RE PUTTING WORDS IN MY MOUTH!
I NEVER SAID...
HM?
PERK
YOU'VE GOT A SLOUCH.
TAKE THAT!
WHAM
HRK—!

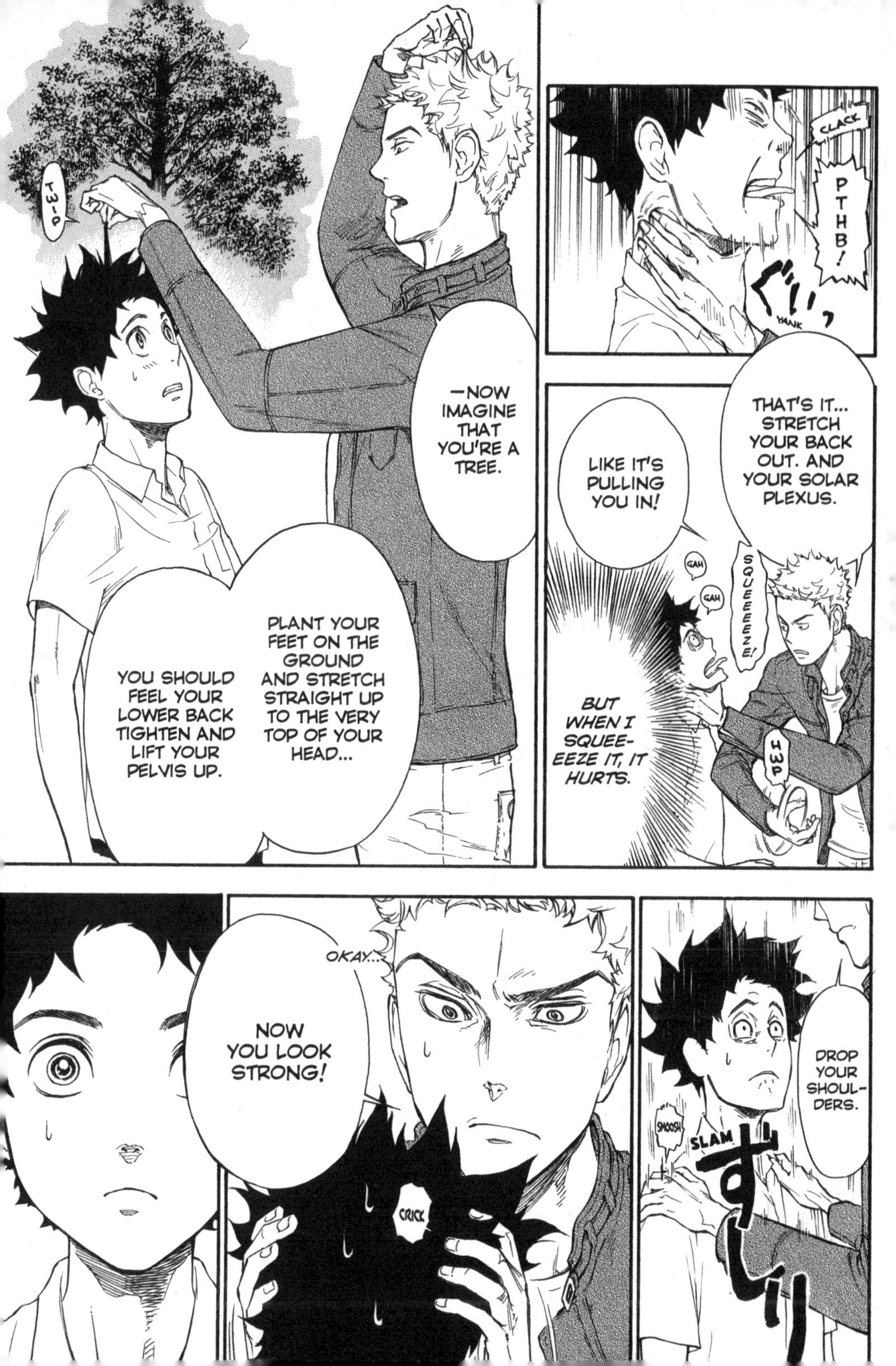
CLACK
PTHB!
YANK
THAT'S IT... STRETCH YOUR BACK OUT. AND YOUR SOLAR PLEXUS.
LIKE IT'S PULLING YOU IN!
GAH
GAH
SQUEEEEEZE!
BUT WHEN I SQUEEEZE IT, IT HURTS.
HUP
—NOW IMAGINE THAT YOU'RE A TREE.
PLANT YOUR FEET ON THE GROUND AND STRETCH STRAIGHT UP TO THE VERY TOP OF YOUR HEAD...
YOU SHOULD FEEL YOUR LOWER BACK TIGHTEN AND LIFT YOUR PELVIS UP.
DROP YOUR SHOULDERS.
SMOOSH
SLAM
OKAY...
NOW YOU LOOK STRONG!
CRICK

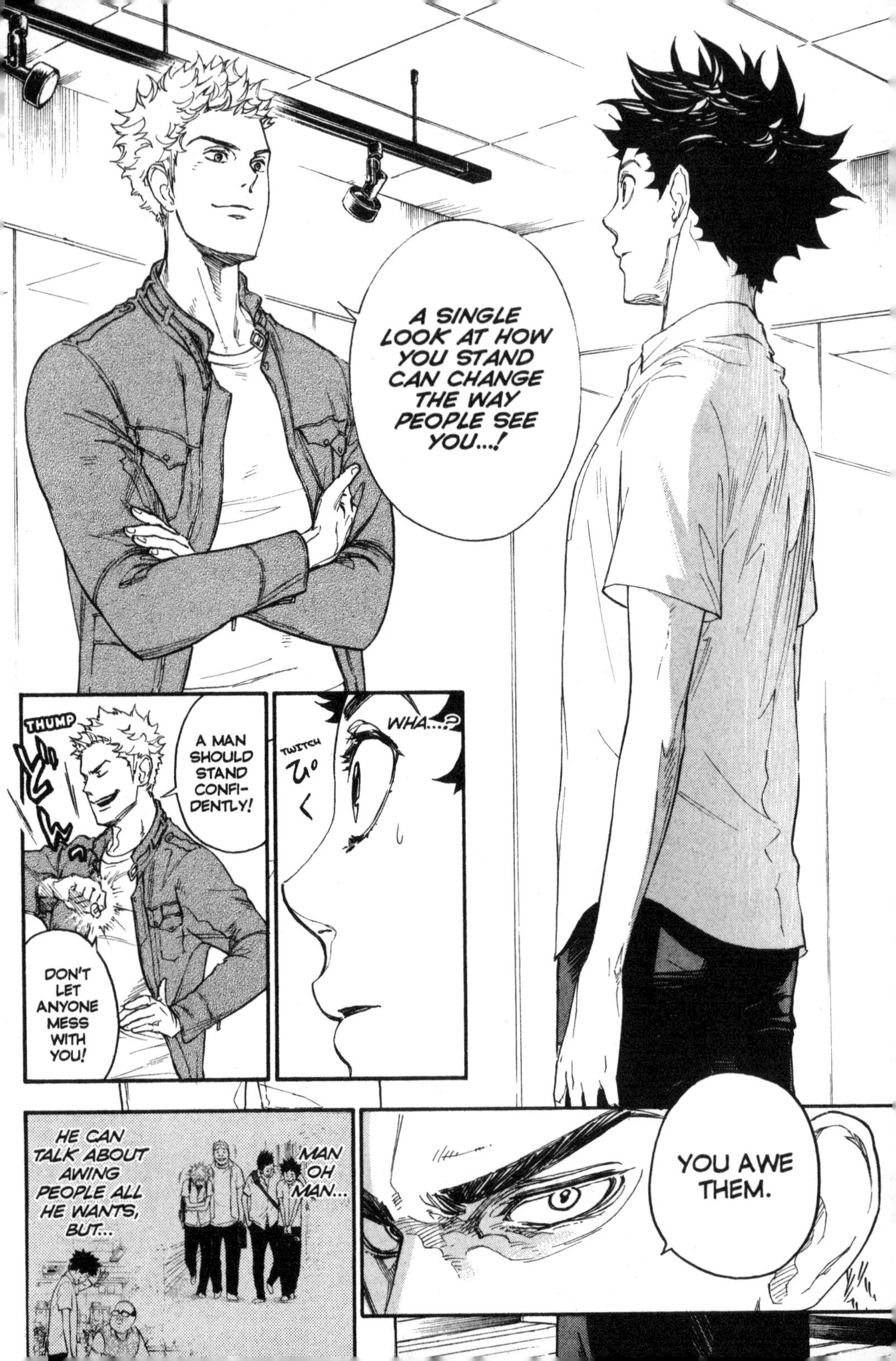

A SINGLE LOOK AT HOW YOU STAND CAN CHANGE THE WAY PEOPLE SEE YOU...!
WHA...?
TWITCH
THUMP
A MAN SHOULD STAND CONFI-DENTLY!
DON'T LET ANYONE MESS WITH YOU!
YOU AWE THEM.
MAN OH MAN...
HE CAN TALK ABOUT AWING PEOPLE ALL HE WANTS, BUT...

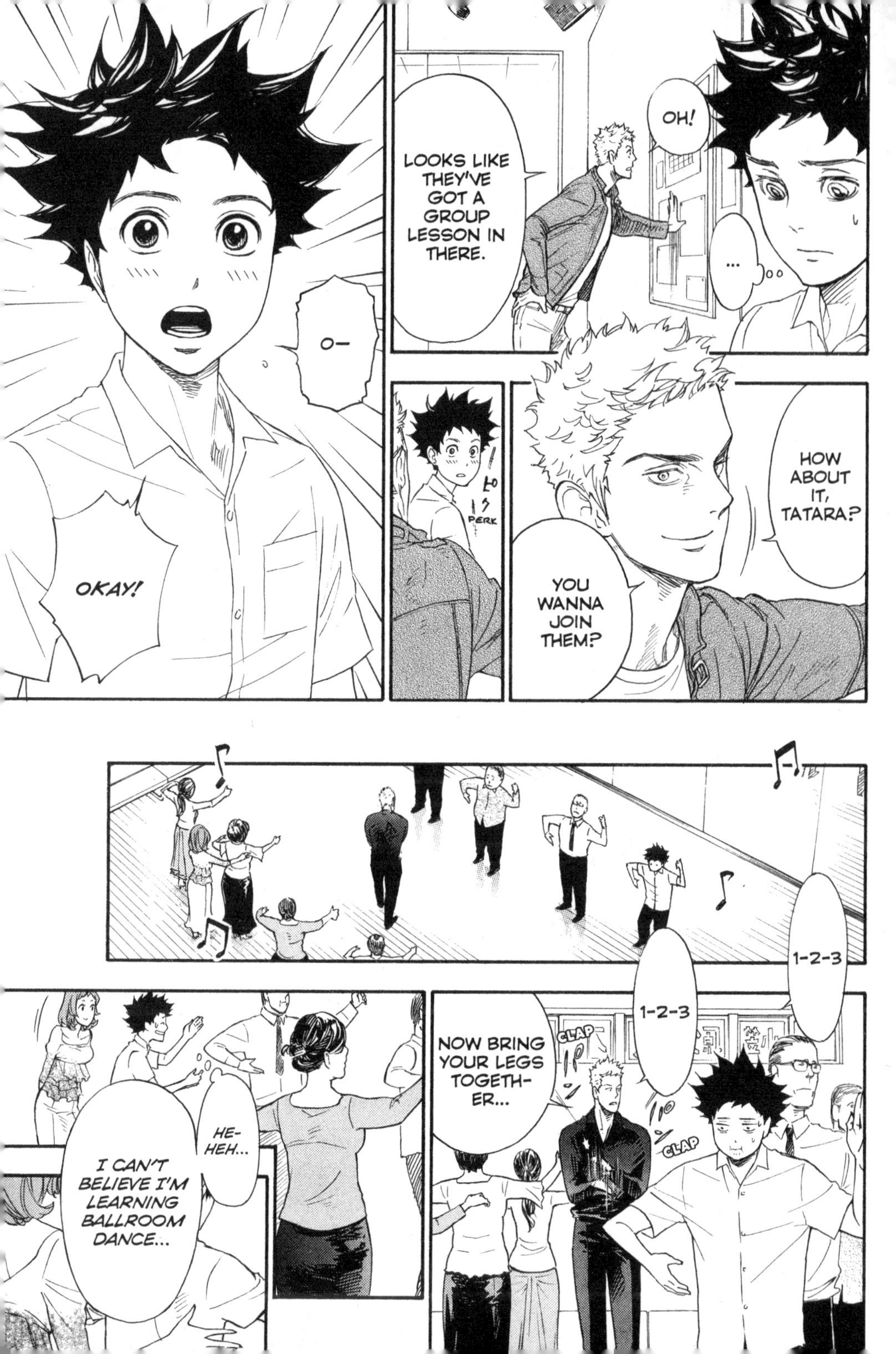
OH!
LOOKS LIKE THEY'VE GOT A GROUP LESSON IN THERE.
...
HOW ABOUT IT, TATARA?
YOU WANNA JOIN THEM?
PERK
O—
OKAY!
1-2-3
1-2-3
NOW BRING YOUR LEGS TOGETH-ER...
CLAP
CLAP
HE-HEH...
I CAN'T BELIEVE I'M LEARNING BALLROOM DANCE...

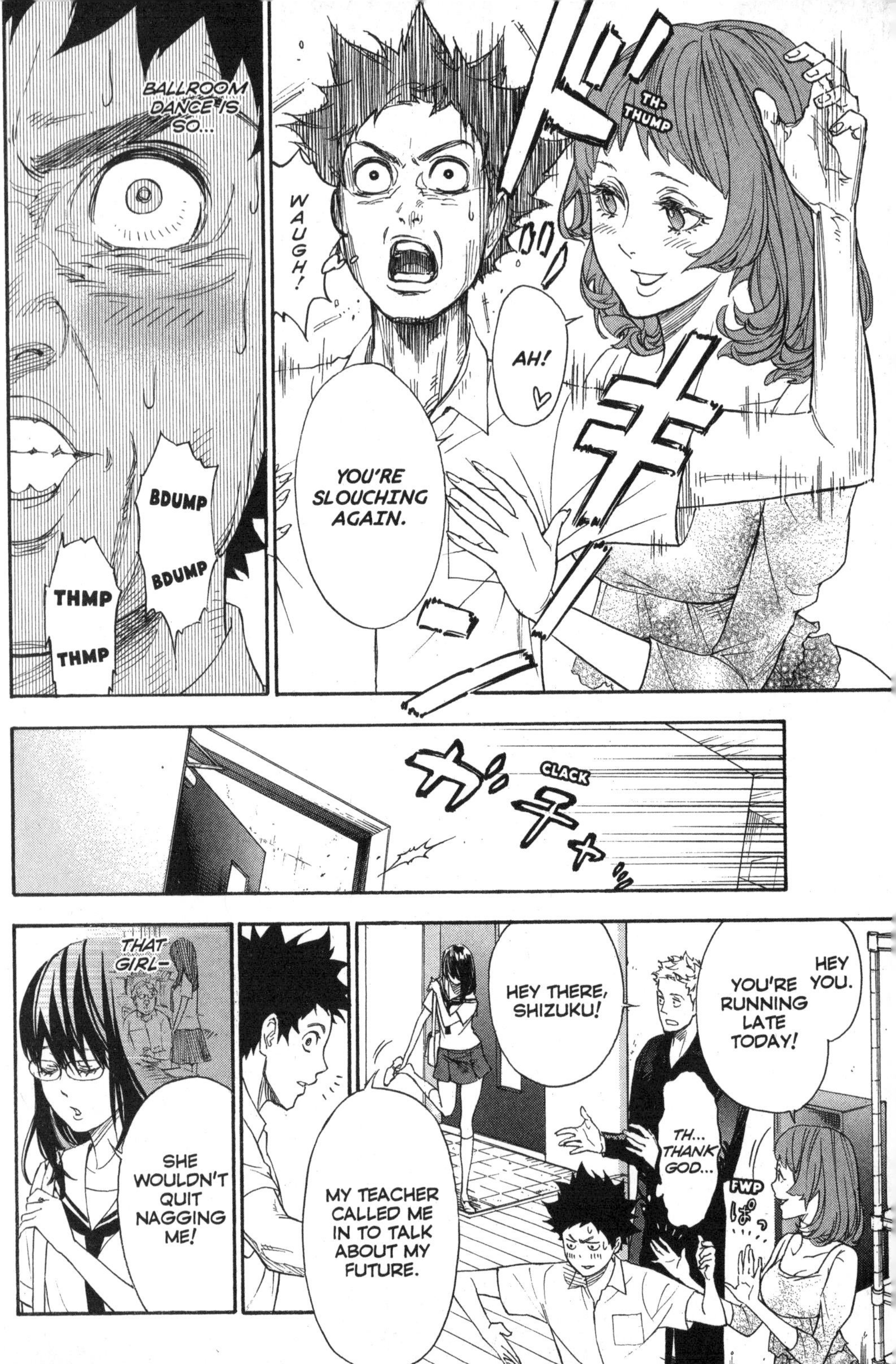
TH-THUMP
AH! ♥
WAUGH!
YOU'RE SLOUCHING AGAIN.
BALLROOM DANCE IS SO...
BDUMP
BDUMP
THMP
THMP
CLACK
HEY YOU. YOU'RE RUNNING LATE TODAY!
HEY THERE, SHIZUKU!
TH... THANK GOD...
FWP
MY TEACHER CALLED ME IN TO TALK ABOUT MY FUTURE.
THAT GIRL-
SHE WOULDN'T QUIT NAGGING ME!

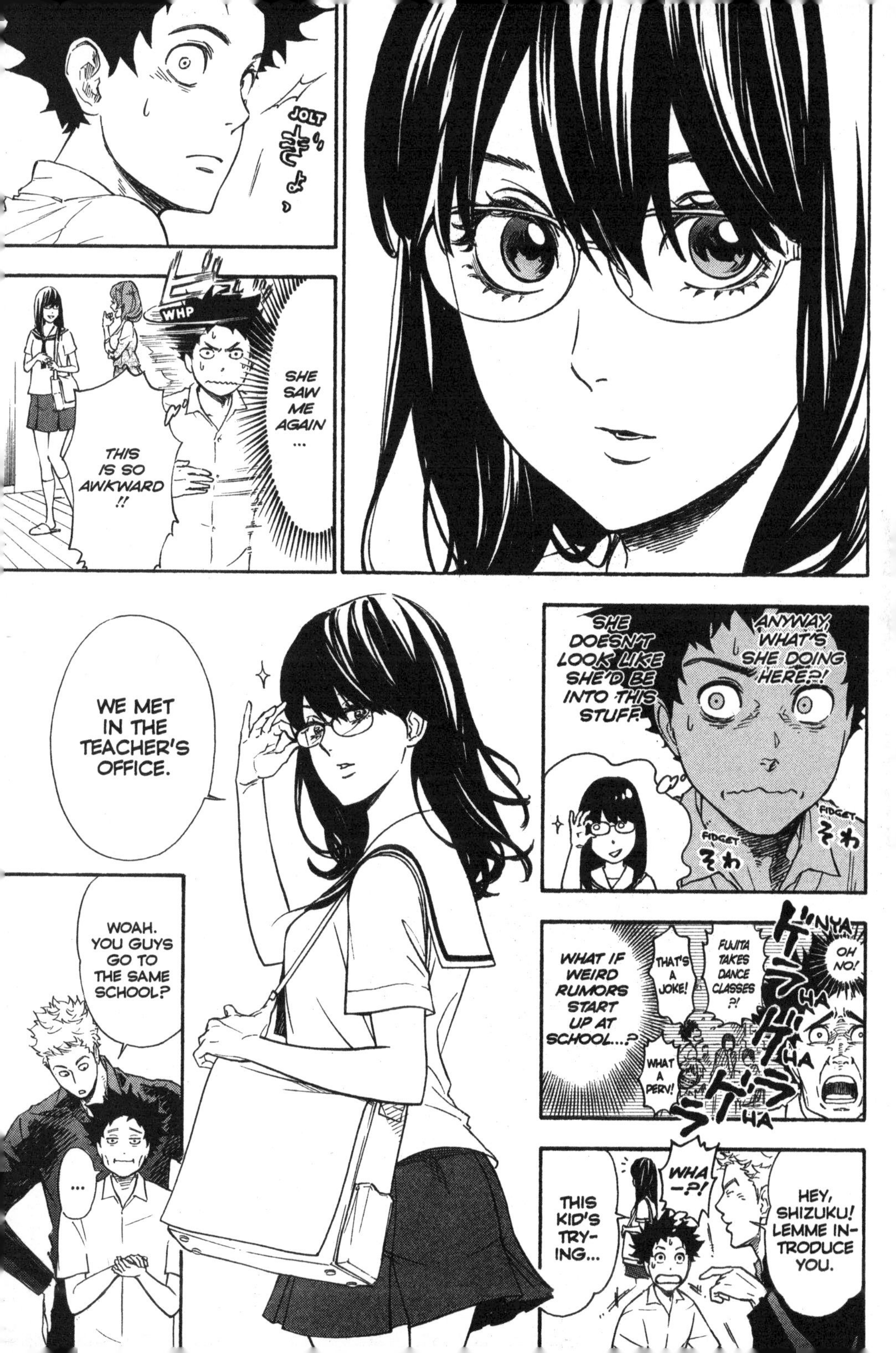
JOLT
WHP
SHE SAW ME AGAIN...
THIS IS SO AWKWARD!!
ANYWAY, WHAT'S SHE DOING HERE?!
SHE DOESN'T LOOK LIKE SHE'D BE INTO THIS STUFF.
FIDGET
FIDGET
GINYA
OH NO!
FUJITA TAKES DANCE CLASSES?!
THAT'S A JOKE!
WHAT IF WEIRD RUMORS START UP AT SCHOOL...?
WHAT A PERV!
HA
HA
HA
HEY, SHIZUKU! LEMME IN-TRODUCE YOU.
WHA-?!
THIS KID'S TRY-ING...
WE MET IN THE TEACHER'S OFFICE.
WOAH. YOU GUYS GO TO THE SAME SCHOOL?
...

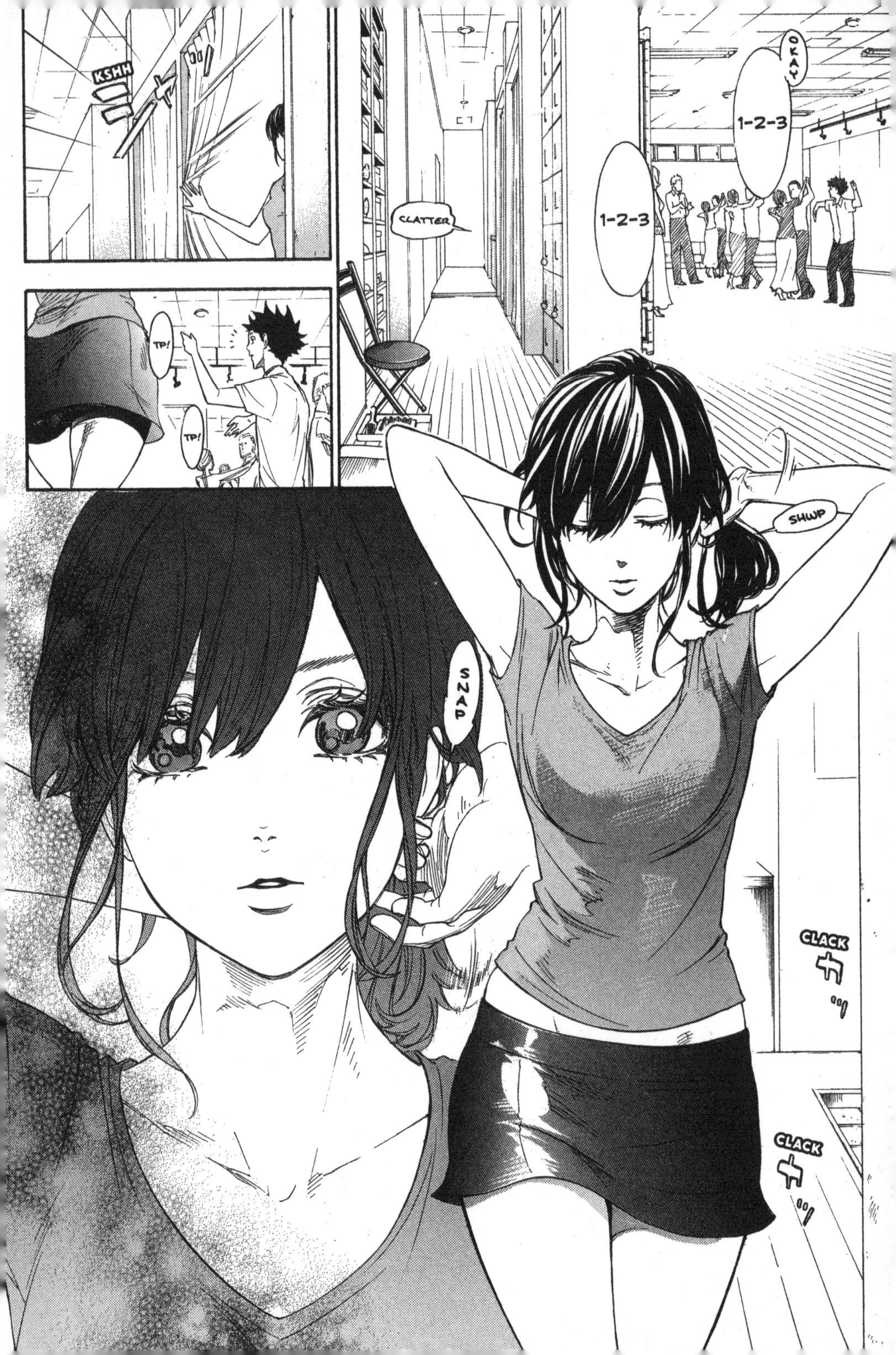
OKAY
1-2-3
1-2-3
CLATTER
KSHH
TP!
TP!
SHWP
SNAP
CLACK
CLACK

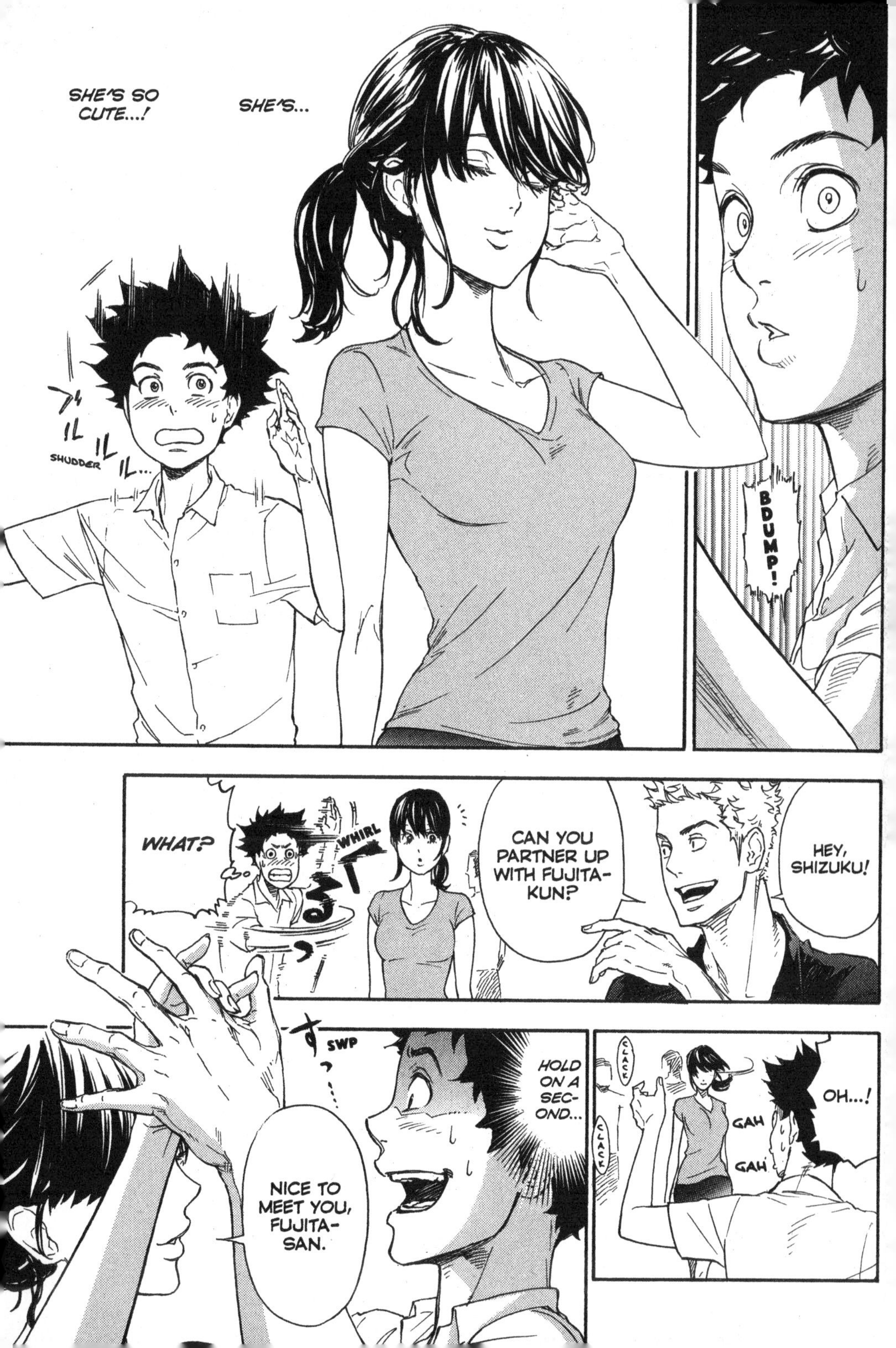
BDUMP!
SHE'S...
SHE'S SO CUTE...!
SHUDDER
HEY, SHIZUKU!
CAN YOU PARTNER UP WITH FUJITA-KUN?
WHIRL
WHAT?
OH...!
GAH
GAH
CLACK
CLACK
HOLD ON A SEC-OND...
SWP
NICE TO MEET YOU, FUJITA-SAN.

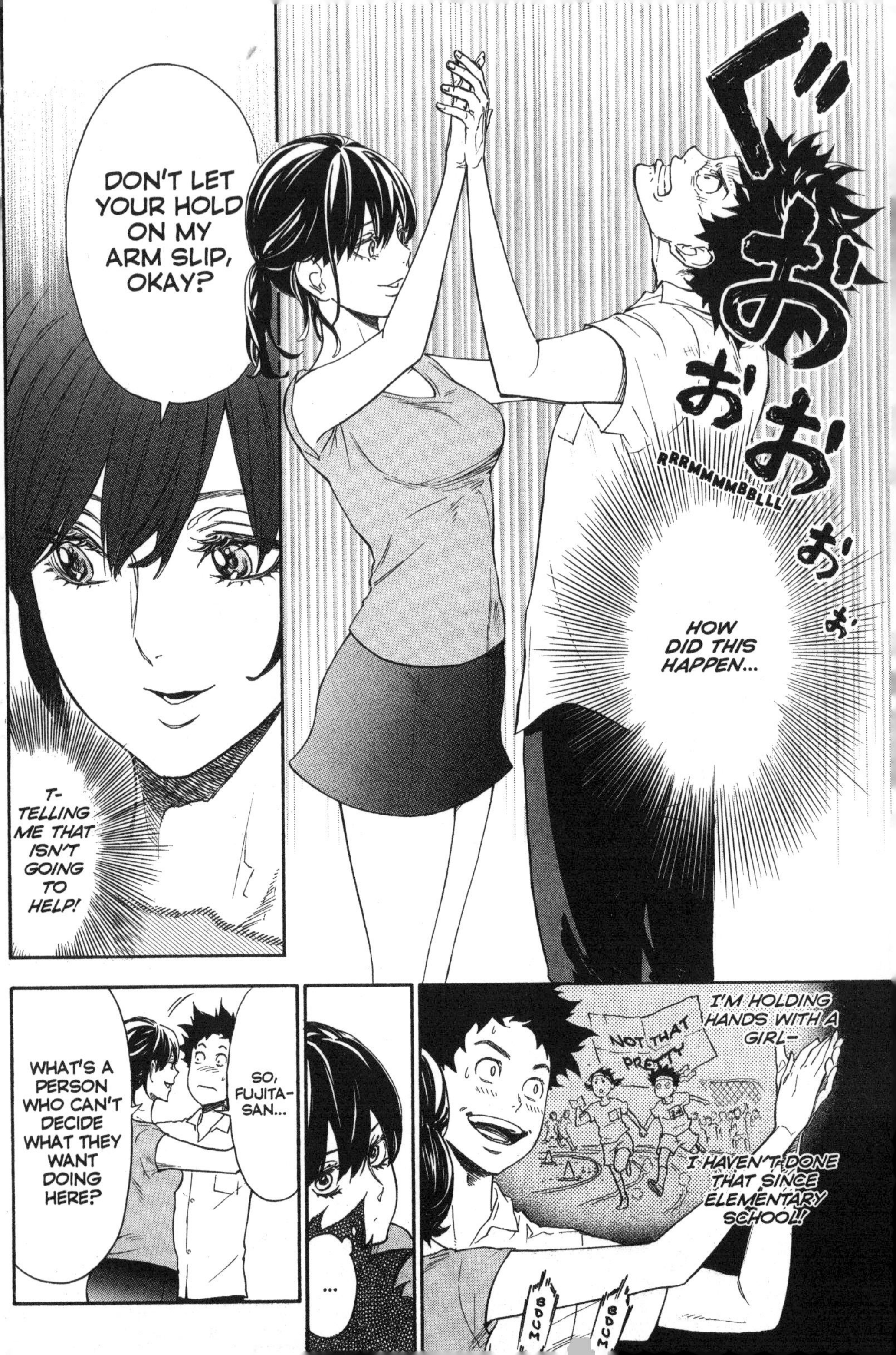
ぐおおおおお
RRRMMMBBLLL
HOW DID THIS HAPPEN...
DON'T LET YOUR HOLD ON MY ARM SLIP, OKAY?
T-TELLING ME THAT ISN'T GOING TO HELP!
I'M HOLDING HANDS WITH A GIRL-
NOT THAT PRETTY
I HAVEN'T DONE THAT SINCE ELEMENTARY SCHOOL!
BDUM
BDUM
...
SO, FUJITA-SAN...
WHAT'S A PERSON WHO CAN'T DECIDE WHAT THEY WANT DOING HERE?

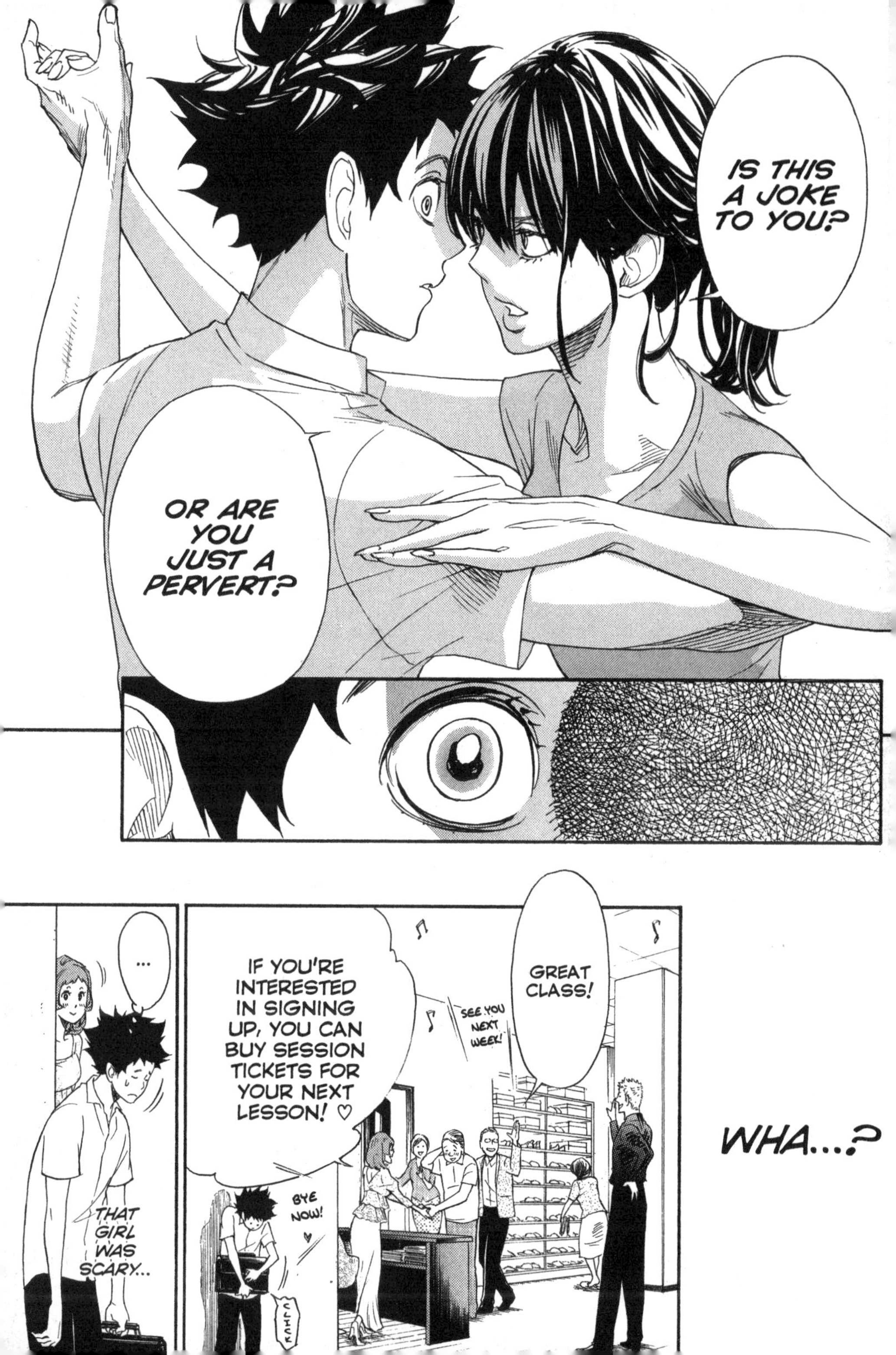
IS THIS A JOKE TO YOU?
OR ARE YOU JUST A PERVERT?
WHA...?
GREAT CLASS!
SEE YOU NEXT WEEK!
IF YOU'RE INTERESTED IN SIGNING UP, YOU CAN BUY SESSION TICKETS FOR YOUR NEXT LESSON! ♡
BYE NOW! ♥
CLICK
...
THAT GIRL WAS SCARY...

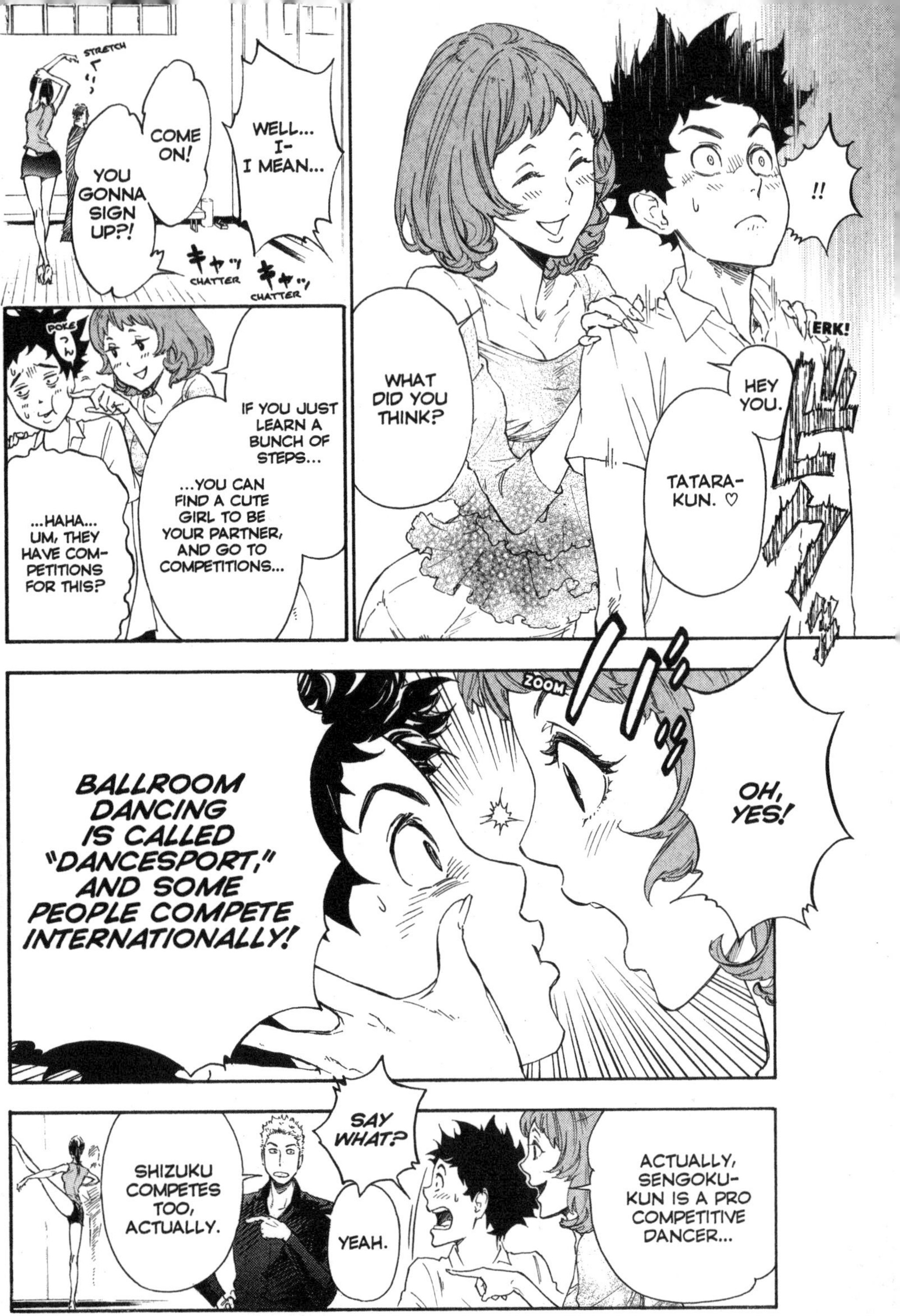
!!
ERK!
HEY YOU.
TATARA-KUN. ♡
WHAT DID YOU THINK?
WELL... I- I MEAN...
COME ON!
YOU GONNA SIGN UP?!
STRETCH
CHATTER
CHATTER
POKE
IF YOU JUST LEARN A BUNCH OF STEPS...
...YOU CAN FIND A CUTE GIRL TO BE YOUR PARTNER, AND GO TO COMPETITIONS...
...HAHA... UM, THEY HAVE COM-PETITIONS FOR THIS?
ZOOM
OH, YES!
BALLROOM DANCING IS CALLED "DANCESPORT," AND SOME PEOPLE COMPETE INTERNATIONALLY!
ACTUALLY, SENGOKU-KUN IS A PRO COMPETITIVE DANCER...
SAY WHAT?
YEAH.
SHIZUKU COMPETES TOO, ACTUALLY.

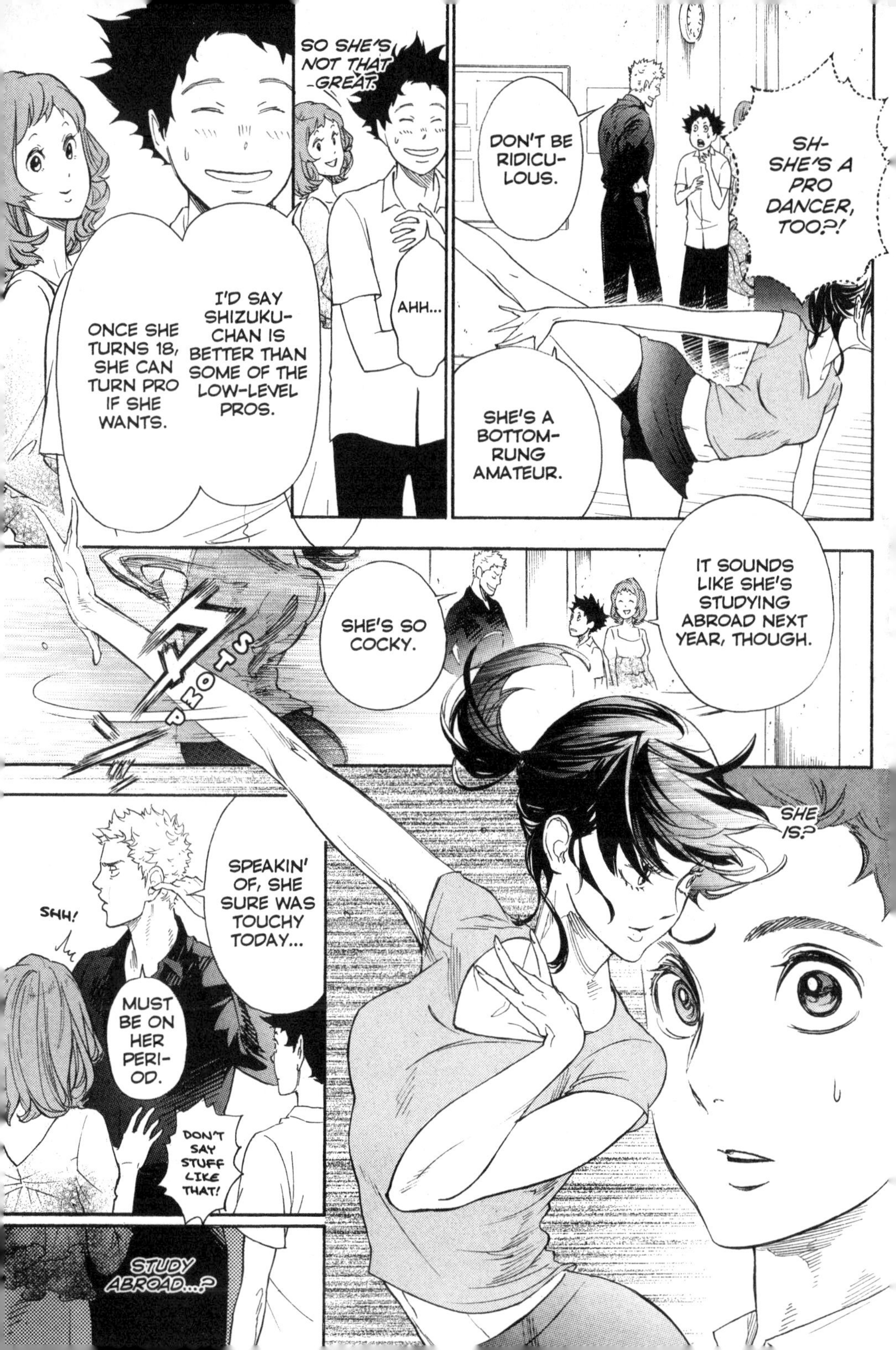
SH- SHE'S A PRO DANCER, TOO?!
DON'T BE RIDICULOUS.
SHE'S A BOTTOM-RUNG AMATEUR.
SO SHE'S NOT THAT GREAT.
AHH...
I'D SAY SHIZUKU-CHAN IS BETTER THAN SOME OF THE LOW-LEVEL PROS.
ONCE SHE TURNS 18, SHE CAN TURN PRO IF SHE WANTS.
IT SOUNDS LIKE SHE'S STUDYING ABROAD NEXT YEAR, THOUGH.
SHE'S SO COCKY.
STOMP
SHE IS?
SPEAKIN' OF, SHE SURE WAS TOUCHY TODAY...
SHH!
MUST BE ON HER PERIOD.
DON'T SAY STUFF LIKE THAT!
STUDY ABROAD...?

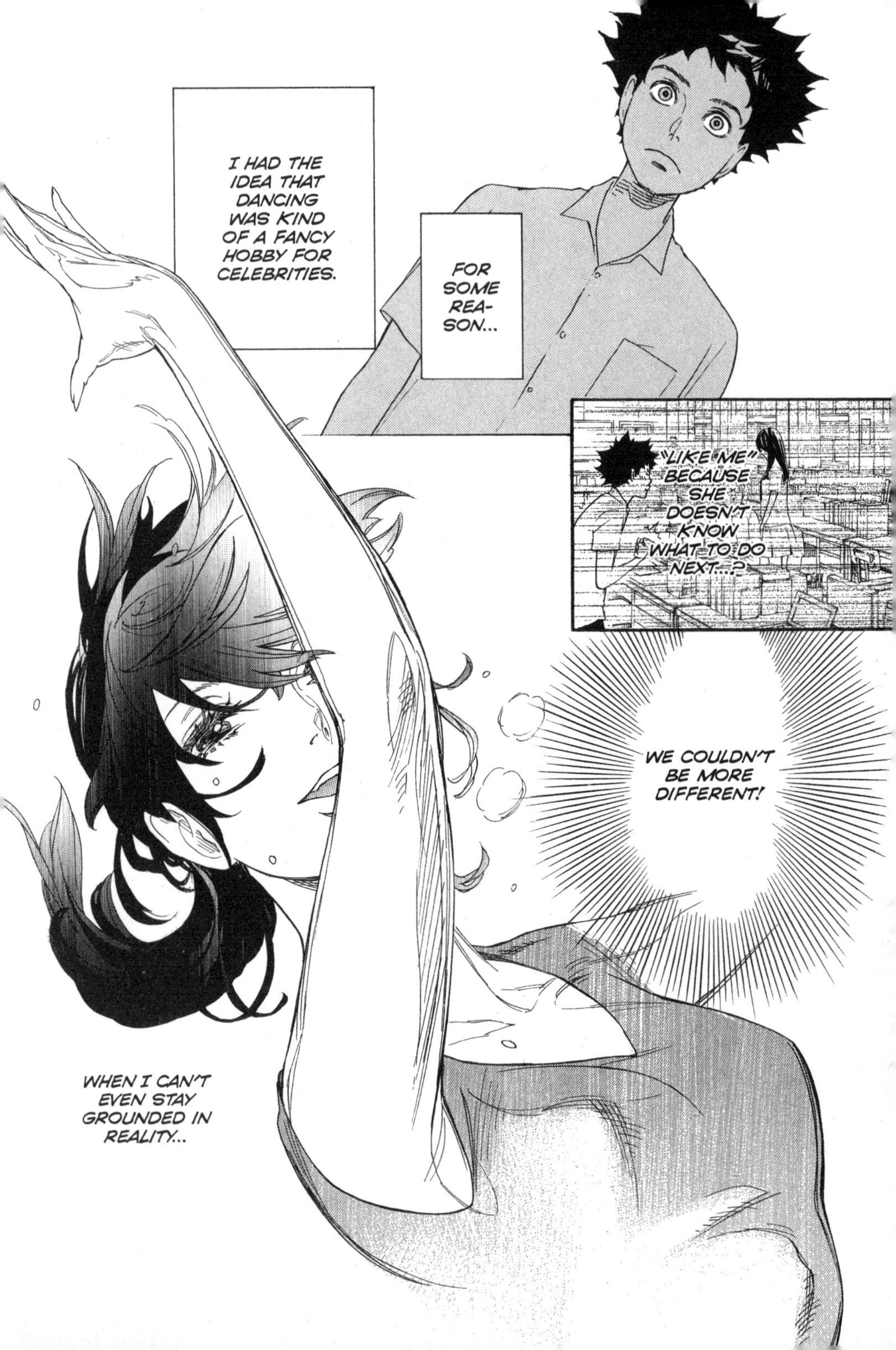
FOR SOME REASON...
I HAD THE IDEA THAT DANCING WAS KIND OF A FANCY HOBBY FOR CELEBRITIES.
"LIKE ME" BECAUSE SHE DOESN'T KNOW WHAT TO DO NEXT...?
WE COULDN'T BE MORE DIFFERENT!
WHEN I CAN'T EVEN STAY GROUNDED IN REALITY...

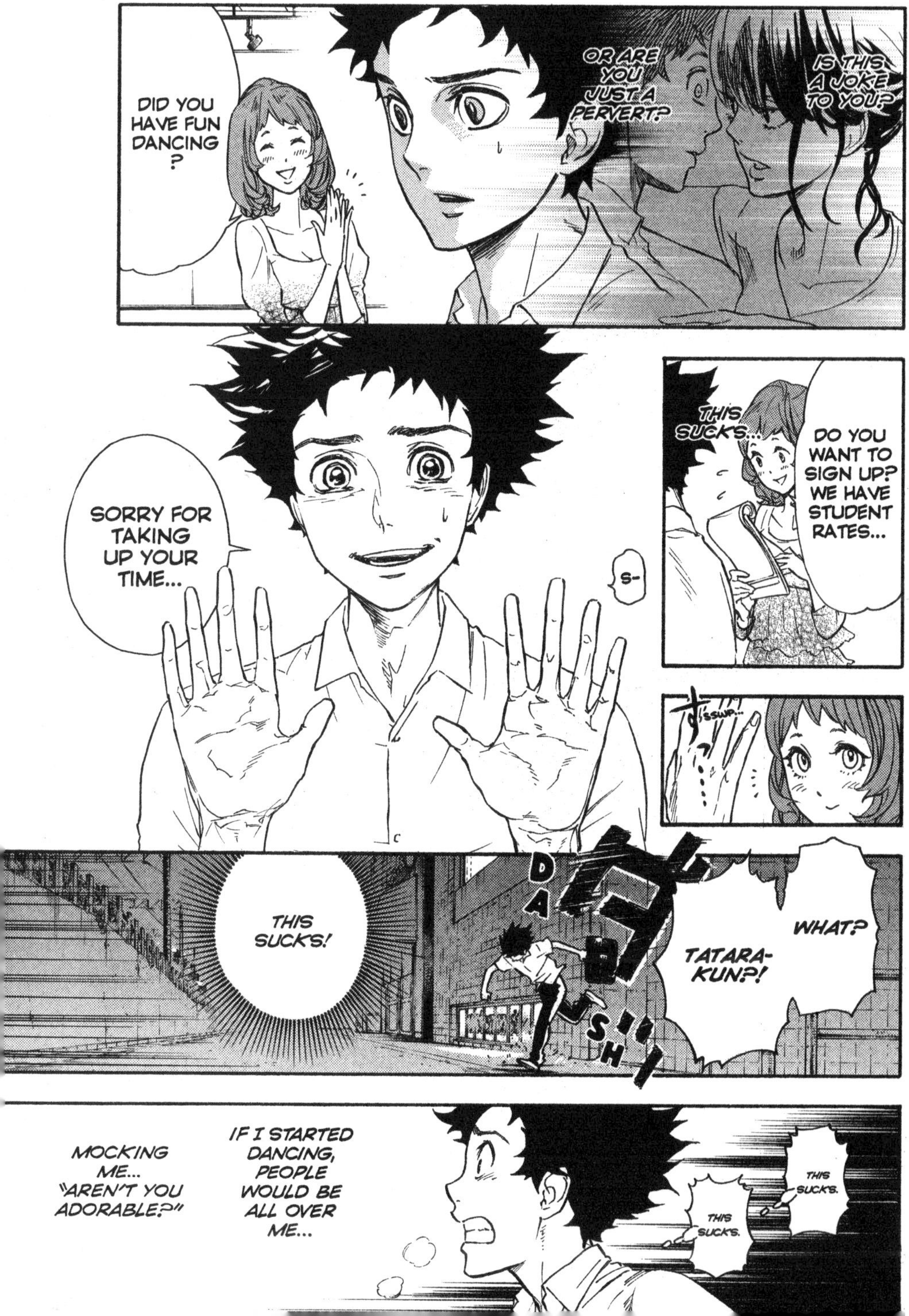
IS THIS A JOKE TO YOU?
OR ARE YOU JUST A PERVERT?
DID YOU HAVE FUN DANCING?
DO YOU WANT TO SIGN UP? WE HAVE STUDENT RATES...
THIS SUCKS...
S-
SORRY FOR TAKING UP YOUR TIME...
WHAT?
TATARA-KUN?!
DASH
THIS SUCKS!
THIS SUCKS.
THIS SUCKS.
IF I STARTED DANCING, PEOPLE WOULD BE ALL OVER ME...
MOCKING ME... "AREN'T YOU ADORABLE?"

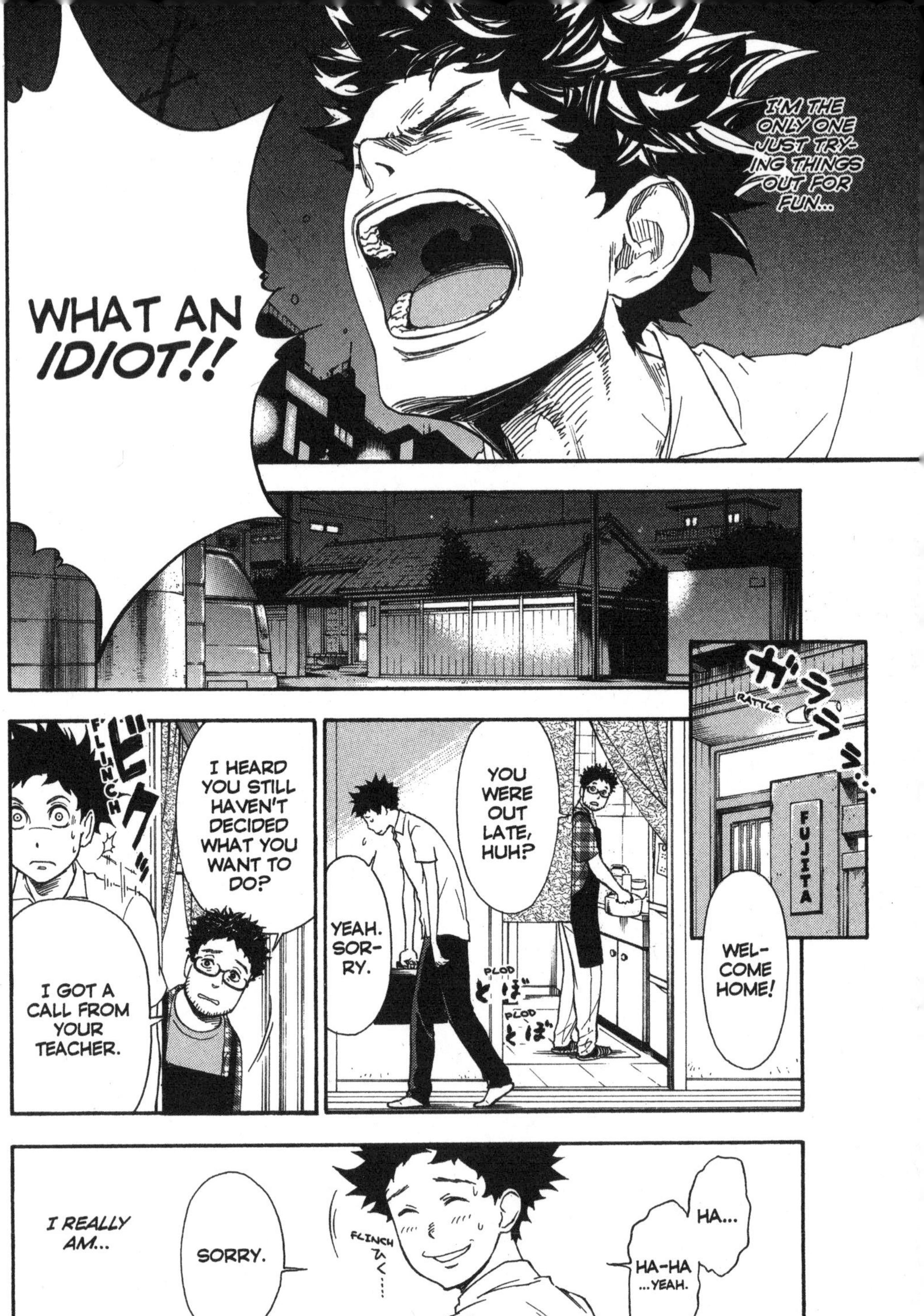
I'M THE ONLY ONE JUST TRYING THINGS OUT FOR FUN...
WHAT AN *IDIOT!!*
ガラララ...
RATTLE
FUJITA
WEL-COME HOME!
YOU WERE OUT LATE, HUH?
YEAH. SOR-RY.
PLOD とぼ
PLOD とぼ
I HEARD YOU STILL HAVEN'T DECIDED WHAT YOU WANT TO DO?
FLINCH ビク
I GOT A CALL FROM YOUR TEACHER.
HA...
HA-HA ...YEAH.
FLINCH ひく...
SORRY.
I REALLY AM...

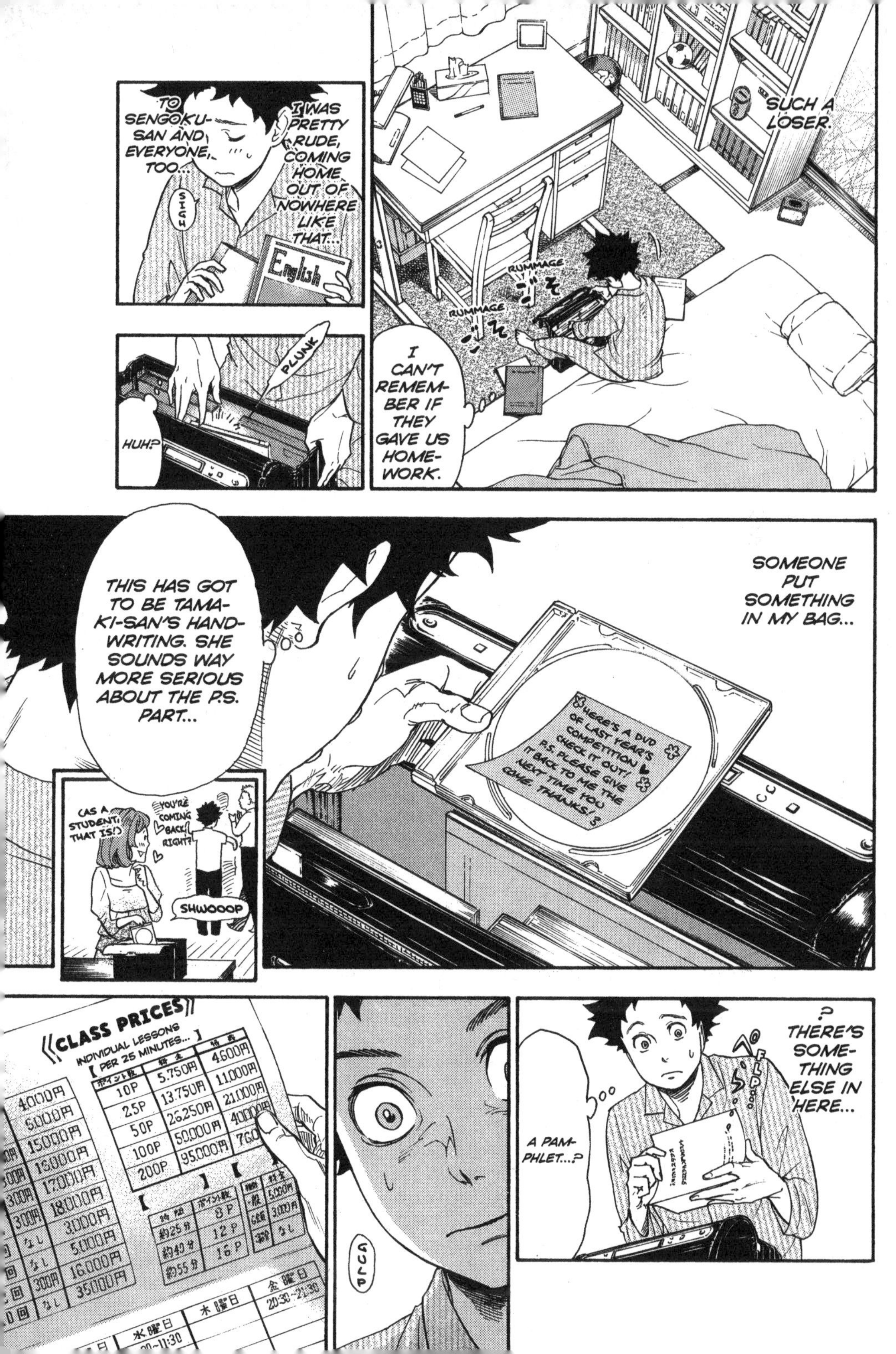
SUCH A LOSER.
RUMMAGE
RUMMAGE
I CAN'T REMEMBER IF THEY GAVE US HOMEWORK.
I WAS PRETTY RUDE, COMING HOME OUT OF NOWHERE LIKE THAT...
TO SENGOKU-SAN AND EVERYONE, TOO...
SIGH
English
PLUNK
HUH?
SOMEONE PUT SOMETHING IN MY BAG...
HERE'S A DVD OF LAST YEAR'S COMPETITION ♥ CHECK IT OUT! P.S. PLEASE GIVE IT BACK TO ME THE NEXT TIME YOU COME. THANKS!
THIS HAS GOT TO BE TAMA-KI-SAN'S HAND-WRITING. SHE SOUNDS WAY MORE SERIOUS ABOUT THE P.S. PART...
YOU'RE COMING BACK, RIGHT?
(AS A STUDENT, THAT IS!)
SHWOOOP
THERE'S SOME-THING ELSE IN HERE...
FLIP
A PAM-PHLET...?
GULP
CLASS PRICES
INDIVIDUAL LESSONS
PER 25 MINUTES...

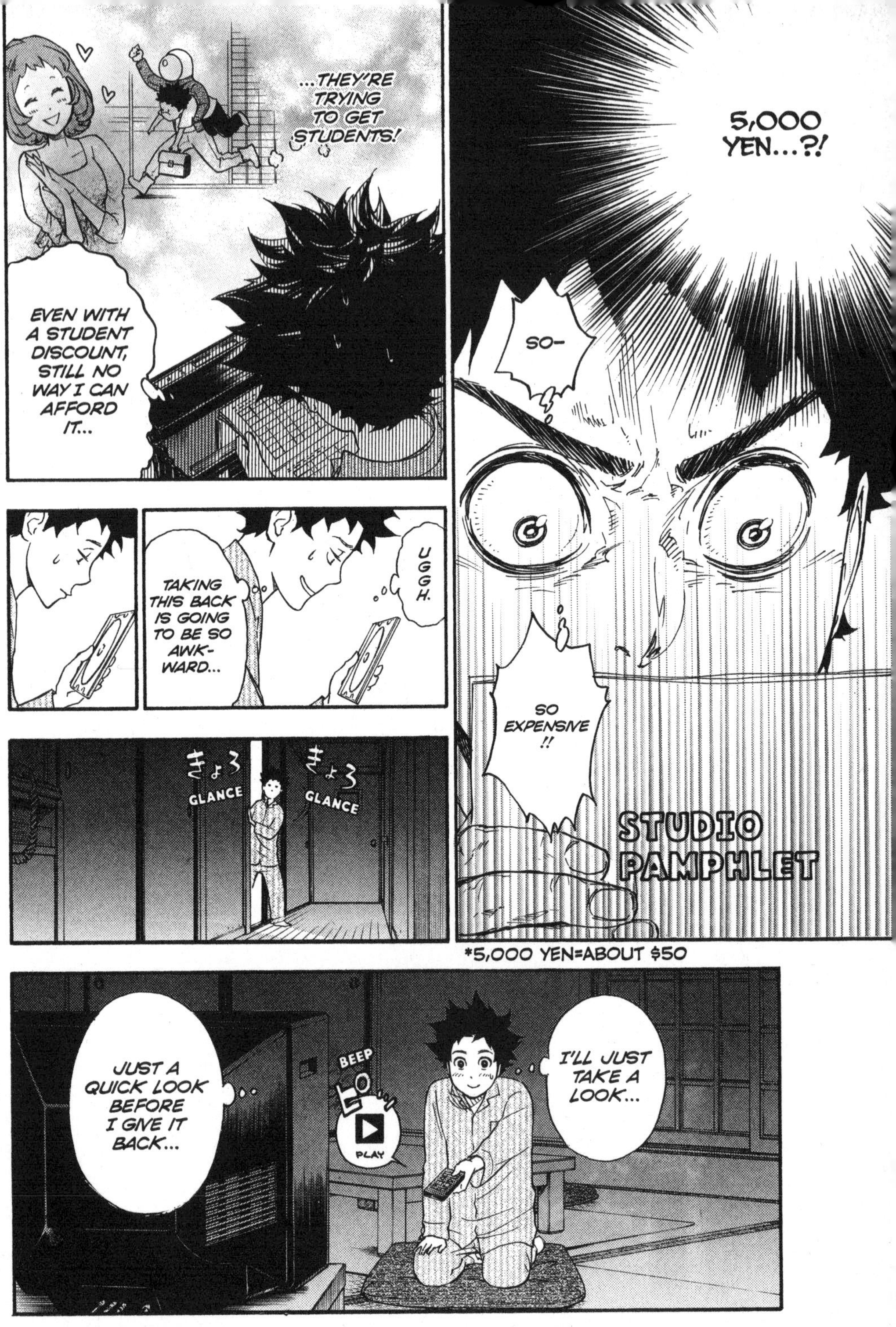
5,000 YEN...?!
SO-
SO EXPENSIVE!!
STUDIO PAMPHLET
...THEY'RE TRYING TO GET STUDENTS!
EVEN WITH A STUDENT DISCOUNT, STILL NO WAY I CAN AFFORD IT...
UGGH.
TAKING THIS BACK IS GOING TO BE SO AWK-WARD...
きょろ GLANCE
きょろ GLANCE
I'LL JUST TAKE A LOOK...
BEEP
PLAY
JUST A QUICK LOOK BEFORE I GIVE IT BACK...

*5,000 YEN=ABOUT $50

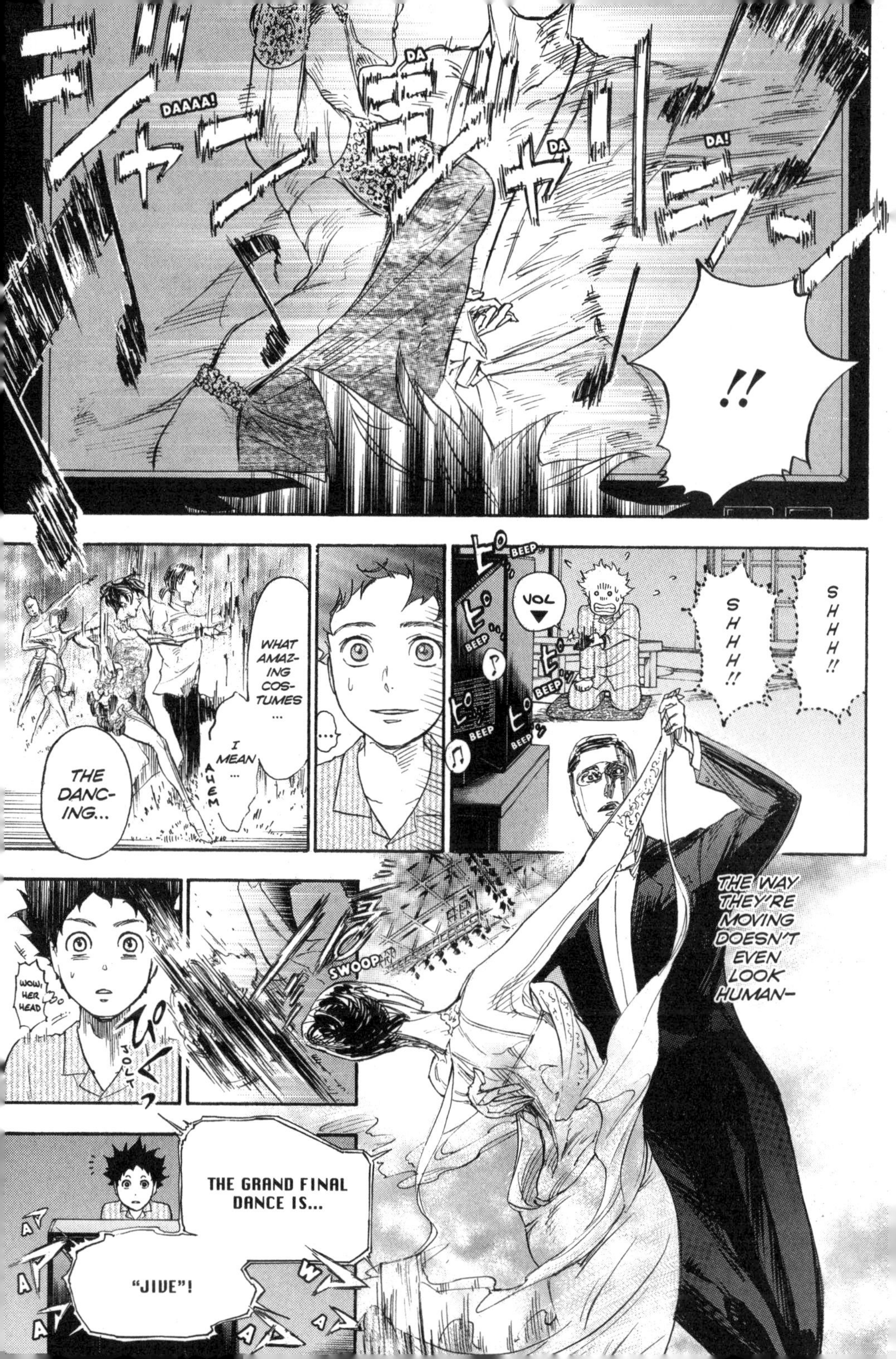

DA!
!!
DA
DA
DAAAA!
SHHHH!!
SHHHH!!
VOL ▼
BEEP
BEEP
BEEP
BEEP
BEEP
...
WHAT AMAZING COSTUMES...
I MEAN...
AHEM
THE DANCING...
THE WAY THEY'RE MOVING DOESN'T EVEN LOOK HUMAN–
SWOOP
WOW, HER HEAD
JOLT
THE GRAND FINAL DANCE IS...
"JIVE"!

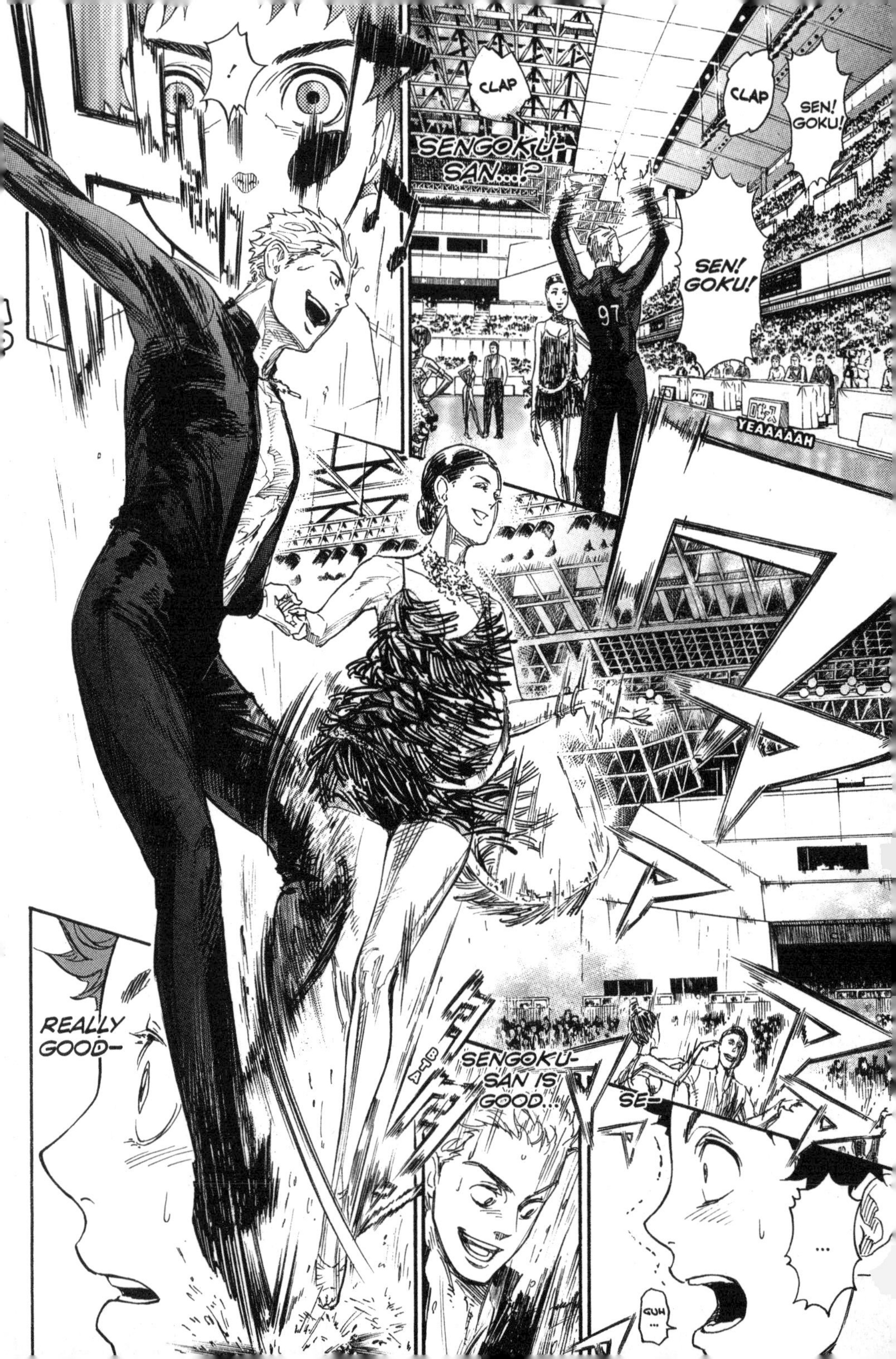
CLAP
SEN! GOKU!
SEN! GOKU!
YEAAAAAH
CLAP
SENGOKU-SAN...?
!
SE-
...
GUH ...
SENGOKU-SAN IS GOOD...
REALLY GOOD-

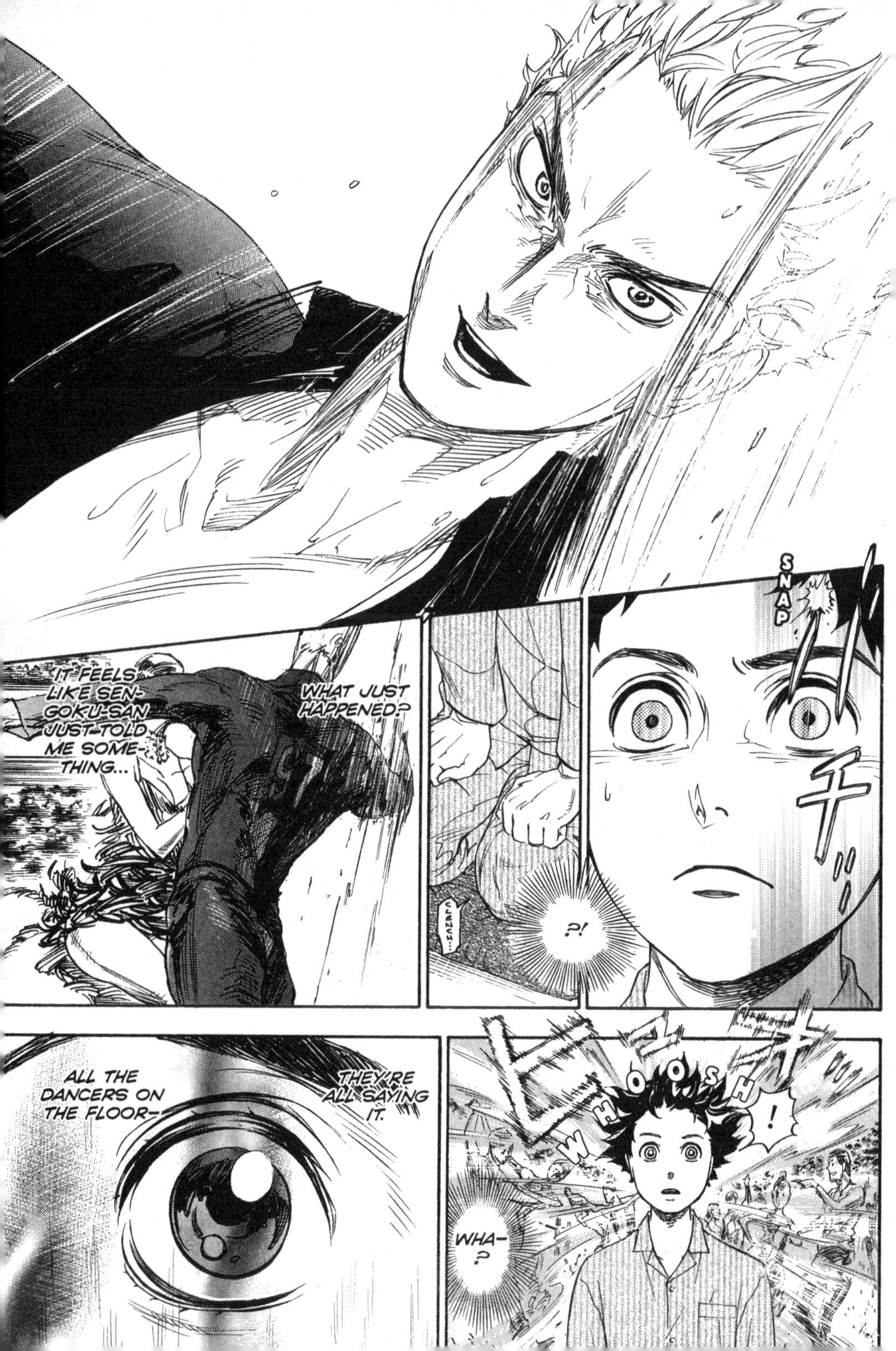
SNAP
?!
WHAT JUST HAPPENED?
IT FEELS LIKE SEN-GOKU-SAN JUST TOLD ME SOME-THING...
WHOOSH
!
WHA-?
THEY'RE ALL SAYING IT.
ALL THE DANCERS ON THE FLOOR-

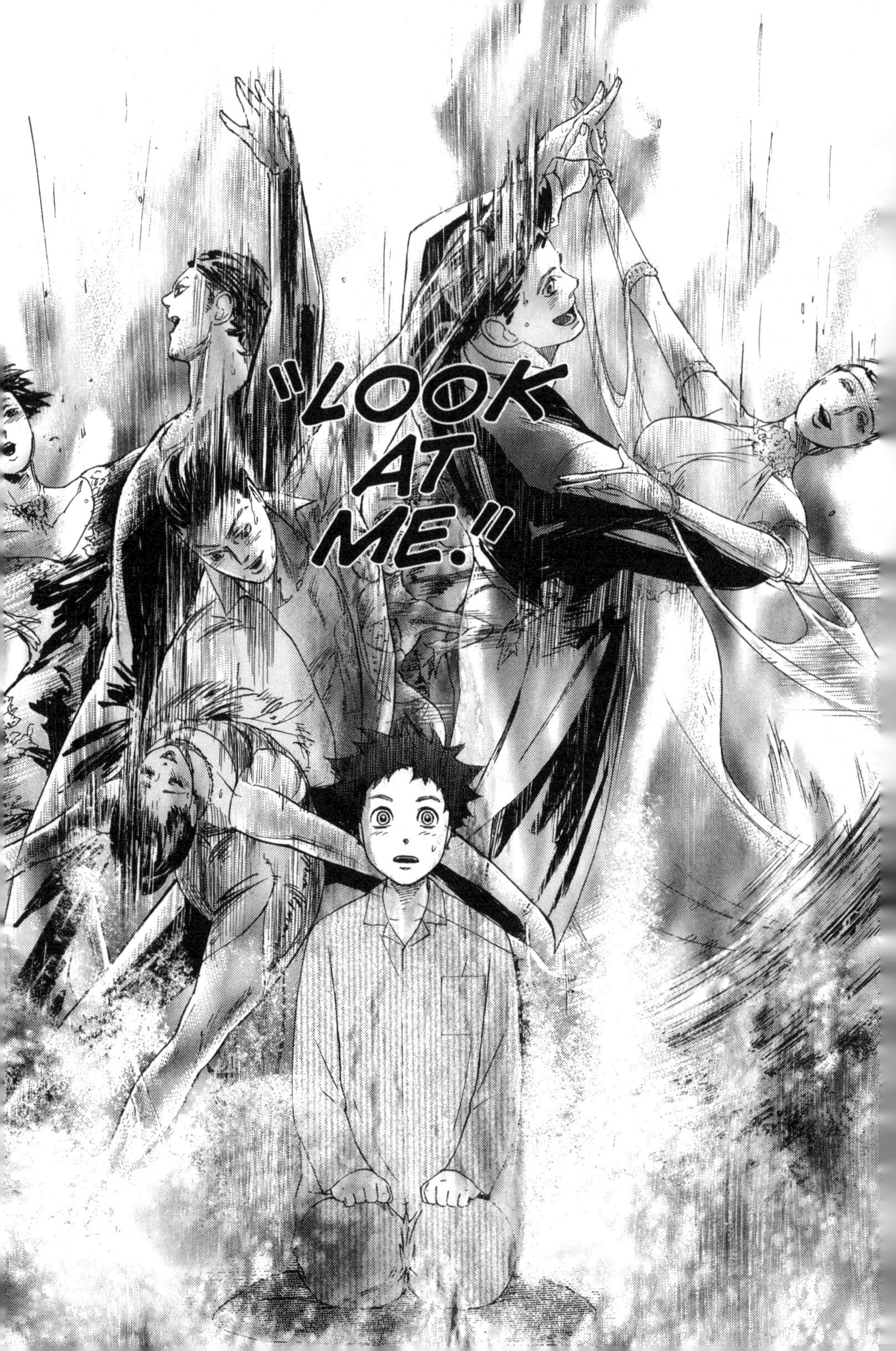
"LOOK AT ME."

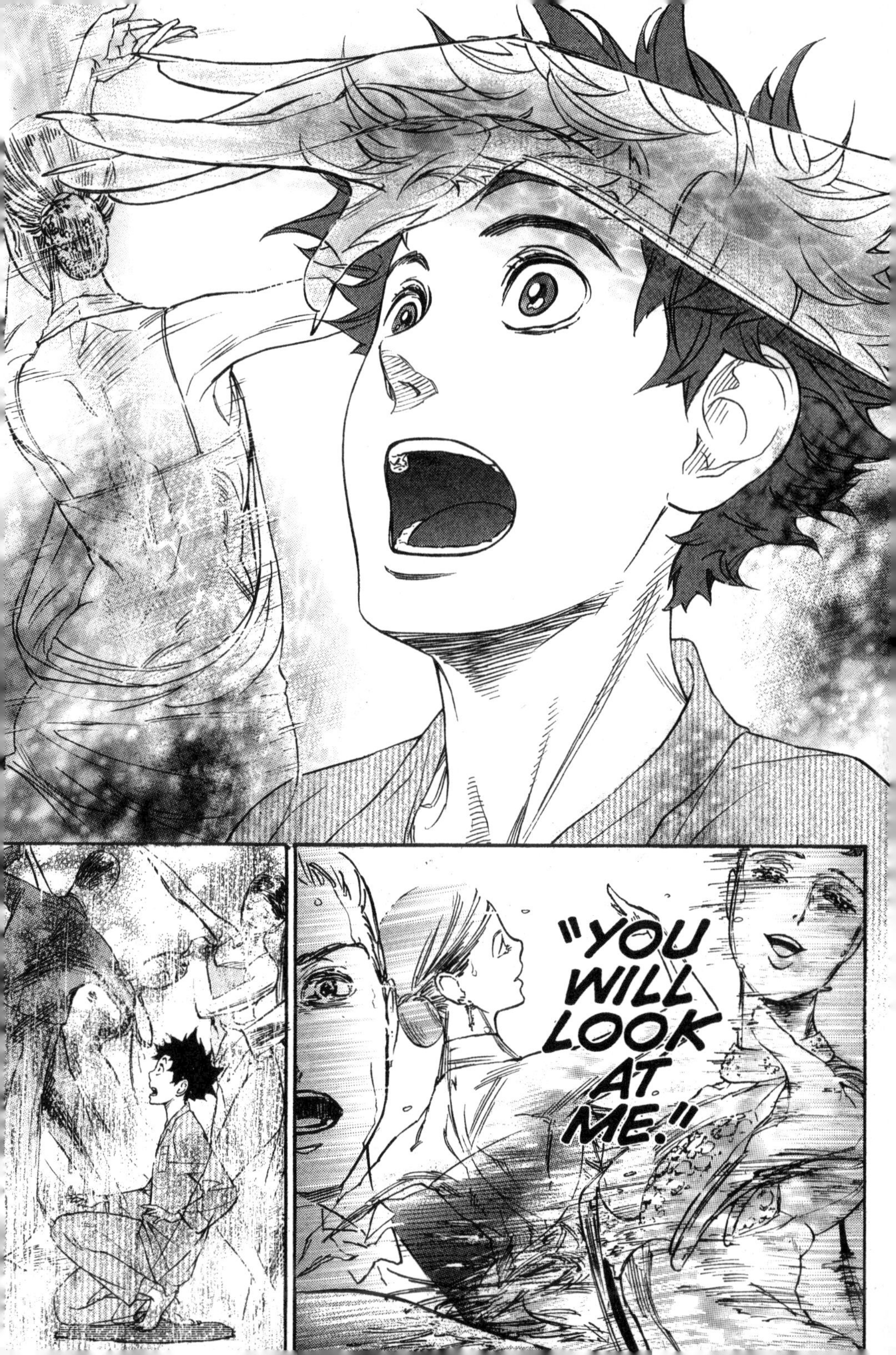
"YOU WILL LOOK AT ME."

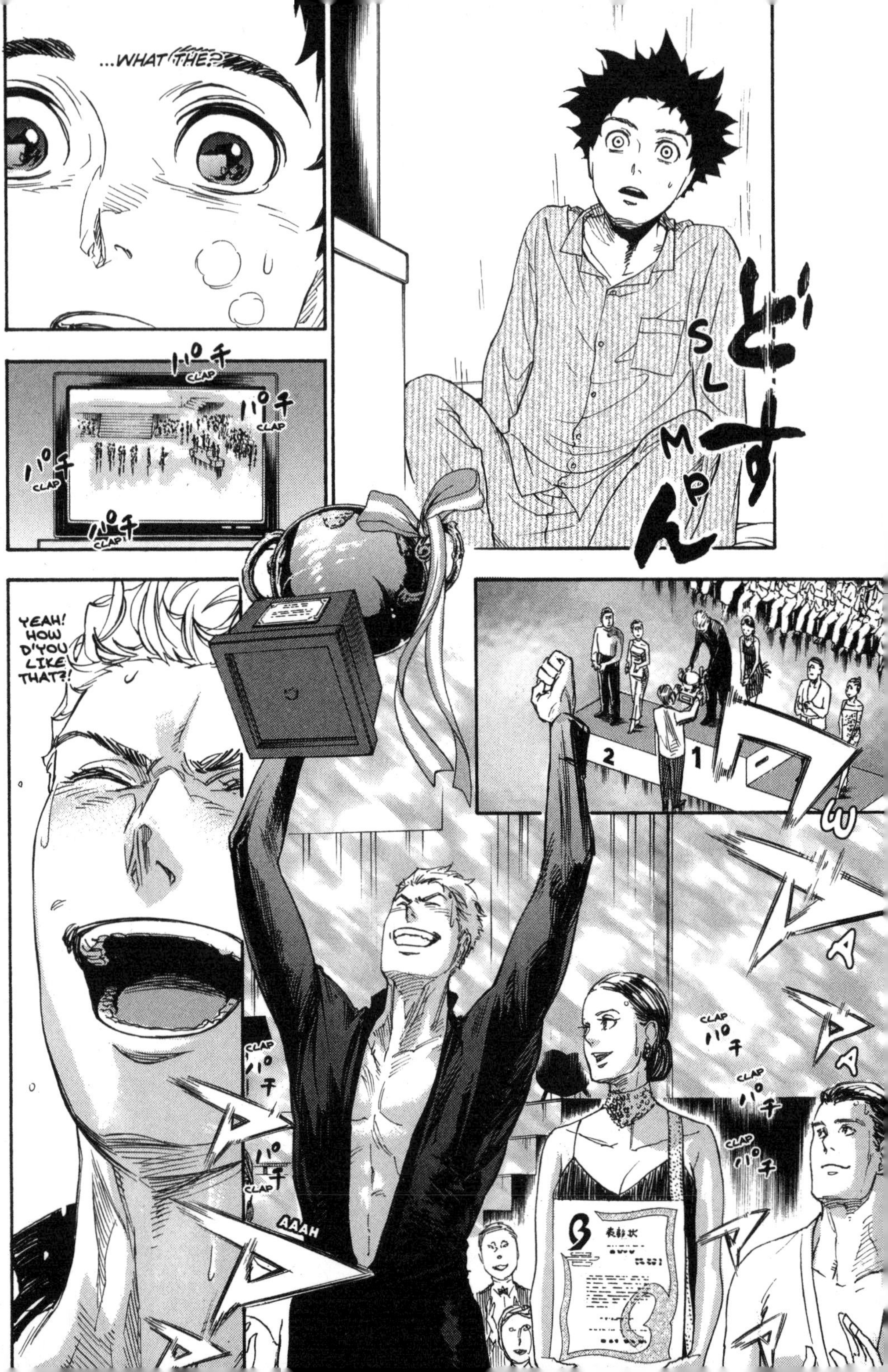

どすん
SLUMP
...WHAT THE?
パチ
CLAP
パチ
CLAP
パチ
CLAP
パチ
CLAP
WAAA
YEAH! HOW D'YOU LIKE THAT?!
パチ
CLAP
パチ
CLAP
パチ
CLAP
パチ
CLAP
パチ
CLAP
AAAH

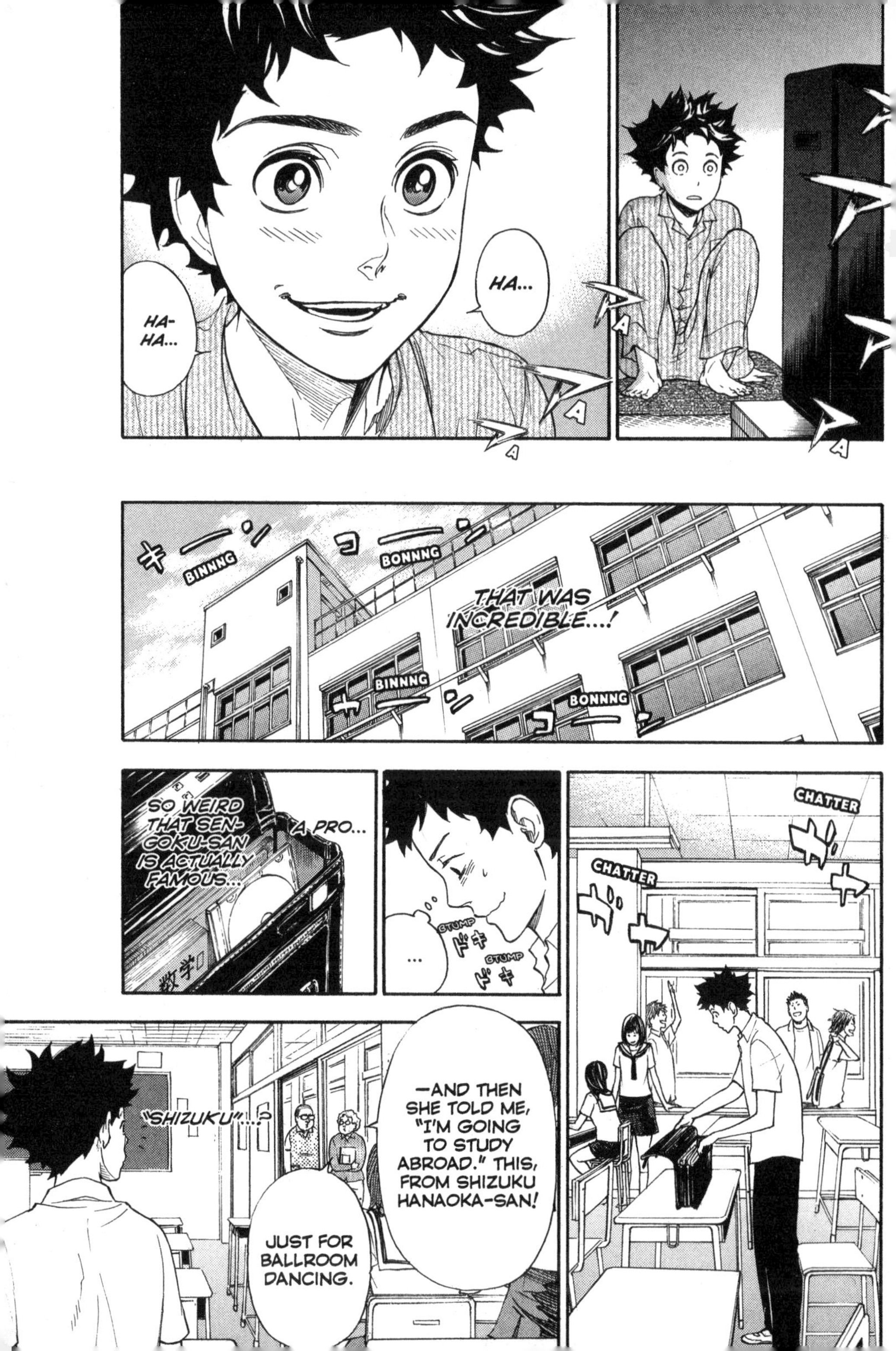
A
A
HA...
HA-HA...
A
A
BINNNG
BONNNG
THAT WAS INCREDIBLE...!
BINNNG
BONNNG
CHATTER
CHATTER
...
BTUMP
BTUMP
A PRO...
SO WEIRD THAT SEN-GOKU-SAN IS ACTUALLY FAMOUS...
—AND THEN SHE TOLD ME, "I'M GOING TO STUDY ABROAD." THIS, FROM SHIZUKU HANAOKA-SAN!
JUST FOR BALLROOM DANCING.
"SHIZUKU"...?

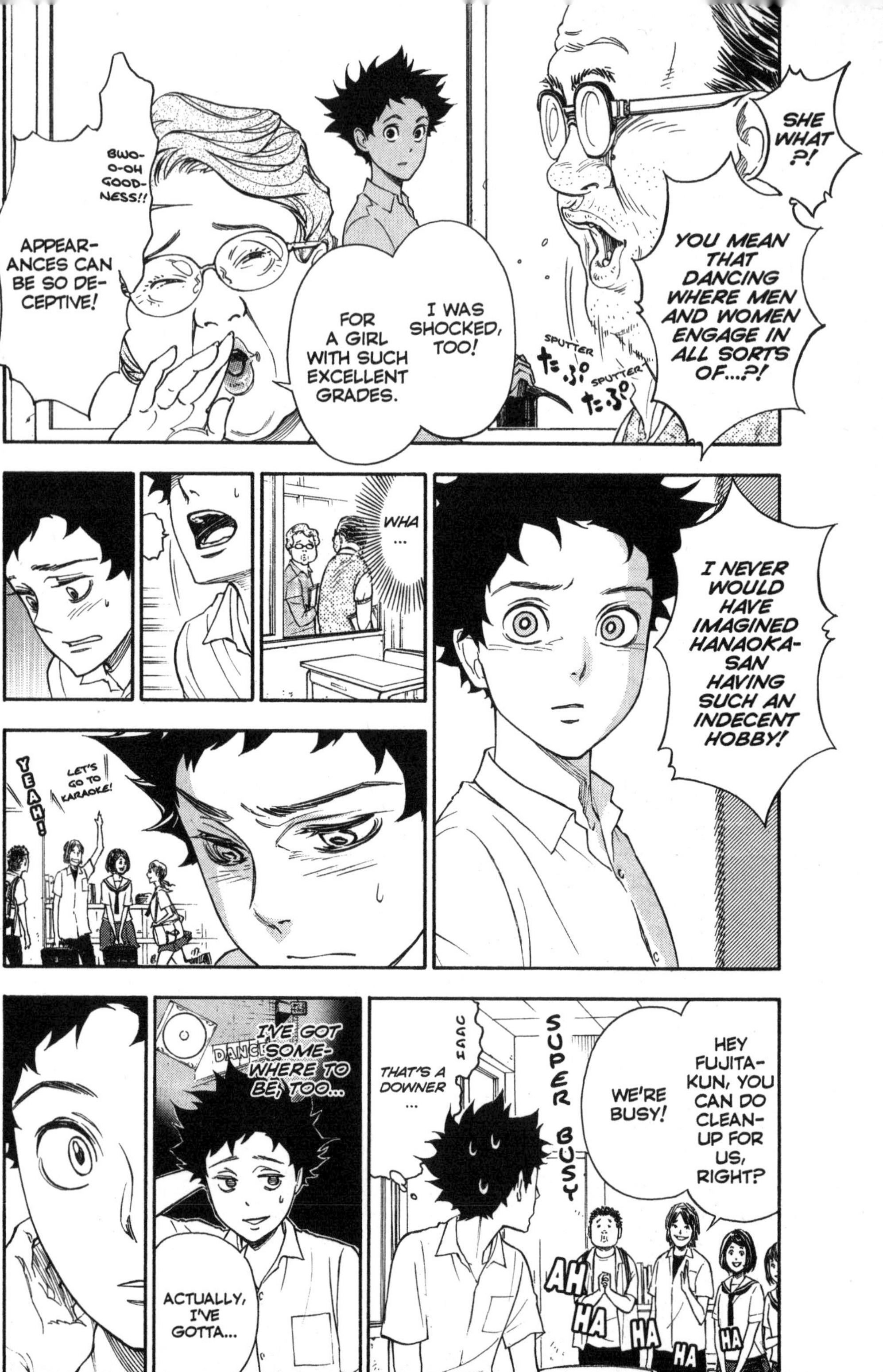

SHE WHAT ?!
YOU MEAN THAT DANCING WHERE MEN AND WOMEN ENGAGE IN ALL SORTS OF...?!
SPUTTER
SPUTTER
I WAS SHOCKED, TOO!
FOR A GIRL WITH SUCH EXCELLENT GRADES.
BWOO-O-OH GOOD-NESS!!
APPEARANCES CAN BE SO DECEPTIVE!
I NEVER WOULD HAVE IMAGINED HANAOKA-SAN HAVING SUCH AN INDECENT HOBBY!
WHA ...
LET'S GO TO KARAOKE!
YEAH!
HEY FUJITA-KUN, YOU CAN DO CLEAN-UP FOR US, RIGHT?
WE'RE BUSY!
SUPER BUSY
AH HA HA HA HA HA
UGH
THAT'S A DOWNER ...
I'VE GOT SOME-WHERE TO BE, TOO...
DANCE
ACTUALLY, I'VE GOTTA...

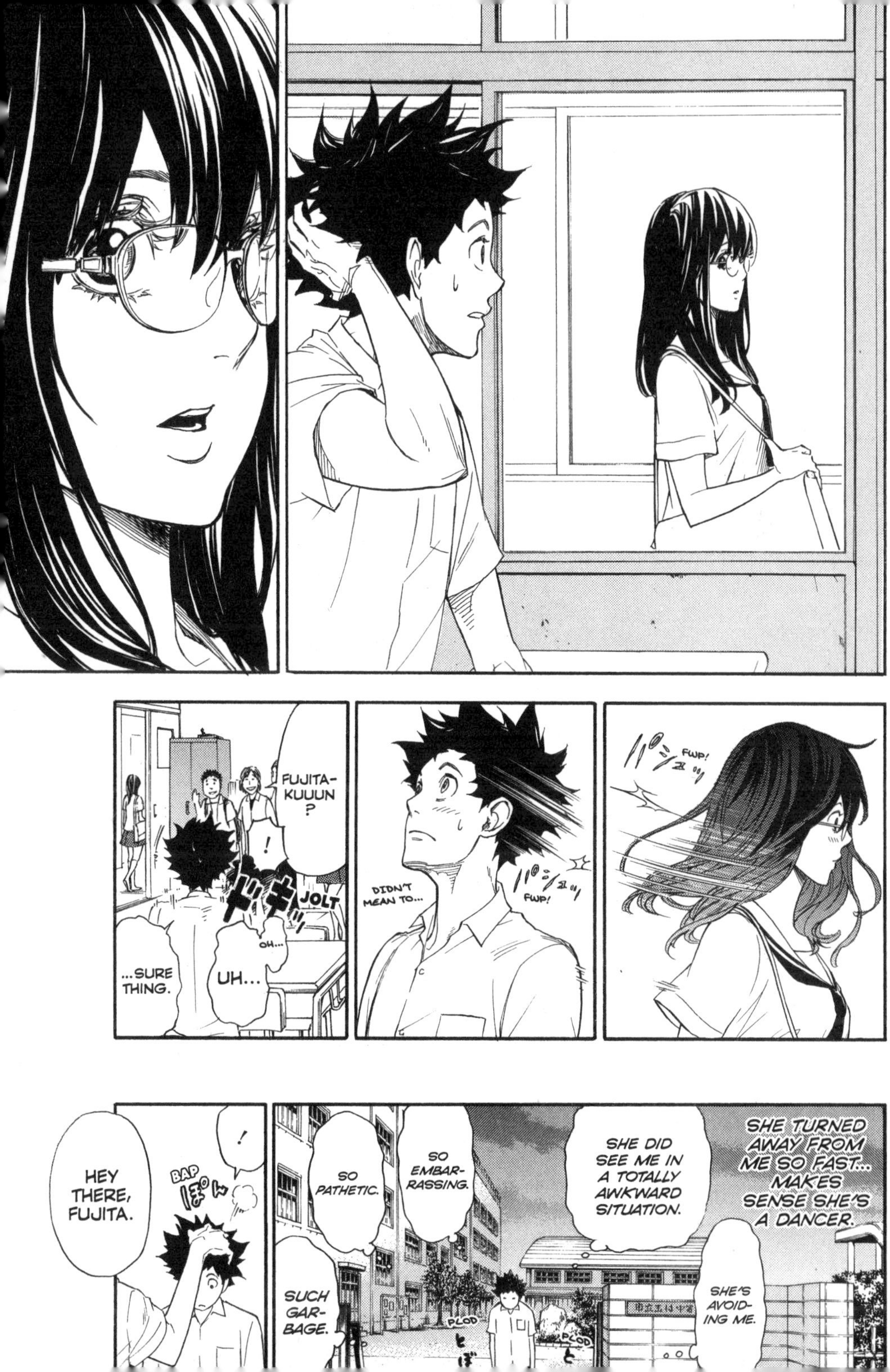
FWP!
DIDN'T MEAN TO...
FWP!
FUJITA-KUUUN?
!
JOLT
OH...
UH...
...SURE THING.
SHE TURNED AWAY FROM ME SO FAST... MAKES SENSE SHE'S A DANCER.
SHE DID SEE ME IN A TOTALLY AWKWARD SITUATION.
SHE'S AVOIDING ME.
SO EMBARRASSING.
SO PATHETIC.
SUCH GARBAGE.
PLOD
PLOD
!
BAP
HEY THERE, FUJITA.

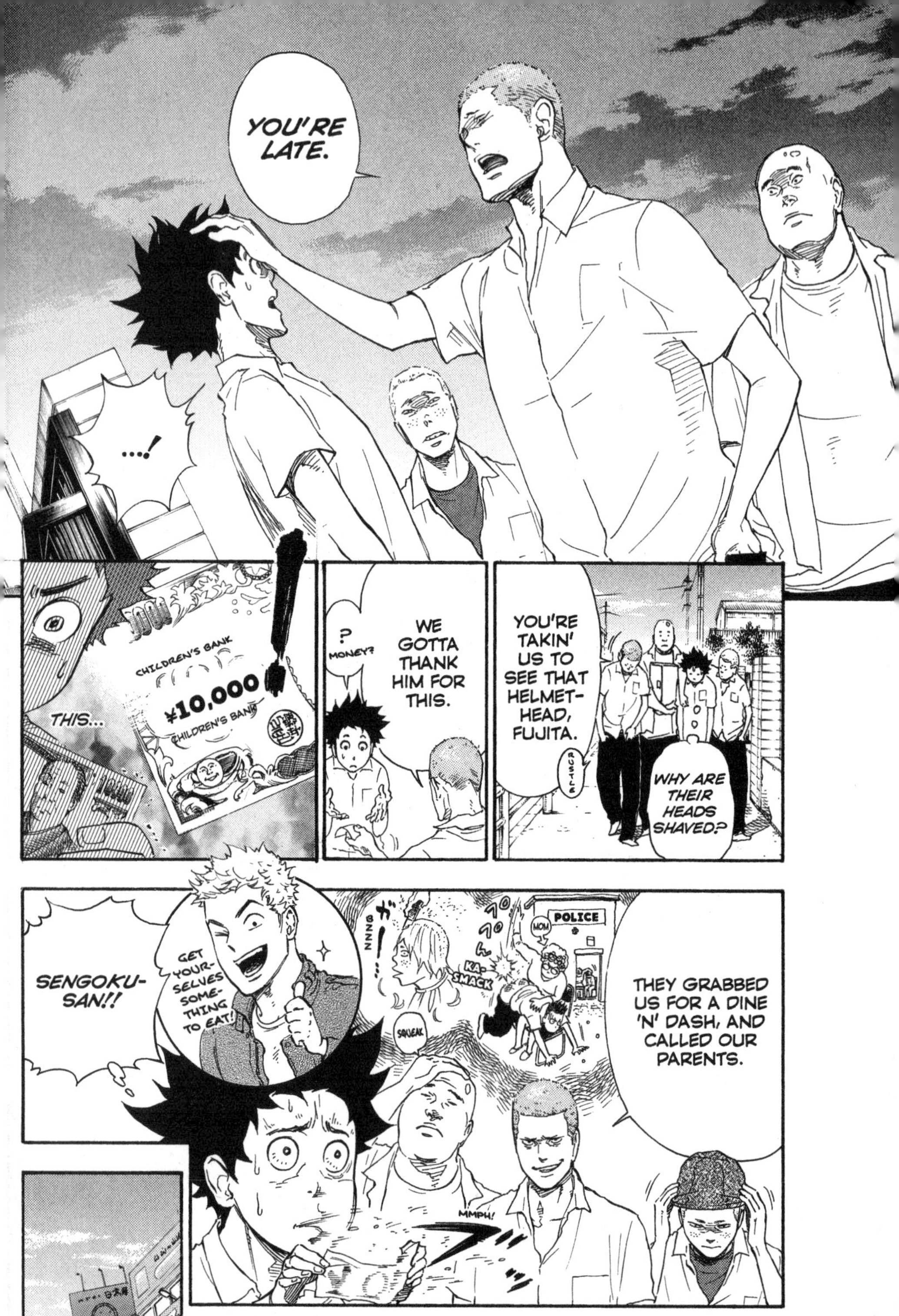
YOU'RE LATE.
...!
YOU'RE TAKIN' US TO SEE THAT HELMET-HEAD, FUJITA.
RUSTLE
WHY ARE THEIR HEADS SHAVED?
WE GOTTA THANK HIM FOR THIS.
? MONEY?
THIS...
CHILDREN'S BANK
¥10,000
CHILDREN'S BANK
THEY GRABBED US FOR A DINE 'N' DASH, AND CALLED OUR PARENTS.
POLICE
MOM
KA-SMACK
SQUEAK
BZZZ
GET YOURSELVES SOMETHING TO EAT!
SENGOKU-SAN!!
MMPH!

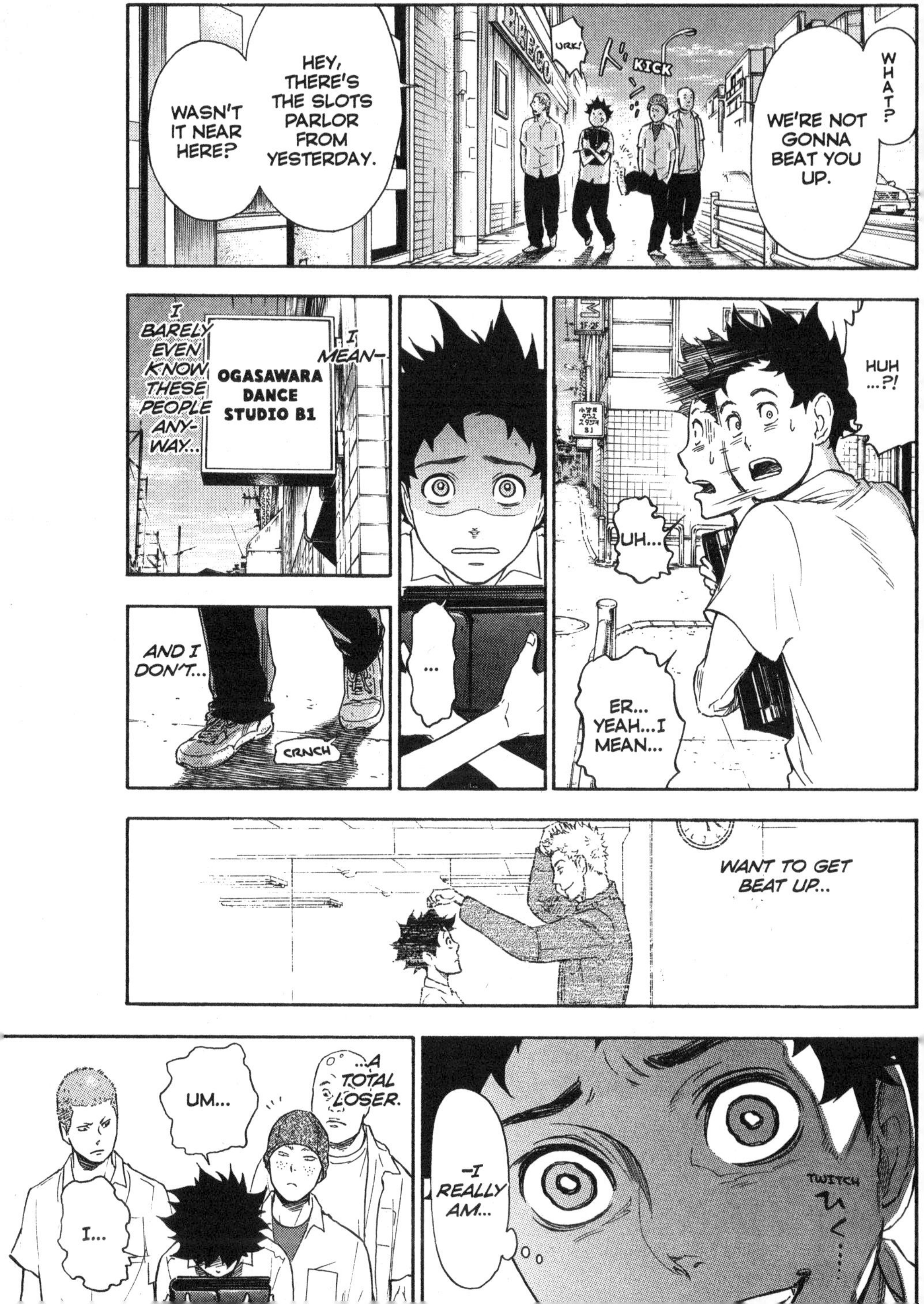
WHAT?
WE'RE NOT GONNA BEAT YOU UP.
KICK
URK!
HEY, THERE'S THE SLOTS PARLOR FROM YESTERDAY.
WASN'T IT NEAR HERE?
HUH ...?!
UH...
ER... YEAH...I MEAN...
I MEAN—
I BARELY EVEN KNOW THESE PEOPLE ANYWAY...
OGASAWARA DANCE STUDIO B1
...
AND I DON'T...
CRNCH
WANT TO GET BEAT UP...
—I REALLY AM...
TWITCH
...A TOTAL LOSER.
UM...
I...

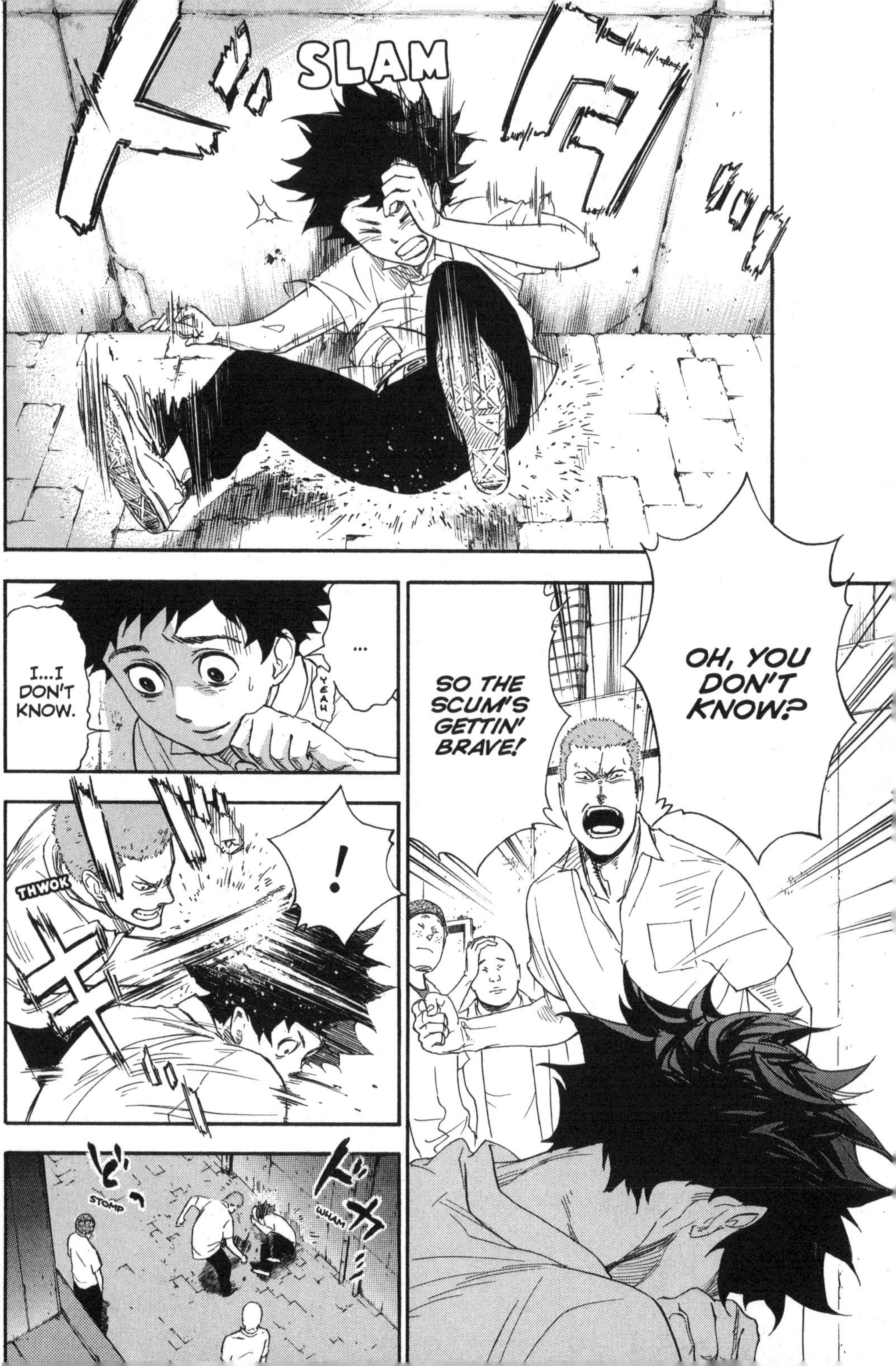
SLAM
OH, YOU DON'T KNOW?
SO THE SCUM'S GETTIN' BRAVE!
...
YEAH
I...I DON'T KNOW.
!
THWOK
WHAM
STOMP

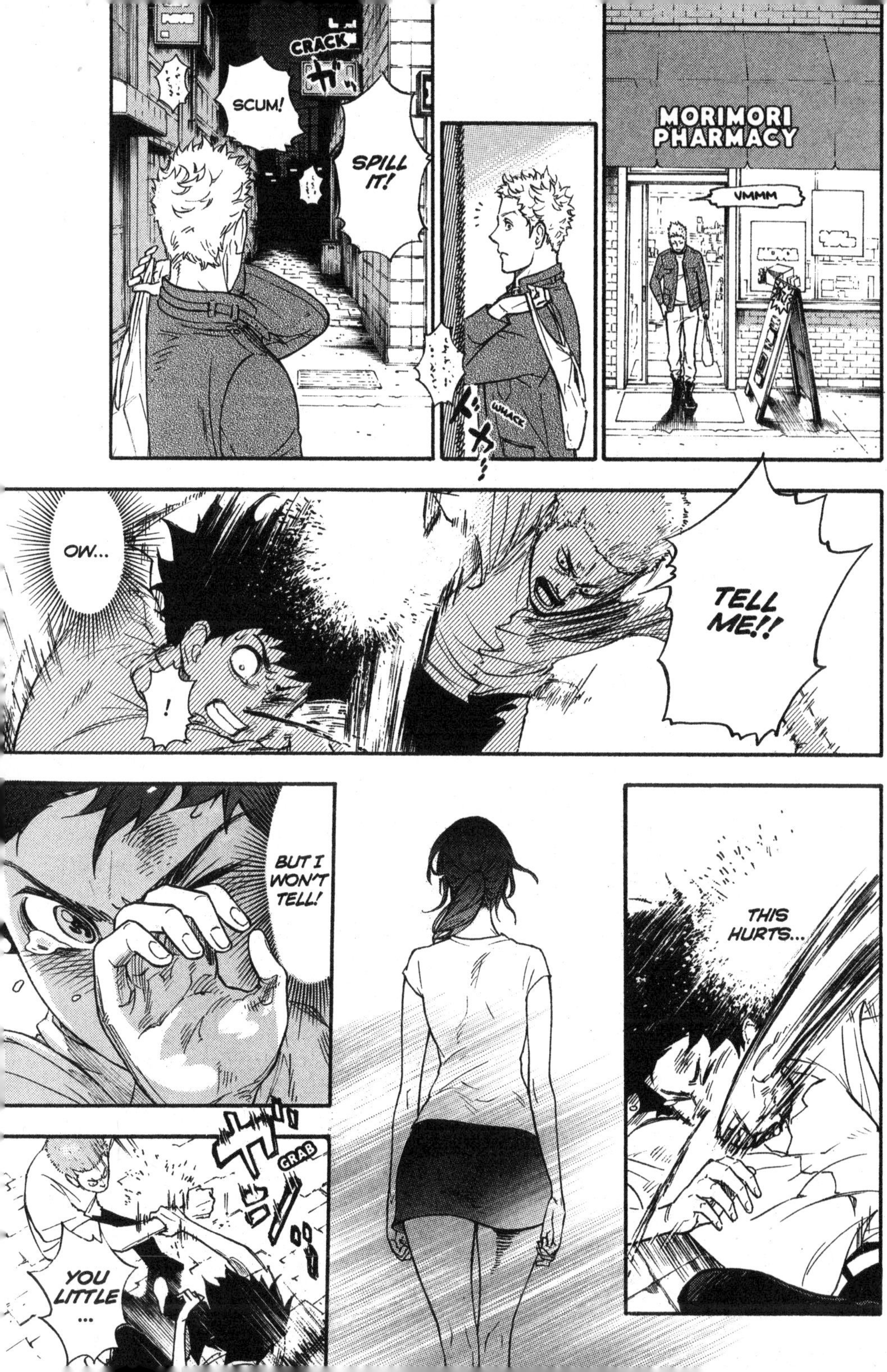
MORIMORI PHARMACY
VMMM
WHACK
CRACK
SCUM!
SPILL IT!
TELL ME!!
OW...
!
THIS HURTS...
BUT I WON'T TELL!
GRAB
YOU LITTLE ...

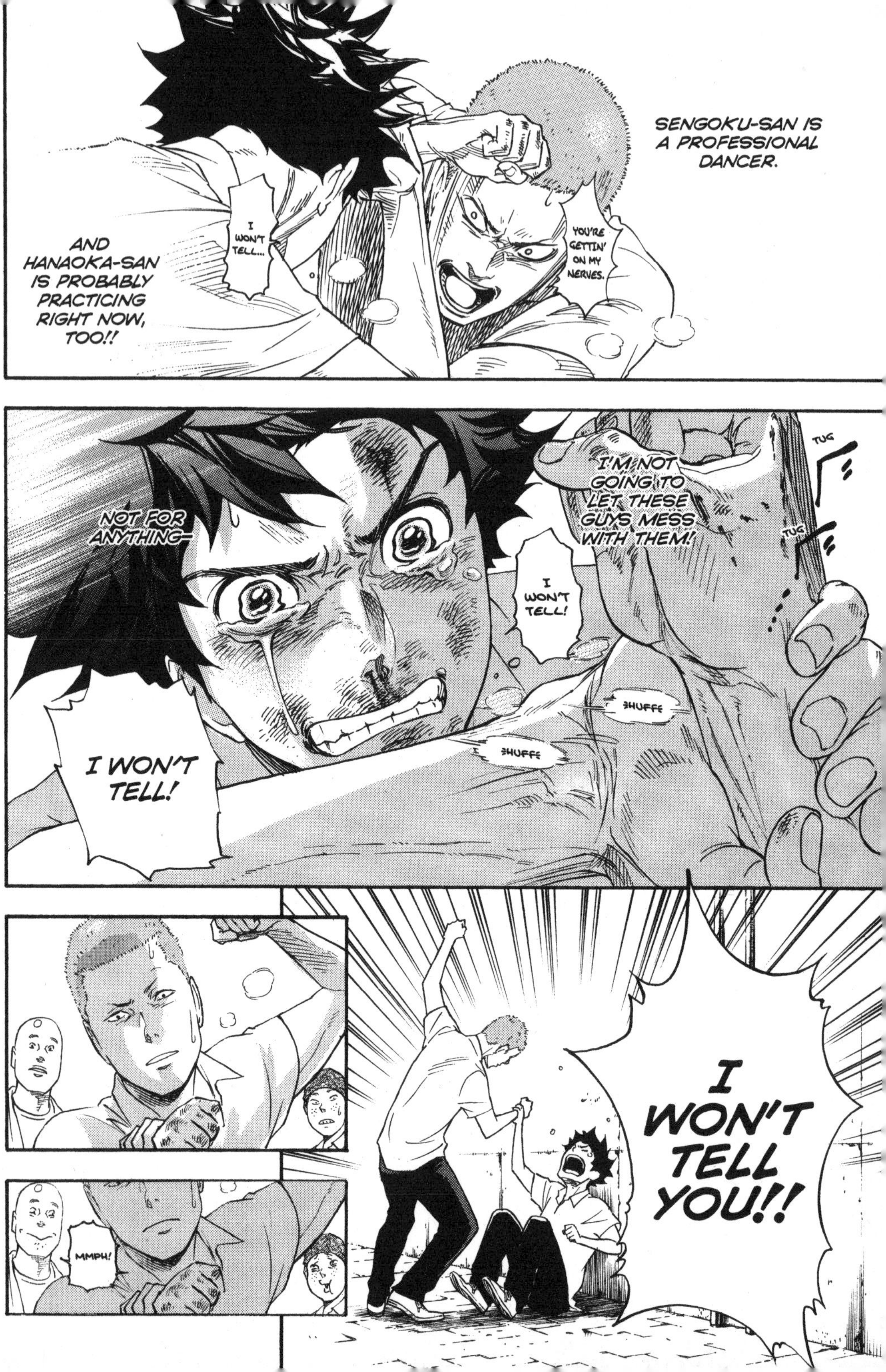
SENGOKU-SAN IS A PROFESSIONAL DANCER.
YOU'RE GETTIN' ON MY NERVES.
I WON'T TELL...
AND HANAOKA-SAN IS PROBABLY PRACTICING RIGHT NOW, TOO!!
TUG
TUG
I'M NOT GOING TO LET THESE GUYS MESS WITH THEM!
NOT FOR ANYTHING—
I WON'T TELL!
HUFF
HUFF
I WON'T TELL!
I WON'T TELL YOU!!
MMPH!

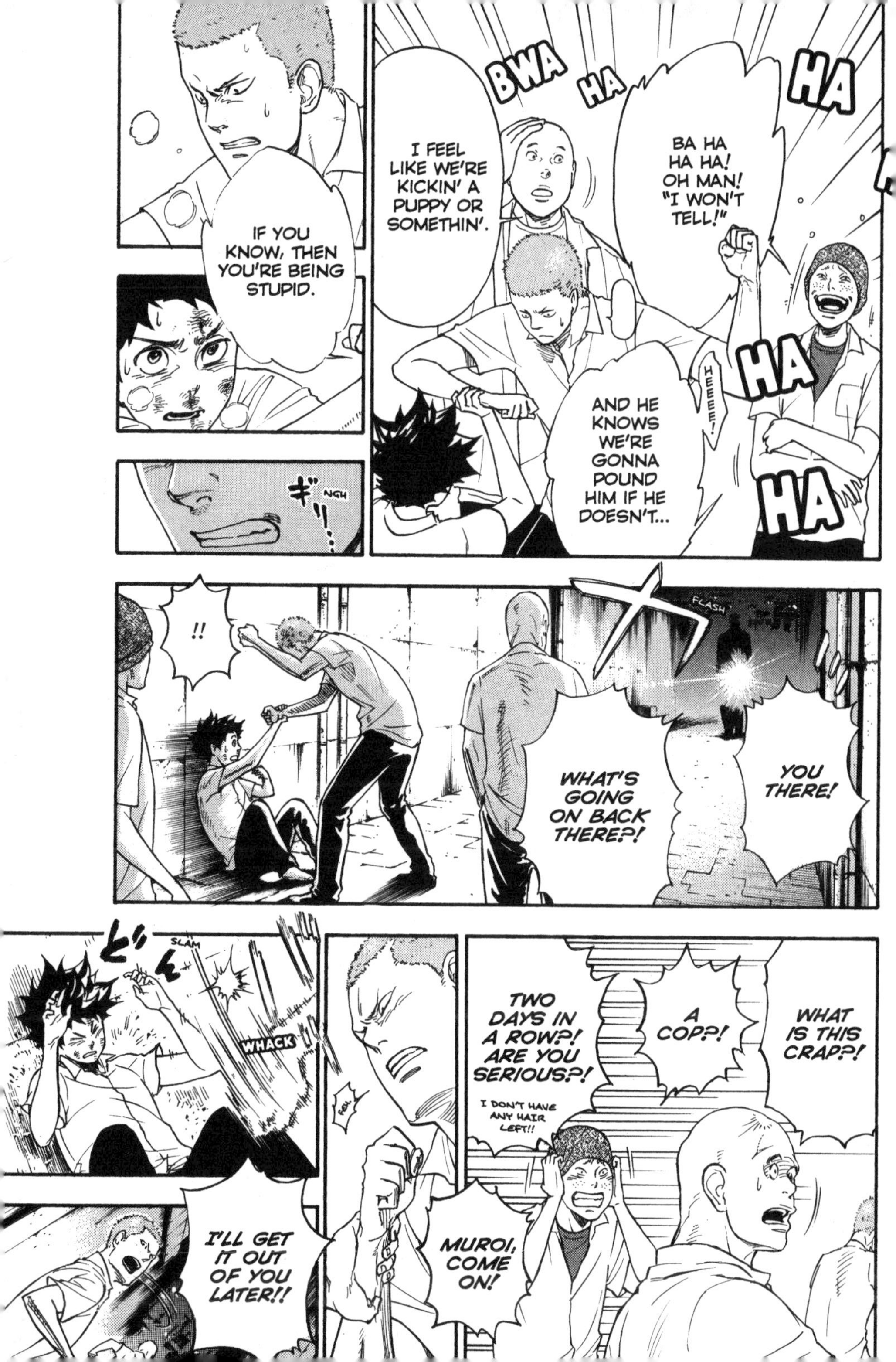
BWA HA HA
BA HA HA HA! OH MAN! "I WON'T TELL!"
I FEEL LIKE WE'RE KICKIN' A PUPPY OR SOMETHIN'.
HEEEE!
AND HE KNOWS WE'RE GONNA POUND HIM IF HE DOESN'T...
HA HA
IF YOU KNOW, THEN YOU'RE BEING STUPID.
NGH
FLASH
YOU THERE!
WHAT'S GOING ON BACK THERE?!
!!
WHAT IS THIS CRAP?!
A COP?!
TWO DAYS IN A ROW?! ARE YOU SERIOUS?!
I DON'T HAVE ANY HAIR LEFT!!
MUROI, COME ON!
FSH
SLAM
WHACK
I'LL GET IT OUT OF YOU LATER!!

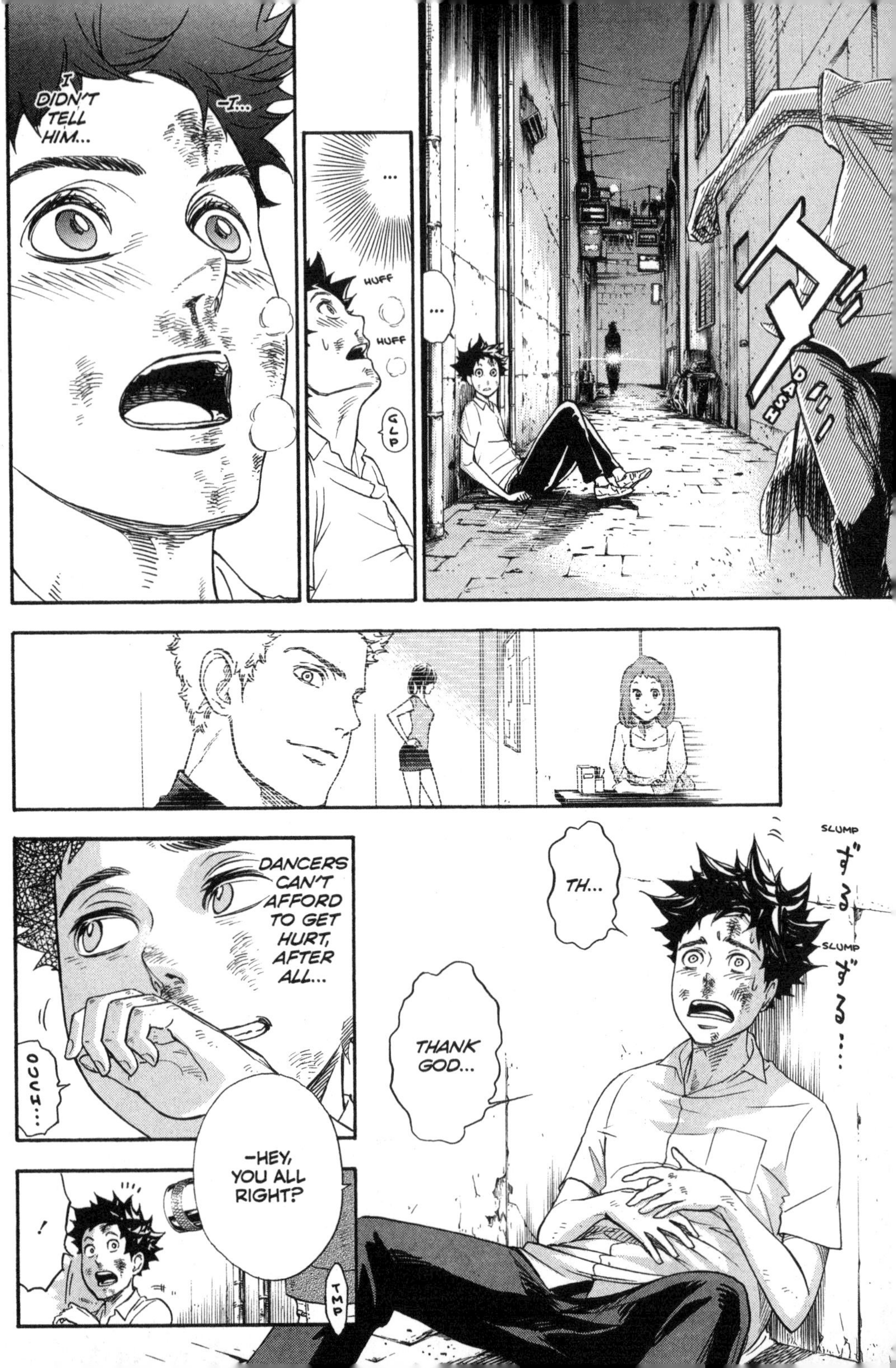
DASH
...
HUFF
HUFF
GLP
...
—I...
I DIDN'T TELL HIM...
SLUMP
SLUMP
TH...
THANK GOD...
DANCERS CAN'T AFFORD TO GET HURT, AFTER ALL...
OUCH...
—HEY, YOU ALL RIGHT?
TMP
!

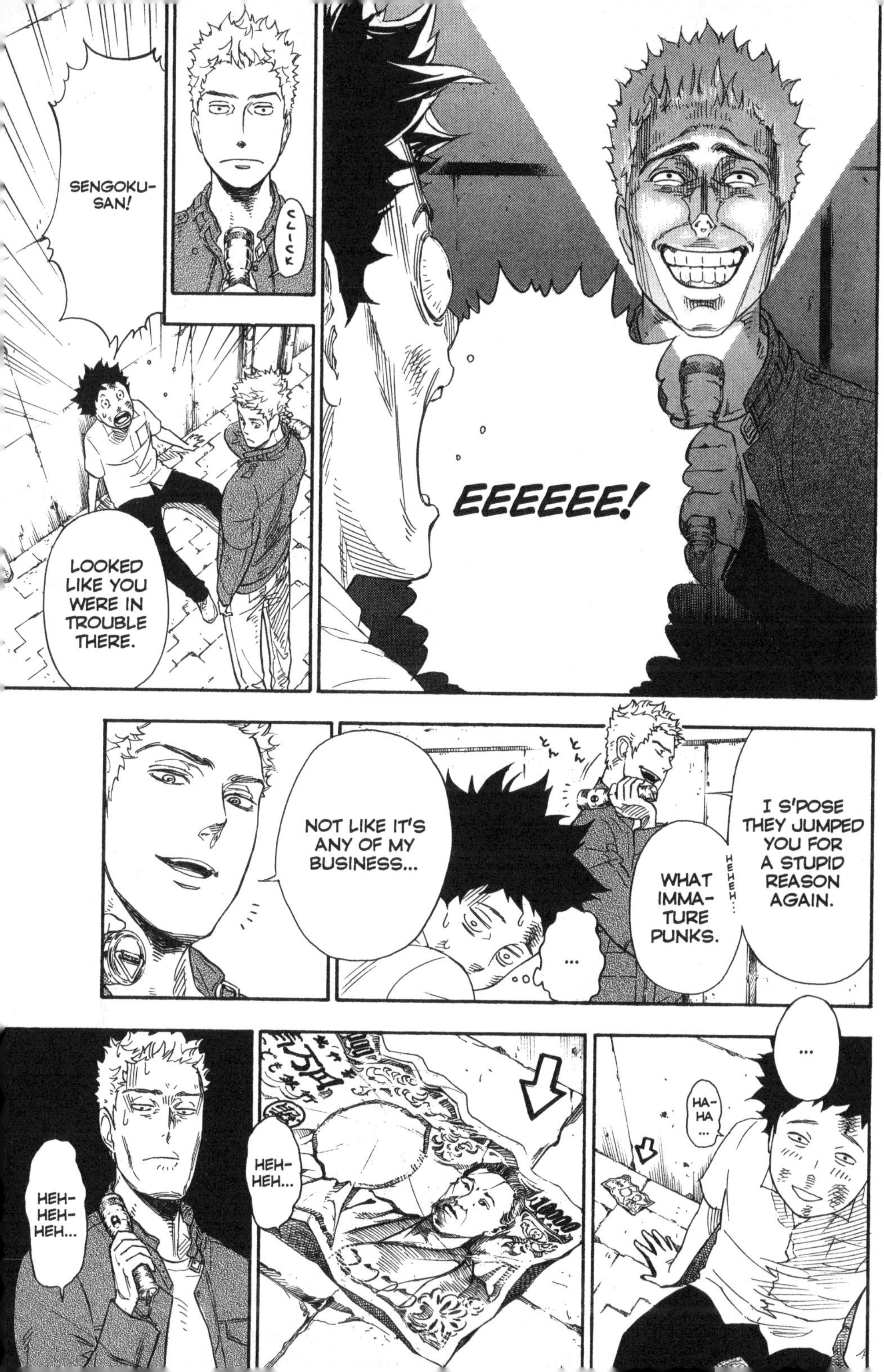
EEEEEE!
SENGOKU-SAN!
CLICK
LOOKED LIKE YOU WERE IN TROUBLE THERE.
I S'POSE THEY JUMPED YOU FOR A STUPID REASON AGAIN.
HEHEH...
WHAT IMMATURE PUNKS.
...
NOT LIKE IT'S ANY OF MY BUSINESS...
...
HA-HA...
HEH-HEH...
HEH-HEH-HEH...

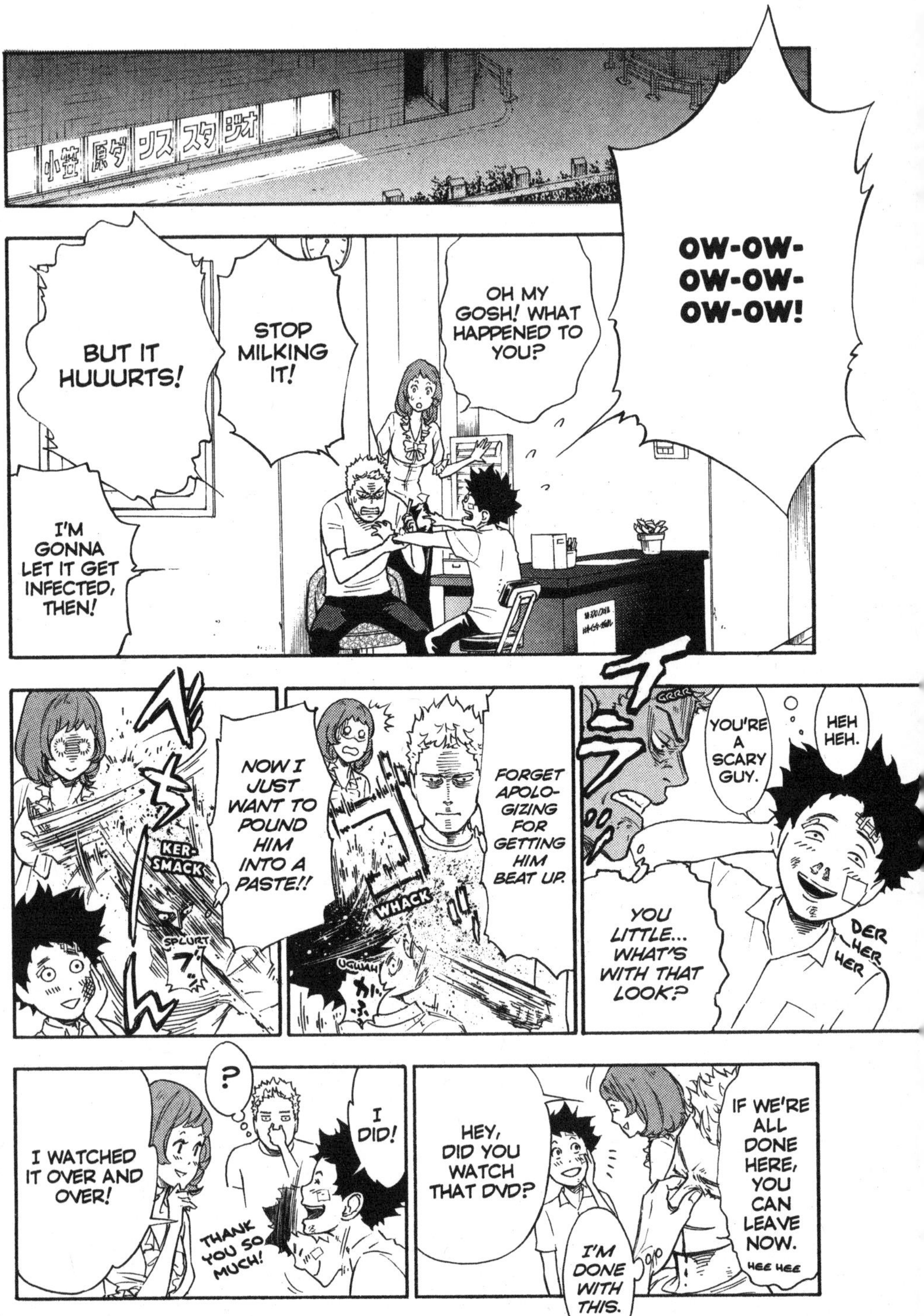
小笠原ダンススタジオ
OW-OW-OW-OW-OW-OW!
OH MY GOSH! WHAT HAPPENED TO YOU?
STOP MILKING IT!
BUT IT HUUURTS!
I'M GONNA LET IT GET INFECTED, THEN!
HEH HEH.
YOU'RE A SCARY GUY.
GRRR
YOU LITTLE... WHAT'S WITH THAT LOOK?
DER HER HER
FORGET APOLOGIZING FOR GETTING HIM BEAT UP.
WHACK
UGUAH
NOW I JUST WANT TO POUND HIM INTO A PASTE!!
KER-SMACK
SPLURT
IF WE'RE ALL DONE HERE, YOU CAN LEAVE NOW.
HEE HEE
HEY, DID YOU WATCH THAT DVD?
I'M DONE WITH THIS.
I DID!
?
THANK YOU SO MUCH!
I WATCHED IT OVER AND OVER!

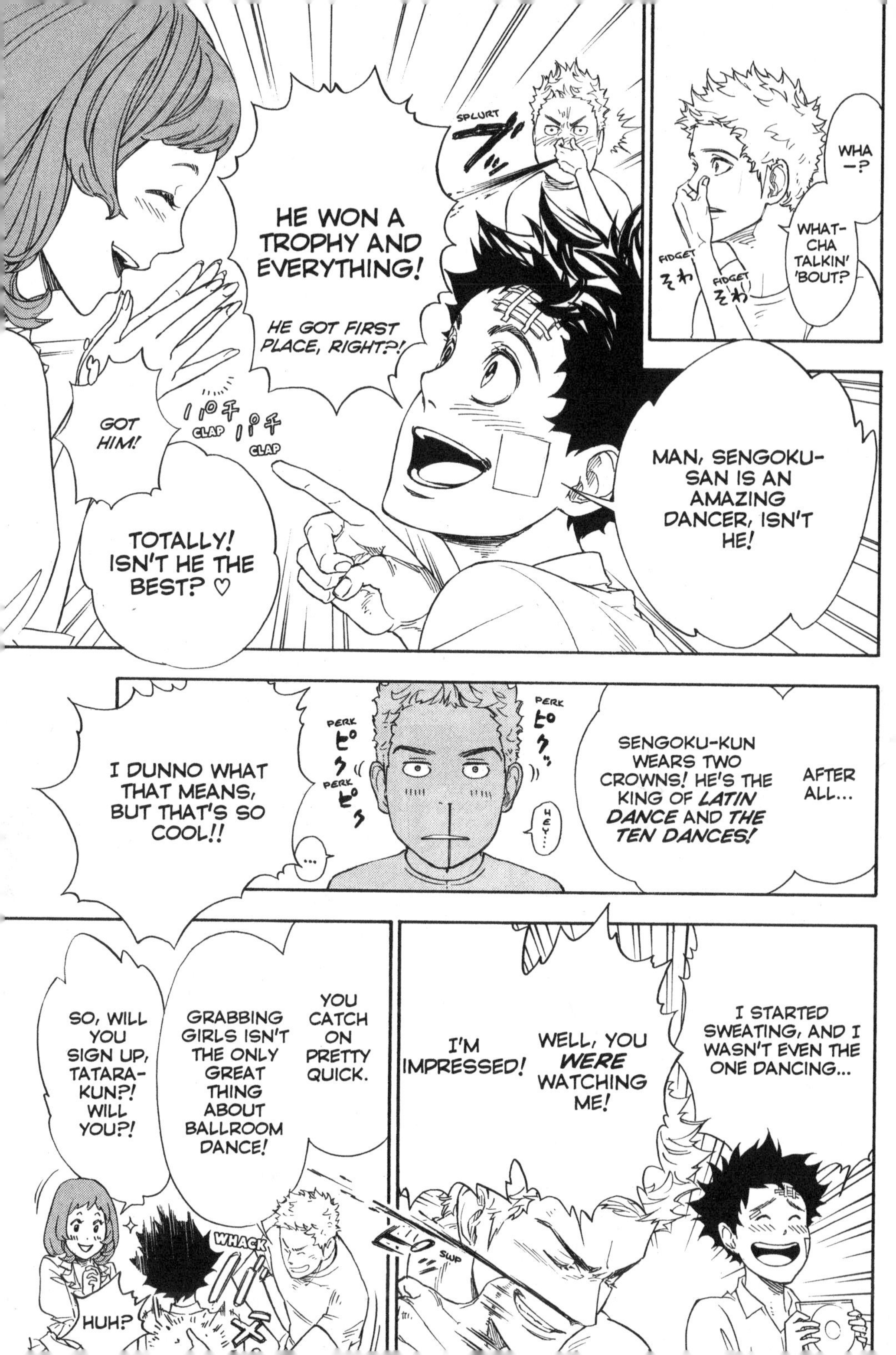
WHA —?
WHAT-CHA TALKIN' 'BOUT?
FIDGET
FIDGET
MAN, SENGOKU-SAN IS AN AMAZING DANCER, ISN'T HE!
TOTALLY! ISN'T HE THE BEST? ♡
GOT HIM!
CLAP
CLAP
HE WON A TROPHY AND EVERYTHING!
HE GOT FIRST PLACE, RIGHT?!
SPLURT
AFTER ALL...
SENGOKU-KUN WEARS TWO CROWNS! HE'S THE KING OF *LATIN DANCE* AND *THE TEN DANCES!*
HEY...
PERK
PERK
PERK
...
I DUNNO WHAT THAT MEANS, BUT THAT'S SO COOL!!
I STARTED SWEATING, AND I WASN'T EVEN THE ONE DANCING...
WELL, YOU *WERE* WATCHING ME!
I'M IMPRESSED!
SWP
YOU CATCH ON PRETTY QUICK.
GRABBING GIRLS ISN'T THE ONLY GREAT THING ABOUT BALLROOM DANCE!
SO, WILL YOU SIGN UP, TATARA-KUN?! WILL YOU?!
WHACK
HUH?

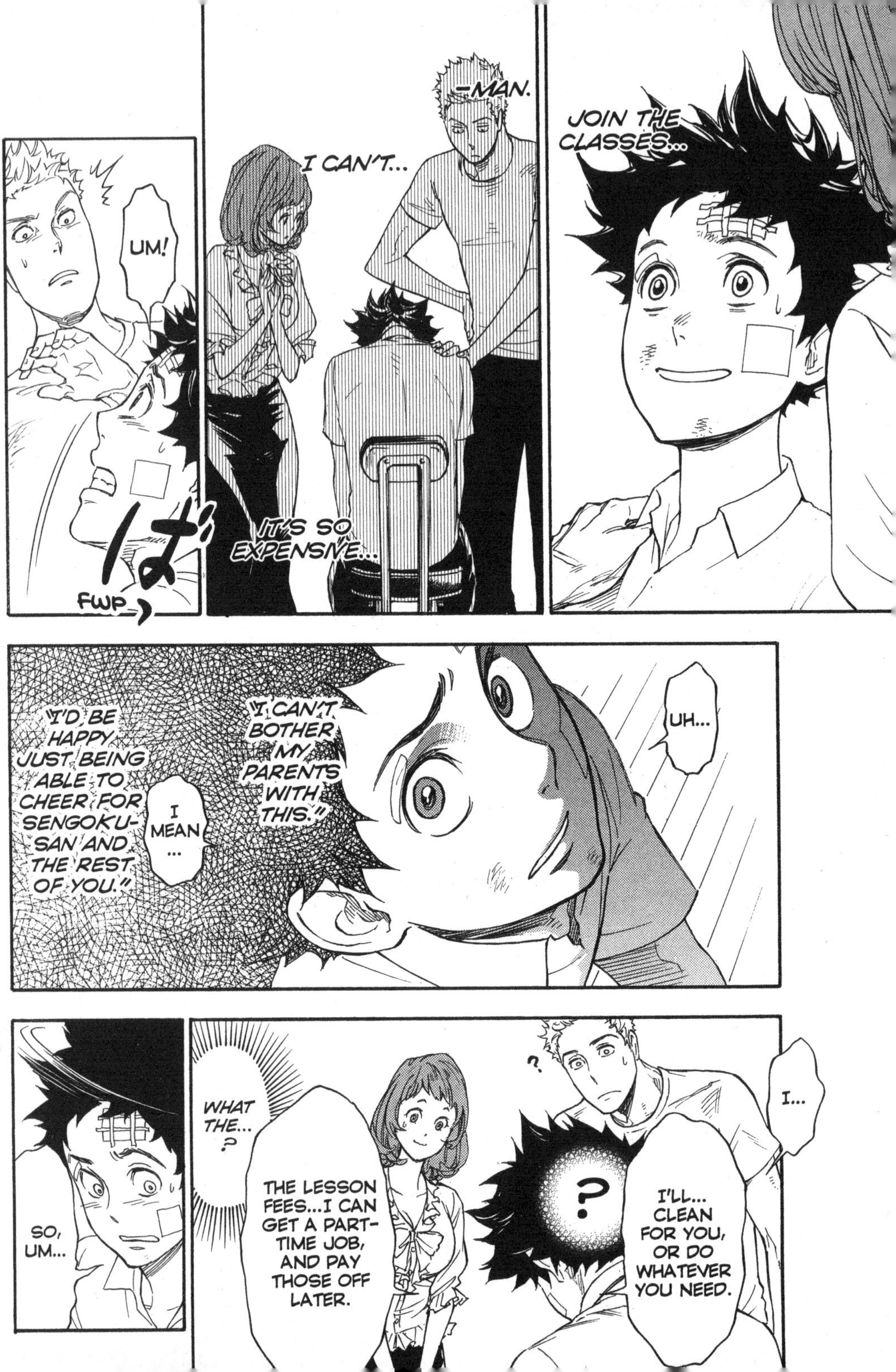
JOIN THE CLASSES...
-MAN.
I CAN'T...
IT'S SO EXPENSIVE...
UM!
ぱ
FWP
UH...
"I CAN'T BOTHER MY PARENTS WITH THIS."
I MEAN...
"I'D BE HAPPY JUST BEING ABLE TO CHEER FOR SENGOKU-SAN AND THE REST OF YOU."
I...
I'LL... CLEAN FOR YOU, OR DO WHATEVER YOU NEED.
?
?
THE LESSON FEES...I CAN GET A PART-TIME JOB, AND PAY THOSE OFF LATER.
WHAT THE...?
SO, UM...

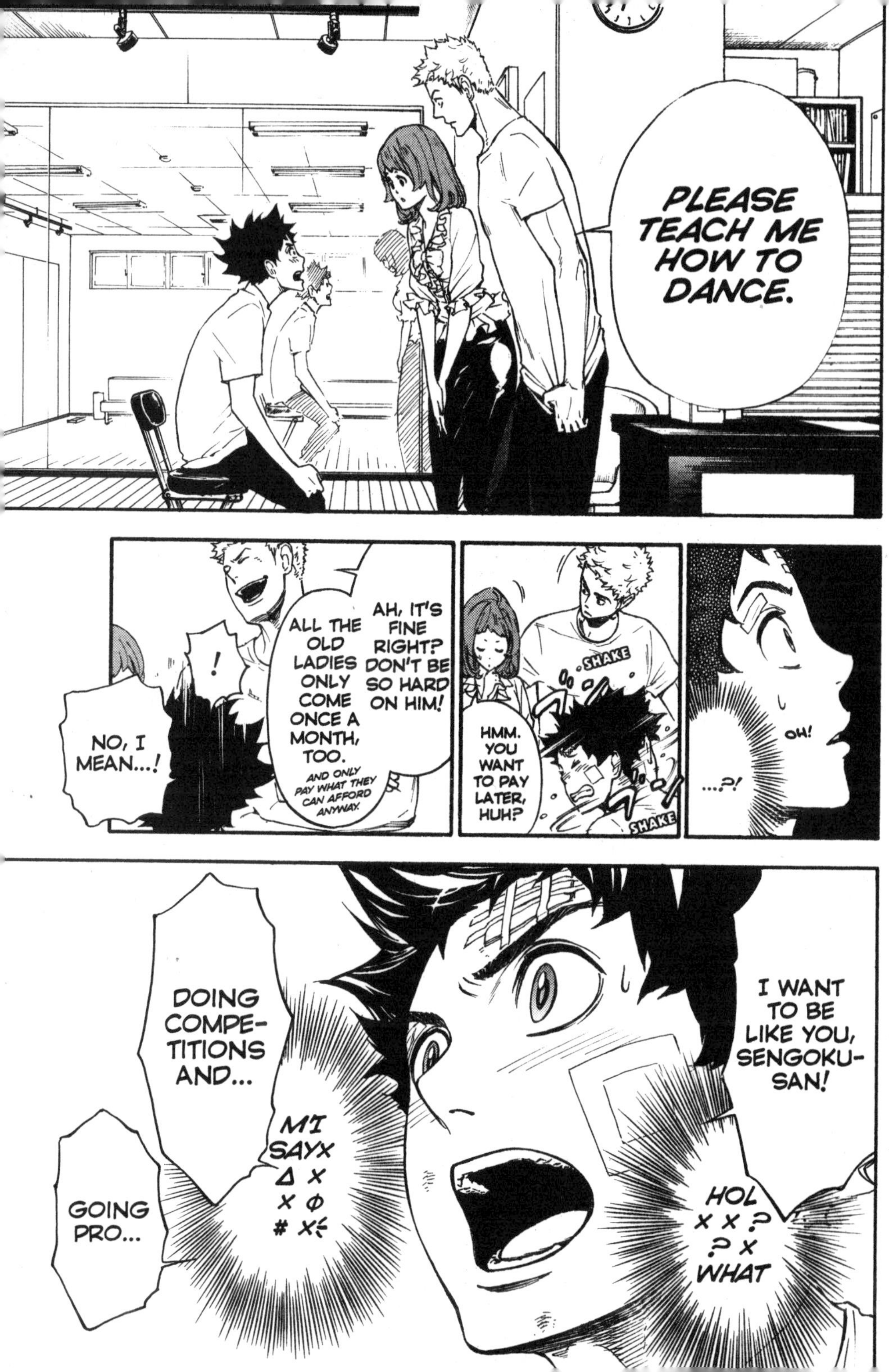
PLEASE TEACH ME HOW TO DANCE.
OH!
...?!
SHAKE
HMM. YOU WANT TO PAY LATER, HUH?
SHAKE
AH, IT'S FINE RIGHT? DON'T BE SO HARD ON HIM!
ALL THE OLD LADIES ONLY COME ONCE A MONTH, TOO.
AND ONLY PAY WHAT THEY CAN AFFORD ANYWAY.
!
NO, I MEAN...!
I WANT TO BE LIKE YOU, SENGOKU-SAN!
HOL × × ? ? × WHAT
M'I SAY× Δ × × Φ # ×
DOING COMPETITIONS AND...
GOING PRO...

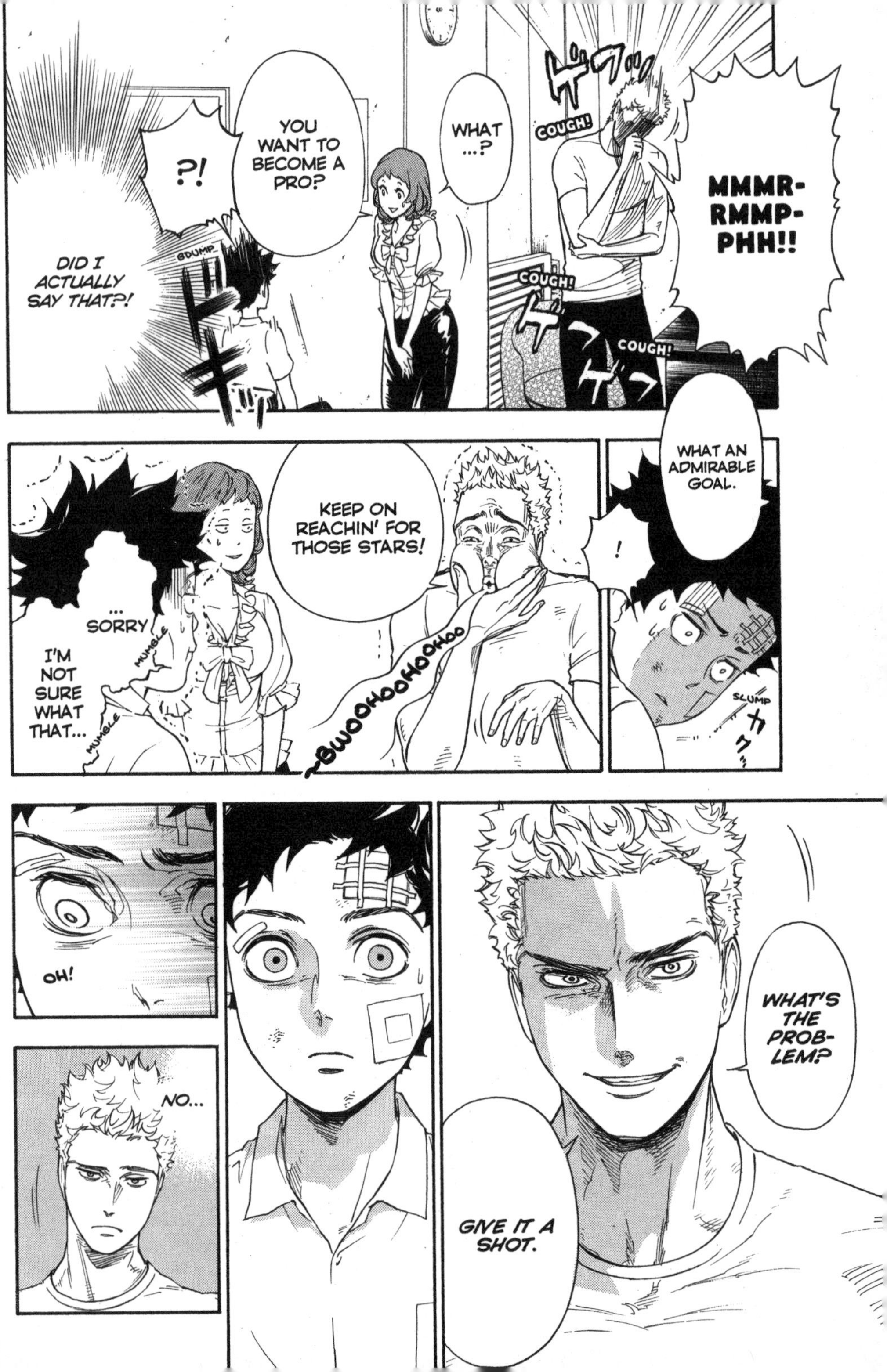
MMMR-RMMP-PHH!!
COUGH!
COUGH!
COUGH!
WHAT ...?
YOU WANT TO BECOME A PRO?
?!
DID I ACTUALLY SAY THAT?!
BDUMP
WHAT AN ADMIRABLE GOAL.
!
SLUMP
KEEP ON REACHIN' FOR THOSE STARS!
~BWOOHOOHOOHOO
... SORRY
MUMBLE
I'M NOT SURE WHAT THAT...
MUMBLE
WHAT'S THE PROB-LEM?
GIVE IT A SHOT.
OH!
NO...

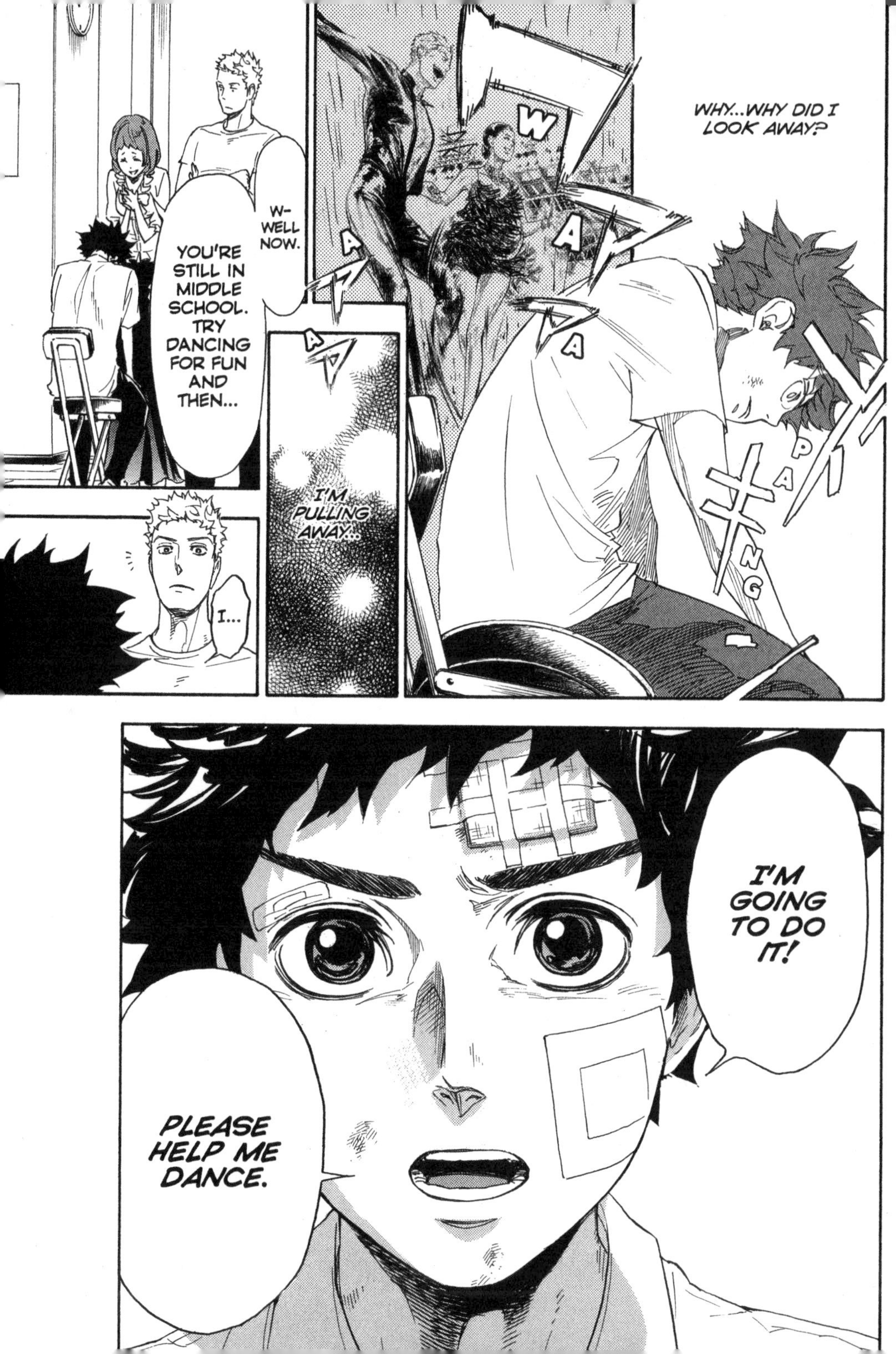
WHY...WHY DID I LOOK AWAY?
WAAAA
PANG
I'M PULLING AWAY...
W-WELL NOW.
YOU'RE STILL IN MIDDLE SCHOOL. TRY DANCING FOR FUN AND THEN...
I...
I'M GOING TO DO IT!
PLEASE HELP ME DANCE.

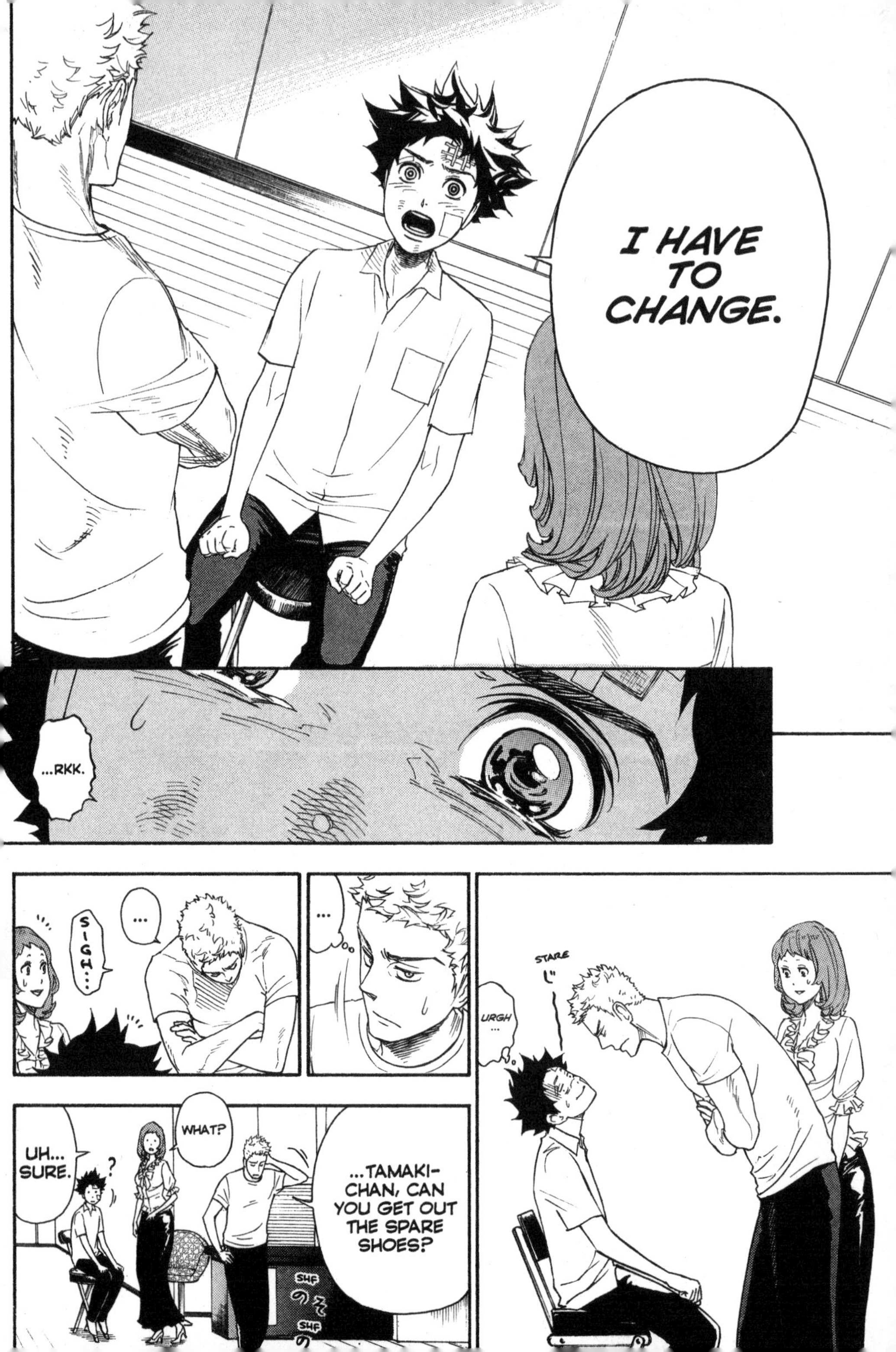

I HAVE TO CHANGE.
...RKK.
STARE
URGH...
...
...
SIGH...
...TAMAKI-CHAN, CAN YOU GET OUT THE SPARE SHOES?
WHAT?
UH... SURE.
SHF
SHF

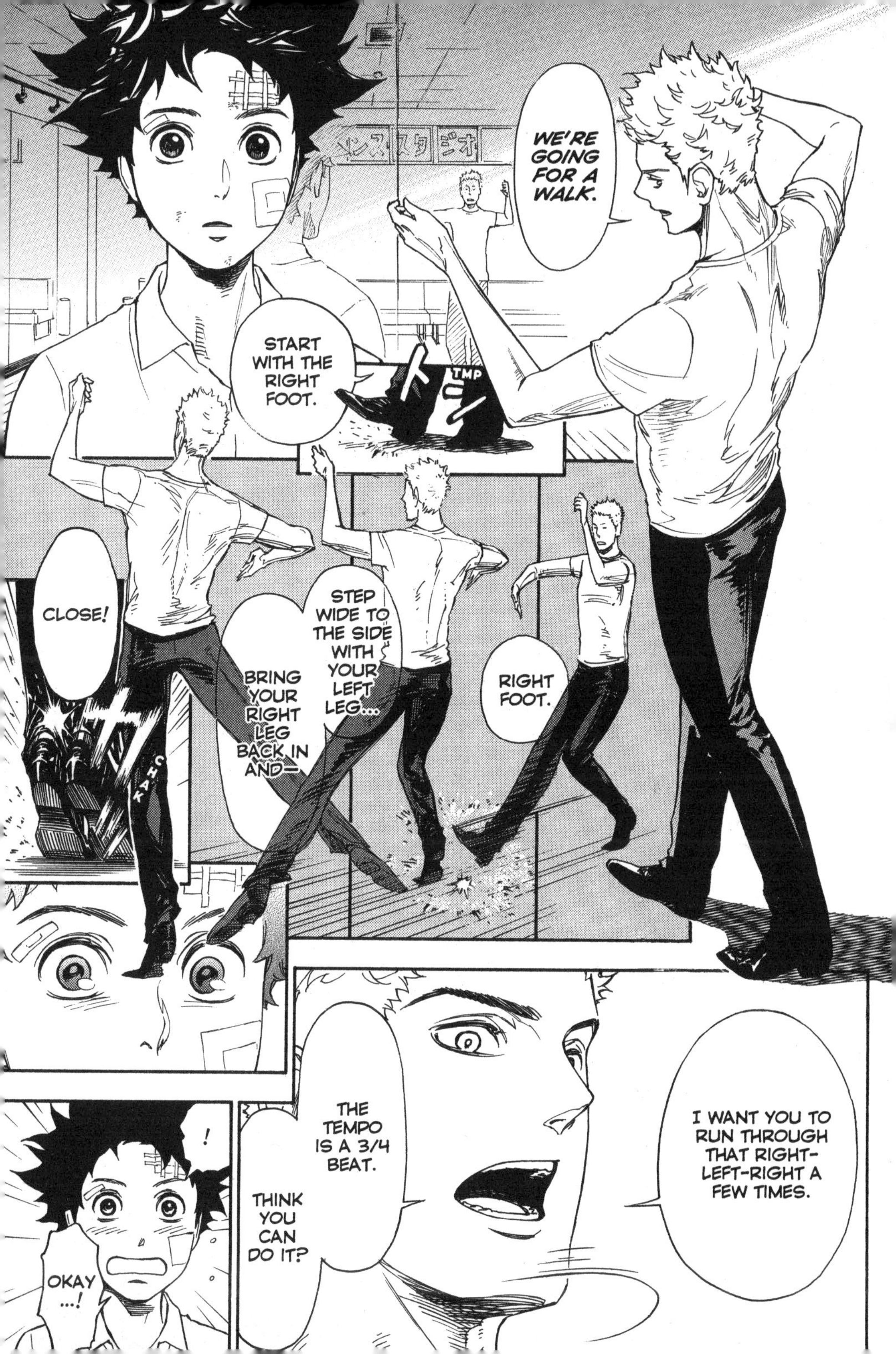

WE'RE GOING FOR A WALK.
START WITH THE RIGHT FOOT.
TMP
RIGHT FOOT.
STEP WIDE TO THE SIDE WITH YOUR LEFT LEG...
BRING YOUR RIGHT LEG BACK IN AND—
CLOSE!
CHAK
I WANT YOU TO RUN THROUGH THAT RIGHT-LEFT-RIGHT A FEW TIMES.
THE TEMPO IS A 3/4 BEAT.
THINK YOU CAN DO IT?
!
OKAY ...!

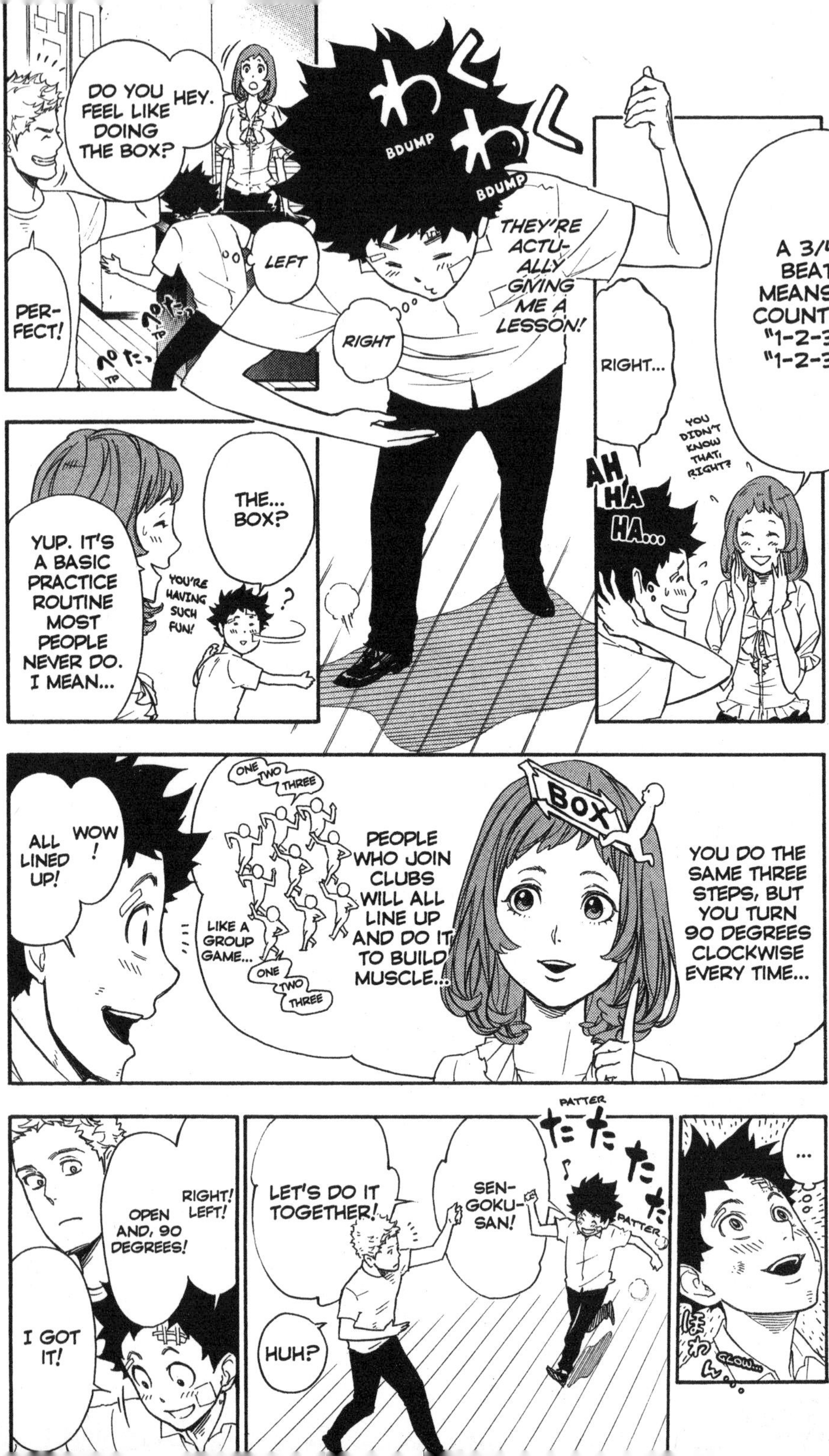
A 3/4 BEAT MEANS A COUNT OF "1-2-3," "1-2-3."
RIGHT...
YOU DIDN'T KNOW THAT, RIGHT?
AH HA HA...
わくわく
BDUMP
BDUMP
THEY'RE ACTU-ALLY GIVING ME A LESSON!
LEFT
RIGHT
HEY.
DO YOU FEEL LIKE DOING THE BOX?
PERFECT!
ぺたっ
TP
ぺたっ
TP
THE... BOX?
YUP. IT'S A BASIC PRACTICE ROUTINE MOST PEOPLE NEVER DO. I MEAN...
YOU'RE HAVING SUCH FUN!
YOU DO THE SAME THREE STEPS, BUT YOU TURN 90 DEGREES CLOCKWISE EVERY TIME...
BOX
PEOPLE WHO JOIN CLUBS WILL ALL LINE UP AND DO IT TO BUILD MUSCLE...
ONE TWO THREE
LIKE A GROUP GAME...
ONE TWO THREE
WOW!
ALL LINED UP!
...
ほわん
GLOW...
PATTER
たたたた
PATTER
SEN-GOKU-SAN!
LET'S DO IT TOGETHER!
HUH?
RIGHT! LEFT!
OPEN AND, 90 DEGREES!
I GOT IT!

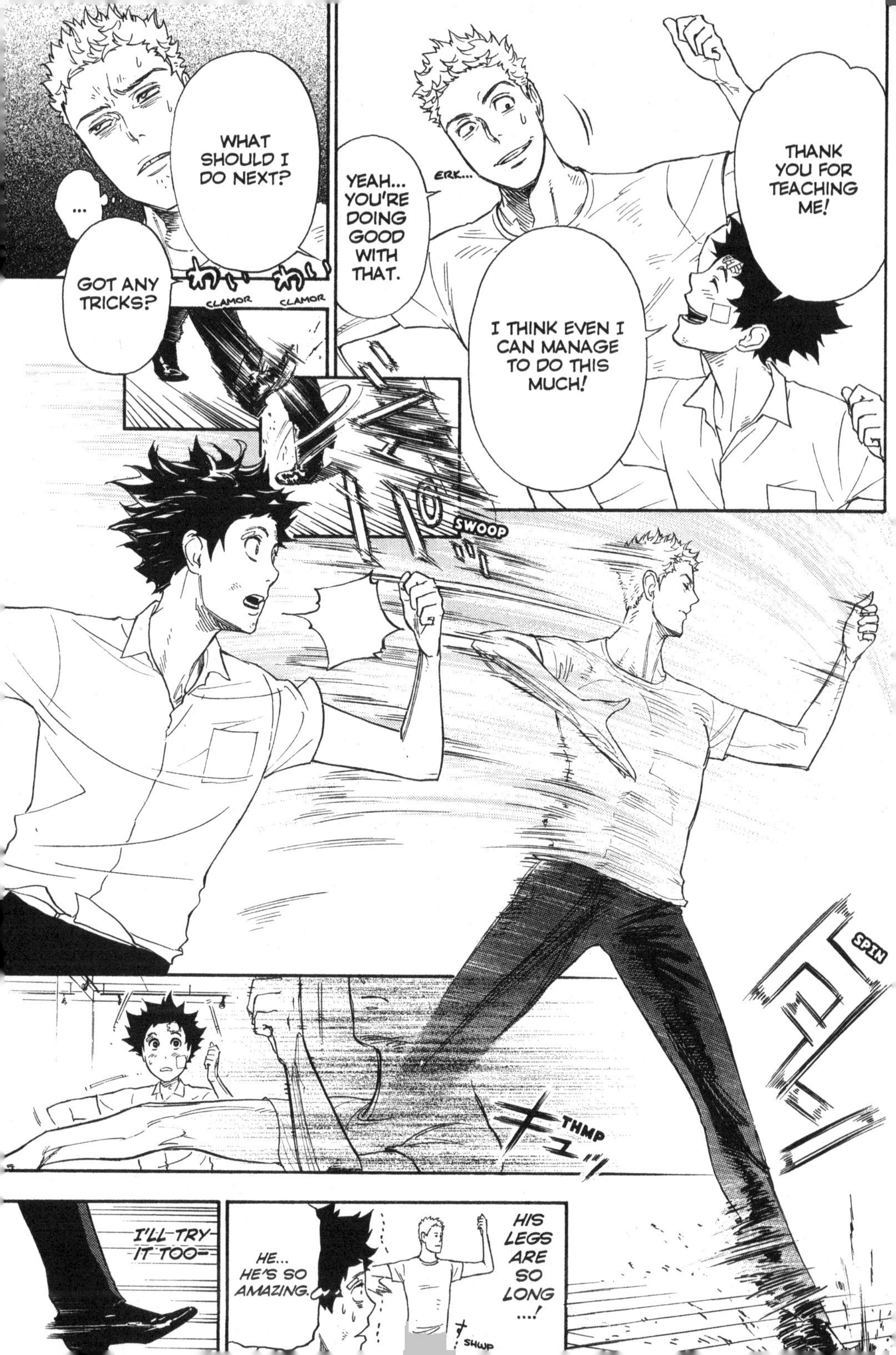
THANK YOU FOR TEACHING ME!
ERK...
YEAH... YOU'RE DOING GOOD WITH THAT.
I THINK EVEN I CAN MANAGE TO DO THIS MUCH!
WHAT SHOULD I DO NEXT?
...
GOT ANY TRICKS?
CLAMOR CLAMOR
SWOOP
SPIN
THMP
HIS LEGS ARE SO LONG ...!
HE... HE'S SO AMAZING.
SHWP
I'LL TRY IT TOO—

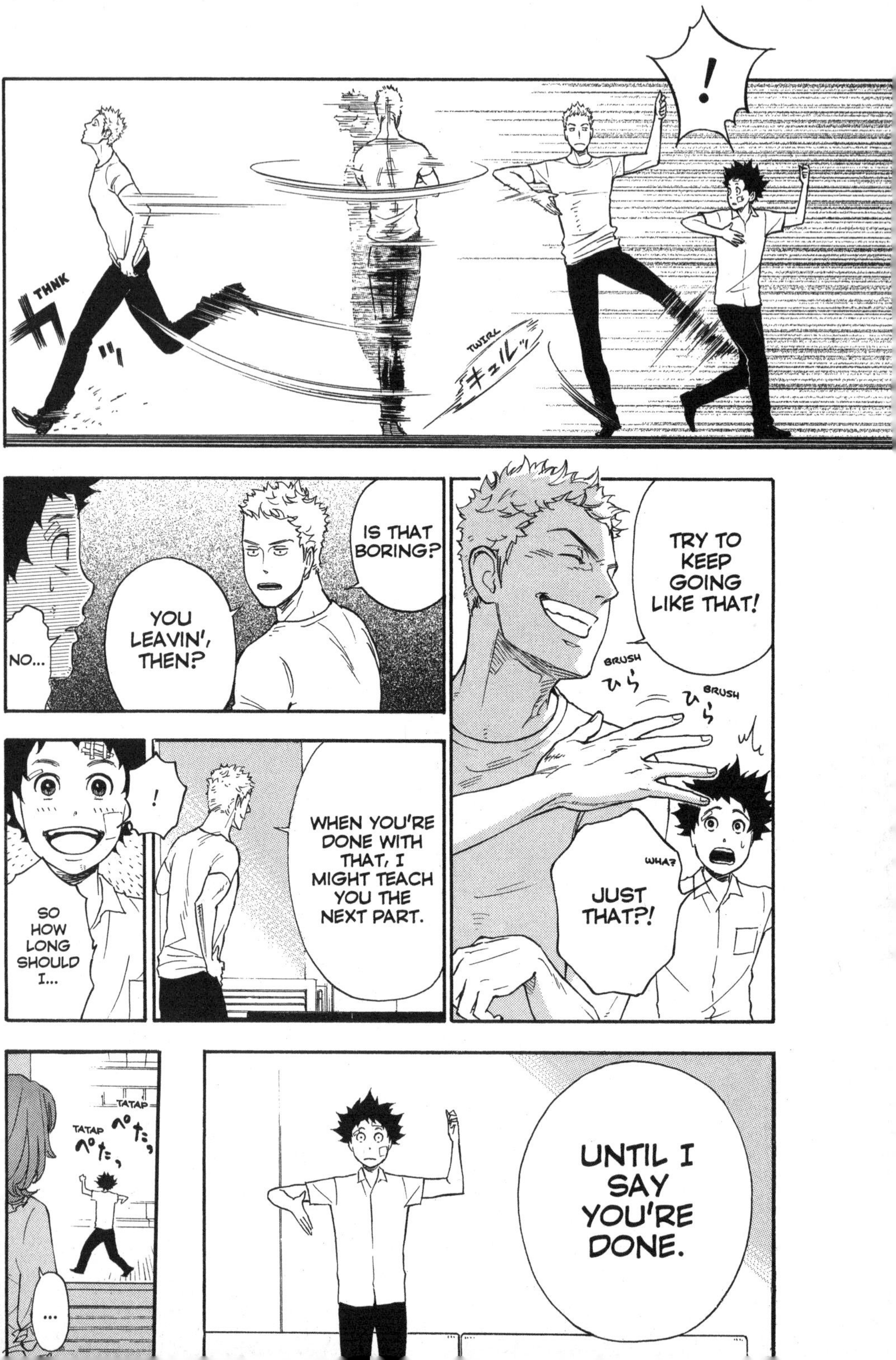
!
TWIRL
キュルッ
THNK
TRY TO KEEP GOING LIKE THAT!
BRUSH
ひら
BRUSH
ひら
WHA?
JUST THAT?!
IS THAT BORING?
YOU LEAVIN', THEN?
NO...
!
WHEN YOU'RE DONE WITH THAT, I MIGHT TEACH YOU THE NEXT PART.
SO HOW LONG SHOULD I...
UNTIL I SAY YOU'RE DONE.
TATAP
ぺたっ
TATAP
ぺたっ
...

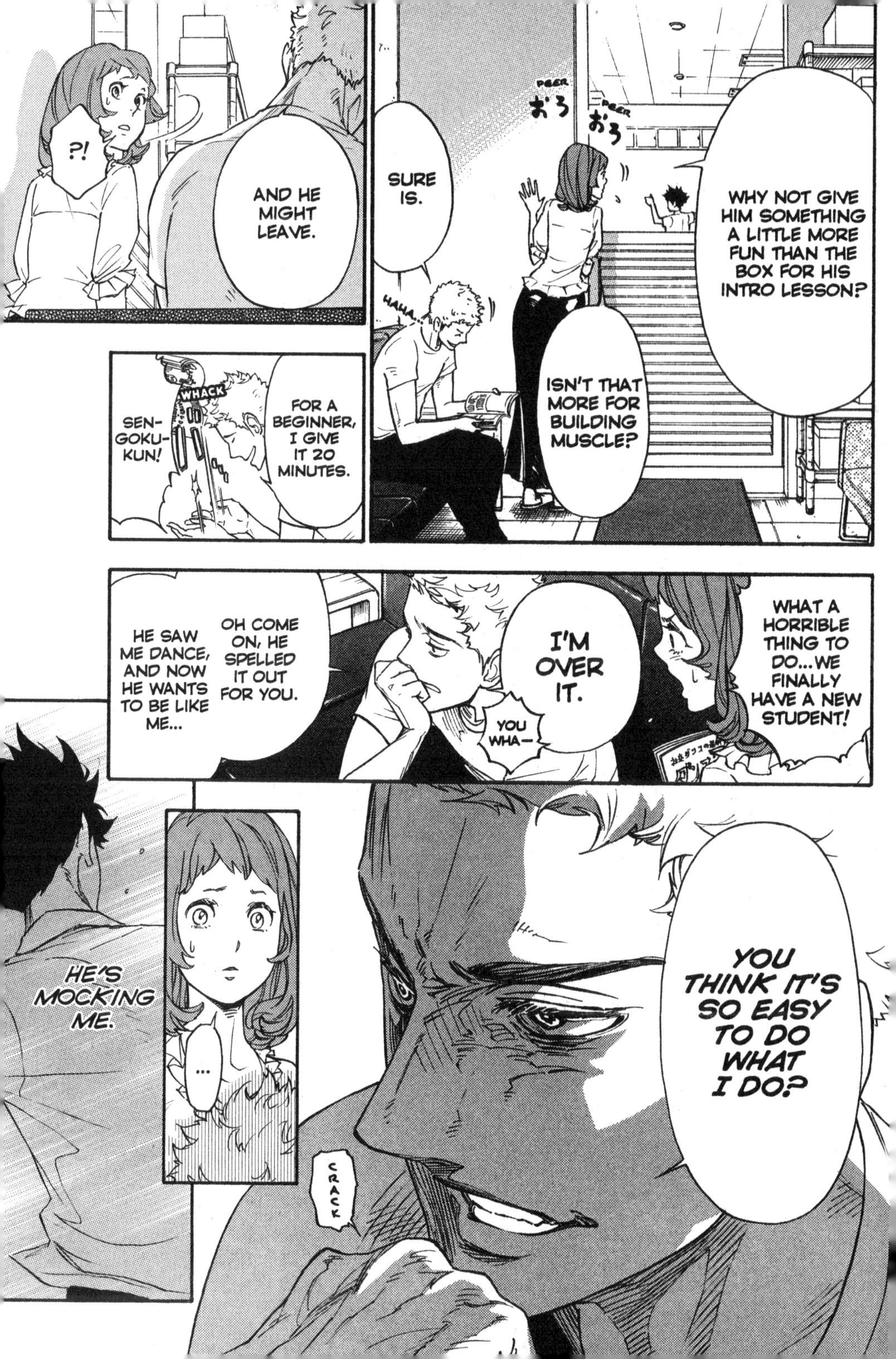
PEER
おろ
PEER
おろ
WHY NOT GIVE HIM SOMETHING A LITTLE MORE FUN THAN THE BOX FOR HIS INTRO LESSON?
ISN'T THAT MORE FOR BUILDING MUSCLE?
HAHA...
SURE IS.
AND HE MIGHT LEAVE.
?!
FOR A BEGINNER, I GIVE IT 20 MINUTES.
WHACK
SEN-GOKU-KUN!
WHAT A HORRIBLE THING TO DO...WE FINALLY HAVE A NEW STUDENT!
I'M OVER IT.
YOU WHA—
OH COME ON, HE SPELLED IT OUT FOR YOU.
HE SAW ME DANCE, AND NOW HE WANTS TO BE LIKE ME...
YOU THINK IT'S SO EASY TO DO WHAT I DO?
CRACK
...
HE'S MOCKING ME.

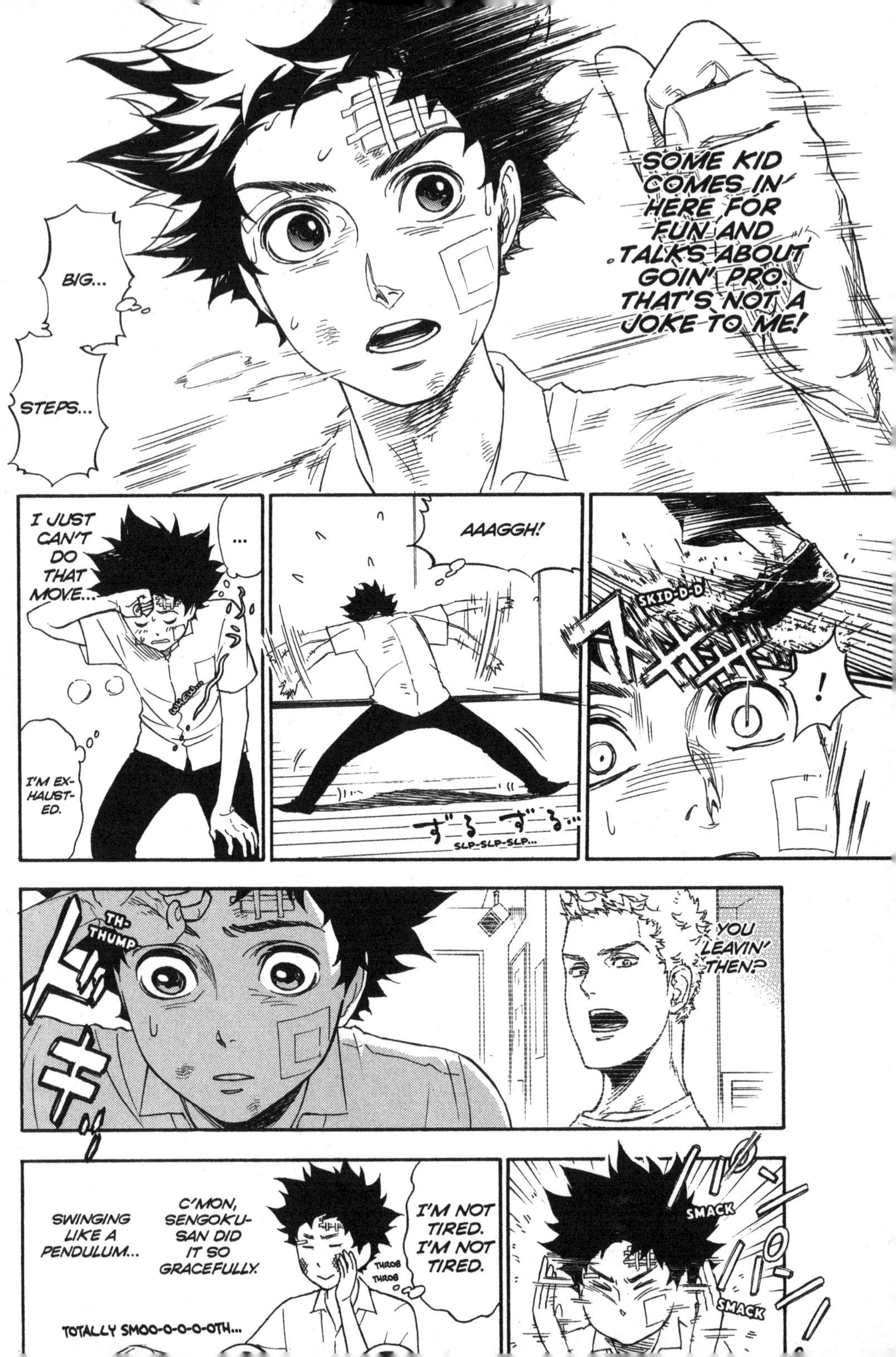
SOME KID COMES IN HERE FOR FUN AND TALKS ABOUT GOIN' PRO. THAT'S NOT A JOKE TO ME!
BIG...
STEPS...
SKID-D-D
!
AAAGGH!
SLP-SLP-SLP...
...
I JUST CAN'T DO THAT MOVE...
I'M EX-HAUST-ED.
YOU LEAVIN' THEN?
TH-THUMP
SMACK
SMACK
I'M NOT TIRED. I'M NOT TIRED.
THROB THROB
C'MON, SENGOKU-SAN DID IT SO GRACEFULLY.
SWINGING LIKE A PENDULUM...
TOTALLY SMOO-O-O-O-OTH...

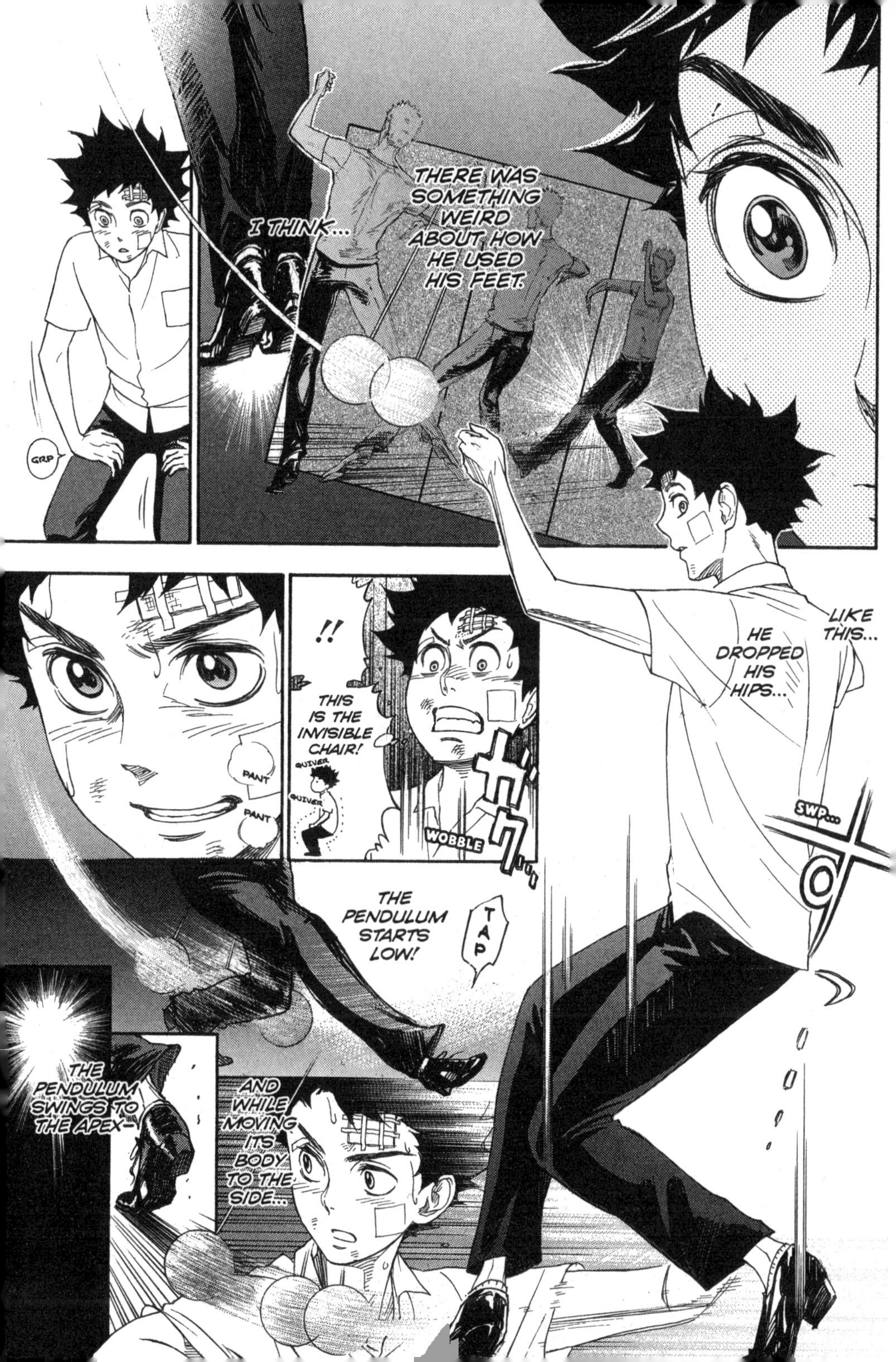
THERE WAS SOMETHING WEIRD ABOUT HOW HE USED HIS FEET.
I THINK...
GRP
LIKE THIS...
HE DROPPED HIS HIPS...
SWP...
!!
THIS IS THE INVISIBLE CHAIR!
QUIVER
QUIVER
WOBBLE
PANT
PANT
THE PENDULUM STARTS LOW!
TAP
AND WHILE MOVING ITS BODY TO THE SIDE...
THE PENDULUM SWINGS TO THE APEX–

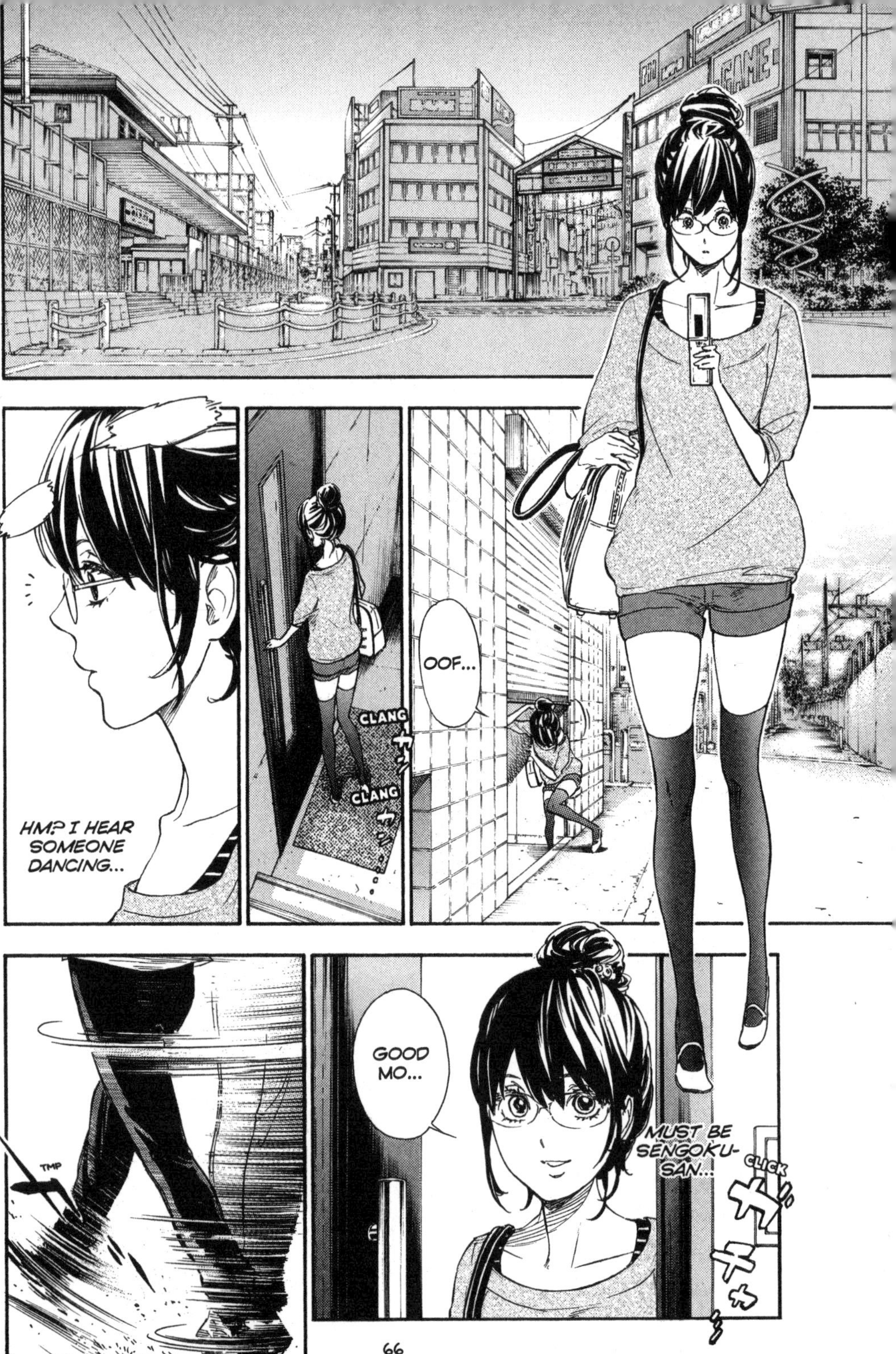

OOF...
CLANG
CLANG
HM? I HEAR SOMEONE DANCING...
CLICK
MUST BE SENGOKU-SAN...
GOOD MO...
TMP

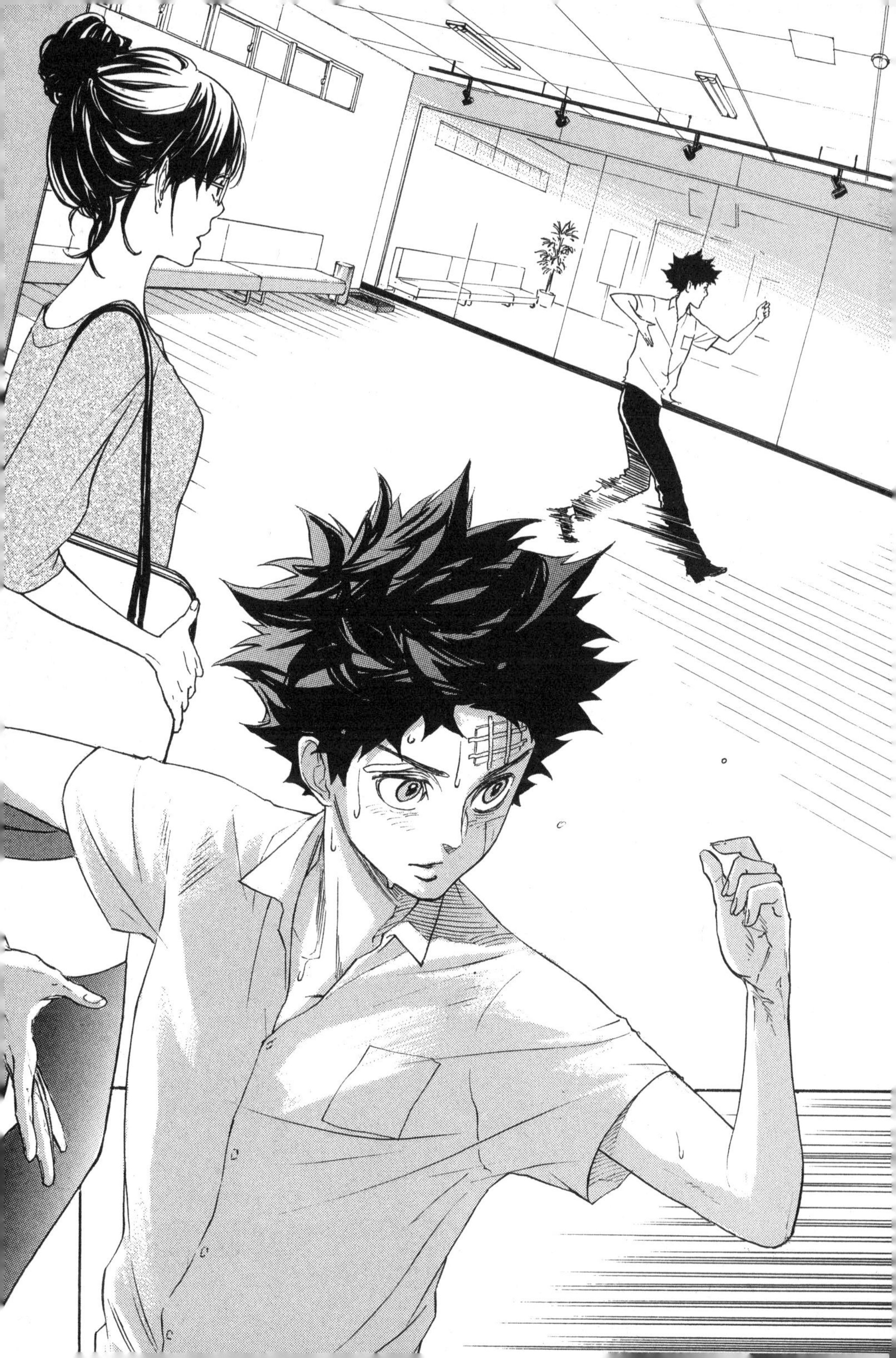

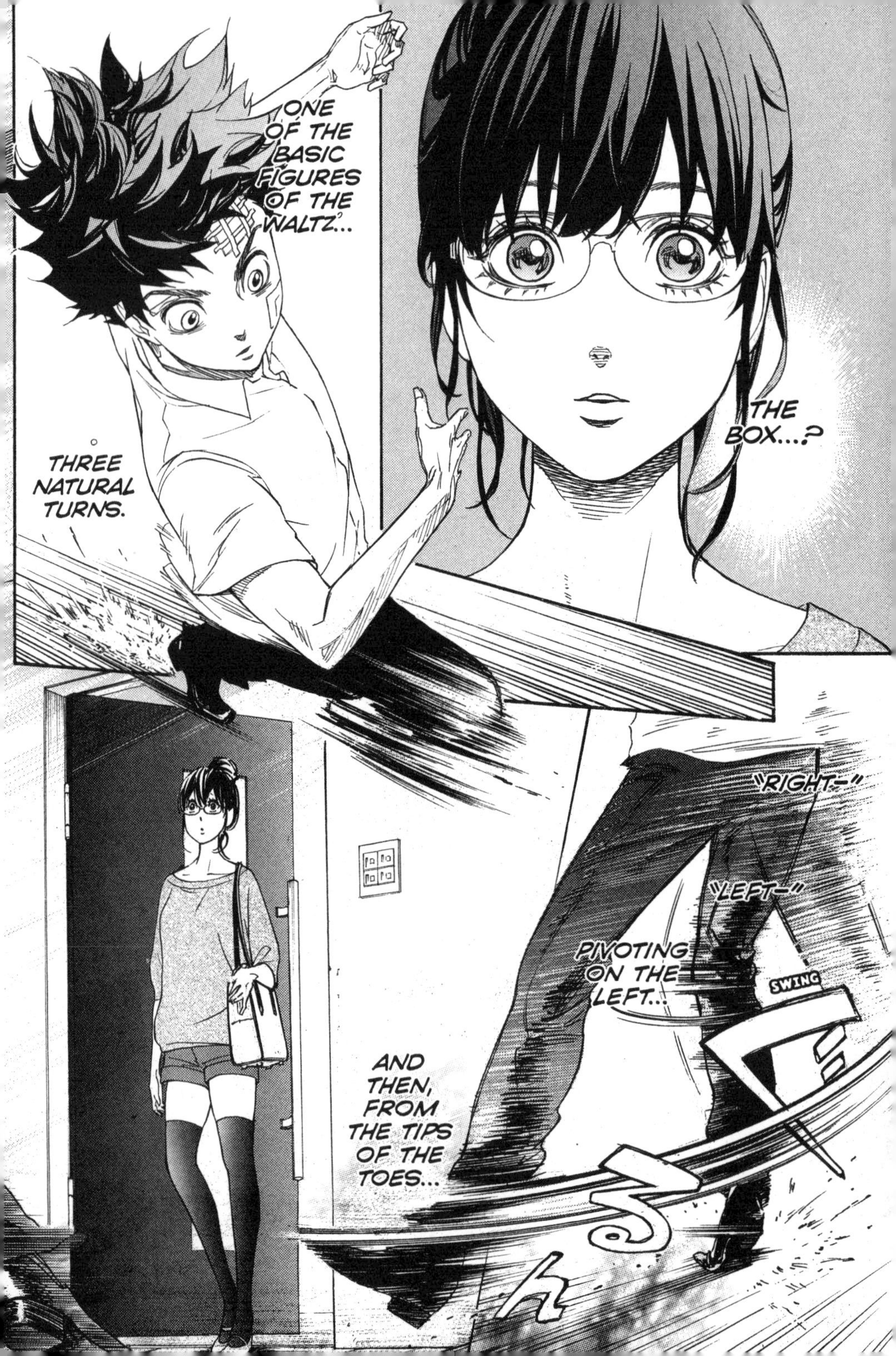
THE BOX...?
ONE OF THE BASIC FIGURES OF THE WALTZ...
THREE NATURAL TURNS.
"RIGHT-"
"LEFT-"
PIVOTING ON THE LEFT...
SWING
AND THEN, FROM THE TIPS OF THE TOES...

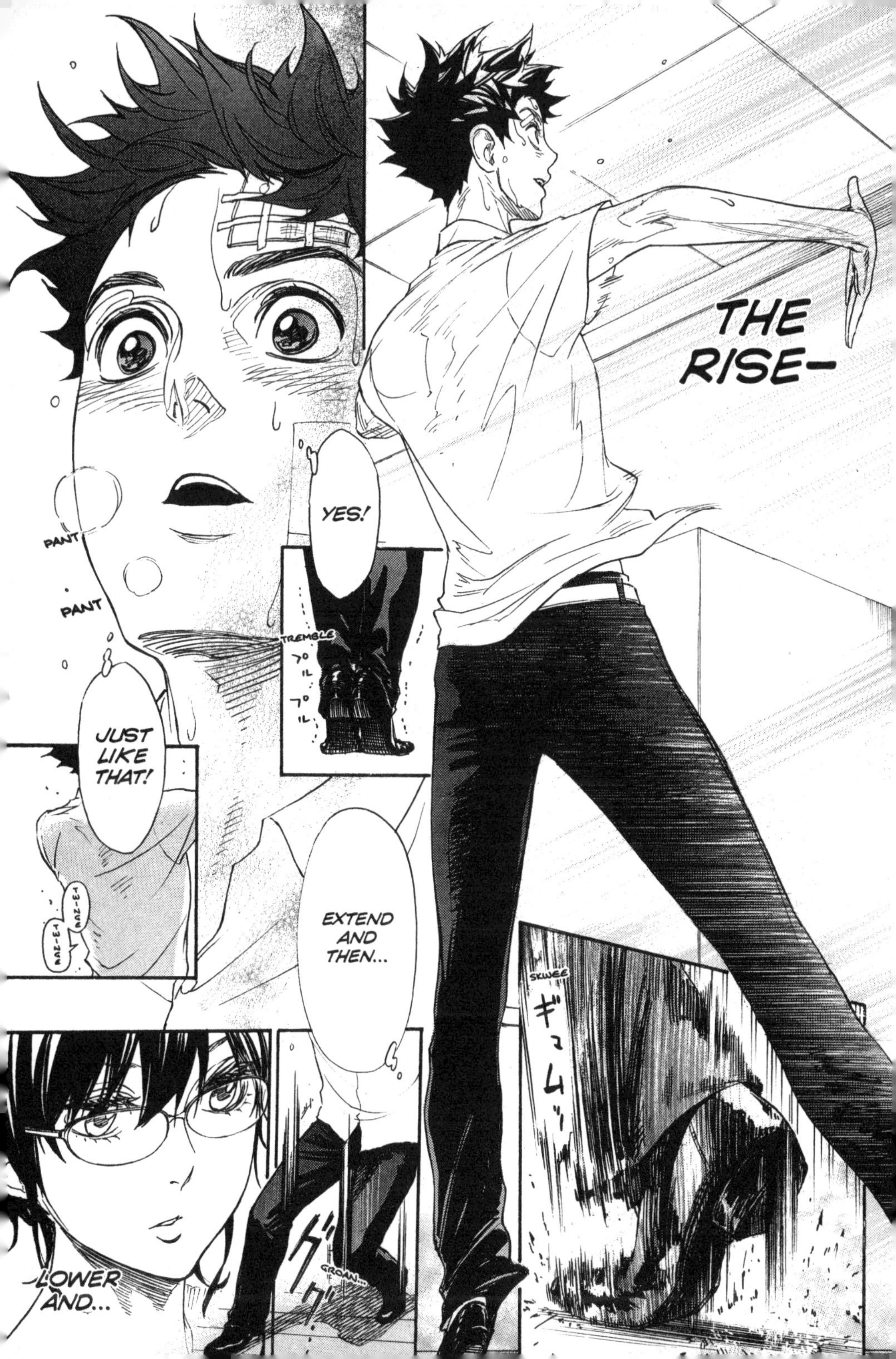
THE RISE-
YES!
PANT
PANT
TREMBLE
JUST LIKE THAT!
TWINGE TWINGE
EXTEND AND THEN...
SKWEE
GROAN...
LOWER AND...

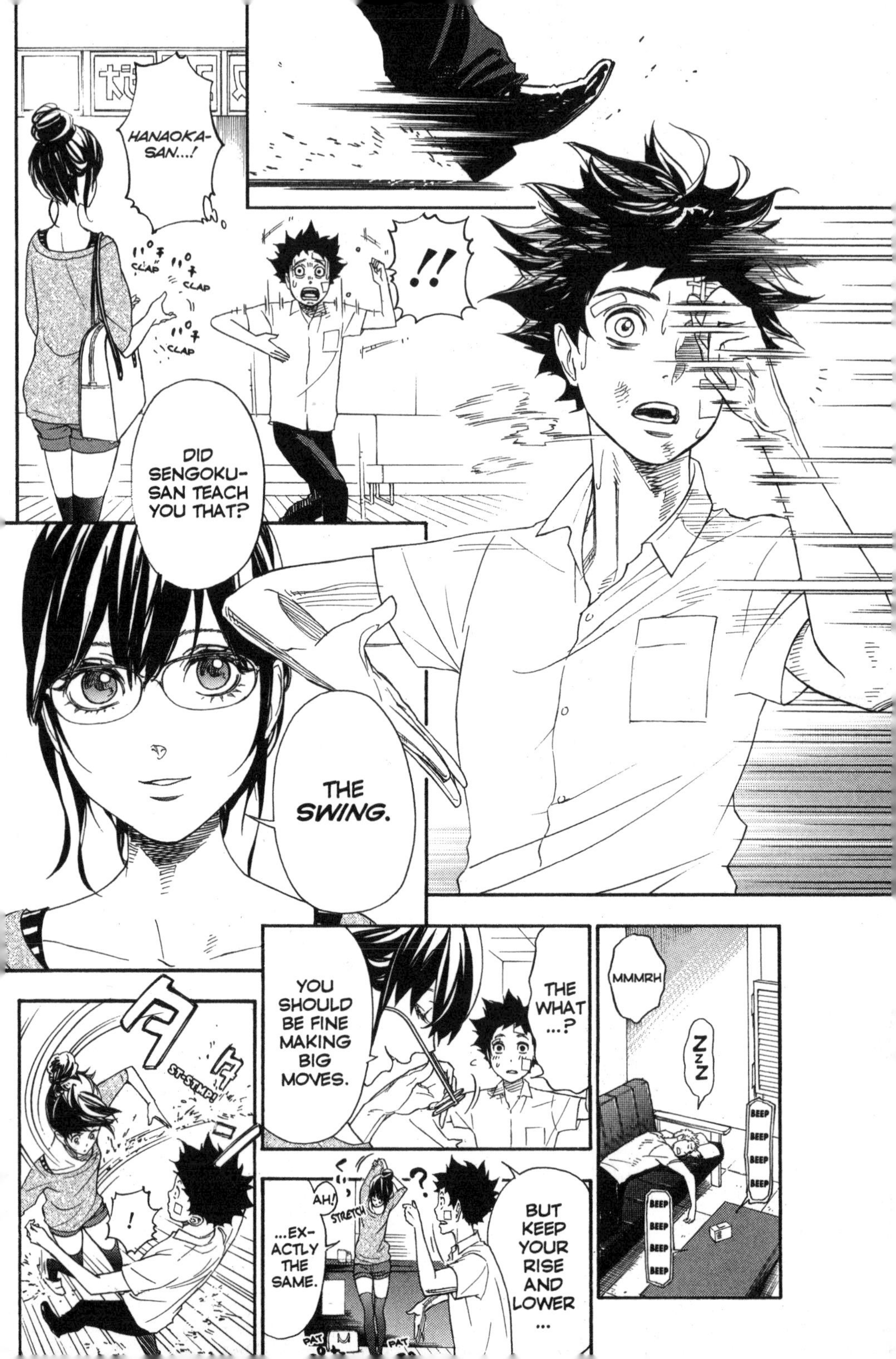

!!
HANAOKA-SAN...!
CLAP CLAP CLAP
DID SENGOKU-SAN TEACH YOU THAT?
THE SWING.
MMMRH
ZzZ
BEEP BEEP BEEP BEEP
BEEP BEEP BEEP BEEP
THE WHAT...?
YOU SHOULD BE FINE MAKING BIG MOVES.
BUT KEEP YOUR RISE AND LOWER...
AH!
STRETCH
...EXACTLY THE SAME.
PAT PAT
ST-STMP!
!

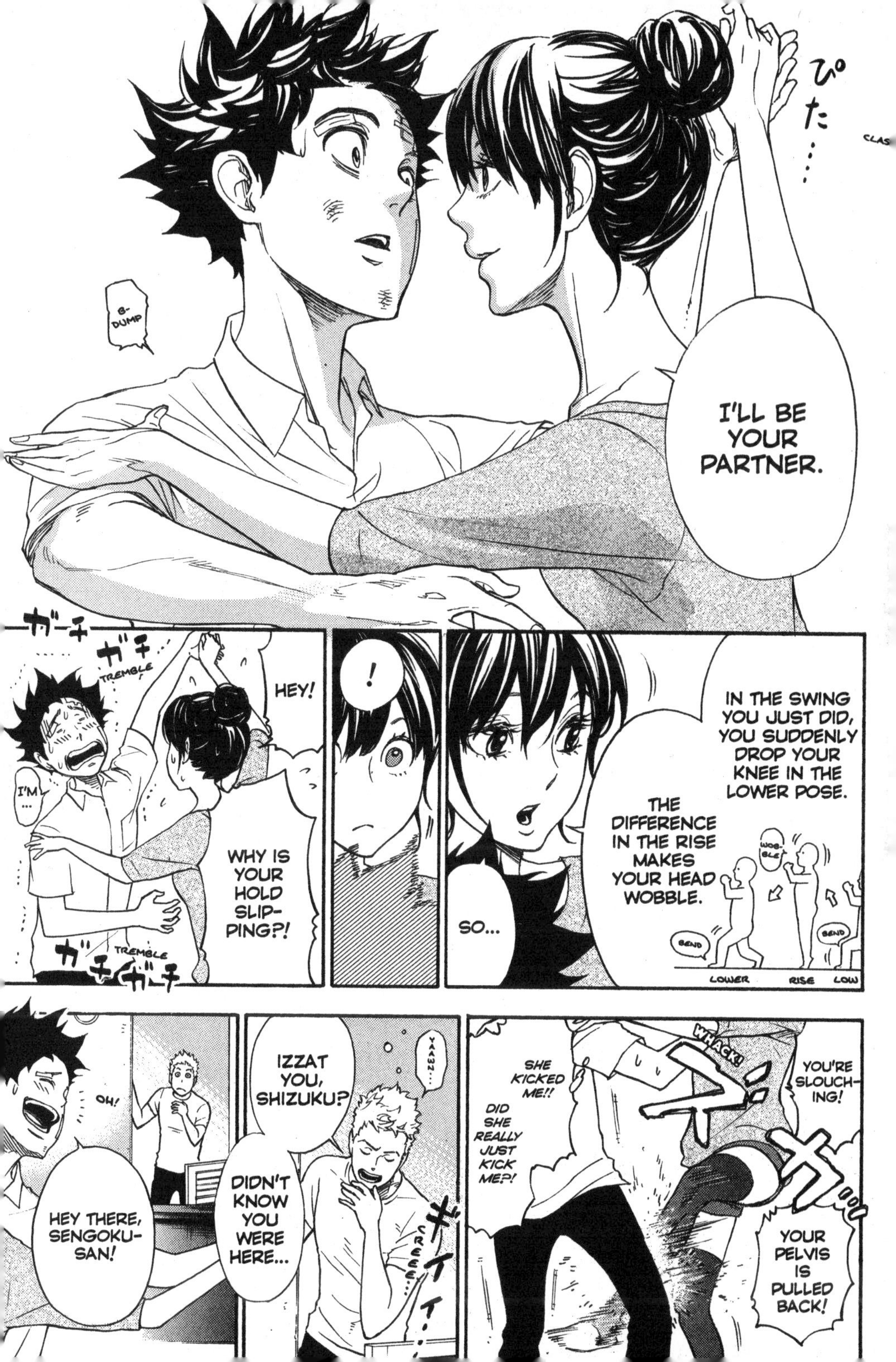

ぴた……
CLAS
I'LL BE YOUR PARTNER.
B-DUMP
IN THE SWING YOU JUST DID, YOU SUDDENLY DROP YOUR KNEE IN THE LOWER POSE.
THE DIFFERENCE IN THE RISE MAKES YOUR HEAD WOBBLE.
WOB-BLE
BEND
BEND
LOWER
RISE
LOW
SO...
!
HEY!
WHY IS YOUR HOLD SLIP-PING?!
ガチ
ガチ
TREMBLE
I'M ...
ガチガチ
TREMBLE
YOU'RE SLOUCH-ING!
WHACK!
SHE KICKED ME!!
DID SHE REALLY JUST KICK ME?!
YOUR PELVIS IS PULLED BACK!
YAAWN...
IZZAT YOU, SHIZUKU?
DIDN'T KNOW YOU WERE HERE...
ギイイ
CREEE...
OH!
HEY THERE, SENGOKU-SAN!

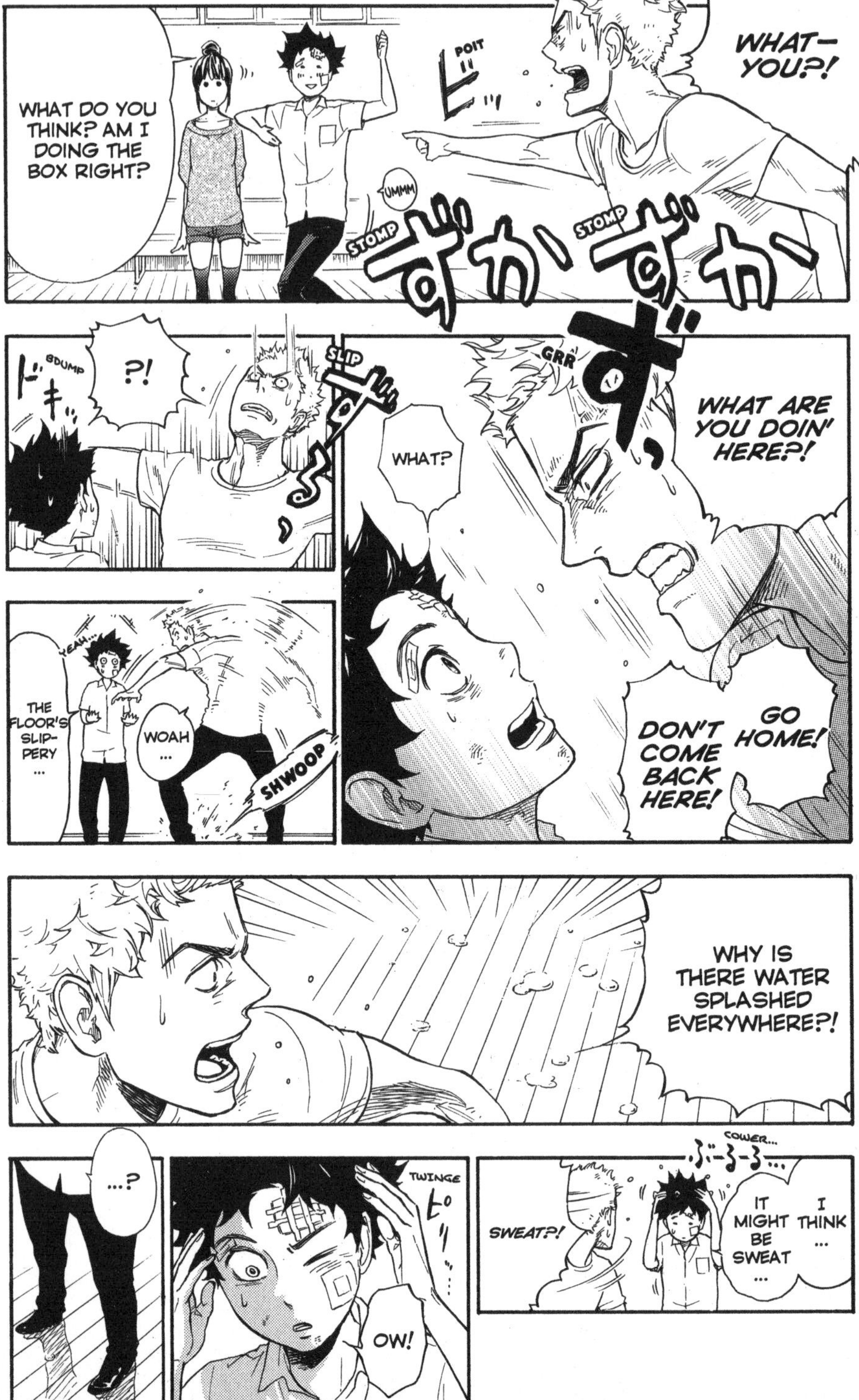
WHAT— YOU?!
POIT
UMMM
STOMP
STOMP
WHAT DO YOU THINK? AM I DOING THE BOX RIGHT?
GRR
WHAT ARE YOU DOIN' HERE?!
WHAT?
GO HOME!
DON'T COME BACK HERE!
SLIP
?!
BDUMP
YEAH...
WOAH ...
SHWOOP
THE FLOOR'S SLIP-PERY ...
WHY IS THERE WATER SPLASHED EVERYWHERE?!
COWER...
I THINK ...
IT MIGHT BE SWEAT ...
SWEAT?!
TWINGE
OW!
...?

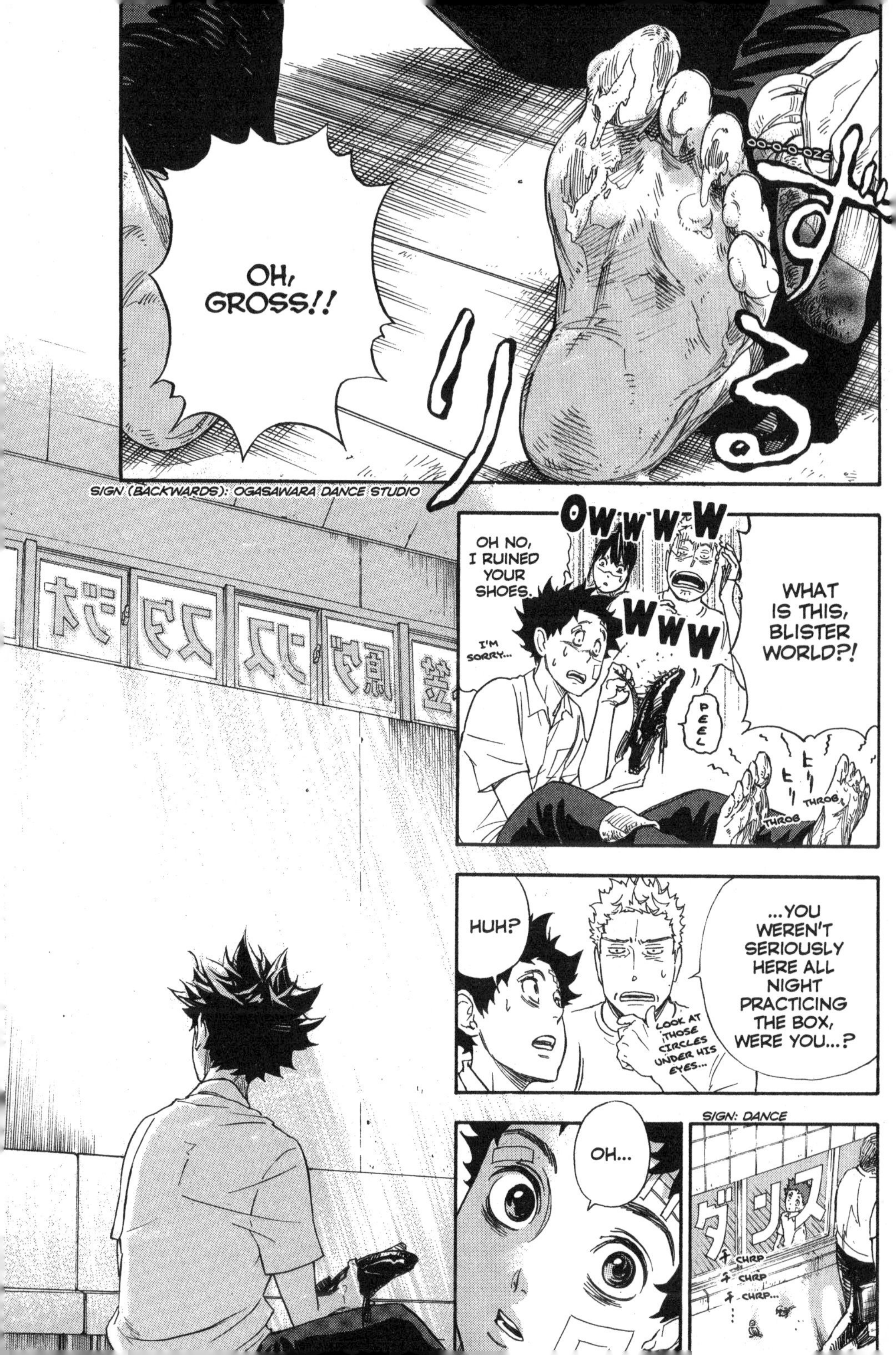
OO-O-O-OZE
OH, GROSS!!
OWWWWWWWW
WHAT IS THIS, BLISTER WORLD?!
OH NO, I RUINED YOUR SHOES.
I'M SORRY...
PEEL
THROB
THROB
...YOU WEREN'T SERIOUSLY HERE ALL NIGHT PRACTICING THE BOX, WERE YOU...?
LOOK AT THOSE CIRCLES UNDER HIS EYES...
HUH?
SIGN: DANCE
ダンス
CHRP
CHRP
CHRP...
OH...
SIGN (BACKWARDS): OGASAWARA DANCE STUDIO

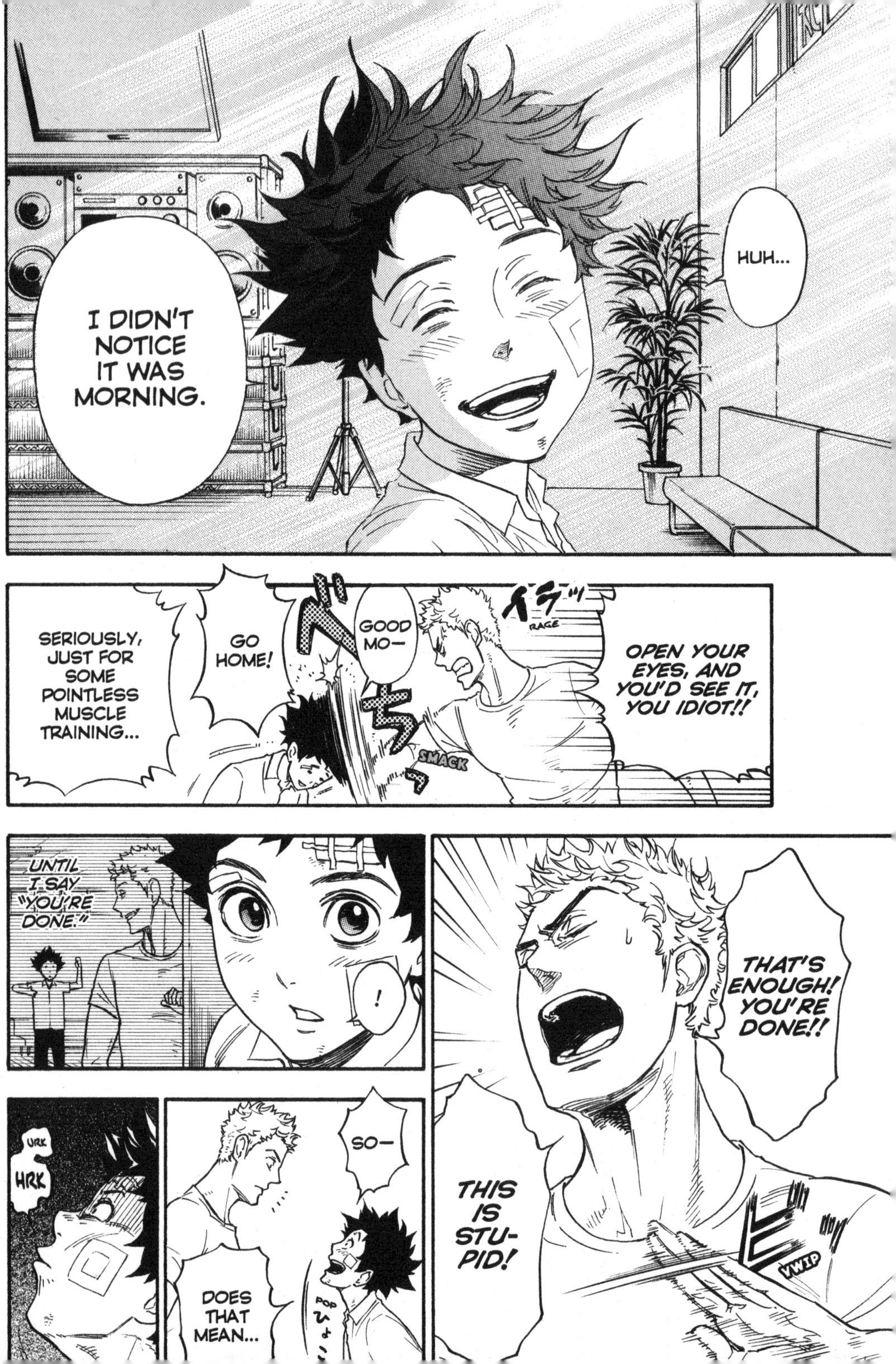
HUH...
I DIDN'T NOTICE IT WAS MORNING.
OPEN YOUR EYES, AND YOU'D SEE IT, YOU IDIOT!!
RAGE
GOOD MO—
GO HOME!
SMACK
SERIOUSLY, JUST FOR SOME POINTLESS MUSCLE TRAINING...
THAT'S ENOUGH! YOU'RE DONE!!
THIS IS STU-PID!
VWIP
!
UNTIL I SAY "YOU'RE DONE."
SO—
DOES THAT MEAN...
POP
URK
HRK

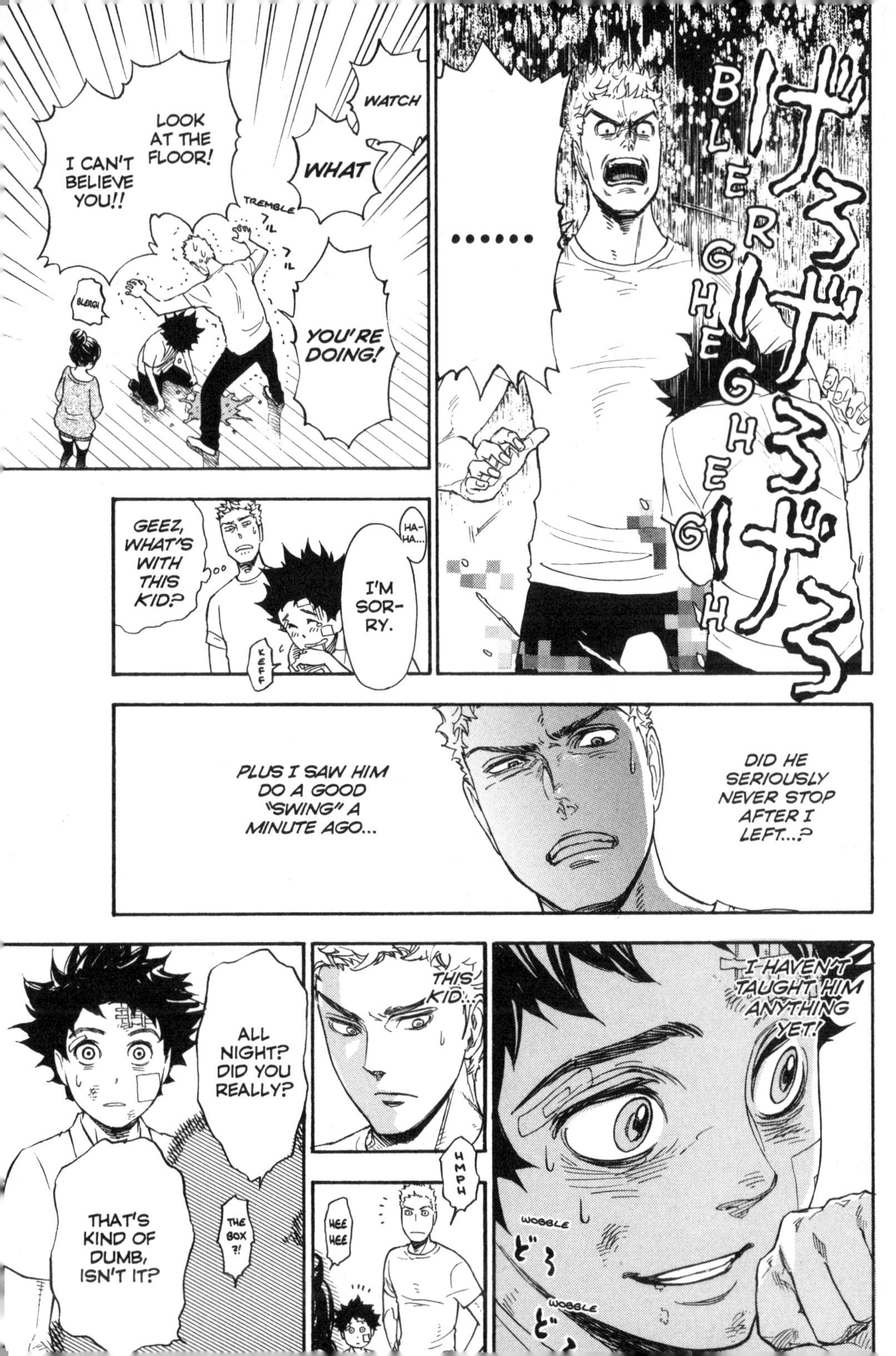
......
BLERGHGHEGHEGH
WATCH WHAT YOU'RE DOING!
LOOK AT THE FLOOR!
I CAN'T BELIEVE YOU!!
TREMBLE
BLERGH
HA-HA...
I'M SORRY.
GEEZ, WHAT'S WITH THIS KID?
KEFF
DID HE SERIOUSLY NEVER STOP AFTER I LEFT...?
PLUS I SAW HIM DO A GOOD "SWING" A MINUTE AGO...
I HAVEN'T TAUGHT HIM ANYTHING YET!
WOBBLE
WOBBLE
THIS KID...
HMPH
HEE HEE
ALL NIGHT? DID YOU REALLY?
THE BOX?!
THAT'S KIND OF DUMB, ISN'T IT?

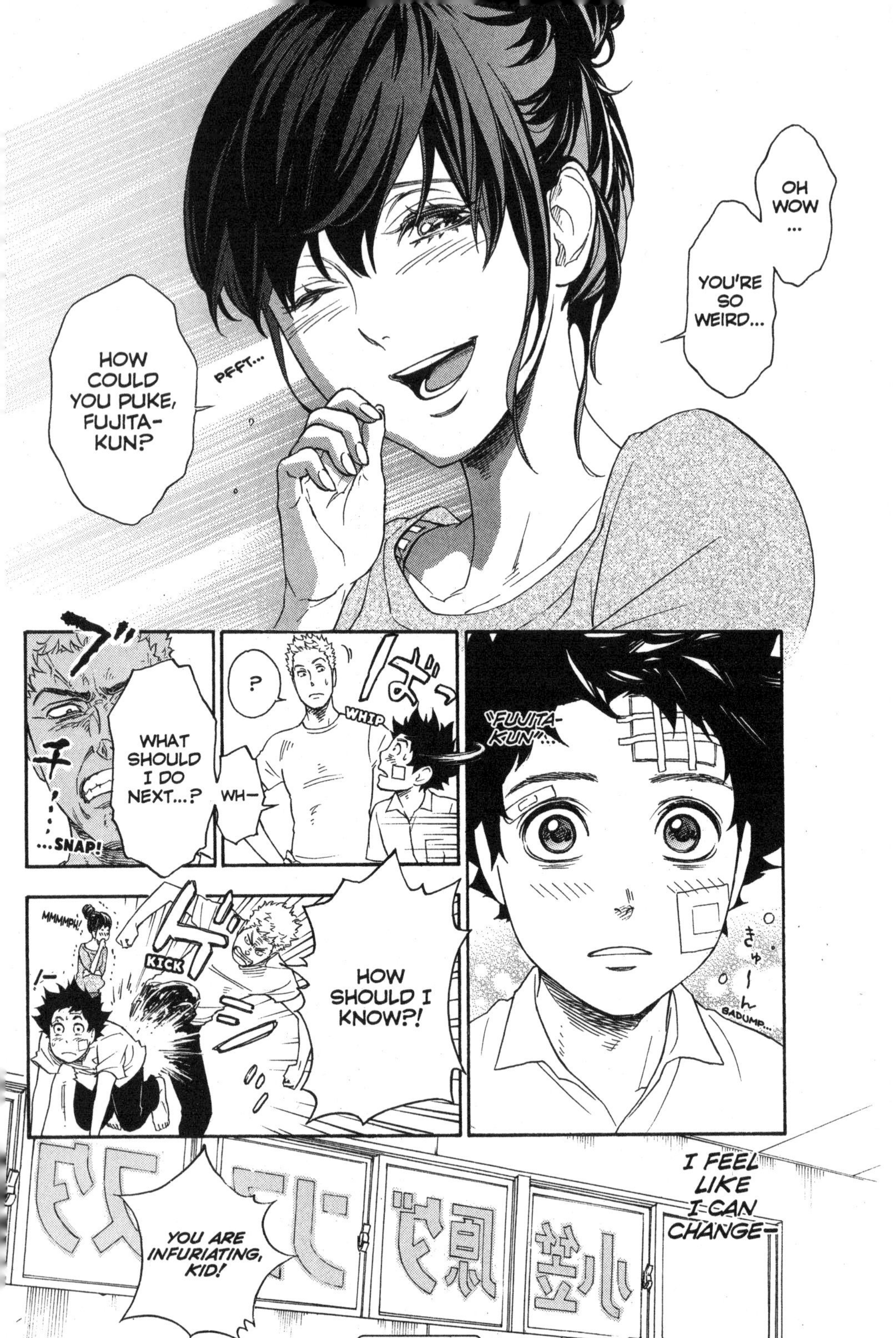
OH WOW ... YOU'RE SO WEIRD...
PFFT...
HOW COULD YOU PUKE, FUJITA-KUN?
"FUJITA-KUN"...
きゅ～ん
BADUMP...
?
ぼっ
WHIP
WH—
WHAT SHOULD I DO NEXT...?
...SNAP!
HOW SHOULD I KNOW?!
KICK
MMMMPH!
!—
I FEEL LIKE I CAN CHANGE—
YOU ARE INFURIATING, KID!

Heat 1: End

WELCOME TO THE BALLROOM

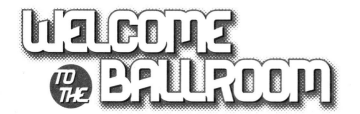

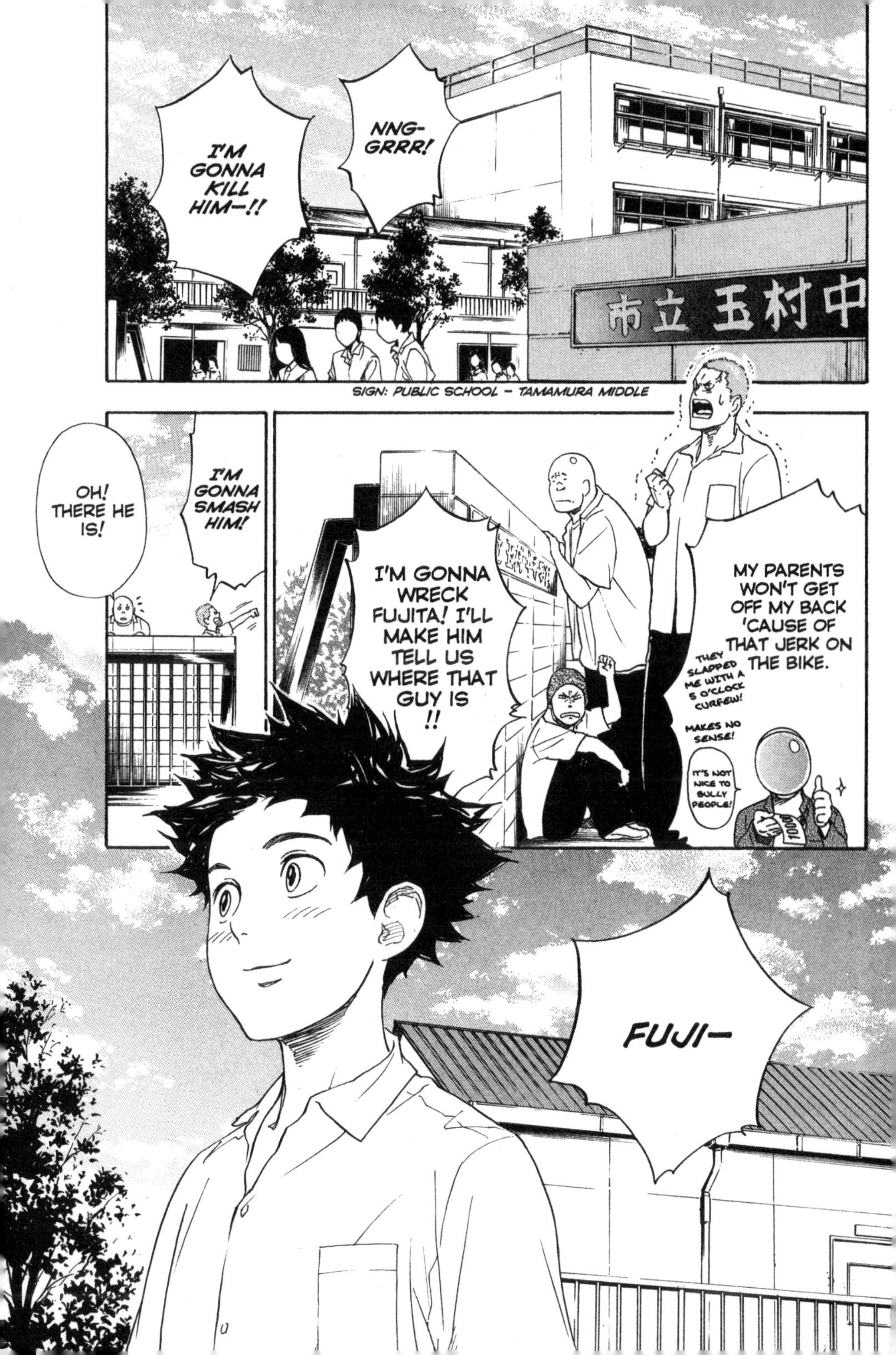
NNG-GRRR!
I'M GONNA KILL HIM--!!
SIGN: PUBLIC SCHOOL - TAMAMURA MIDDLE
MY PARENTS WON'T GET OFF MY BACK 'CAUSE OF THAT JERK ON THE BIKE.
THEY SLAPPED ME WITH A 5 O'CLOCK CURFEW!
MAKES NO SENSE!
I'M GONNA WRECK FUJITA! I'LL MAKE HIM TELL US WHERE THAT GUY IS!!
IT'S NOT NICE TO BULLY PEOPLE!
I'M GONNA SMASH HIM!
OH! THERE HE IS!
FUJI-

Heat 2
Shadowing Basics

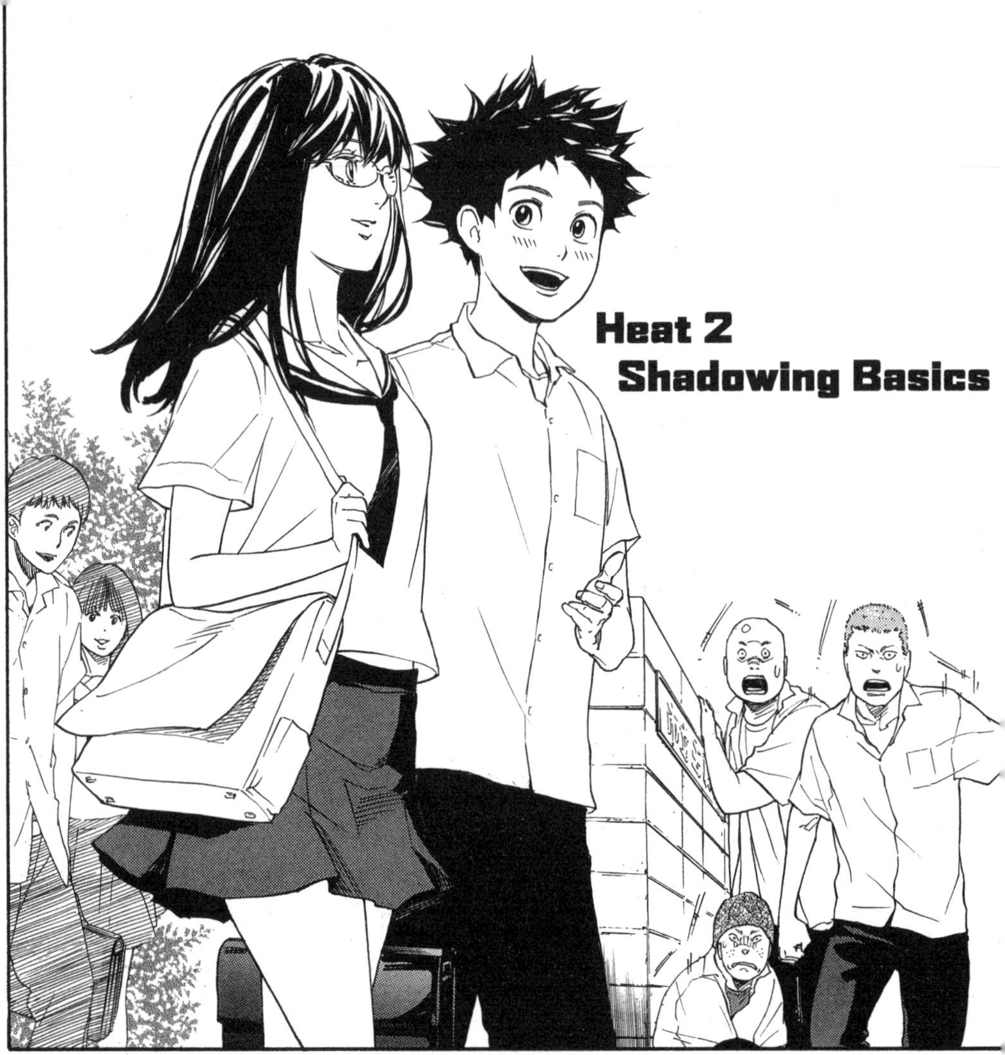

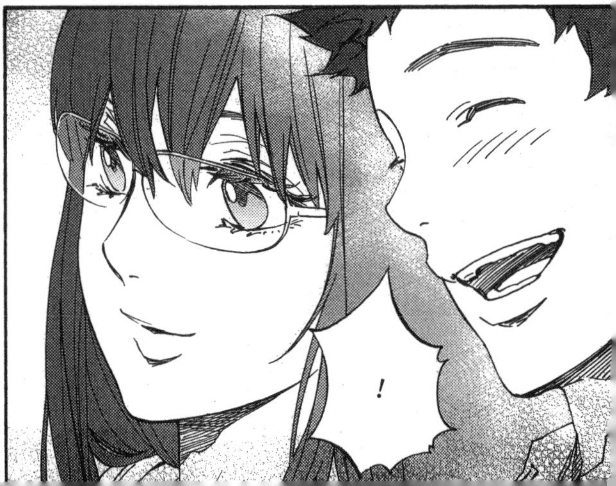
!

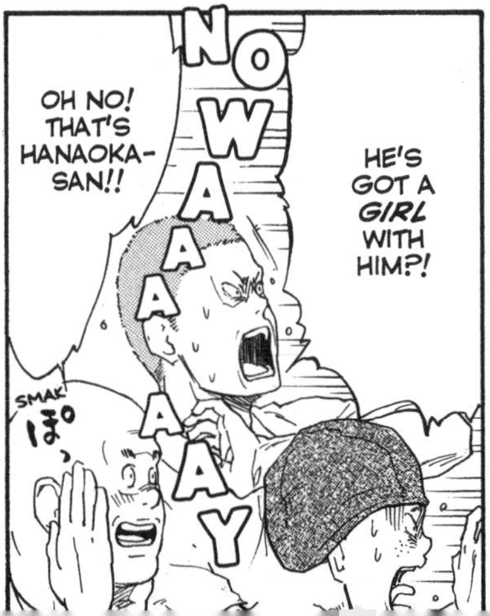
NOWAAAAAAAY
HE'S GOT A *GIRL* WITH HIM?!
OH NO! THAT'S HANAOKA-SAN!!
SMAK
ぽっ

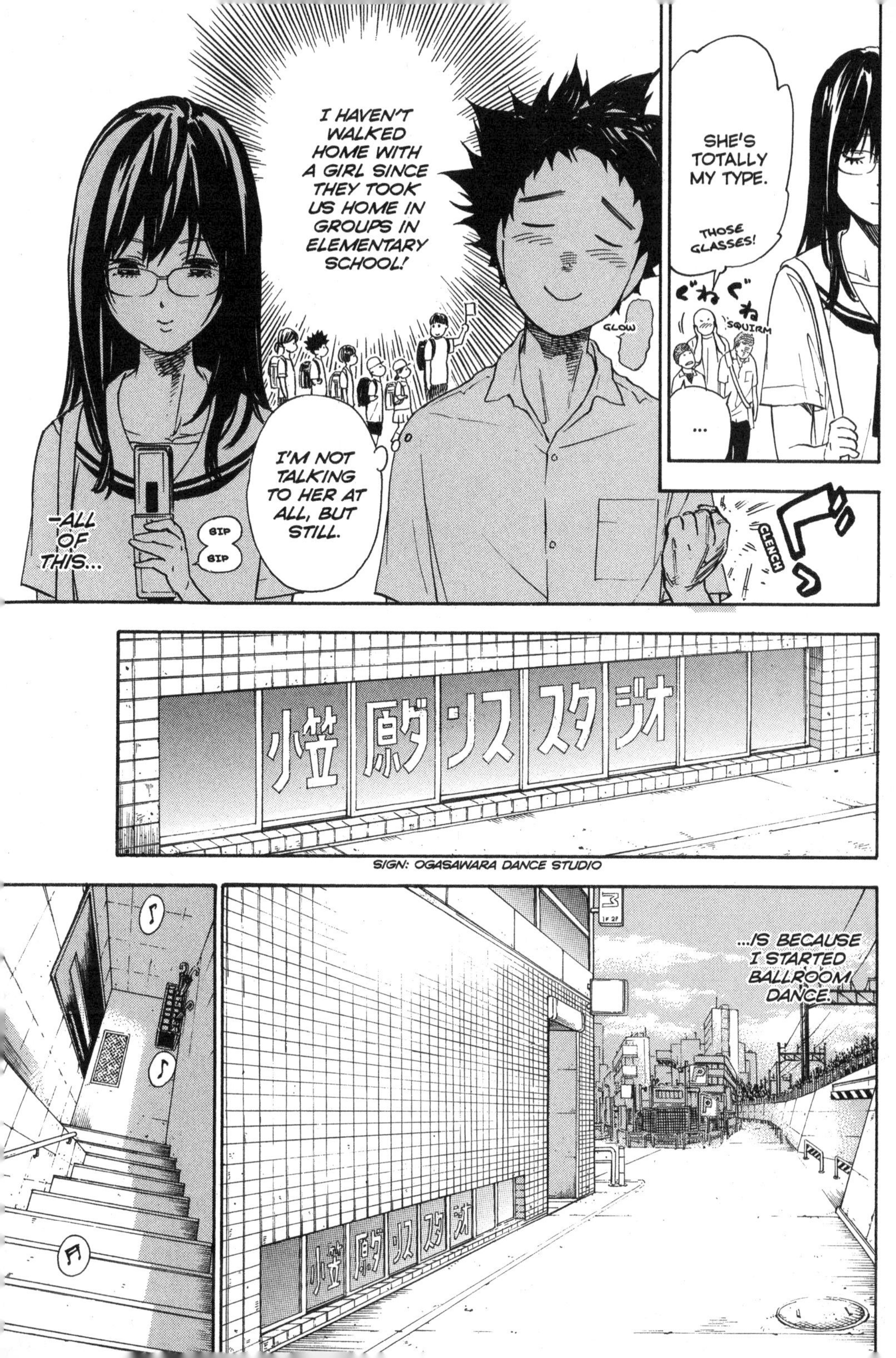

SHE'S TOTALLY MY TYPE.
THOSE GLASSES!
ぐねぐね
SQUIRM
...
I HAVEN'T WALKED HOME WITH A GIRL SINCE THEY TOOK US HOME IN GROUPS IN ELEMENTARY SCHOOL!
GLOW
I'M NOT TALKING TO HER AT ALL, BUT STILL.
CLENCH
SIP SIP
-ALL OF THIS...
小笠原ダンススタジオ
SIGN: OGASAWARA DANCE STUDIO
...IS BECAUSE I STARTED BALLROOM DANCE.

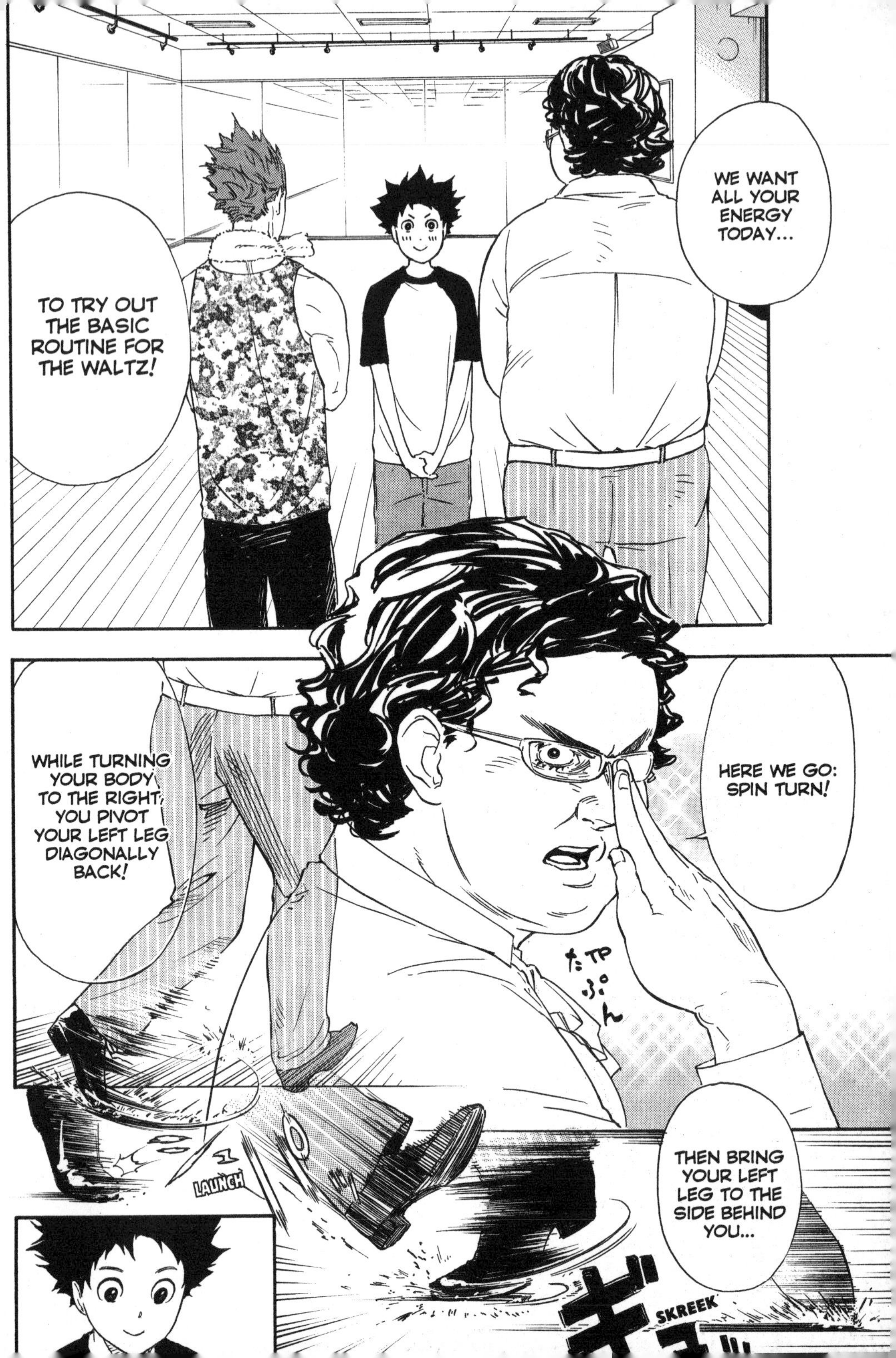
WE WANT ALL YOUR ENERGY TODAY...
TO TRY OUT THE BASIC ROUTINE FOR THE WALTZ!
HERE WE GO: SPIN TURN!
WHILE TURNING YOUR BODY TO THE RIGHT, YOU PIVOT YOUR LEFT LEG DIAGONALLY BACK!
TP
THEN BRING YOUR LEFT LEG TO THE SIDE BEHIND YOU...
LAUNCH
SKREEK

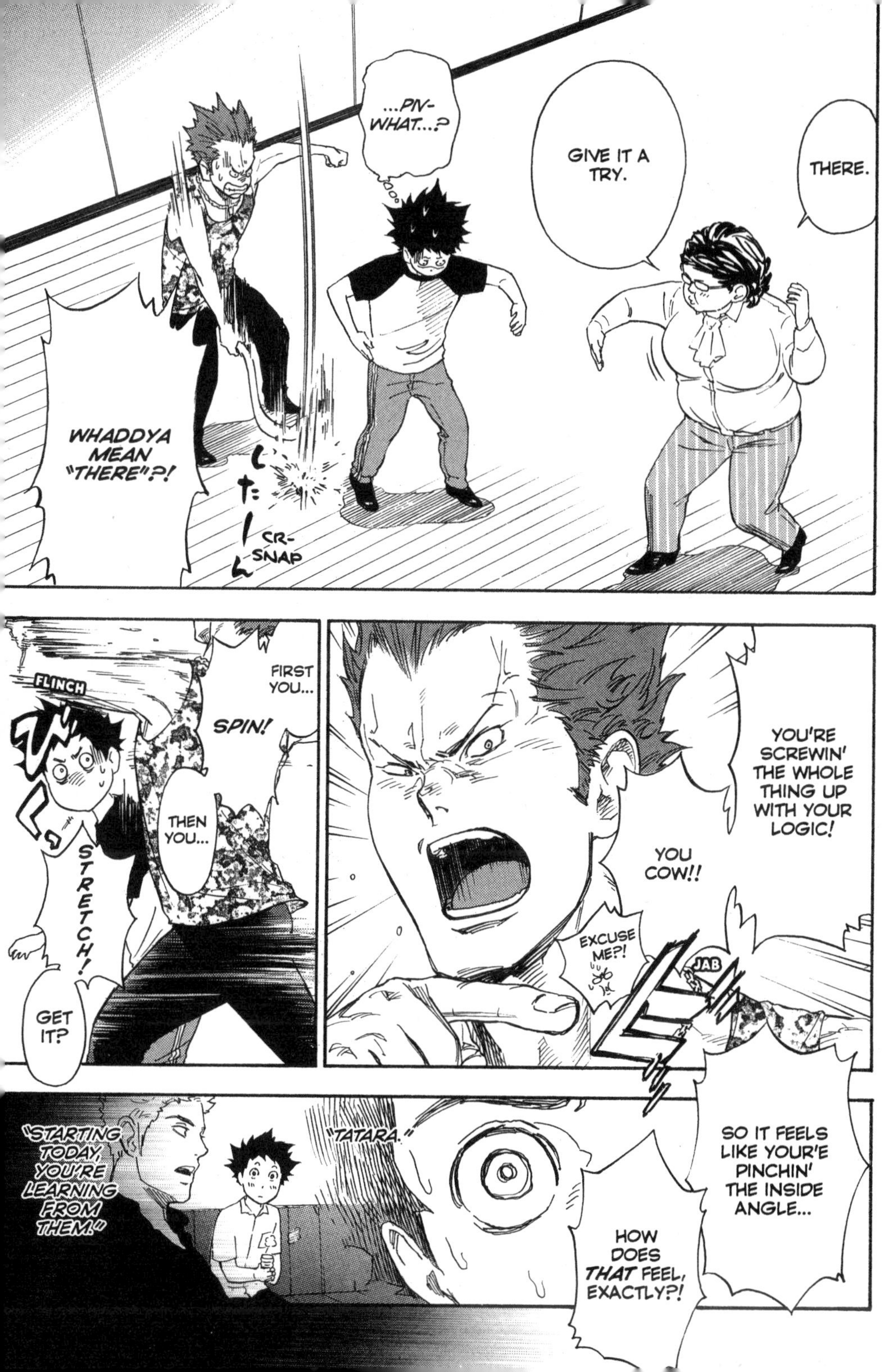
THERE.
GIVE IT A TRY.
...PIN-WHAT...?
WHADDYA MEAN "THERE"?!
CR-SNAP
YOU'RE SCREWIN' THE WHOLE THING UP WITH YOUR LOGIC!
YOU COW!!
EXCUSE ME?!
JAB
FIRST YOU...
SPIN!
FLINCH
THEN YOU...
STRETCH!
GET IT?
SO IT FEELS LIKE YOUR'E PINCHIN' THE INSIDE ANGLE...
HOW DOES *THAT* FEEL, EXACTLY?!
"TATARA."
"STARTING TODAY, YOU'RE LEARNING FROM THEM."

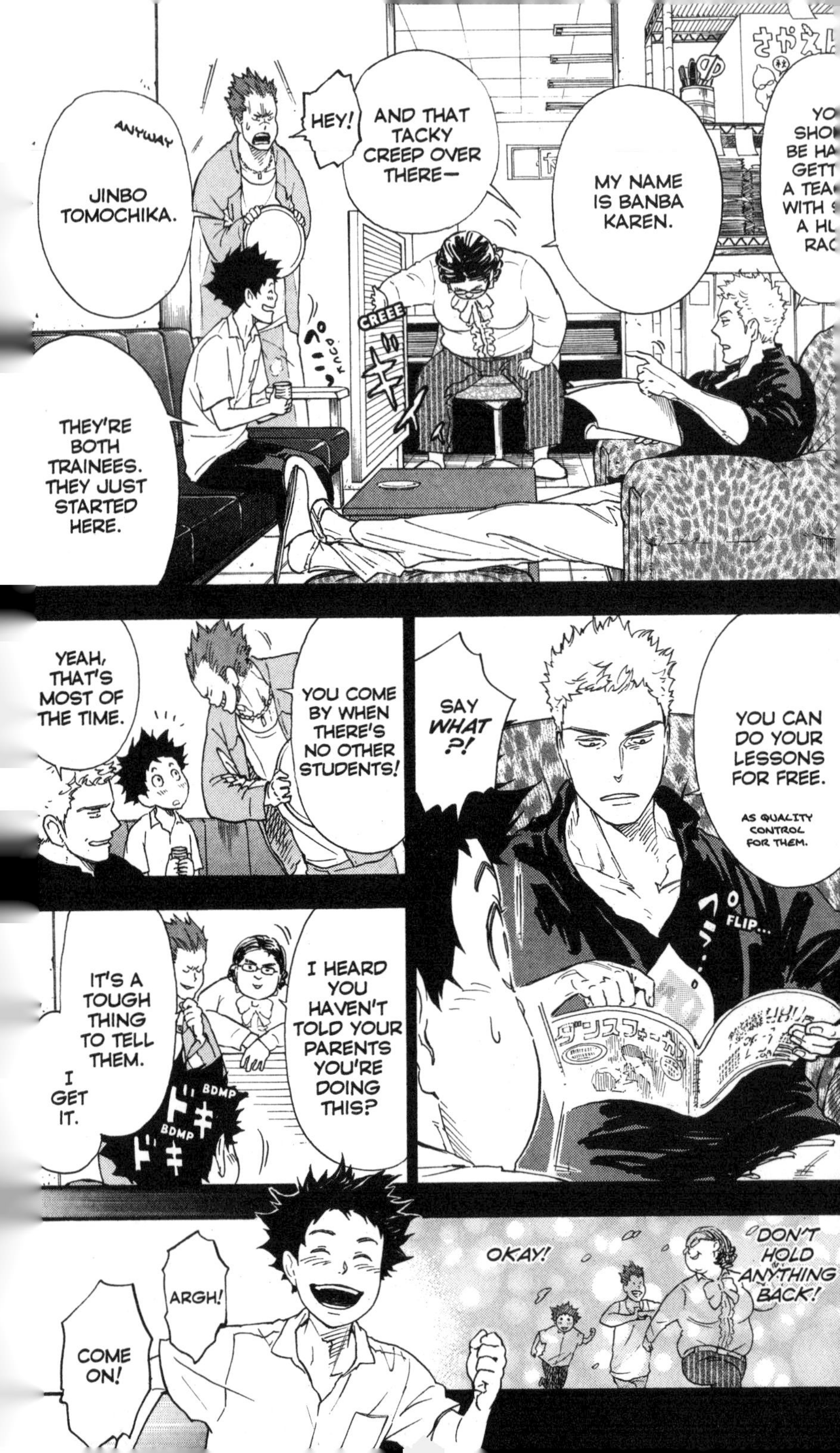
MY NAME IS BANBA KAREN.
AND THAT TACKY CREEP OVER THERE—
HEY!
ANYWAY
JINBO TOMOCHIKA.
CREEE
THEY'RE BOTH TRAINEES. THEY JUST STARTED HERE.
YOU CAN DO YOUR LESSONS FOR FREE.
AS QUALITY CONTROL FOR THEM.
SAY WHAT?!
FLIP...
YOU COME BY WHEN THERE'S NO OTHER STUDENTS!
YEAH, THAT'S MOST OF THE TIME.
I HEARD YOU HAVEN'T TOLD YOUR PARENTS YOU'RE DOING THIS?
IT'S A TOUGH THING TO TELL THEM.
I GET IT.
BDMP
BDMP
DON'T HOLD ANYTHING BACK!
OKAY!
ARGH!
COME ON!

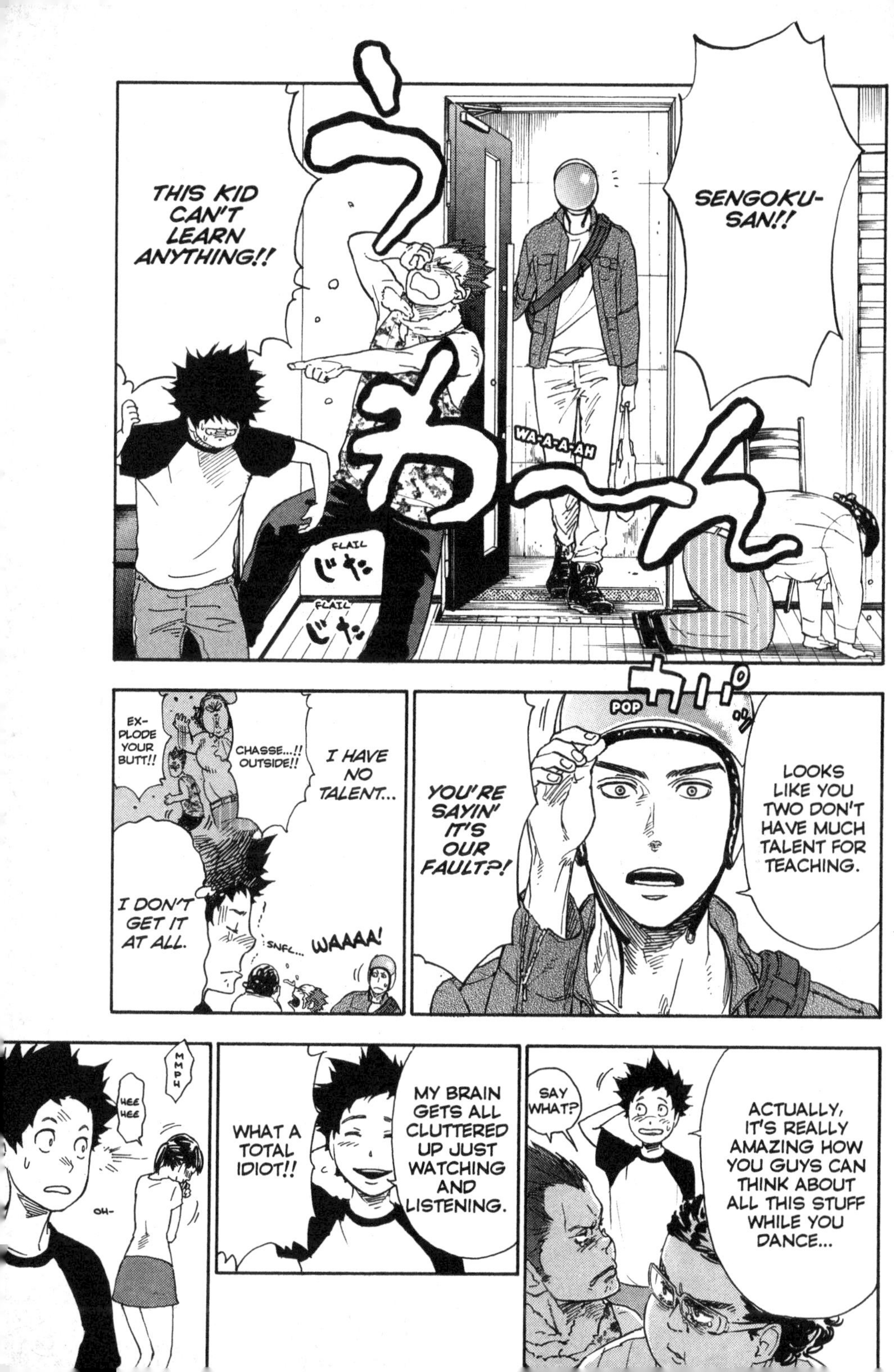
SENGOKU-SAN!!
WA-A-A-AH
THIS KID CAN'T LEARN ANYTHING!!
FLAIL
FLAIL
POP
LOOKS LIKE YOU TWO DON'T HAVE MUCH TALENT FOR TEACHING.
YOU'RE SAYIN' IT'S OUR FAULT?!
I HAVE NO TALENT...
CHASSE...!! OUTSIDE!!
EX-PLODE YOUR BUTT!!
I DON'T GET IT AT ALL.
WAAAA!
SNFL...
ACTUALLY, IT'S REALLY AMAZING HOW YOU GUYS CAN THINK ABOUT ALL THIS STUFF WHILE YOU DANCE...
SAY WHAT?
MY BRAIN GETS ALL CLUTTERED UP JUST WATCHING AND LISTENING.
WHAT A TOTAL IDIOT!!
MMPH
HEE HEE
OH-

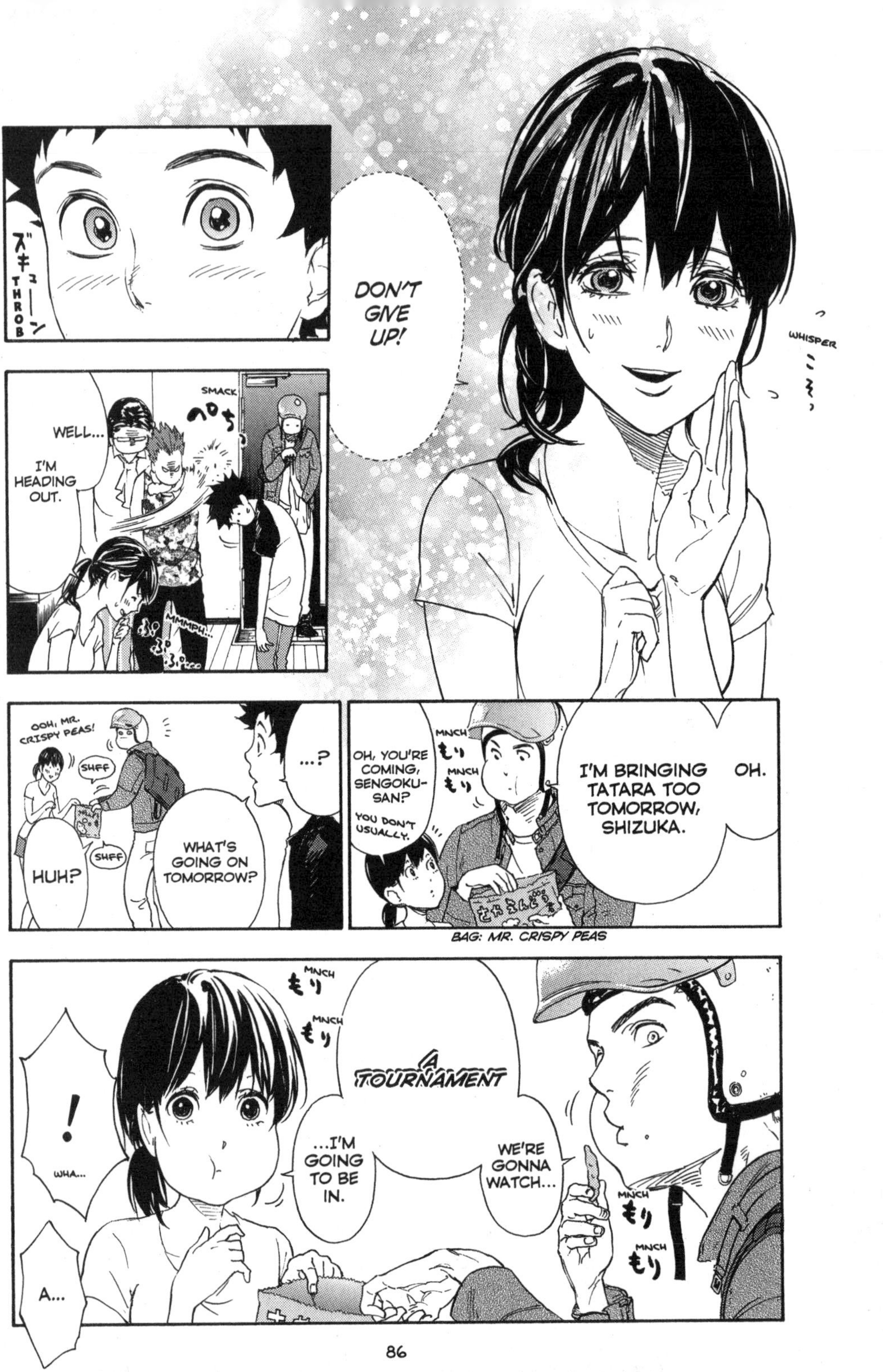
DON'T GIVE UP!
WHISPER
THROB
WELL...
I'M HEADING OUT.
SMACK
MMMPH...
OH.
I'M BRINGING TATARA TOO TOMORROW, SHIZUKA.
MNCH
もり
MNCH
もり
OH, YOU'RE COMING, SENGOKU-SAN?
YOU DON'T USUALLY.
BAG: MR. CRISPY PEAS
...?
WHAT'S GOING ON TOMORROW?
OOH, MR. CRISPY PEAS!
SHFF
SHFF
HUH?
MNCH
もり
MNCH
もり
WE'RE GONNA WATCH...
A TOURNAMENT
...I'M GOING TO BE IN.
MNCH
もり
MNCH
もり
!
WHA...
A...

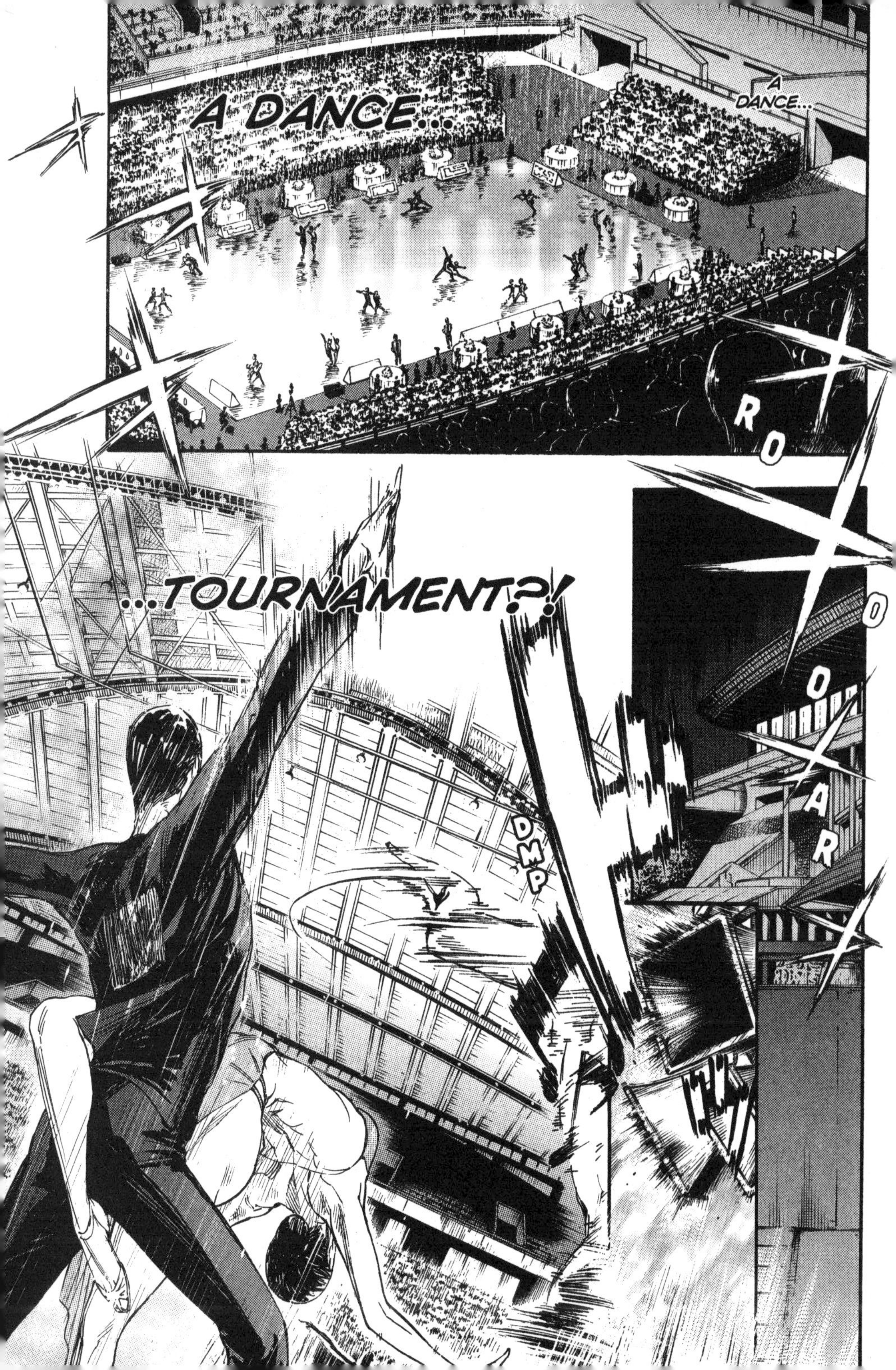

A DANCE...
A DANCE...
ROOOOAR
...TOURNAMENT?!
DMP

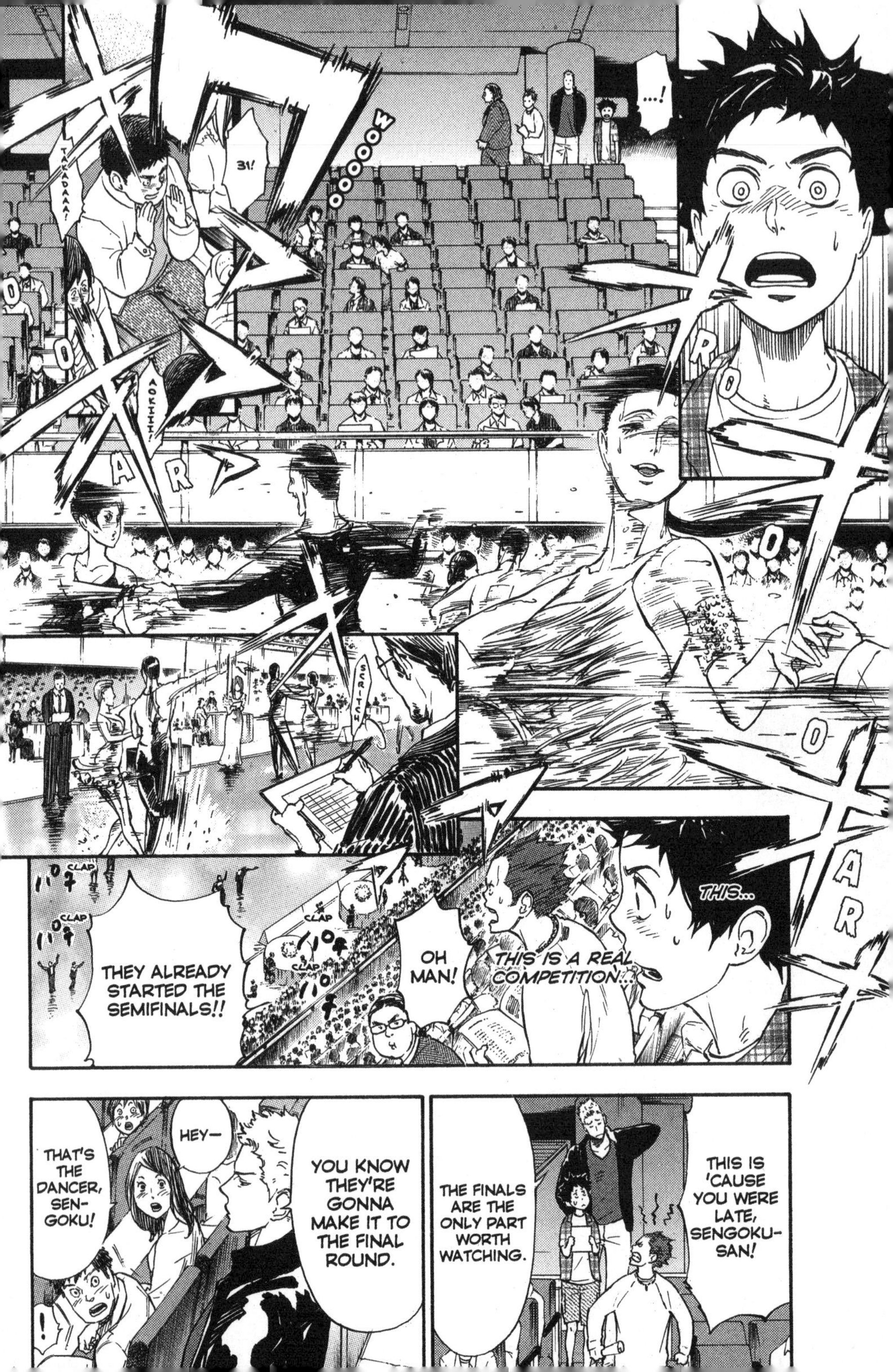

...!
WOOOOOO
31!
TAKADAAA!
AOKIII!
SCRITCH
THIS...
THIS IS A REAL COMPETITION...
OH MAN!
THEY ALREADY STARTED THE SEMIFINALS!!
CLAP
CLAP
CLAP
CLAP
THIS IS 'CAUSE YOU WERE LATE, SENGOKU-SAN!
THE FINALS ARE THE ONLY PART WORTH WATCHING.
YOU KNOW THEY'RE GONNA MAKE IT TO THE FINAL ROUND.
HEY—
THAT'S THE DANCER, SENGOKU!
!

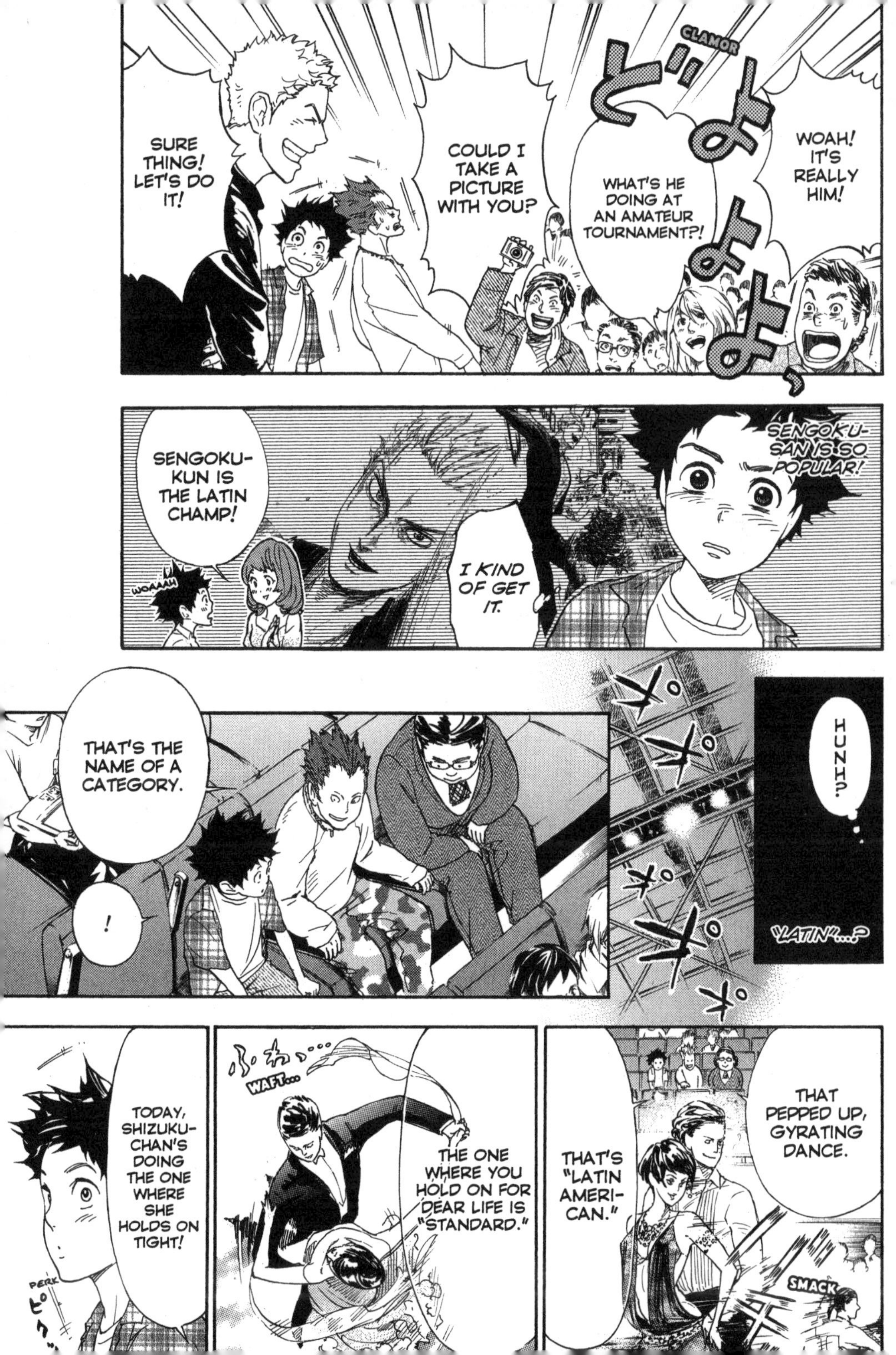
WOAH! IT'S REALLY HIM!
CLAMOR
WHAT'S HE DOING AT AN AMATEUR TOURNAMENT?!
COULD I TAKE A PICTURE WITH YOU?
SURE THING! LET'S DO IT!
SENGOKU-SAN IS SO POPULAR!
I KIND OF GET IT.
SENGOKU-KUN IS THE LATIN CHAMP!
WOAAAH
HUNH?
"LATIN"...?
THAT'S THE NAME OF A CATEGORY.
!
THAT PEPPED UP, GYRATING DANCE.
THAT'S "LATIN AMERICAN."
SMACK
THE ONE WHERE YOU HOLD ON FOR DEAR LIFE IS "STANDARD."
WAFT...
TODAY, SHIZUKU-CHAN'S DOING THE ONE WHERE SHE HOLDS ON TIGHT!
PERK

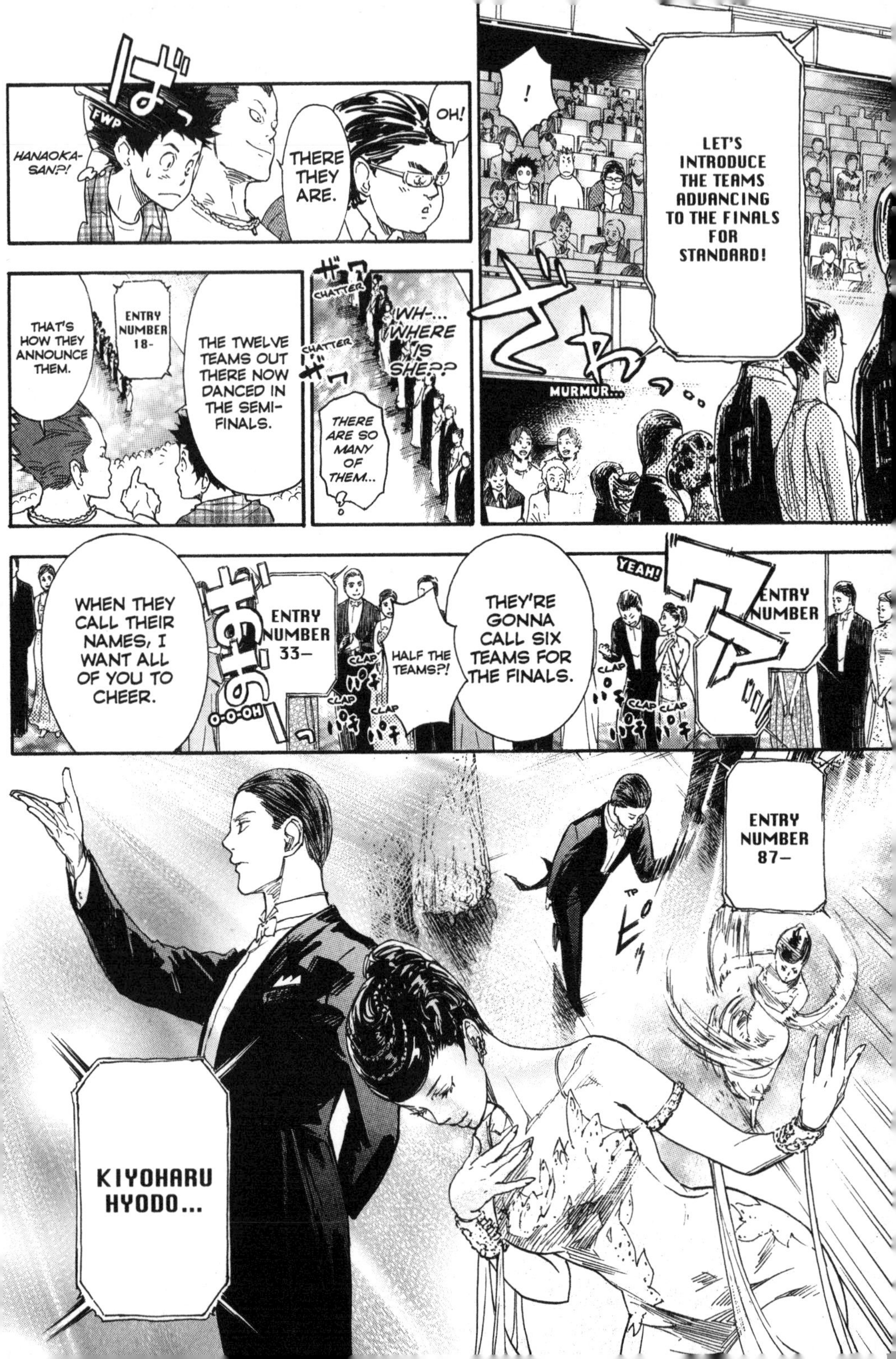
!
LET'S INTRODUCE THE TEAMS ADVANCING TO THE FINALS FOR STANDARD!
MURMUR...
OH!
THERE THEY ARE.
FWP
HANAOKA-SAN?!
CHATTER
WH-... WHERE IS SHE??
CHATTER
THERE ARE SO MANY OF THEM...
?
THE TWELVE TEAMS OUT THERE NOW DANCED IN THE SEMI-FINALS.
ENTRY NUMBER 18-
THAT'S HOW THEY ANNOUNCE THEM.
ENTRY NUMBER —
YEAH!
CLAP
CLAP
CLAP
THEY'RE GONNA CALL SIX TEAMS FOR THE FINALS.
HALF THE TEAMS?!
CLAP
CLAP
CLAP
ENTRY NUMBER 33—
O-O-OH
WHEN THEY CALL THEIR NAMES, I WANT ALL OF YOU TO CHEER.
ENTRY NUMBER 87—
TP
KIYOHARU HYODO...

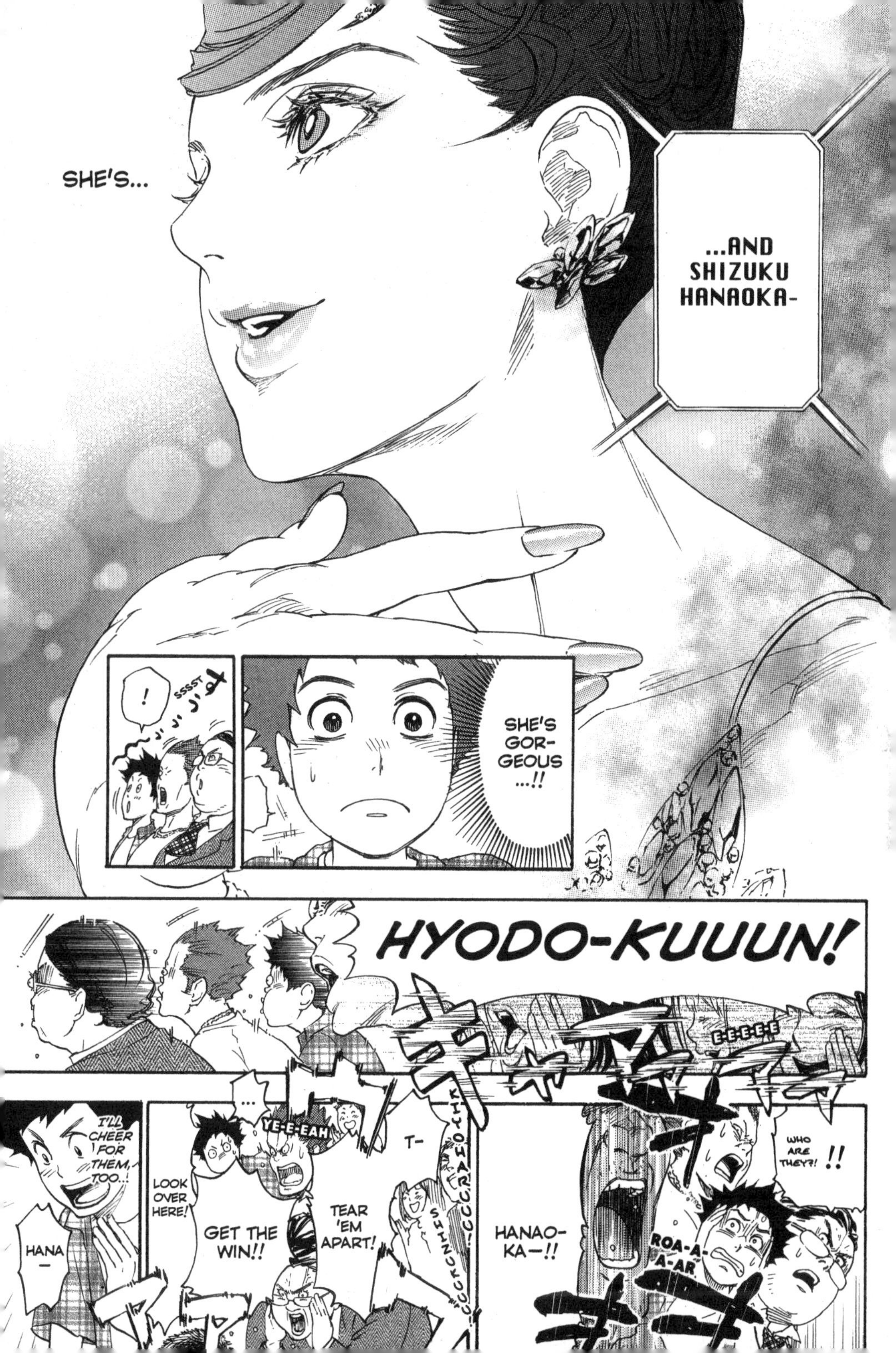
...AND SHIZUKU HANAOKA-
SHE'S...
SHE'S GORGEOUS ...!!
!
SSSST
HYODO-KUUUN!
E-E-E-E-E
WHO ARE THEY?!
!!
ROA-A-A-AR
HANAOKA—!!
KHYOHARCCCC—!!
SHIINCCCCCC—!!
T-
TEAR 'EM APART!
...
YE-E-EAH
LOOK OVER HERE!
GET THE WIN!!
I'LL CHEER FOR THEM, TOO...!
HANA—

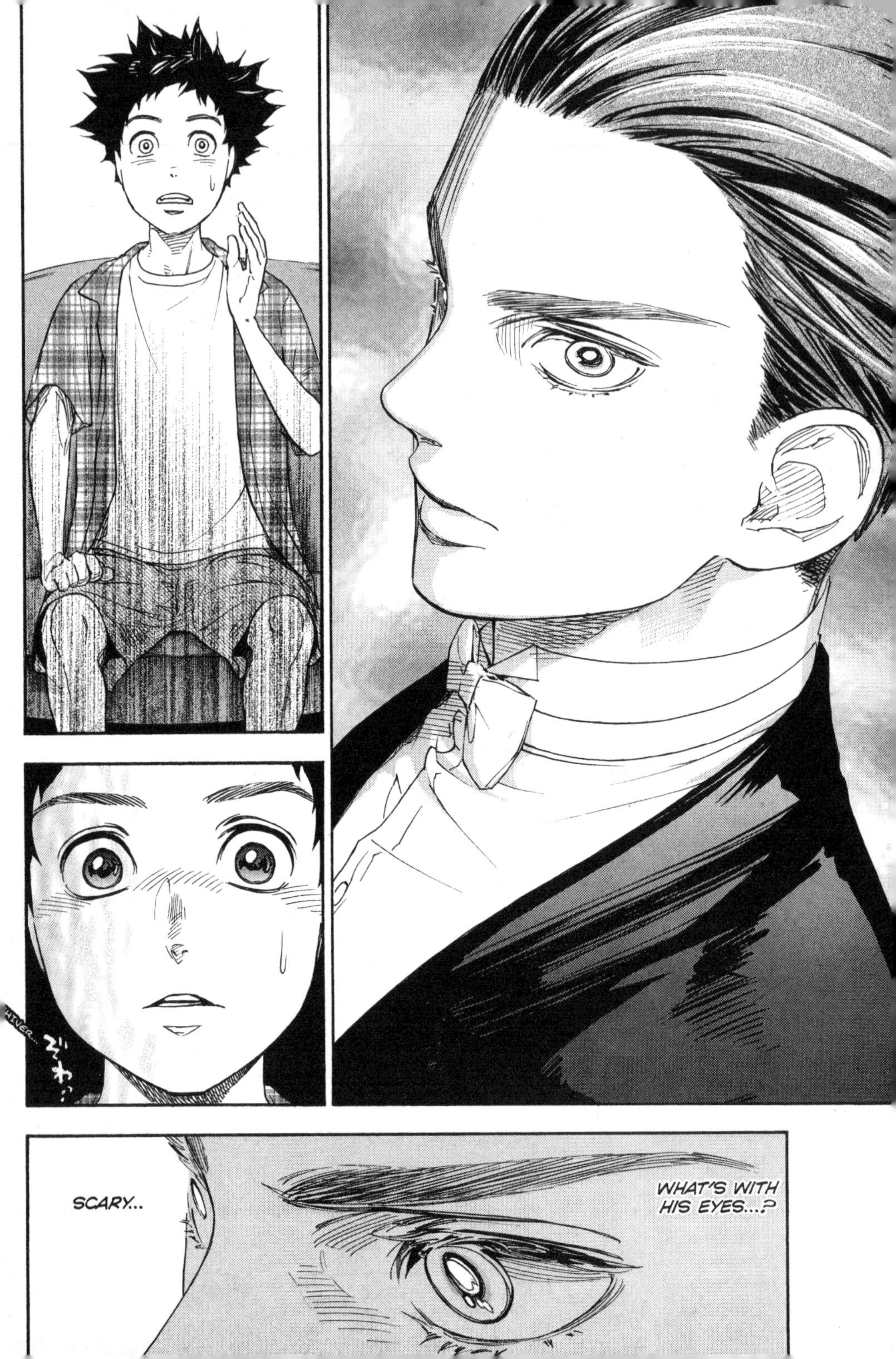
HIVER...
ぞわっ
WHAT'S WITH HIS EYES...?
SCARY...

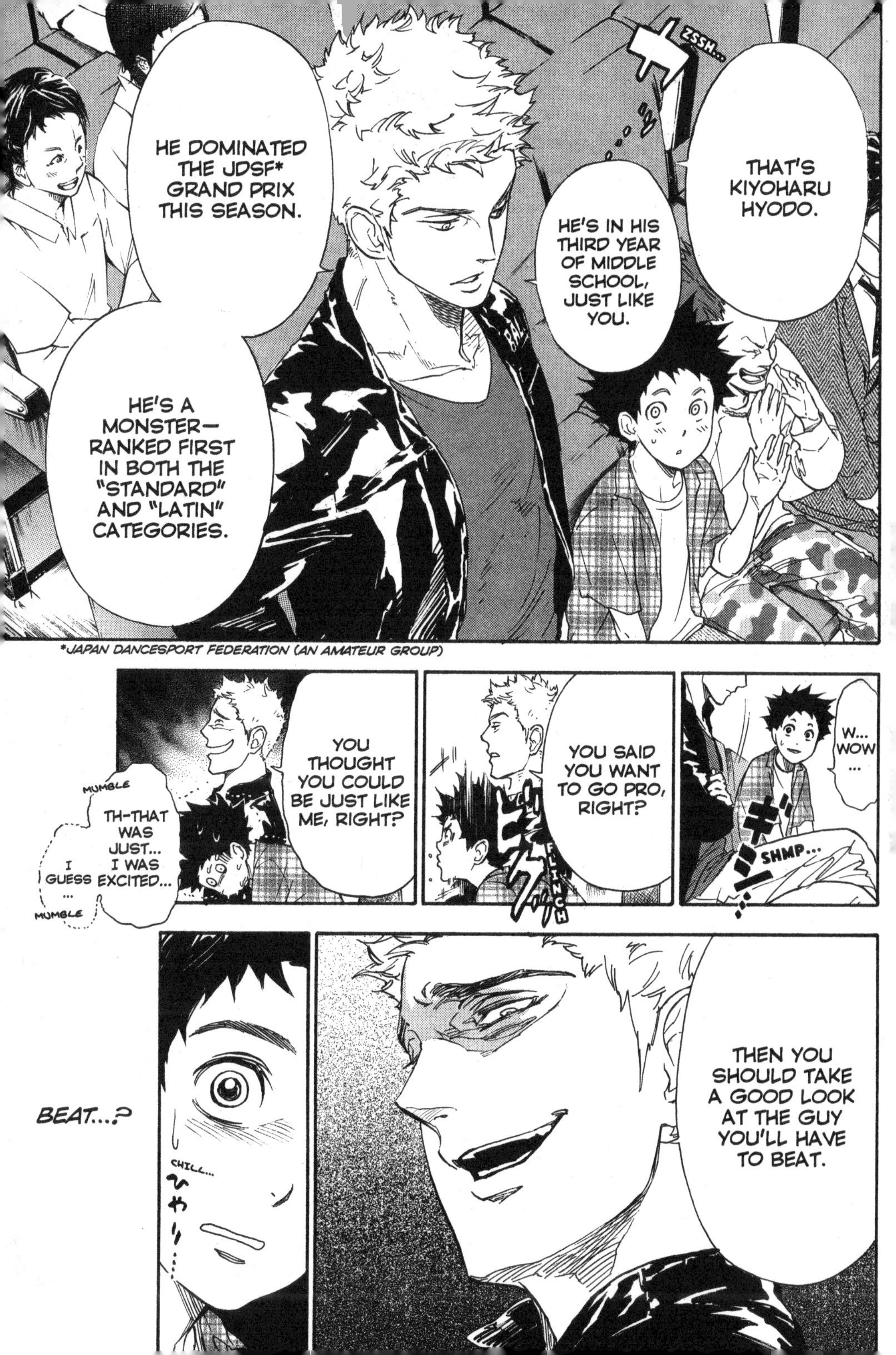
ZSSH...
THAT'S KIYOHARU HYODO.
HE'S IN HIS THIRD YEAR OF MIDDLE SCHOOL, JUST LIKE YOU.
HE DOMINATED THE JDSF* GRAND PRIX THIS SEASON.
HE'S A MONSTER—RANKED FIRST IN BOTH THE "STANDARD" AND "LATIN" CATEGORIES.
*JAPAN DANCESPORT FEDERATION (AN AMATEUR GROUP)
SHMP...
W... WOW...
YOU SAID YOU WANT TO GO PRO, RIGHT?
FLINCH
YOU THOUGHT YOU COULD BE JUST LIKE ME, RIGHT?
MUMBLE
TH-THAT WAS JUST... I WAS EXCITED...
I GUESS...
MUMBLE
THEN YOU SHOULD TAKE A GOOD LOOK AT THE GUY YOU'LL HAVE TO BEAT.
BEAT...?
CHILL...

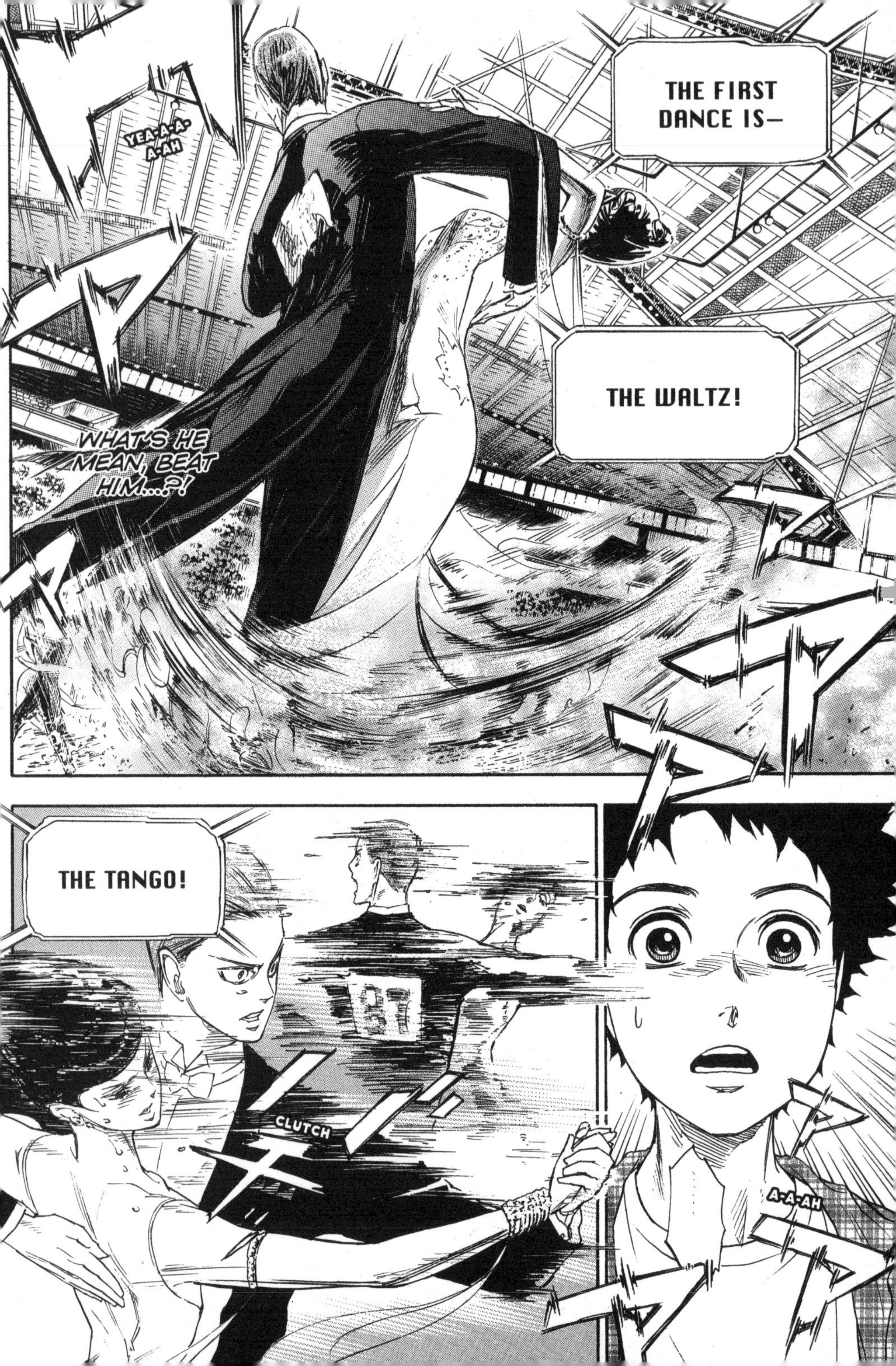
THE FIRST DANCE IS—
YEA-A-A-A-AH
THE WALTZ!
WHAT'S HE MEAN, BEAT HIM...?!
A-A-AH
THE TANGO!
CLUTCH

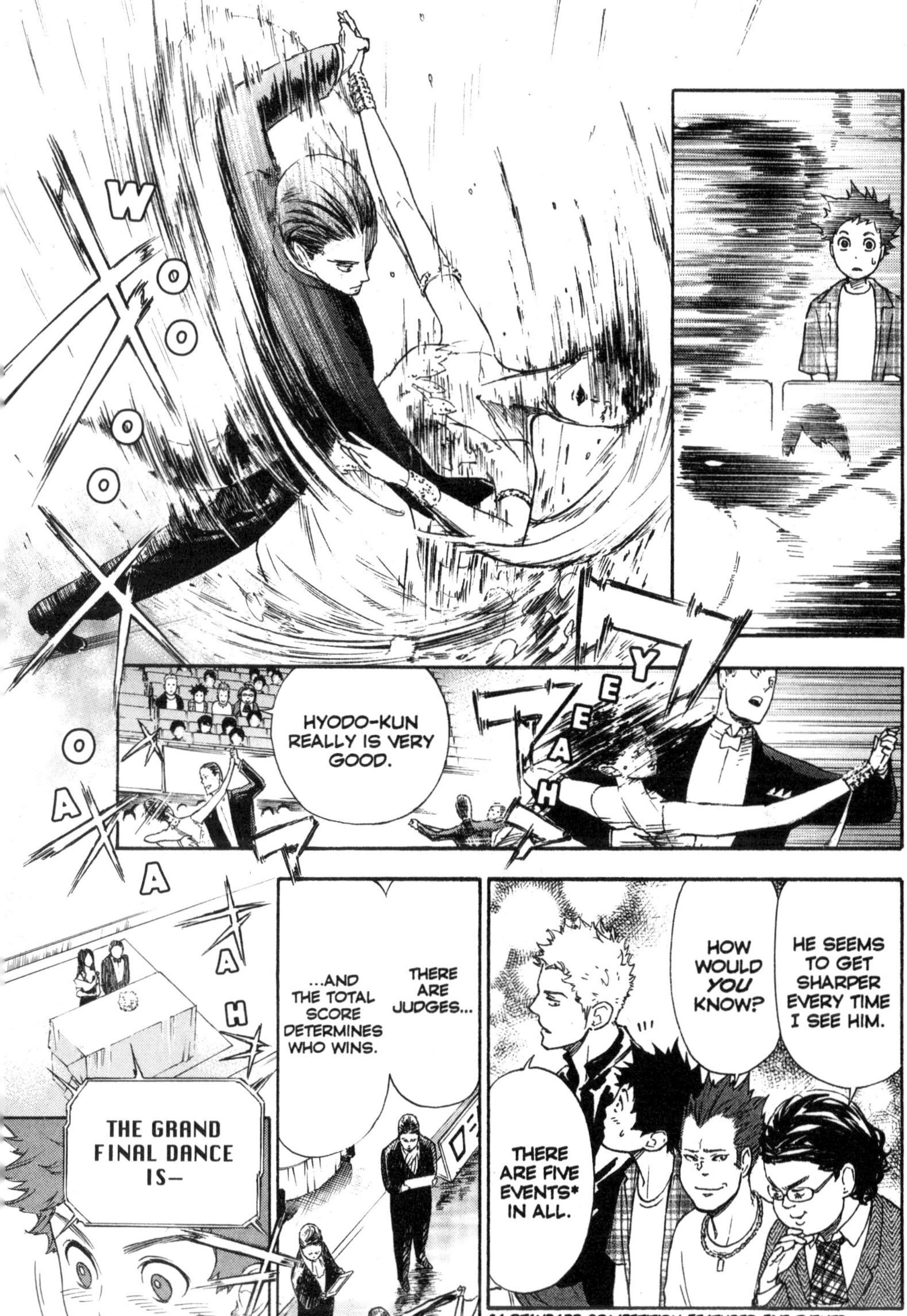
WOOOOOAAAH
YEEAH
HYODO-KUN REALLY IS VERY GOOD.
HE SEEMS TO GET SHARPER EVERY TIME I SEE HIM.
HOW WOULD *YOU* KNOW?
THERE ARE FIVE EVENTS* IN ALL.
THERE ARE JUDGES...
...AND THE TOTAL SCORE DETERMINES WHO WINS.
THE GRAND FINAL DANCE IS—

*A STANDARD COMPETITION FEATURES FIVE EVENTS: WALTZ, TANGO, VIENNESE WALTZ, SLOW FOXTROT, AND QUICKSTEP.

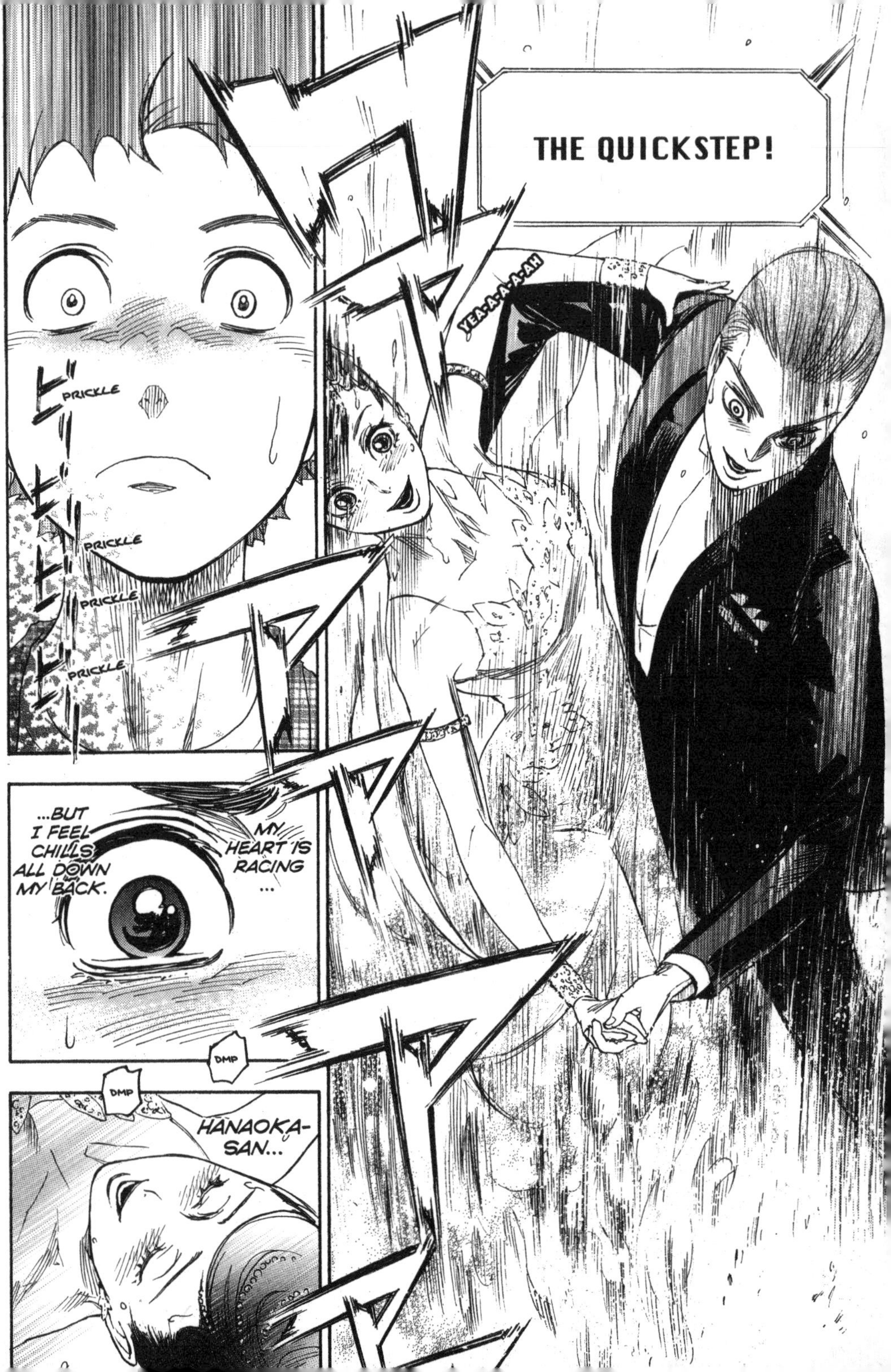
THE QUICKSTEP!
YEA-A-A-A-AH
PRICKLE
PRICKLE
PRICKLE
PRICKLE
MY HEART IS RACING...
...BUT I FEEL CHILLS ALL DOWN MY BACK.
DMP
DMP
HANAOKA-SAN...

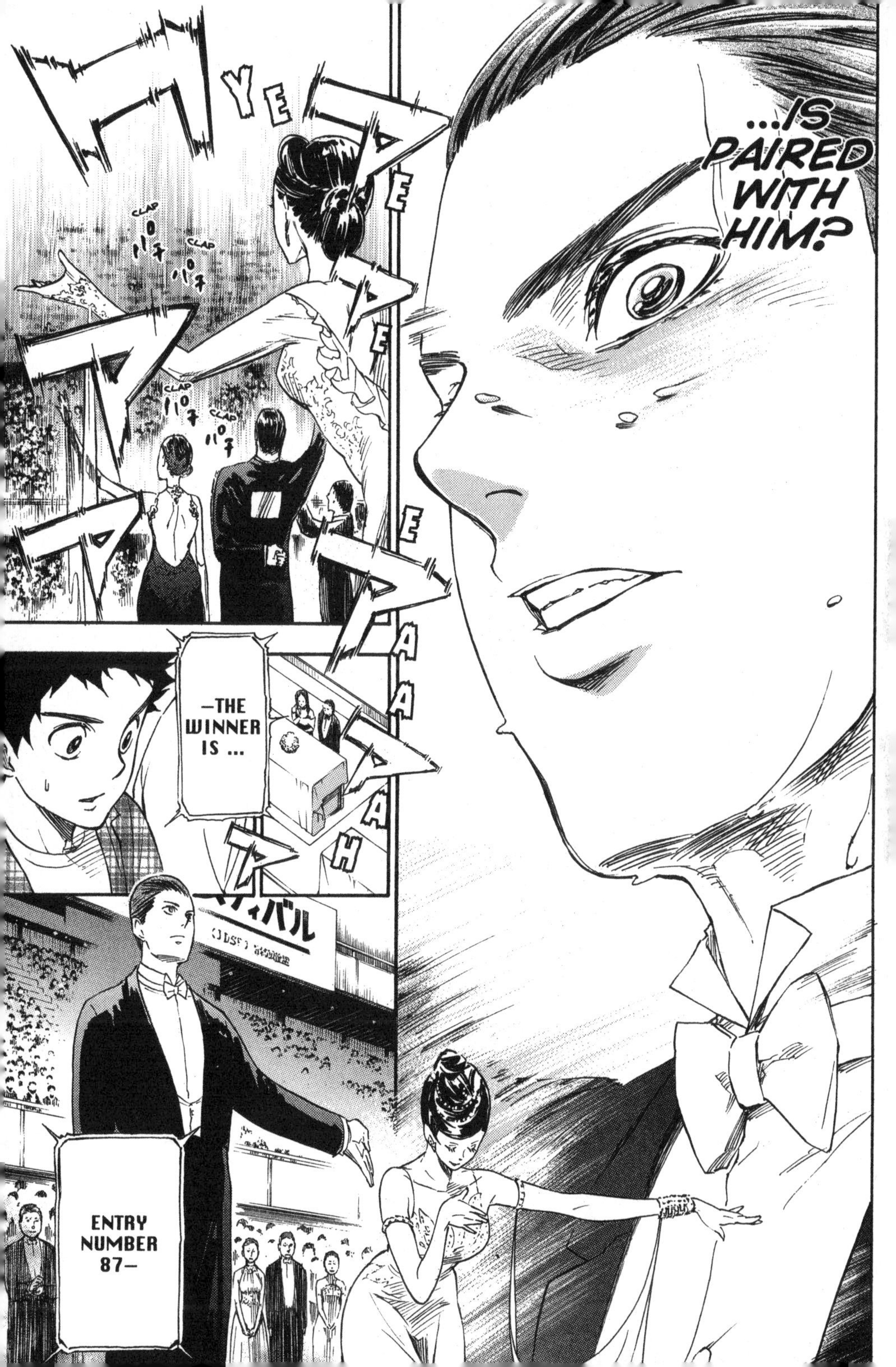
...IS PAIRED WITH HIM?
YEEEEAAAH
CLAP
パチ
CLAP
パチ
CLAP
パチ
CLAP
パチ
—THE WINNER IS ...
ENTRY NUMBER 87—

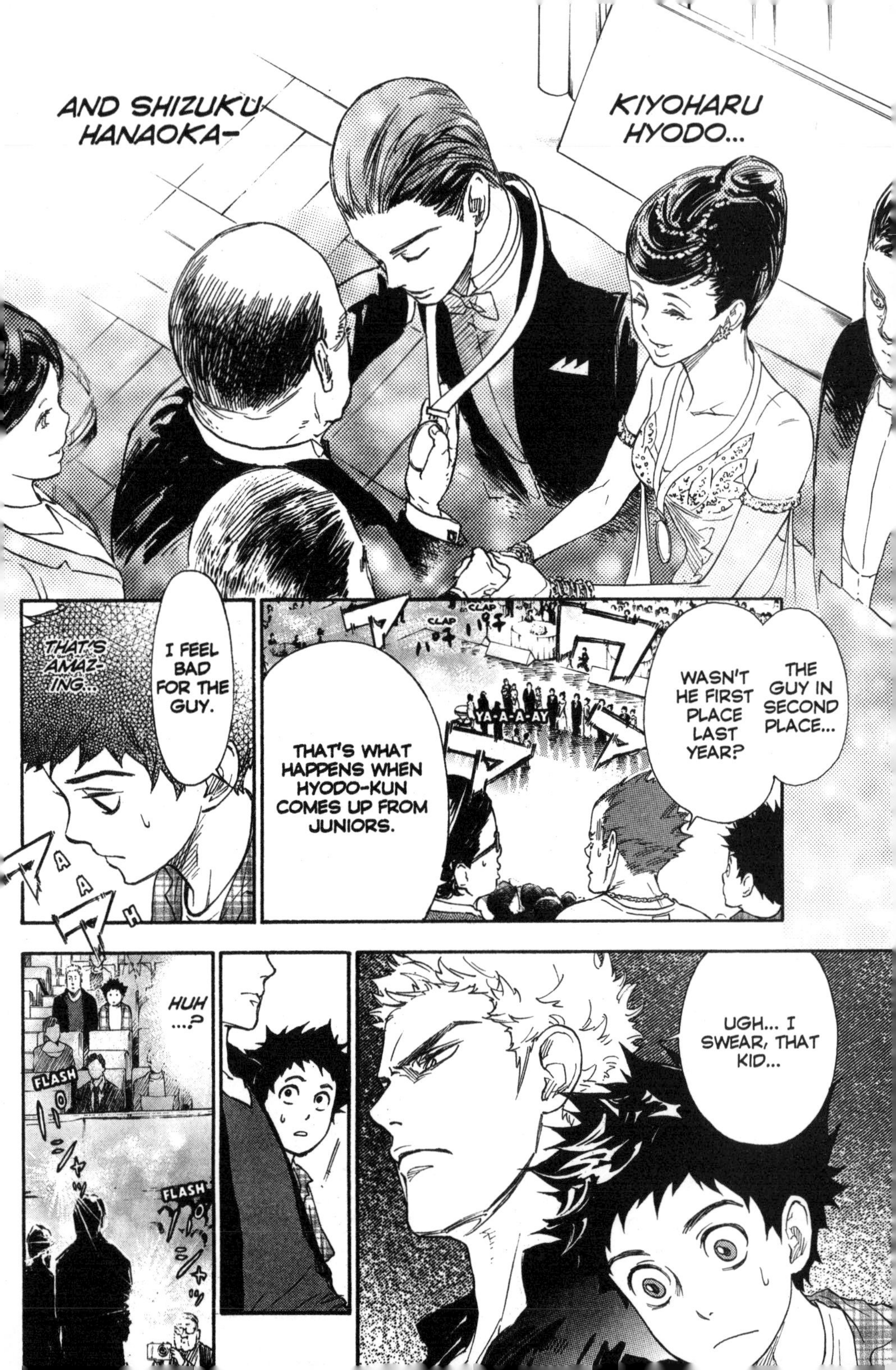
KIYOHARU HYODO...
AND SHIZUKU HANAOKA-
CLAP
CLAP
THE GUY IN SECOND PLACE...
WASN'T HE FIRST PLACE LAST YEAR?
YA-A-A-AY
THAT'S WHAT HAPPENS WHEN HYODO-KUN COMES UP FROM JUNIORS.
I FEEL BAD FOR THE GUY.
THAT'S AMAZ-ING...
AAAH
UGH... I SWEAR, THAT KID...
HUH ...?
FLASH
FLASH

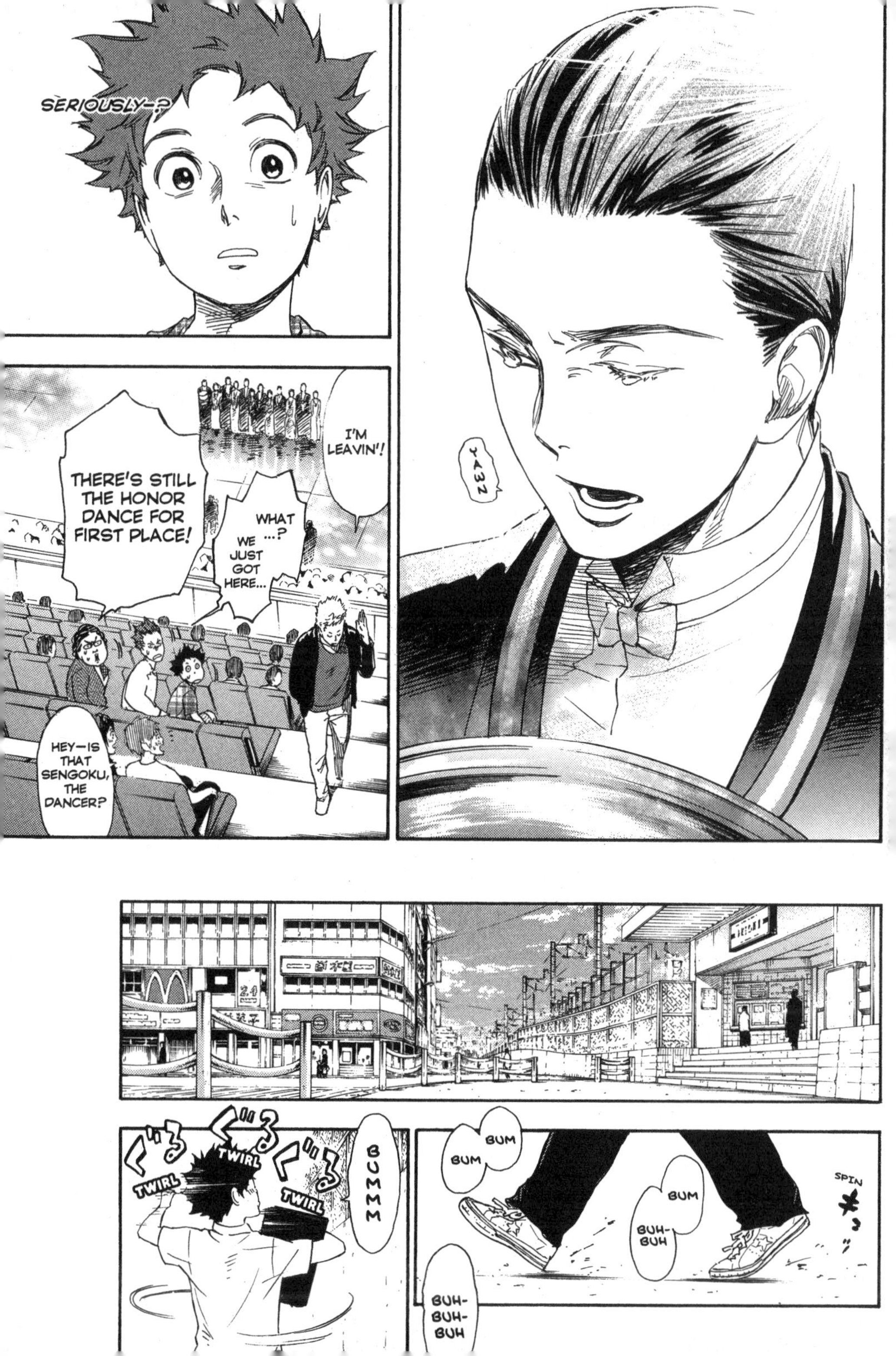
YAWN
SERIOUSLY—?
I'M LEAVIN'!
WHAT ...?
WE JUST GOT HERE...
THERE'S STILL THE HONOR DANCE FOR FIRST PLACE!
HEY—IS THAT SENGOKU, THE DANCER?
SPIN
BUM
BUM
BUM
BUH-BUH
BUH-BUH-BUH
BUMMM
TWIRL
TWIRL
TWIRL

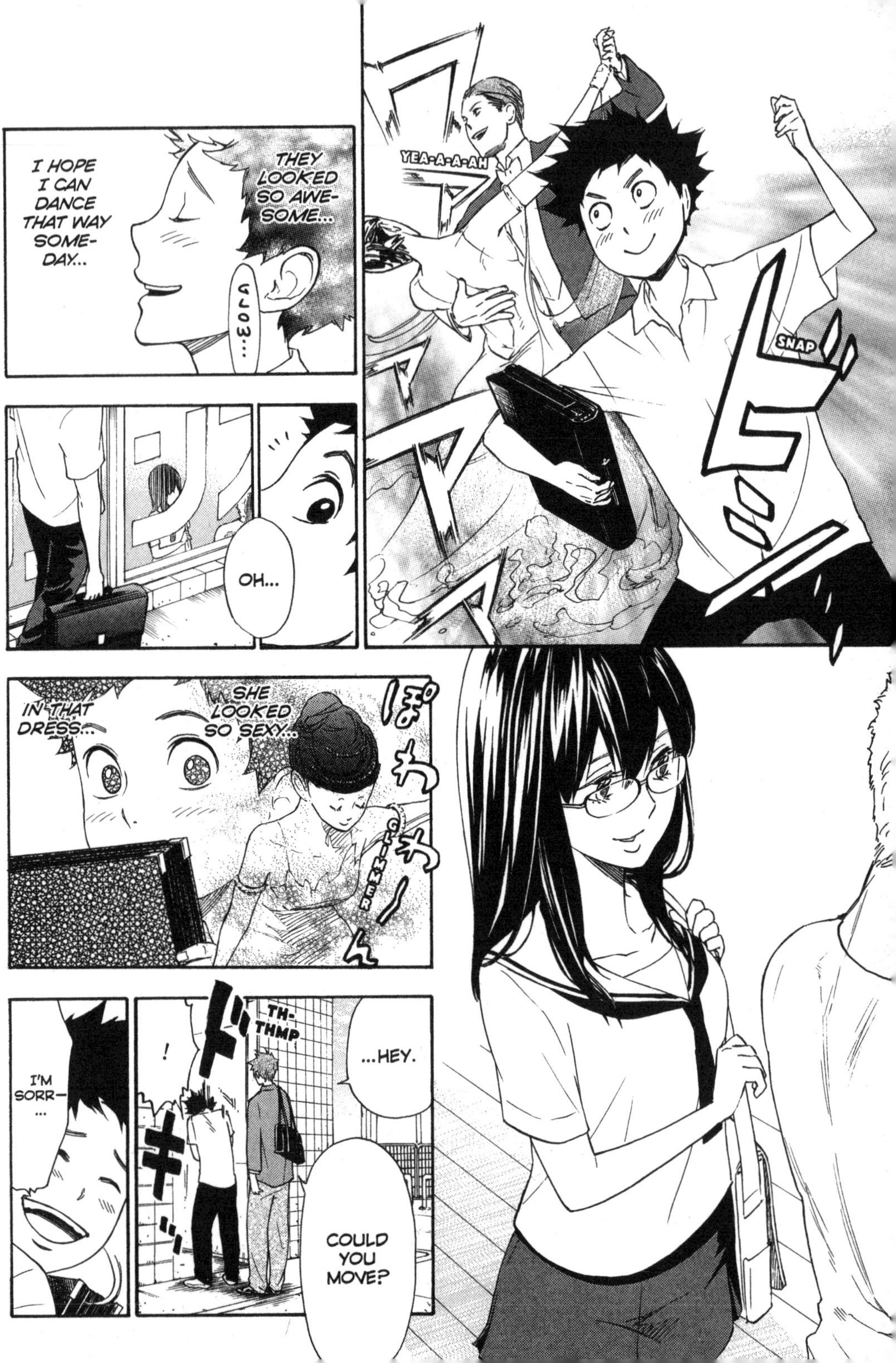
YEA-A-A-AH
SNAP
THEY LOOKED SO AWE-SOME...
I HOPE I CAN DANCE THAT WAY SOME-DAY...
GLOW...
OH...
...HEY.
COULD YOU MOVE?
SHE LOOKED SO SEXY...
IN THAT DRESS...
GLIMMER
TH-THMP
!
I'M SORR-...

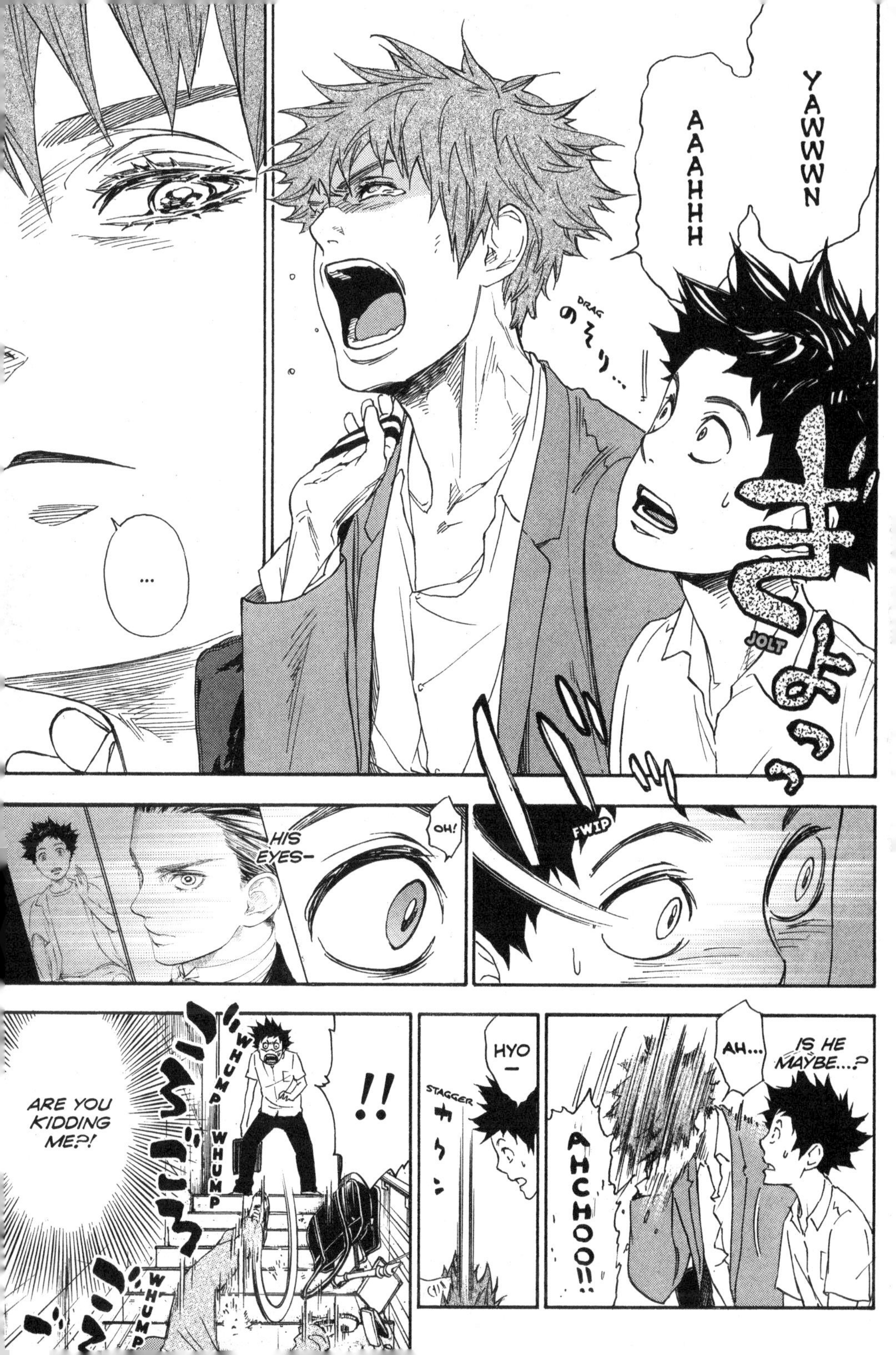
YAWWWN AAAHHH
DRAG
のそり…
JOLT
...
FWIP
OH!
HIS EYES–
AH...
IS HE MAYBE...?
AHCHOO!!
HYO–
STAGGER
!!
WHUMP
WHUMP
WHUMP
WHUMP
ARE YOU KIDDING ME?!

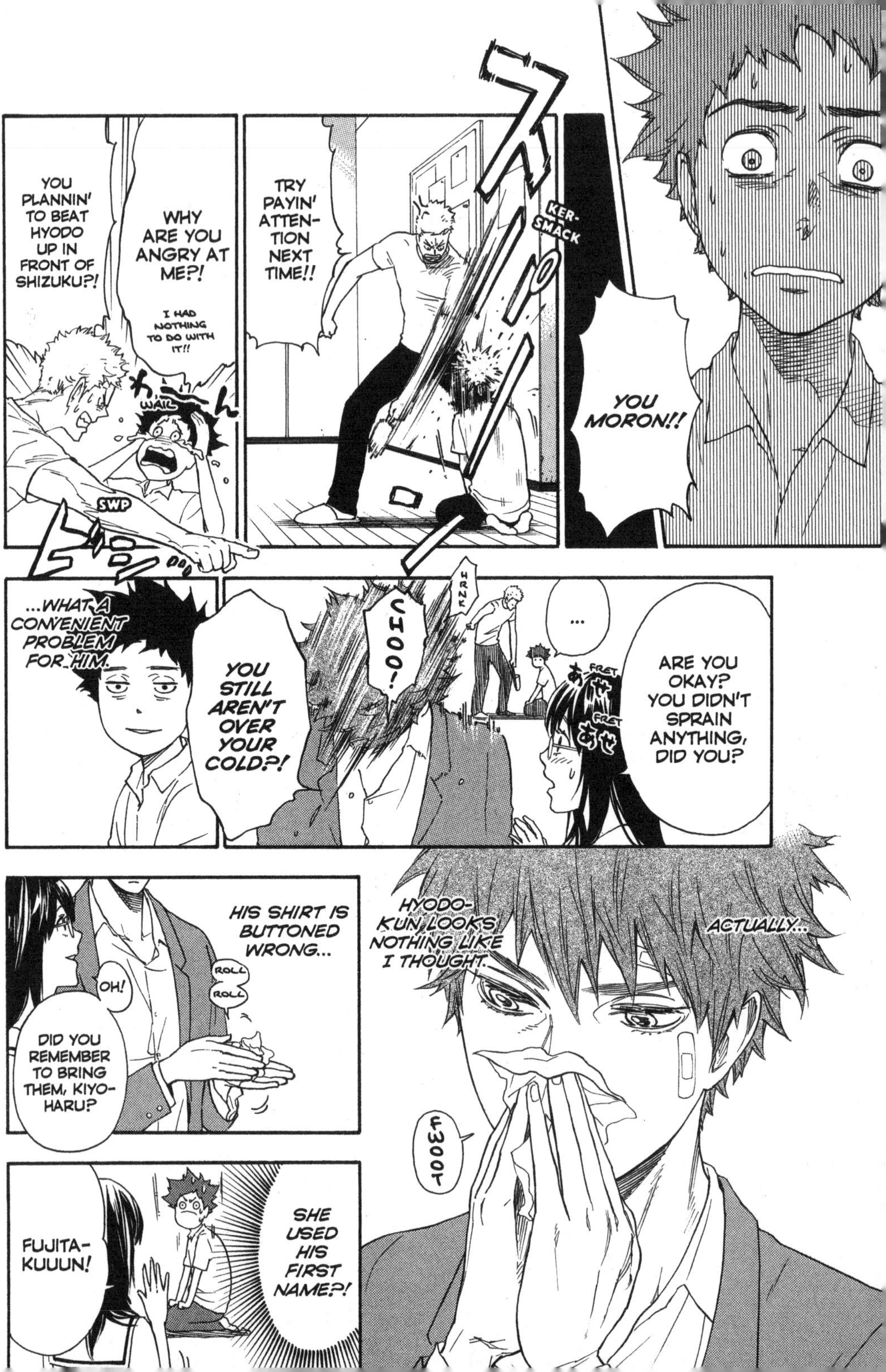
YOU MORON!!
KER-SMACK
TRY PAYIN' ATTENTION NEXT TIME!!
WHY ARE YOU ANGRY AT ME?!
I HAD NOTHING TO DO WITH IT!!
YOU PLANNIN' TO BEAT HYODO UP IN FRONT OF SHIZUKU?!
WAIL
SWP
ARE YOU OKAY? YOU DIDN'T SPRAIN ANYTHING, DID YOU?
FRET
FRET
...
HRNK
CHOO!
YOU STILL AREN'T OVER YOUR COLD?!
...WHAT A CONVENIENT PROBLEM FOR HIM.
ACTUALLY...
HYODO-KUN LOOKS NOTHING LIKE I THOUGHT.
FWOOT
HIS SHIRT IS BUTTONED WRONG...
ROLL
ROLL
OH!
DID YOU REMEMBER TO BRING THEM, KIYO-HARU?
SHE USED HIS FIRST NAME?!
FUJITA-KUUUN!

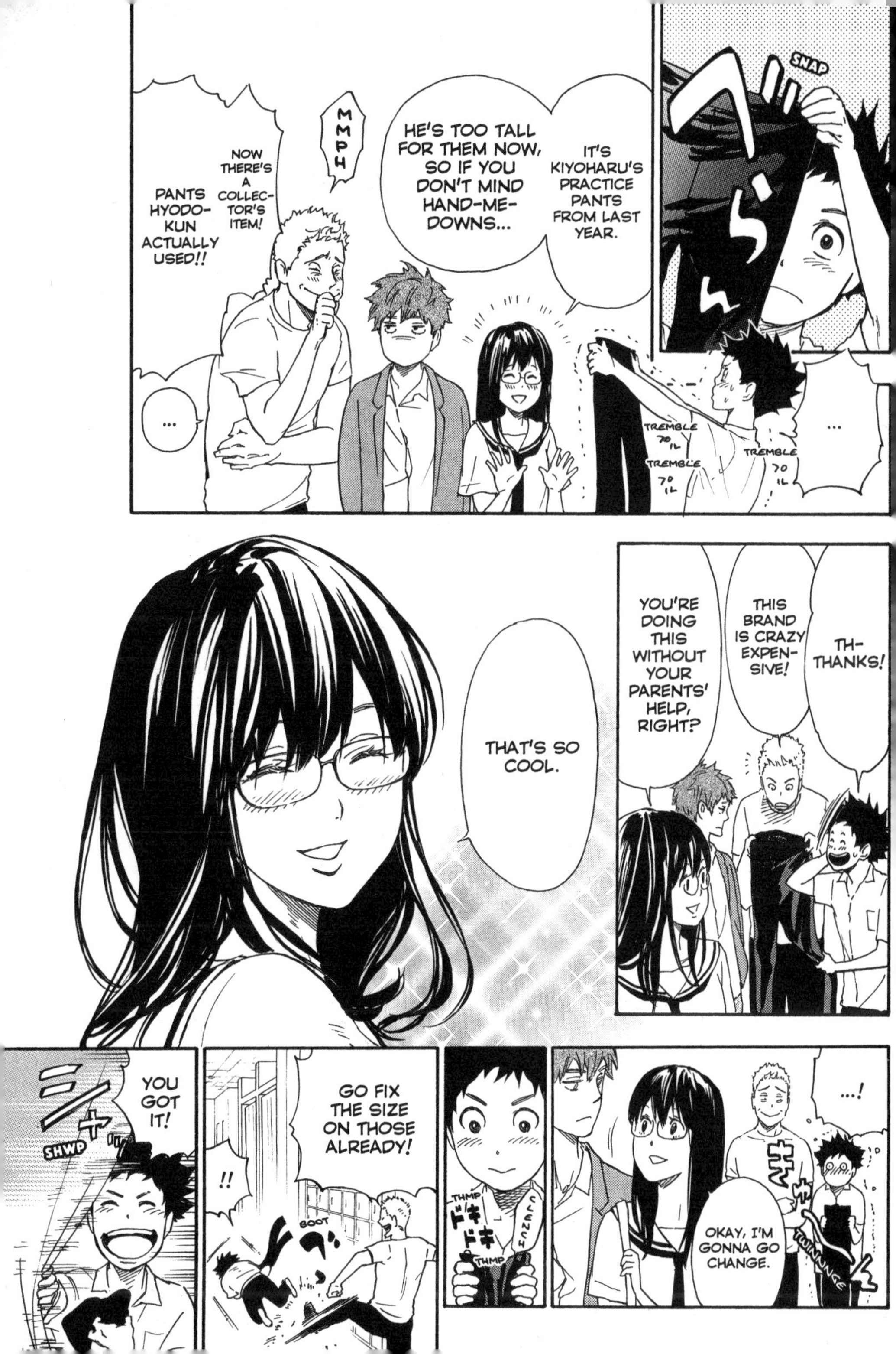
SNAP
IT'S KIYOHARU'S PRACTICE PANTS FROM LAST YEAR.
HE'S TOO TALL FOR THEM NOW, SO IF YOU DON'T MIND HAND-ME-DOWNS...
MMPH
NOW THERE'S A COLLECTOR'S ITEM!
PANTS HYODO-KUN ACTUALLY USED!!
...
TREMBLE
TREMBLE
TREMBLE
...
TH-THANKS!
THIS BRAND IS CRAZY EXPENSIVE!
YOU'RE DOING THIS WITHOUT YOUR PARENTS' HELP, RIGHT?
THAT'S SO COOL.
...!
TWINNNGE
OKAY, I'M GONNA GO CHANGE.
THMP
CLENCH
THMP
GO FIX THE SIZE ON THOSE ALREADY!
!!
BOOT
YOU GOT IT!
SHWP

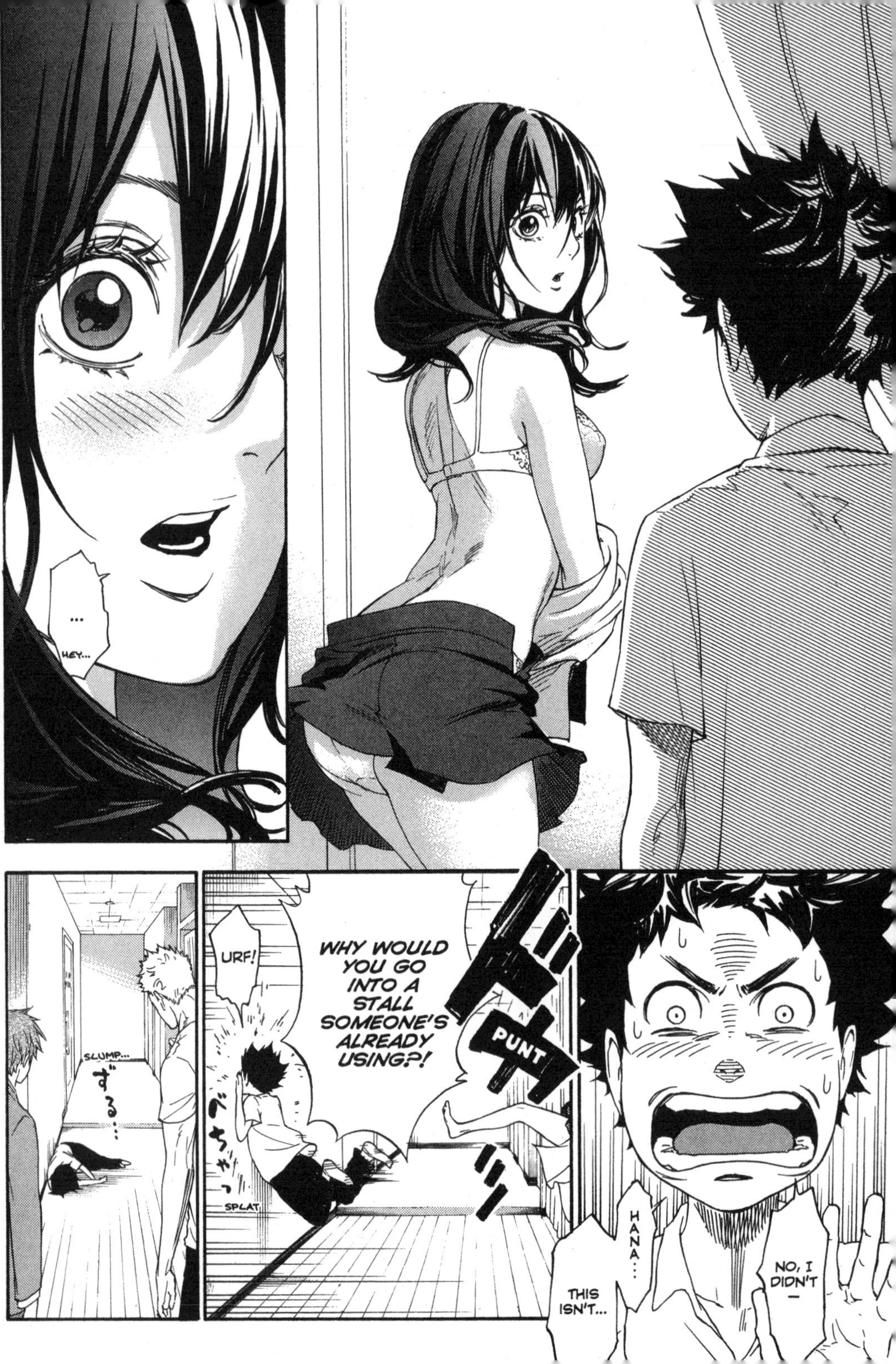
...
HEY...
NO, I DIDN'T —
HANA...
THIS ISN'T...
PUNT
WHY WOULD YOU GO INTO A STALL SOMEONE'S ALREADY USING?!
URF!
SPLAT
SLUMP...
ずる…

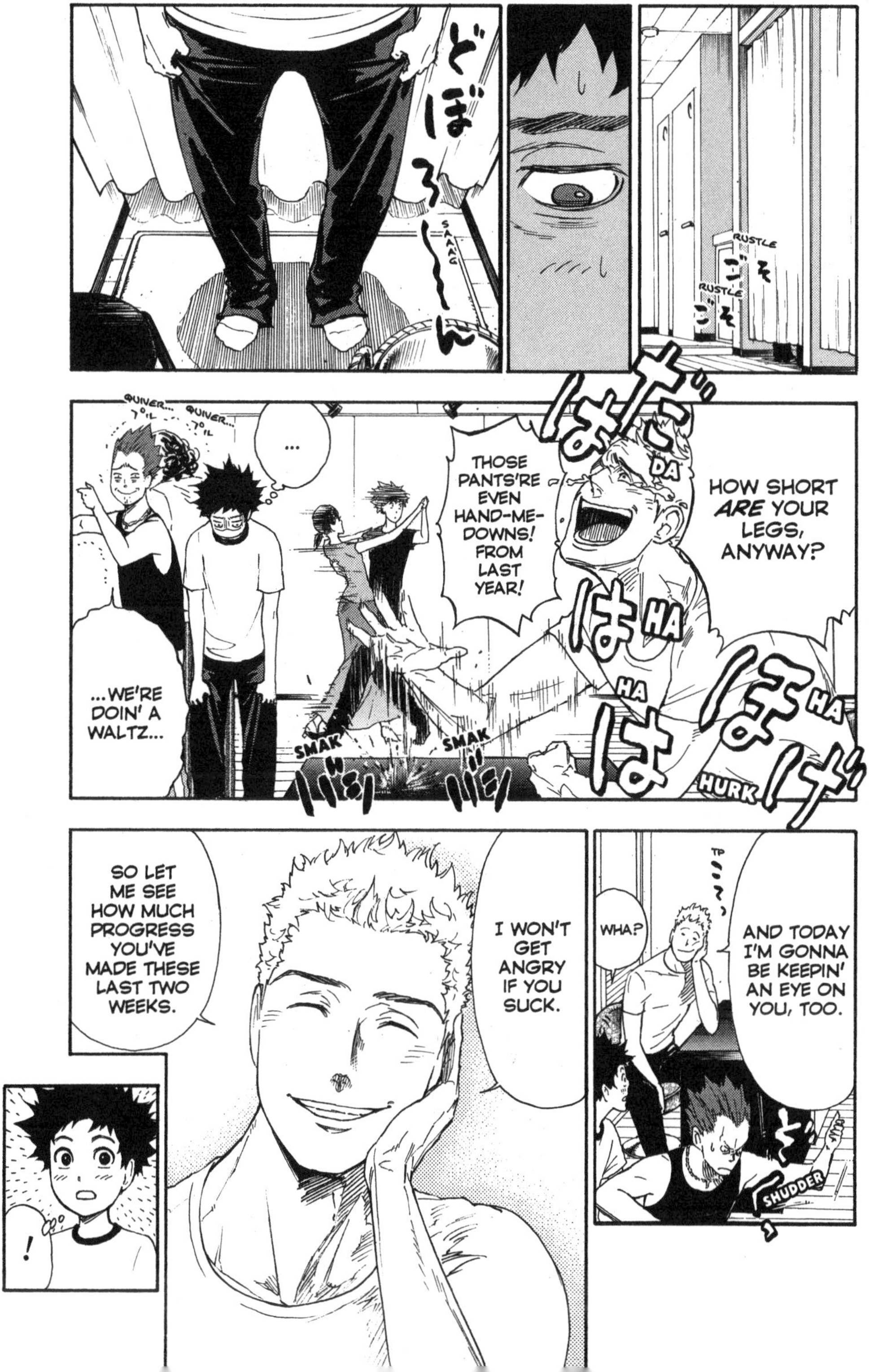
RUSTLE
RUSTLE
SAAAG
HOW SHORT *ARE* YOUR LEGS, ANYWAY?
DA
THOSE PANTS'RE EVEN HAND-ME-DOWNS! FROM LAST YEAR!
...
QUIVER...
QUIVER...
HA
HA
HA
HURK
...WE'RE DOIN' A WALTZ...
SMAK
SMAK
AND TODAY I'M GONNA BE KEEPIN' AN EYE ON YOU, TOO.
TP
WHA?
SHUDDER
I WON'T GET ANGRY IF YOU SUCK.
SO LET ME SEE HOW MUCH PROGRESS YOU'VE MADE THESE LAST TWO WEEKS.
!

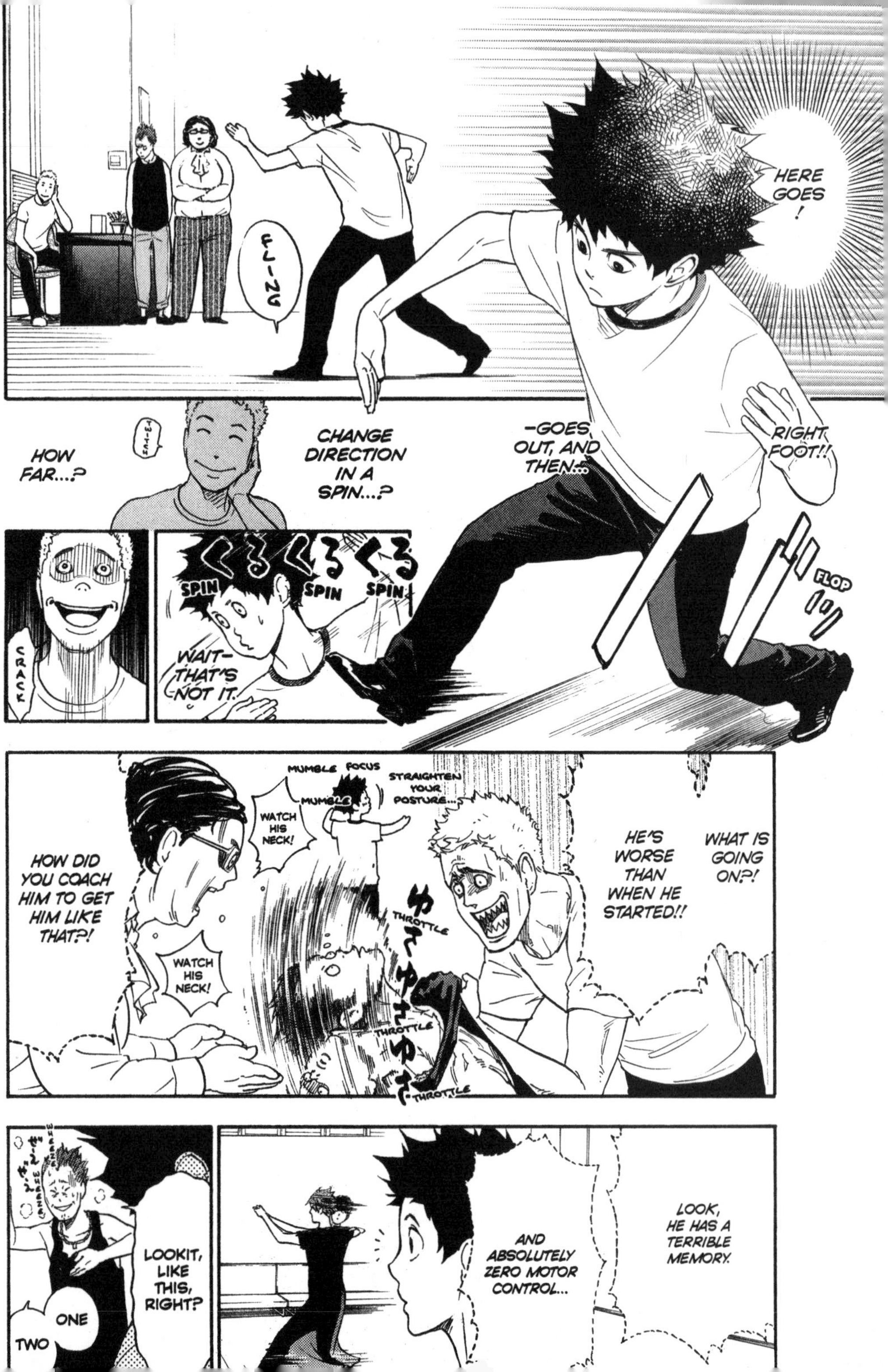

HERE GOES!
FLING
RIGHT FOOT!!
FLOP
-GOES OUT, AND THEN...
CHANGE DIRECTION IN A SPIN...?
HOW FAR...?
くるくるくる
SPIN SPIN SPIN
WAIT- THAT'S NOT IT.
CRACK
WHAT IS GOING ON?!
HE'S WORSE THAN WHEN HE STARTED!!
STRAIGHTEN YOUR POSTURE...
MUMBLE FOCUS MUMBLE
WATCH HIS NECK!
HOW DID YOU COACH HIM TO GET HIM LIKE THAT?!
WATCH HIS NECK!
ゆさゆさゆさ
THROTTLE THROTTLE THROTTLE
LOOK, HE HAS A TERRIBLE MEMORY.
AND ABSOLUTELY ZERO MOTOR CONTROL...
LOOKIT, LIKE THIS, RIGHT?
ONE
TWO

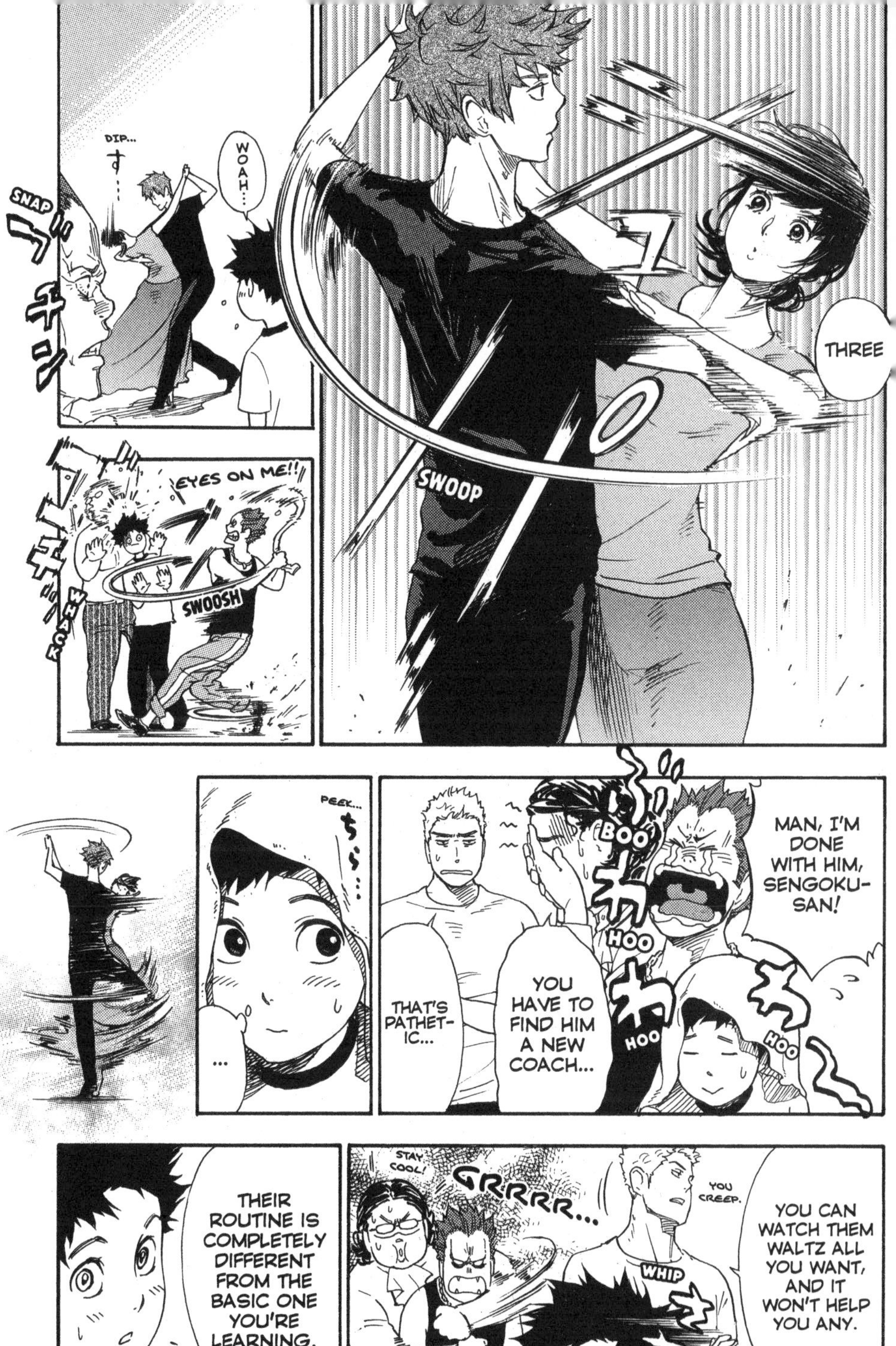
THREE
SWOOP
WOAH...
DIP...
す…
SNAP
EYES ON ME!!
SWOOSH
WHACK
MAN, I'M DONE WITH HIM, SENGOKU-SAN!
BOO
HOO
HOO
HOO
YOU HAVE TO FIND HIM A NEW COACH...
THAT'S PATHETIC...
PEEK...
ちら…
...
YOU CAN WATCH THEM WALTZ ALL YOU WANT, AND IT WON'T HELP YOU ANY.
YOU CREEP.
GRRRRR...
STAY COOL!
WHIP
THEIR ROUTINE IS COMPLETELY DIFFERENT FROM THE BASIC ONE YOU'RE LEARNING.

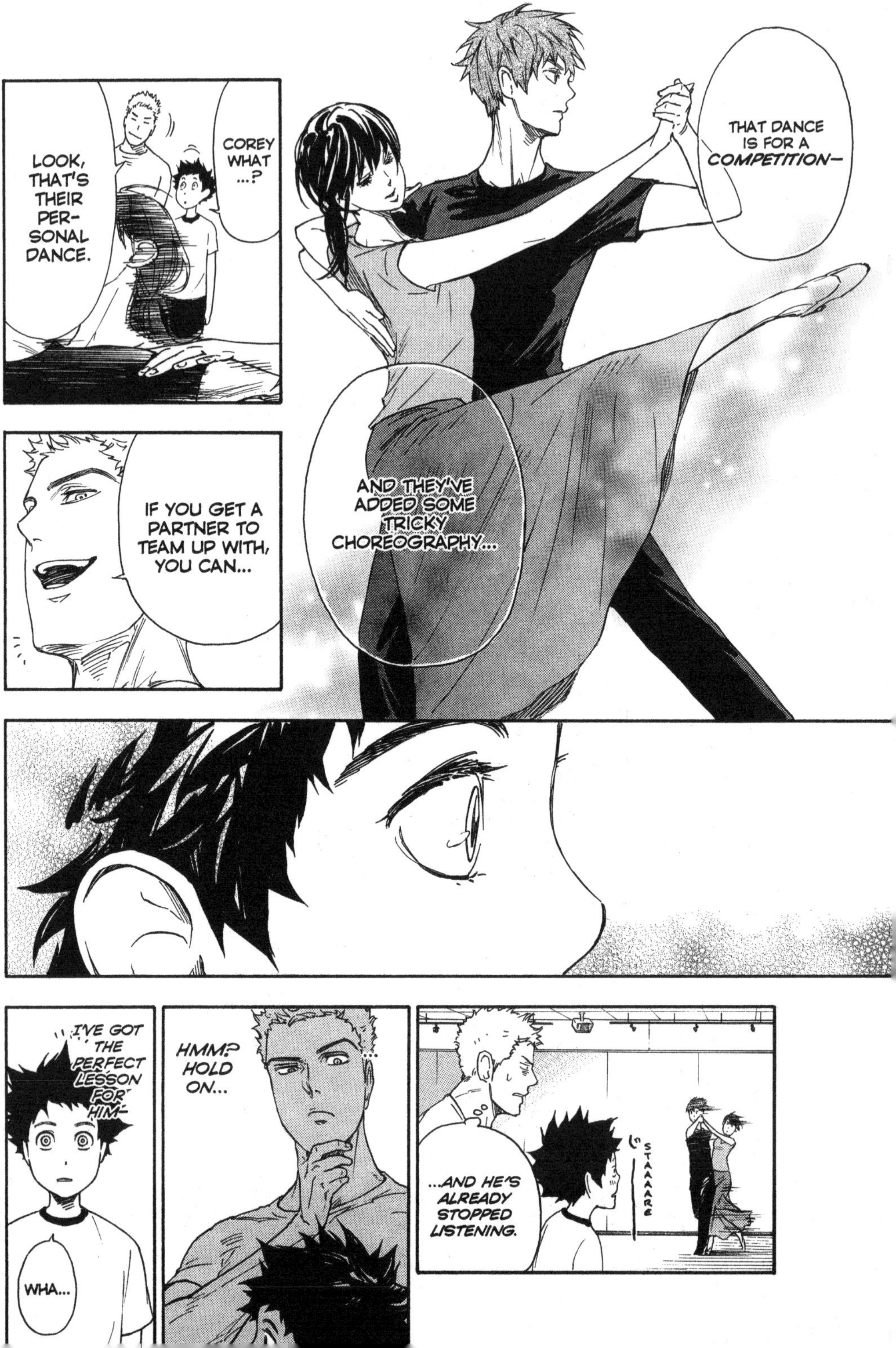
THAT DANCE IS FOR A COMPETITION—
AND THEY'VE ADDED SOME TRICKY CHOREOGRAPHY...
COREY WHAT ...?
LOOK, THAT'S THEIR PERSONAL DANCE.
IF YOU GET A PARTNER TO TEAM UP WITH, YOU CAN...
STAAAARE
...AND HE'S ALREADY STOPPED LISTENING.
HMM? HOLD ON...
I'VE GOT THE PERFECT LESSON FOR HIM—
WHA...

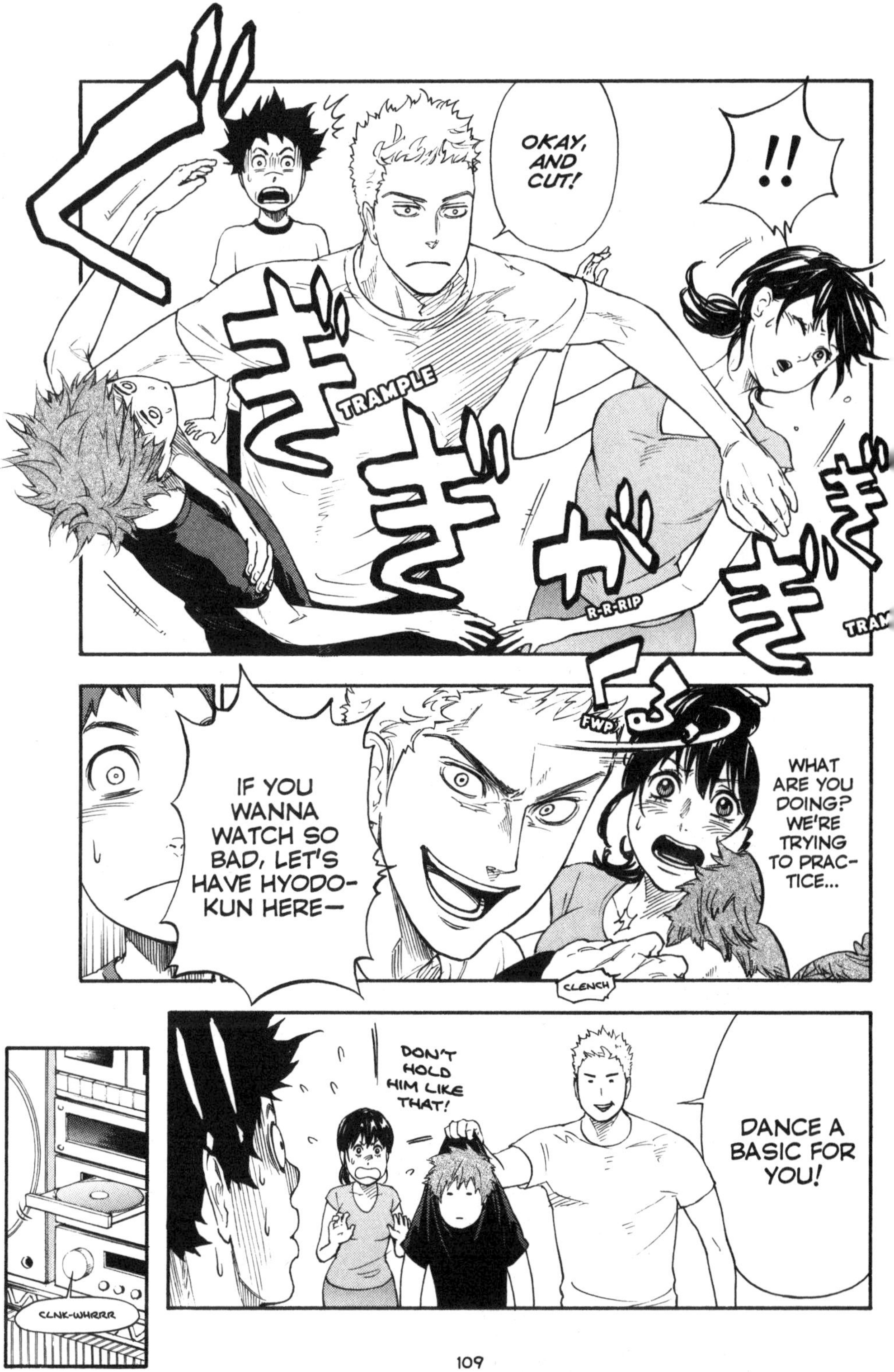
!!
OKAY, AND CUT!
TRAM
R-R-RIP
TRAMPLE
WHAT ARE YOU DOING? WE'RE TRYING TO PRAC-TICE...
FWP
CLENCH
IF YOU WANNA WATCH SO BAD, LET'S HAVE HYODO-KUN HERE—
DANCE A BASIC FOR YOU!
DON'T HOLD HIM LIKE THAT!
CLNK-WHRRR

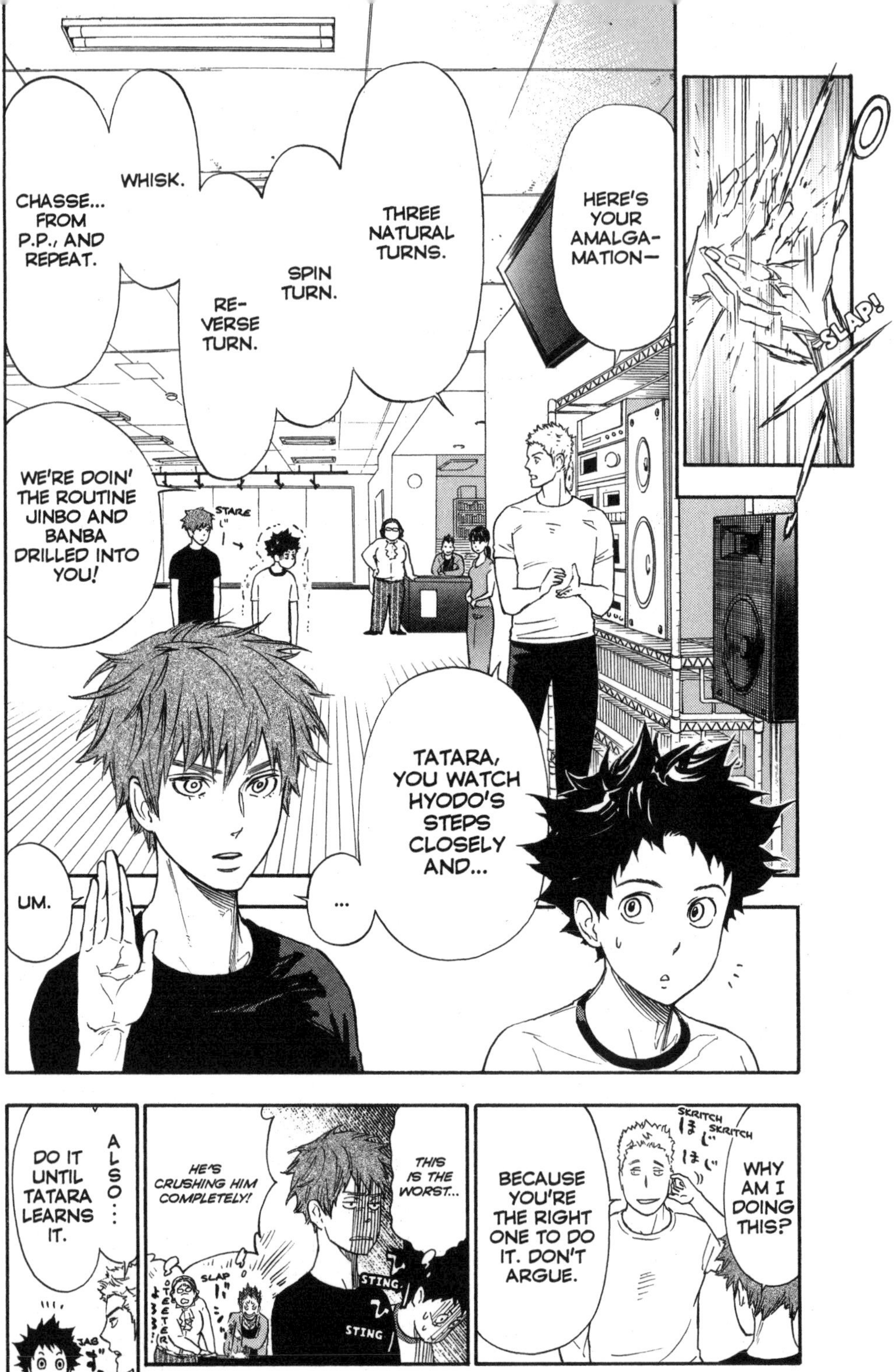
SLAP!
HERE'S YOUR AMALGAMATION—
THREE NATURAL TURNS.
SPIN TURN.
RE-VERSE TURN.
WHISK.
CHASSE... FROM P.P., AND REPEAT.
STARE
WE'RE DOIN' THE ROUTINE JINBO AND BANBA DRILLED INTO YOU!
TATARA, YOU WATCH HYODO'S STEPS CLOSELY AND...
...
UM.
SKRITCH
SKRITCH
WHY AM I DOING THIS?
BECAUSE YOU'RE THE RIGHT ONE TO DO IT. DON'T ARGUE.
THIS IS THE WORST...
STING
STING
HE'S CRUSHING HIM COMPLETELY!
SLAP
TEETER
ALSO...
DO IT UNTIL TATARA LEARNS IT.
JAB

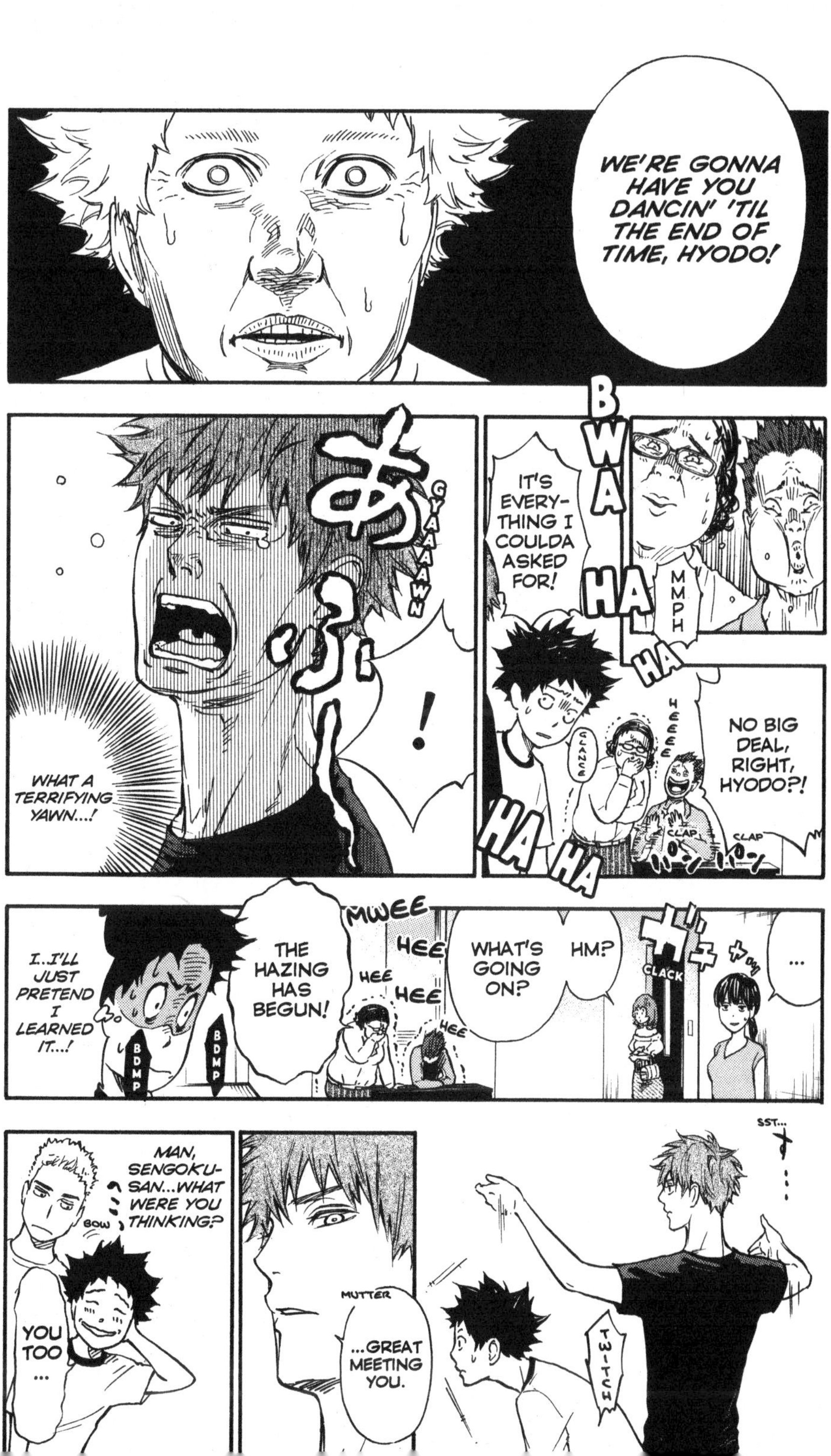
WE'RE GONNA HAVE YOU DANCIN' 'TIL THE END OF TIME, HYODO!
BWA
IT'S EVERYTHING I COULDA ASKED FOR!
MMPH
HA
HA
NO BIG DEAL, RIGHT, HYODO?!
HEEEE
GLANCE
CLAP
CLAP
HA
HA
HA
あふ
GYAAAAAWN
!
WHAT A TERRIFYING YAWN...!
...
CLACK
HM?
WHAT'S GOING ON?
MWEE
HEE
HEE
HEE
HEE
THE HAZING HAS BEGUN!
I..I'LL JUST PRETEND I LEARNED IT...!
BDMP
BDMP
SST...
す...
TWITCH
MUTTER
...GREAT MEETING YOU.
MAN, SENGOKU-SAN...WHAT WERE YOU THINKING?
BOW
YOU TOO ...

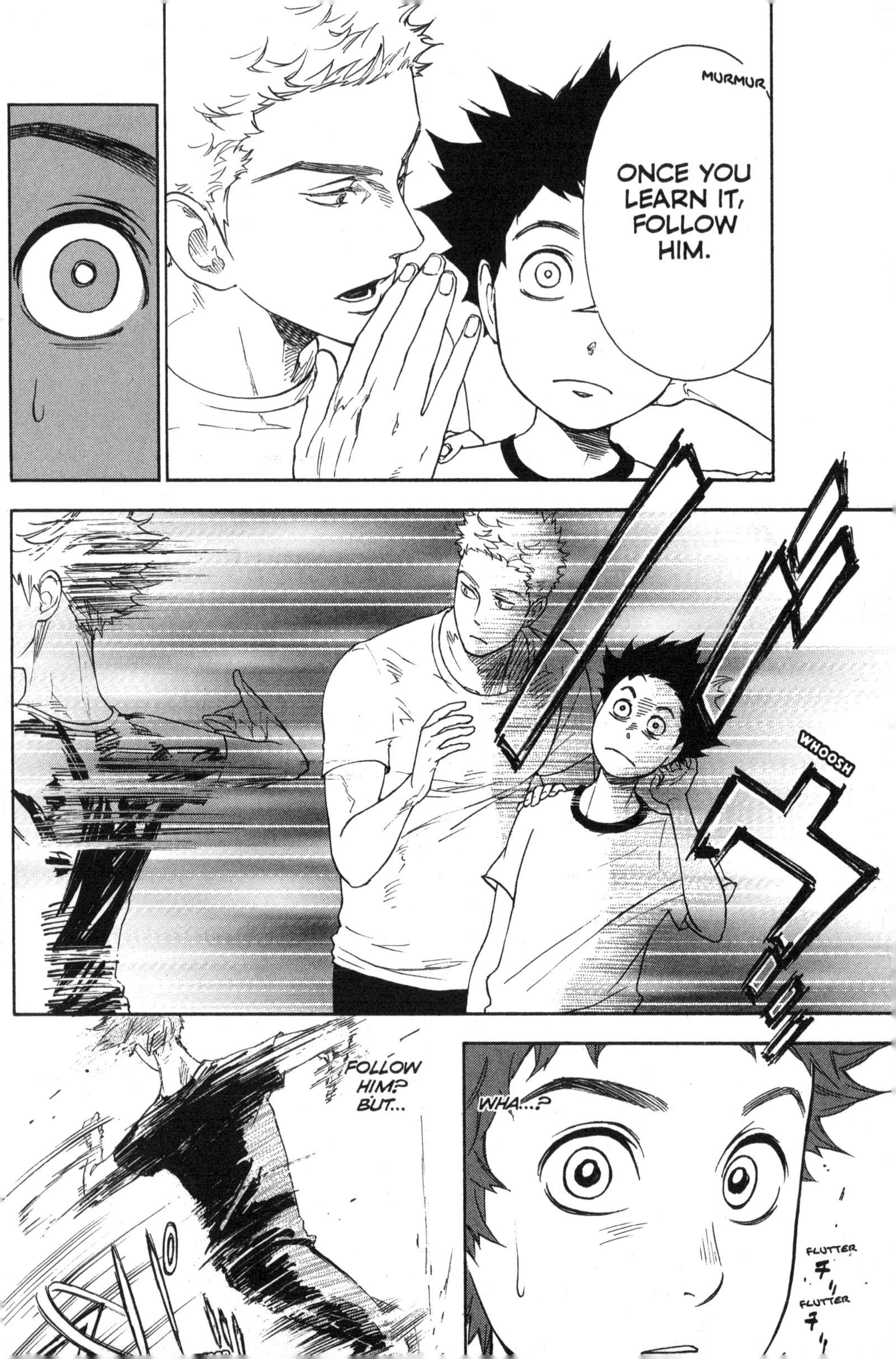
MURMUR
ONCE YOU LEARN IT, FOLLOW HIM.
WHOOSH
WHA...?
FLUTTER
FLUTTER
FOLLOW HIM? BUT...

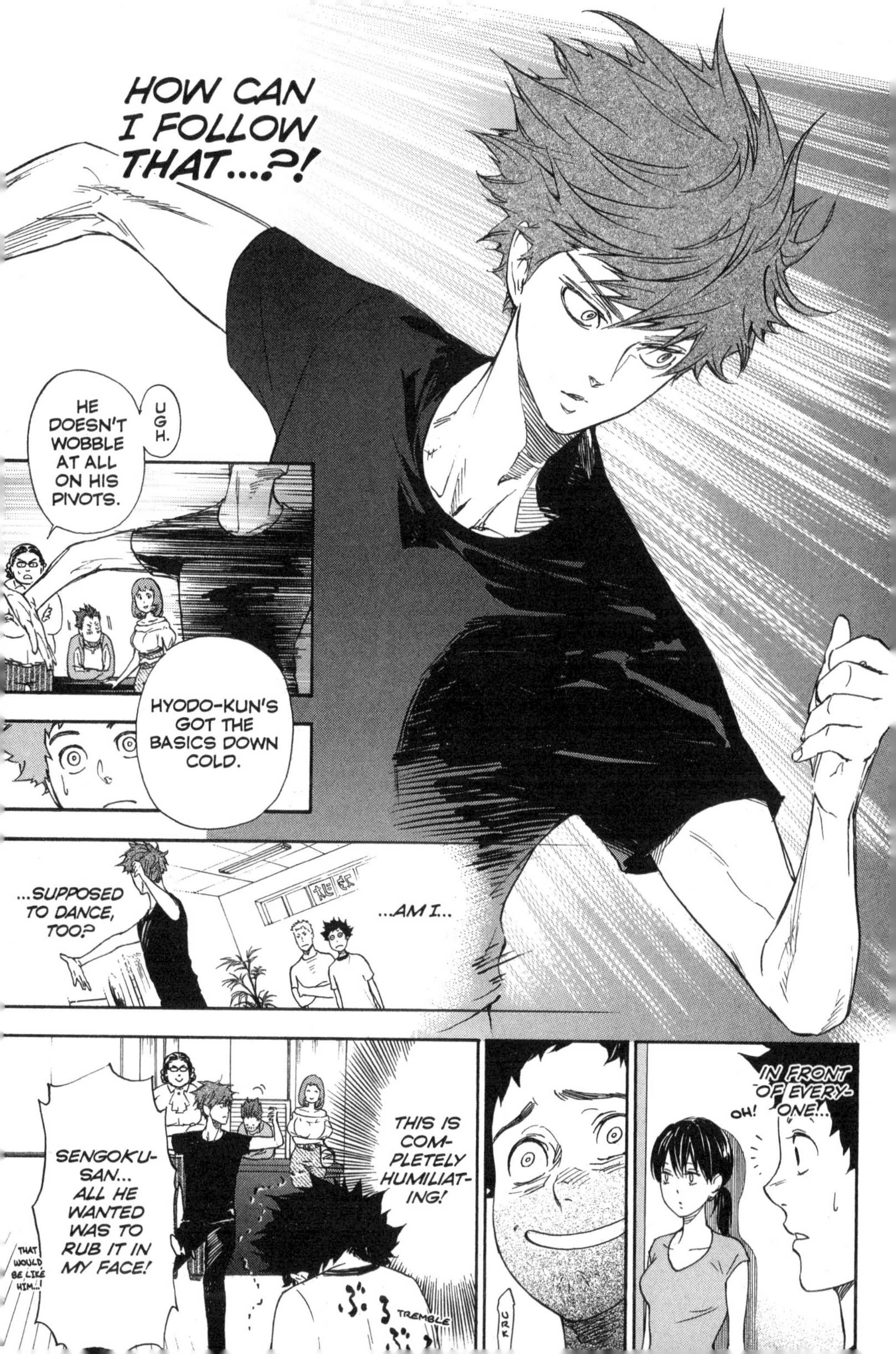
HOW CAN I FOLLOW THAT...?!
UGH.
HE DOESN'T WOBBLE AT ALL ON HIS PIVOTS.
HYODO-KUN'S GOT THE BASICS DOWN COLD.
...AM I...
...SUPPOSED TO DANCE, TOO?
IN FRONT OF EVERY-ONE...
OH!
KRC
THIS IS COM-PLETELY HUMILIAT-ING!
SENGOKU-SAN... ALL HE WANTED WAS TO RUB IT IN MY FACE!
THAT WOULD BE LIKE HIM...
TREMBLE

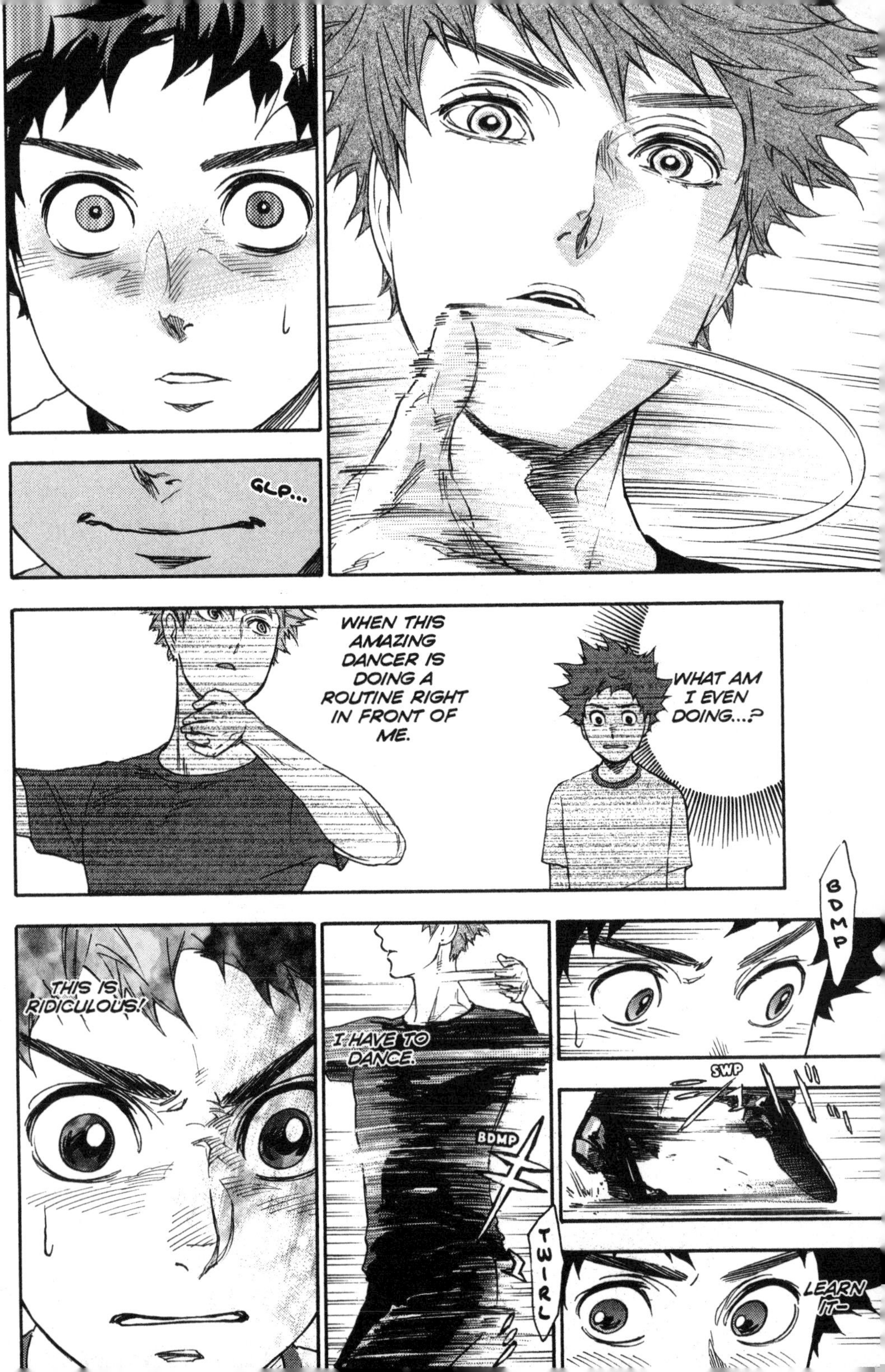
GLP...
WHAT AM I EVEN DOING...?
WHEN THIS AMAZING DANCER IS DOING A ROUTINE RIGHT IN FRONT OF ME.
BDMP
SWP
LEARN IT—
I HAVE TO DANCE.
BDMP
TWIRL
THIS IS RIDICULOUS!

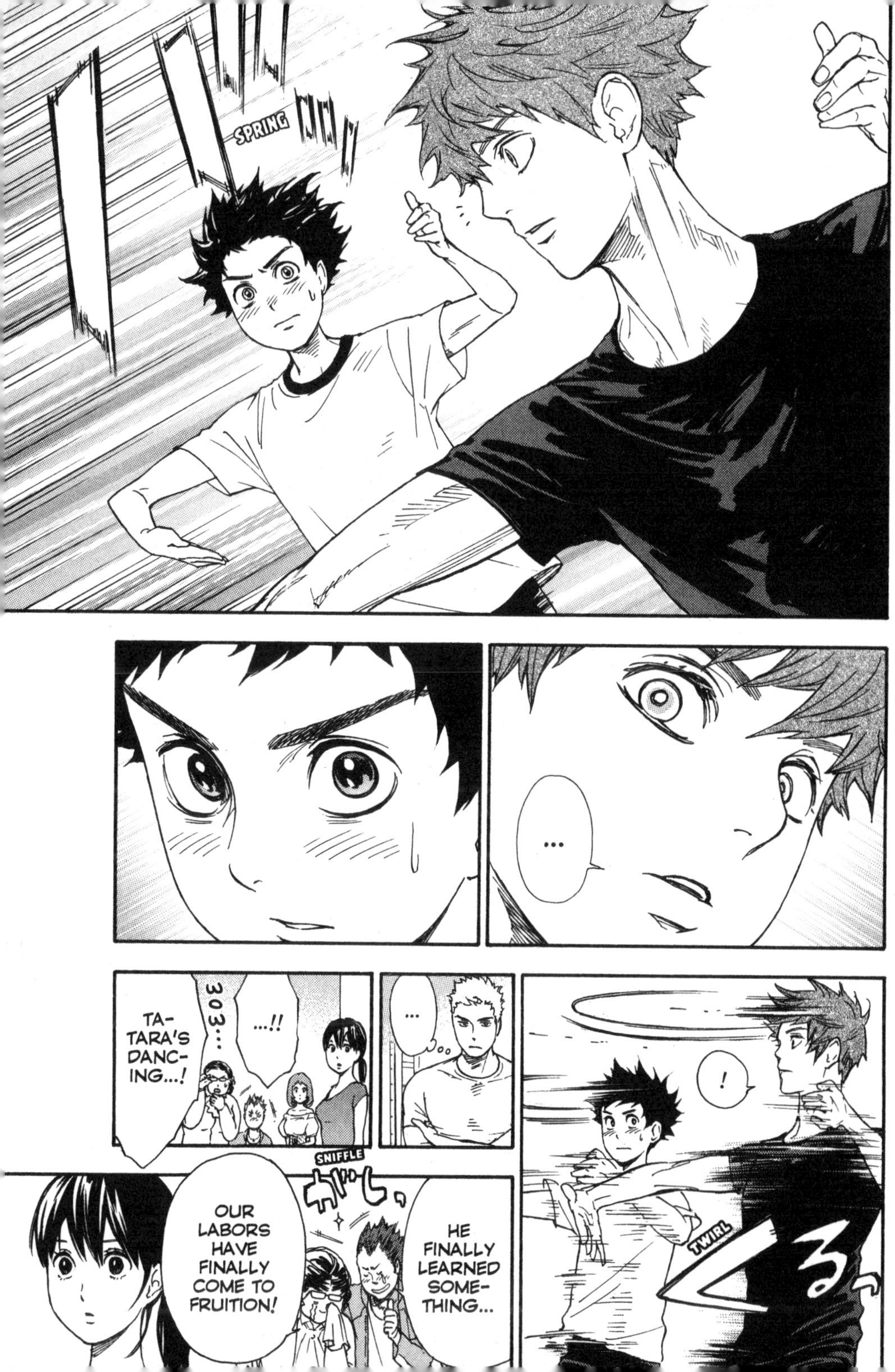
SPRING
...
!
TWIRL
...
...!!
TA-TARA'S DANCING...!
SNIFFLE
HE FINALLY LEARNED SOMETHING...
OUR LABORS HAVE FINALLY COME TO FRUITION!

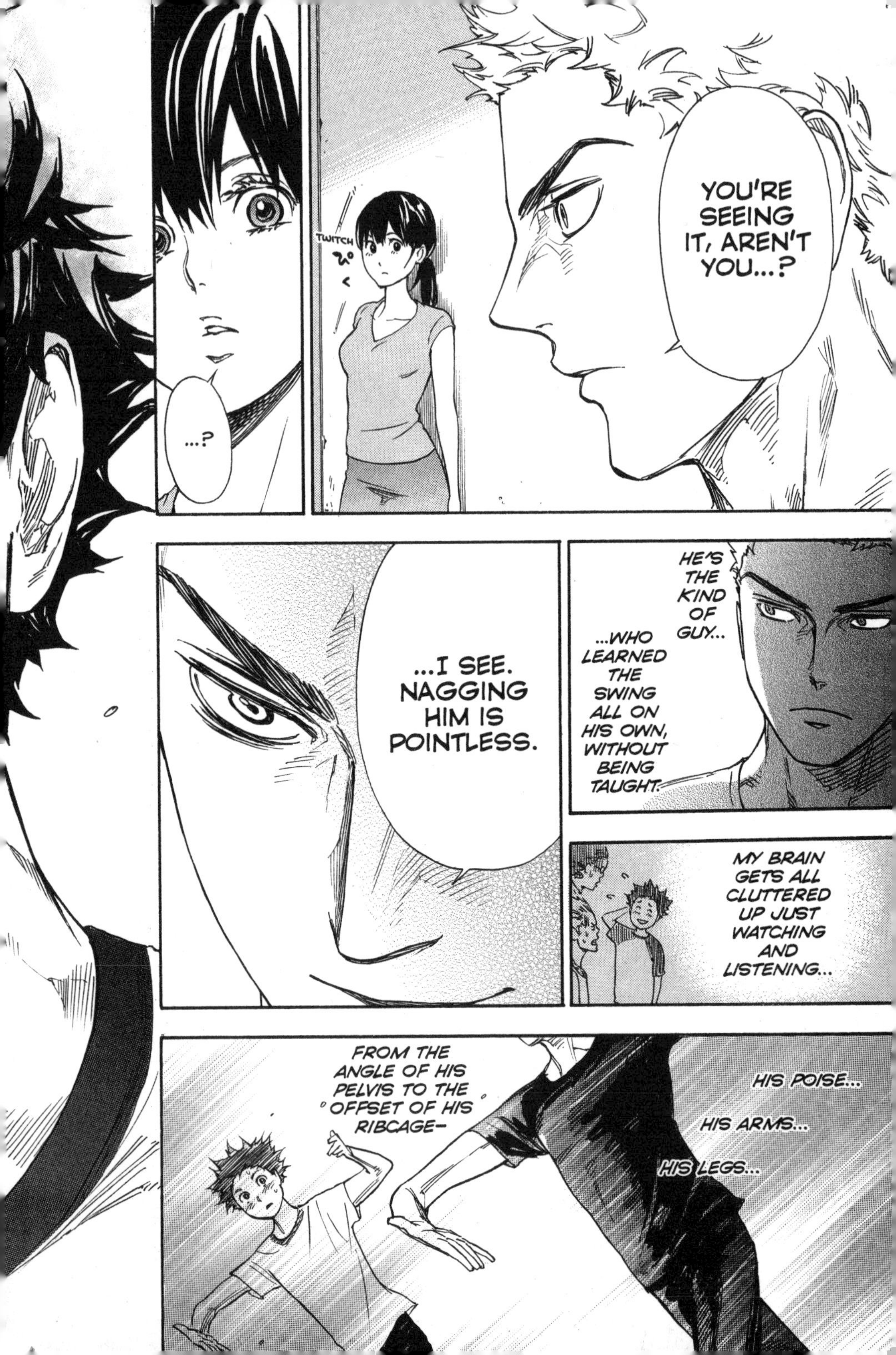

YOU'RE SEEING IT, AREN'T YOU...?
TWITCH
ぴく
...?
HE'S THE KIND OF GUY...
...WHO LEARNED THE SWING ALL ON HIS OWN, WITHOUT BEING TAUGHT.
MY BRAIN GETS ALL CLUTTERED UP JUST WATCHING AND LISTENING...
...I SEE. NAGGING HIM IS POINTLESS.
HIS POISE...
HIS ARMS...
HIS LEGS...
FROM THE ANGLE OF HIS PELVIS TO THE OFFSET OF HIS RIBCAGE–

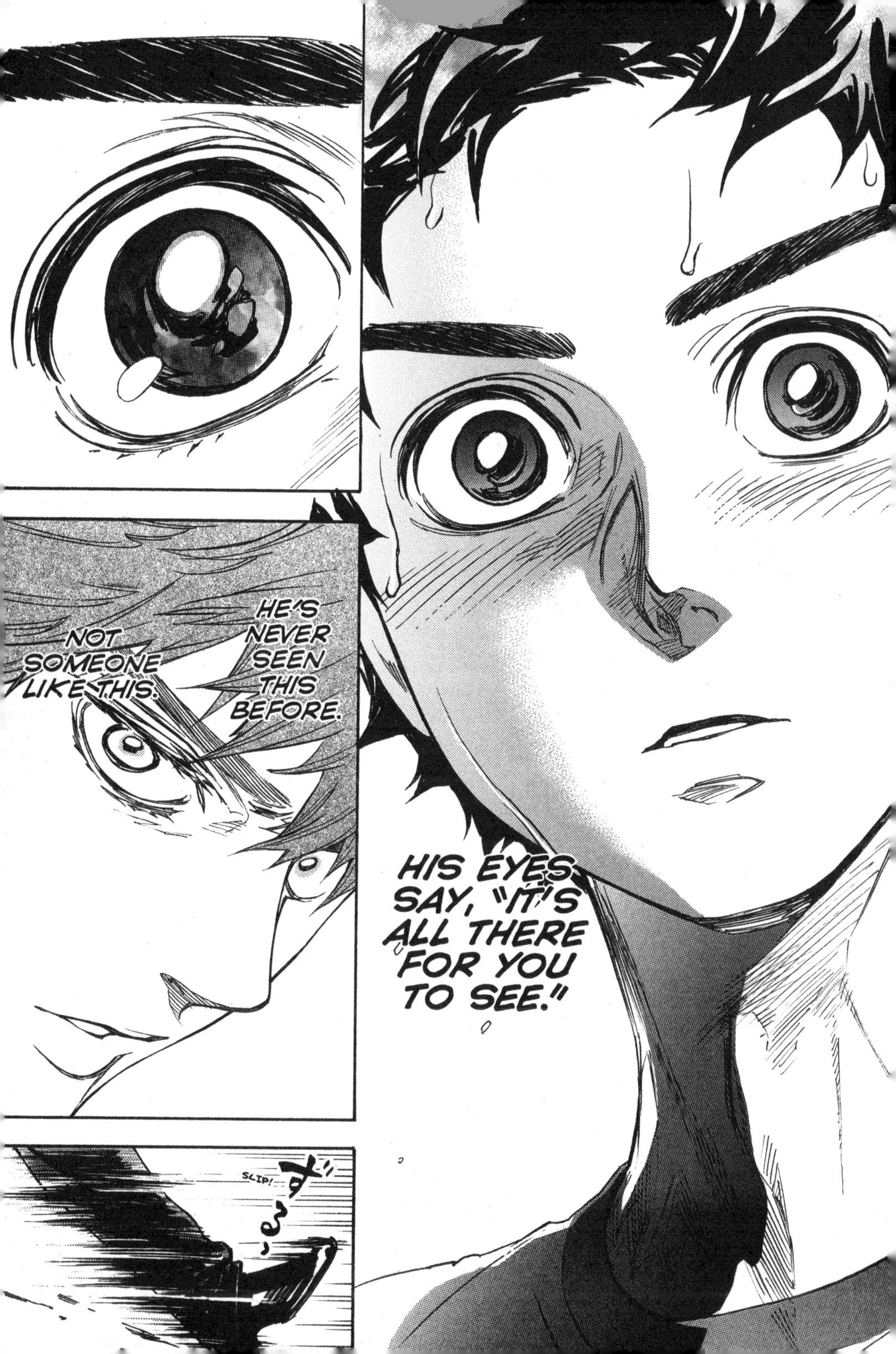
HIS EYES SAY, "IT'S ALL THERE FOR YOU TO SEE."
HE'S NEVER SEEN THIS BEFORE.
NOT SOMEONE LIKE THIS.
SLIP!

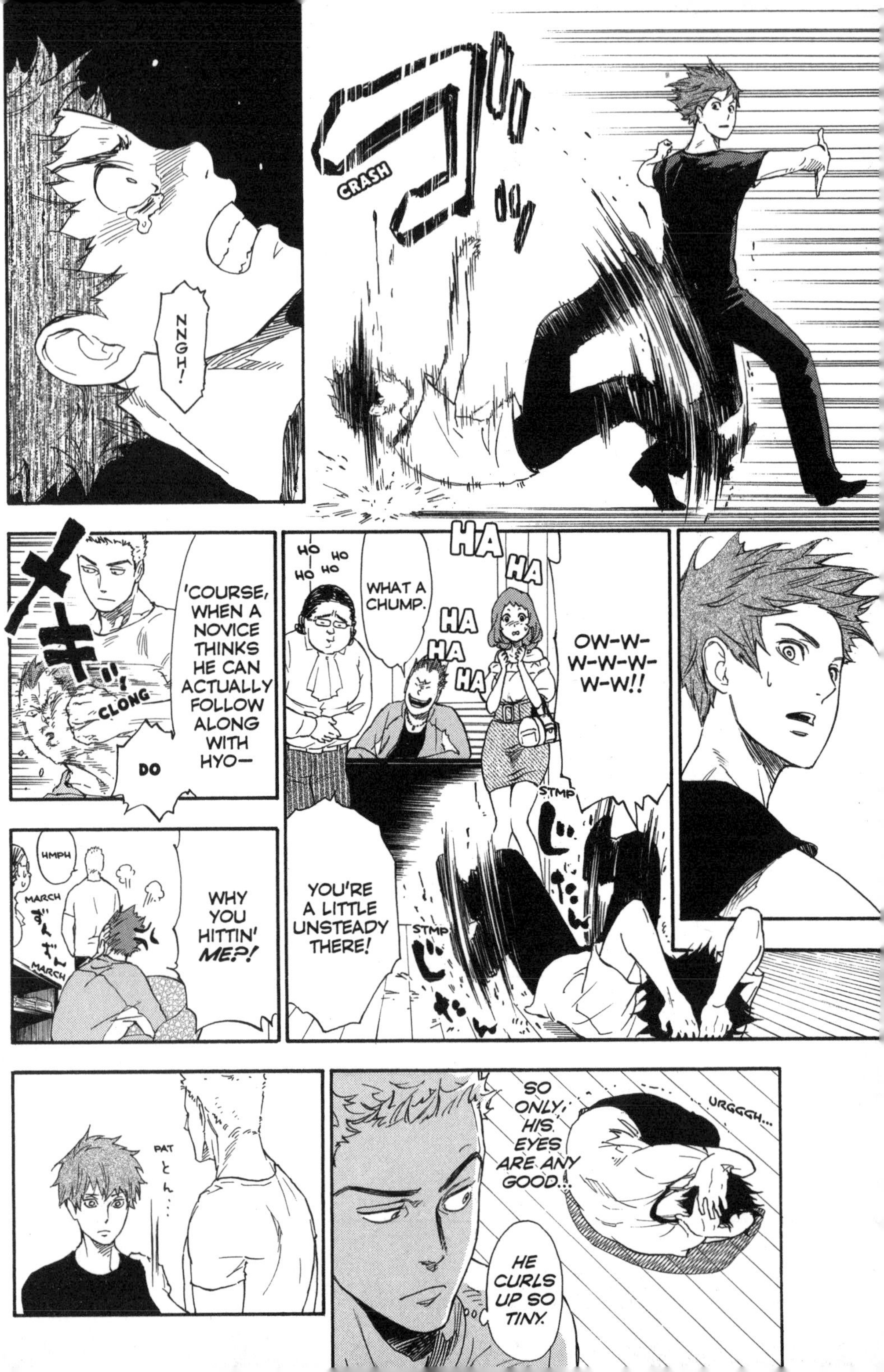
CRASH
NNGH!
OW-W-W-W-W-W-W!!
HO HO HO HO
WHAT A CHUMP.
HA HA HA HA HA
STMP
YOU'RE A LITTLE UNSTEADY THERE!
STMP
CLONG
'COURSE, WHEN A NOVICE THINKS HE CAN ACTUALLY FOLLOW ALONG WITH HYO—
DO
HMPH
MARCH ずんずん MARCH
WHY YOU HITTIN' ME?!
SO ONLY HIS EYES ARE ANY GOOD...
URGGGH...
HE CURLS UP SO TINY.
PAT とん...

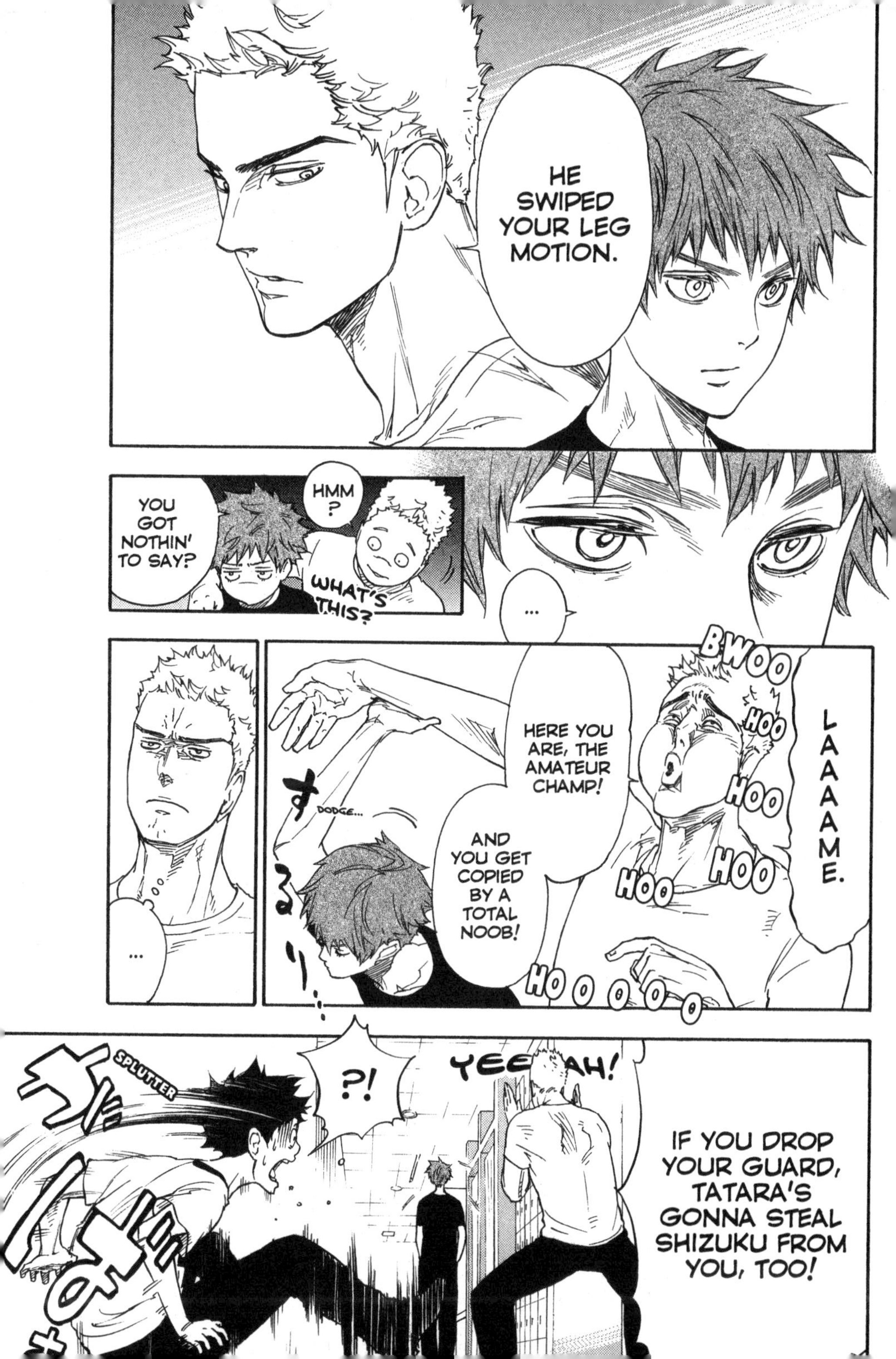
HE SWIPED YOUR LEG MOTION.
...
HMM ?
YOU GOT NOTHIN' TO SAY?
WHAT'S THIS?
LAAAAAME.
BWOO HOO HOO HOO HOO
HERE YOU ARE, THE AMATEUR CHAMP!
AND YOU GET COPIED BY A TOTAL NOOB!
HOOOOOOO
DODGE...
...
IF YOU DROP YOUR GUARD, TATARA'S GONNA STEAL SHIZUKU FROM YOU, TOO!
YEE AH!
?!
SPLUTTER

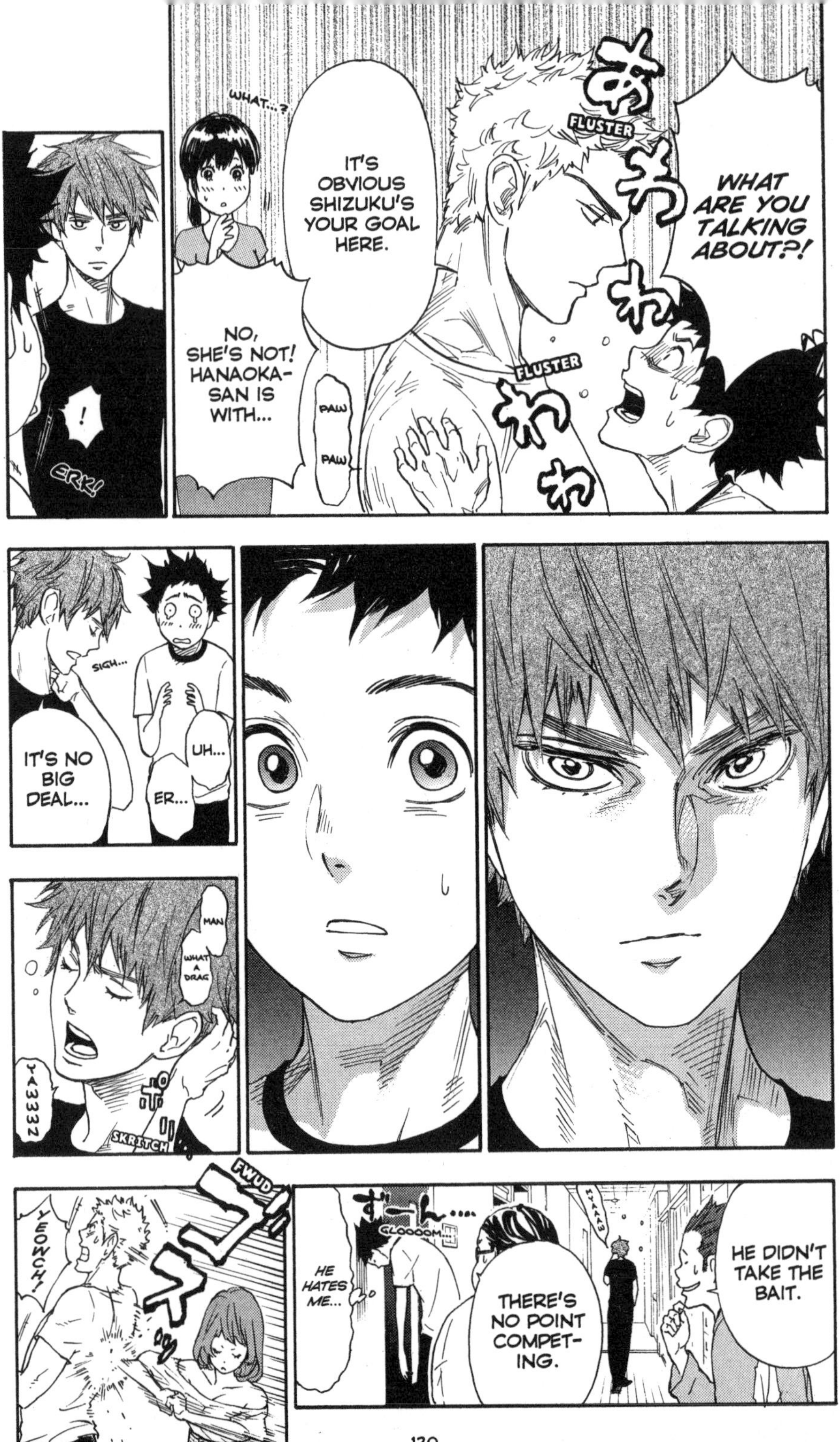

WHAT ARE YOU TALKING ABOUT?!
あわわわ
FLUSTER
FLUSTER
IT'S OBVIOUS SHIZUKU'S YOUR GOAL HERE.
WHAT...?
PAW
PAW
NO, SHE'S NOT! HANAOKA-SAN IS WITH...
!
ERK!
SIGH...
UH...
ER...
IT'S NO BIG DEAL...
MAN
WHAT A DRAG
YAWWWN
SKRITCH
HE DIDN'T TAKE THE BAIT.
MYAAAW
GLOOOOM...
THERE'S NO POINT COMPETING.
HE HATES ME...
FWUD
YEOWCH!

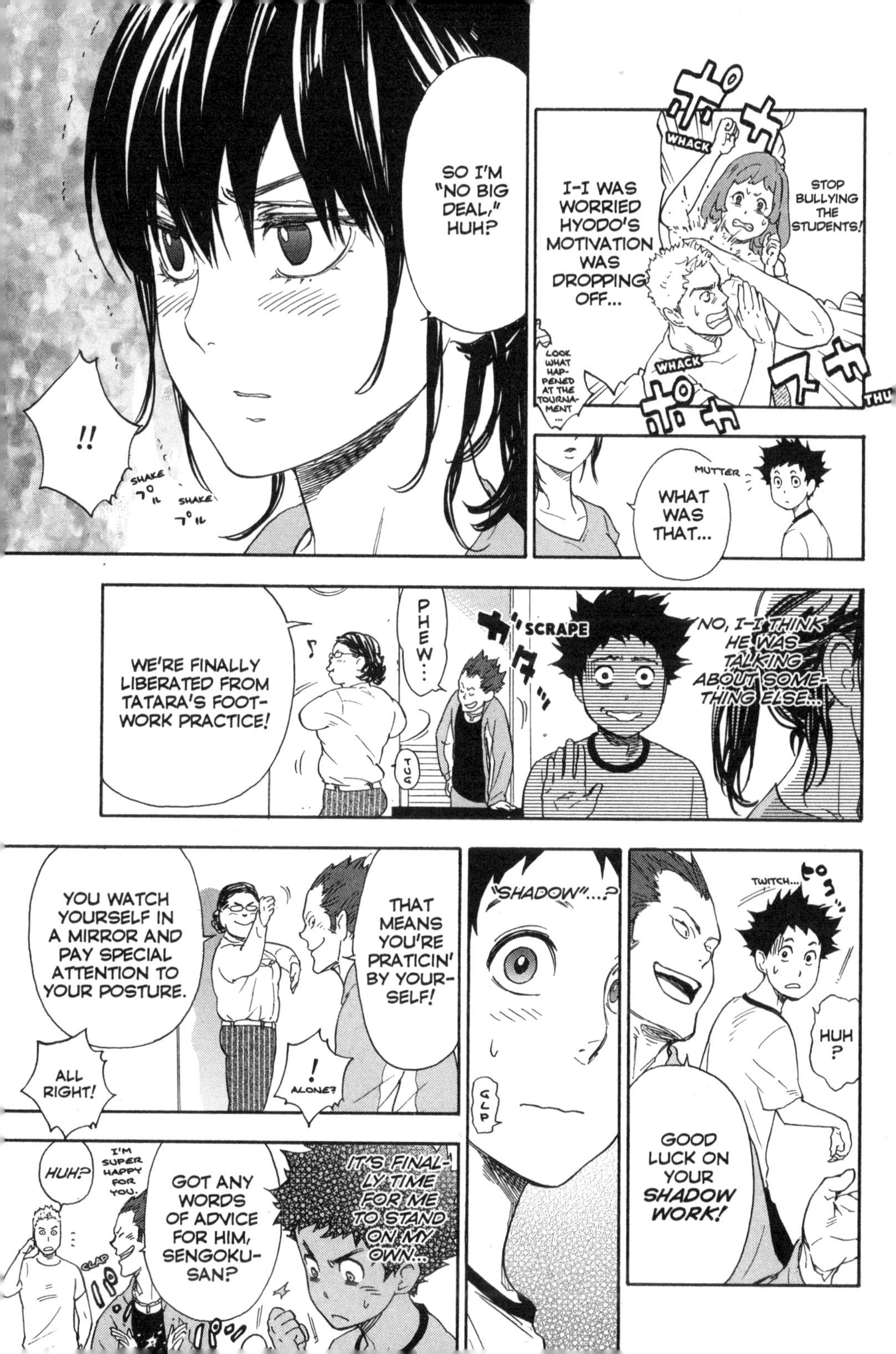
WHACK
I-I WAS WORRIED HYODO'S MOTIVATION WAS DROPPING OFF...
STOP BULLYING THE STUDENTS!
WHACK
LOOK WHAT HAPPENED AT THE TOURNAMENT...
THU
MUTTER
WHAT WAS THAT...
SO I'M "NO BIG DEAL," HUH?
!!
SHAKE
SHAKE
NO, I-I THINK HE WAS TALKING ABOUT SOMETHING ELSE...
SCRAPE
PHEW...
TUG
WE'RE FINALLY LIBERATED FROM TATARA'S FOOTWORK PRACTICE!
TWITCH...
HUH?
GOOD LUCK ON YOUR SHADOW WORK!
"SHADOW"...?
GLP
THAT MEANS YOU'RE PRATICIN' BY YOURSELF!
YOU WATCH YOURSELF IN A MIRROR AND PAY SPECIAL ATTENTION TO YOUR POSTURE.
!
ALONE?
ALL RIGHT!
IT'S FINALLY TIME FOR ME TO STAND ON MY OWN...
GOT ANY WORDS OF ADVICE FOR HIM, SENGOKU-SAN?
I'M SUPER HAPPY FOR YOU.
HUH?
CLAP

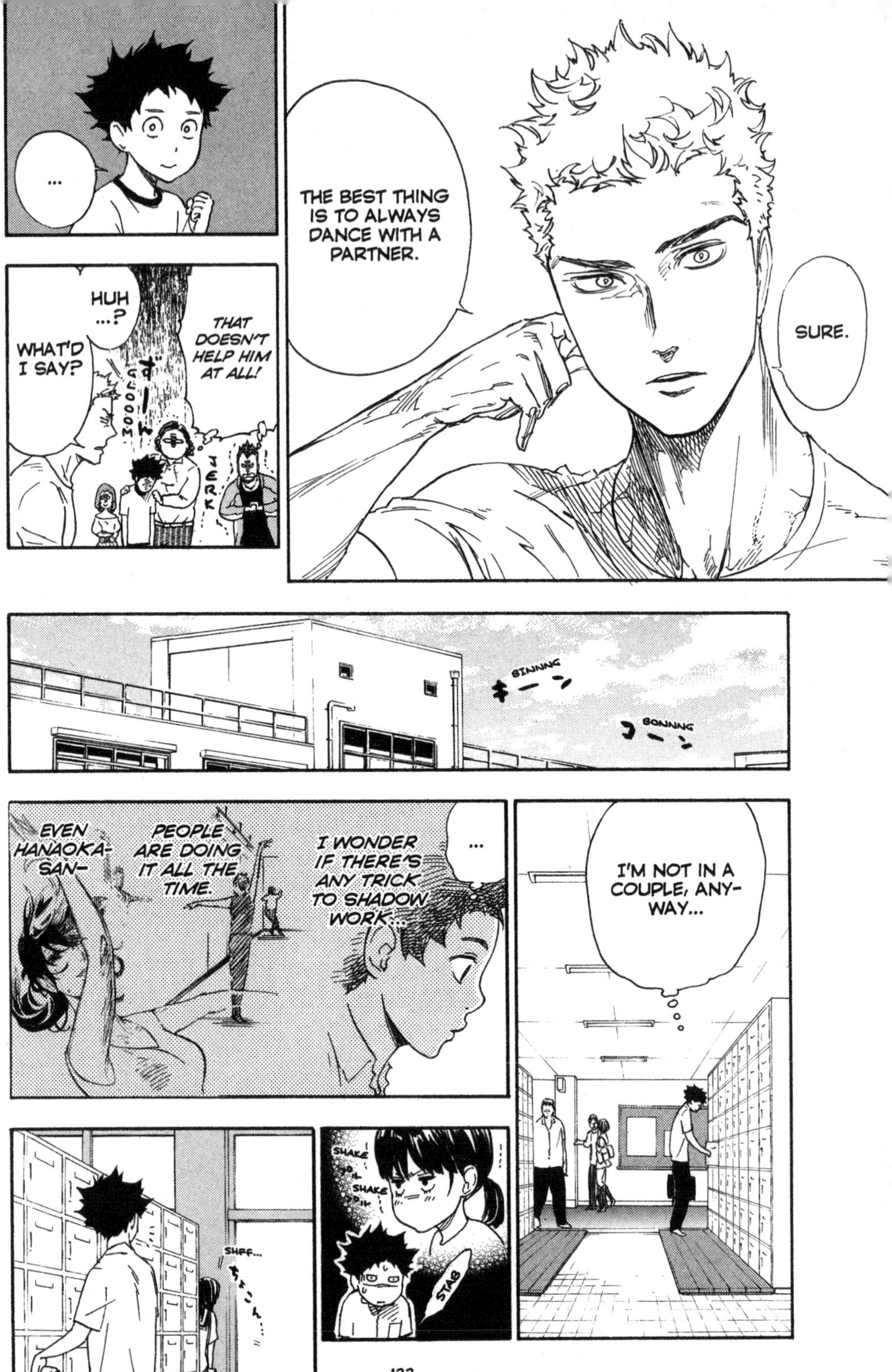
SURE.
THE BEST THING IS TO ALWAYS DANCE WITH A PARTNER.
...
THAT DOESN'T HELP HIM AT ALL!
JERK
GLOOOM
HUH ...?
WHAT'D I SAY?
BINNNG
BONNNG
I'M NOT IN A COUPLE, ANY-WAY...
...
I WONDER IF THERE'S ANY TRICK TO SHADOW WORK...
PEOPLE ARE DOING IT ALL THE TIME.
EVEN HANAOKA-SAN-
SHAKE
SHAKE
STAG
SHFF...

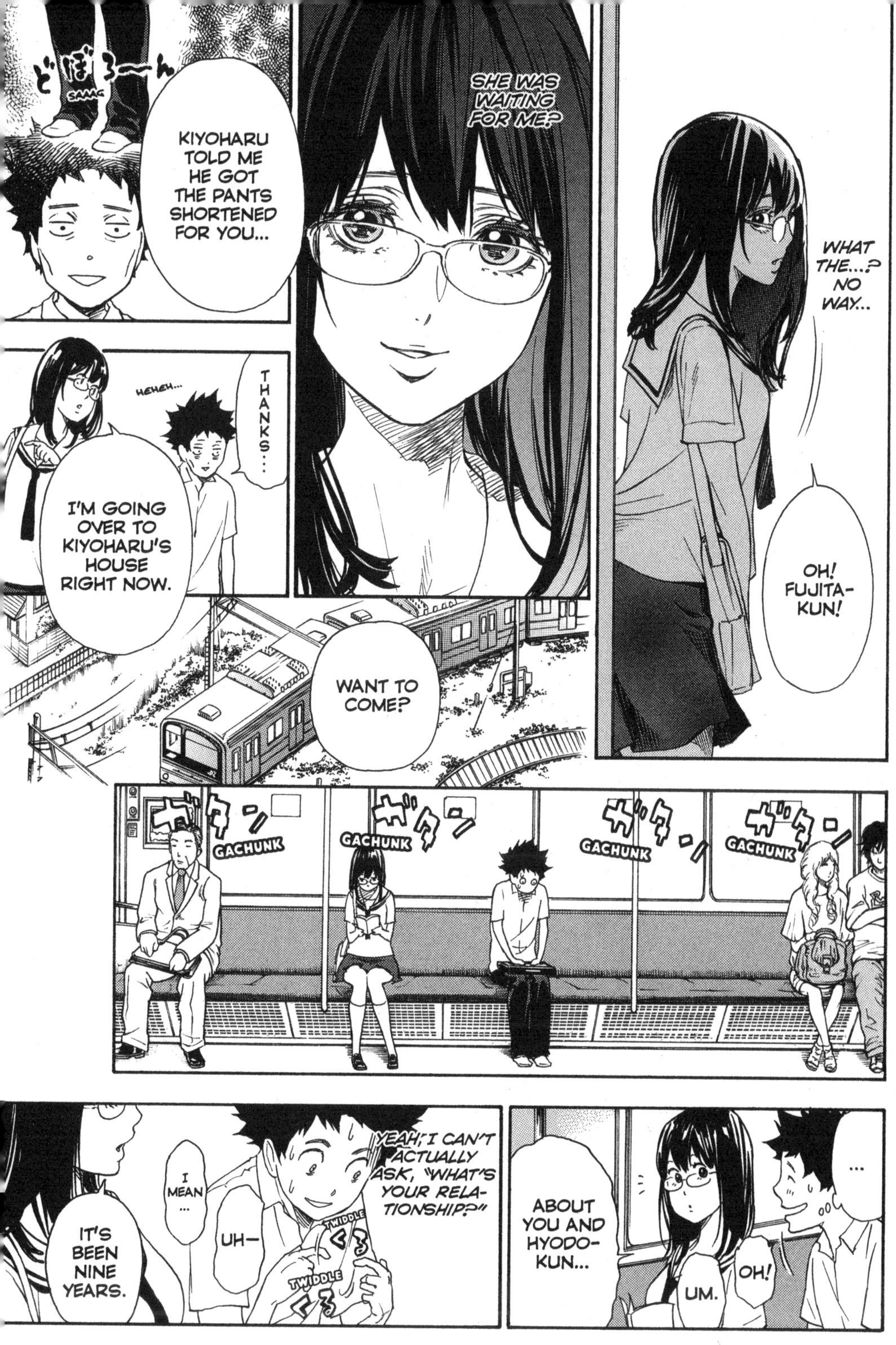
WHAT THE...? NO WAY...
OH! FUJITA-KUN!
SHE WAS WAITING FOR ME?
SAAAG
KIYOHARU TOLD ME HE GOT THE PANTS SHORTENED FOR YOU...
THANKS...
HEHEH...
I'M GOING OVER TO KIYOHARU'S HOUSE RIGHT NOW.
WANT TO COME?
GACHUNK
GACHUNK
GACHUNK
GACHUNK
...
ABOUT YOU AND HYODO-KUN...
OH!
UM.
YEAH, I CAN'T ACTUALLY ASK, "WHAT'S YOUR RELATIONSHIP?"
I MEAN...
TWIDDLE
TWIDDLE
UH—
IT'S BEEN NINE YEARS.

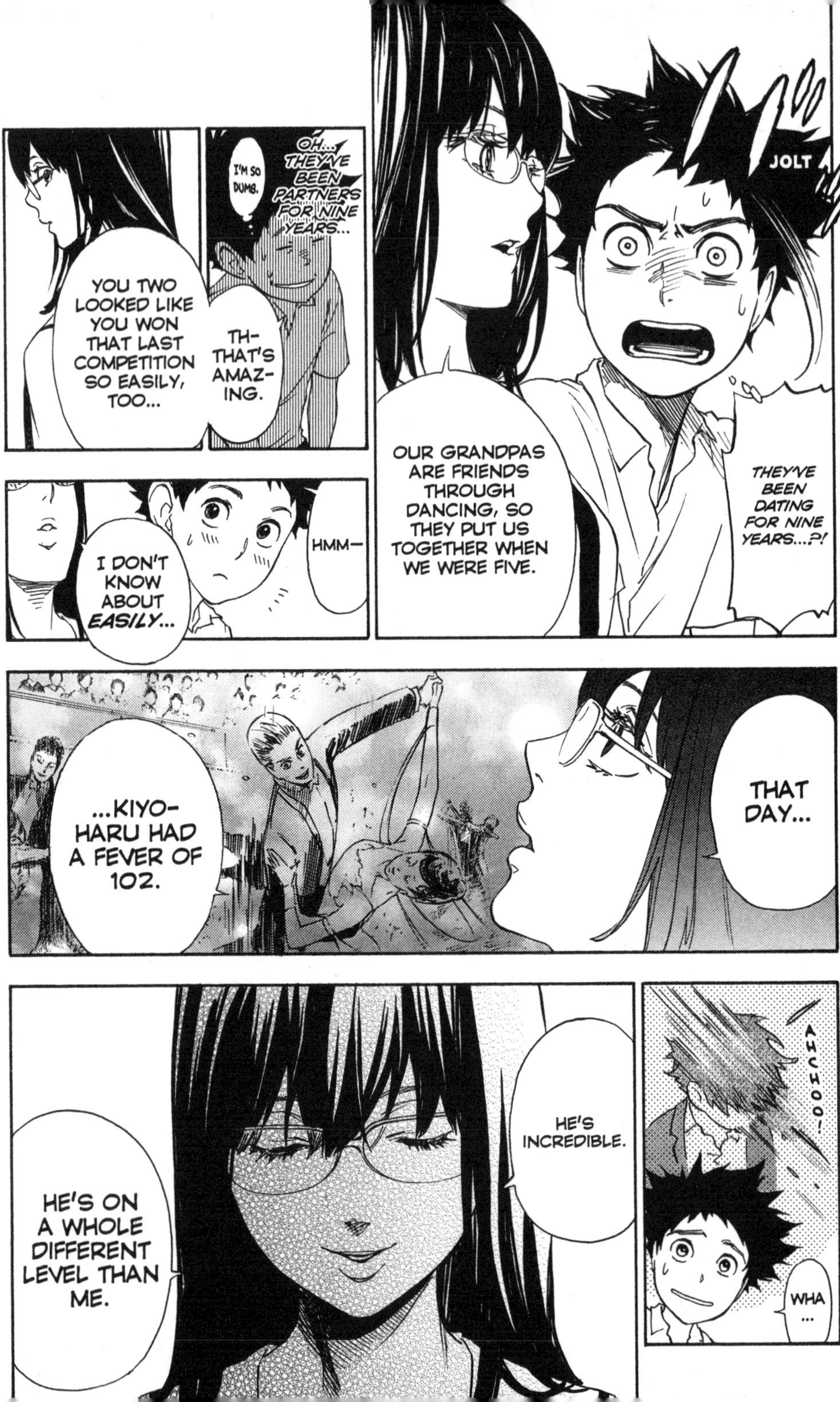

JOLT
OUR GRANDPAS ARE FRIENDS THROUGH DANCING, SO THEY PUT US TOGETHER WHEN WE WERE FIVE.
THEY'VE BEEN DATING FOR NINE YEARS...?!
OH... THEY'VE BEEN PARTNERS FOR NINE YEARS...
I'M SO DUMB.
TH-THAT'S AMAZ-ING.
YOU TWO LOOKED LIKE YOU WON THAT LAST COMPETITION SO EASILY, TOO...
HMM—
I DON'T KNOW ABOUT *EASILY*...
THAT DAY...
...KIYO-HARU HAD A FEVER OF 102.
AHCHOO!
WHA...
HE'S INCREDIBLE.
HE'S ON A WHOLE DIFFERENT LEVEL THAN ME.

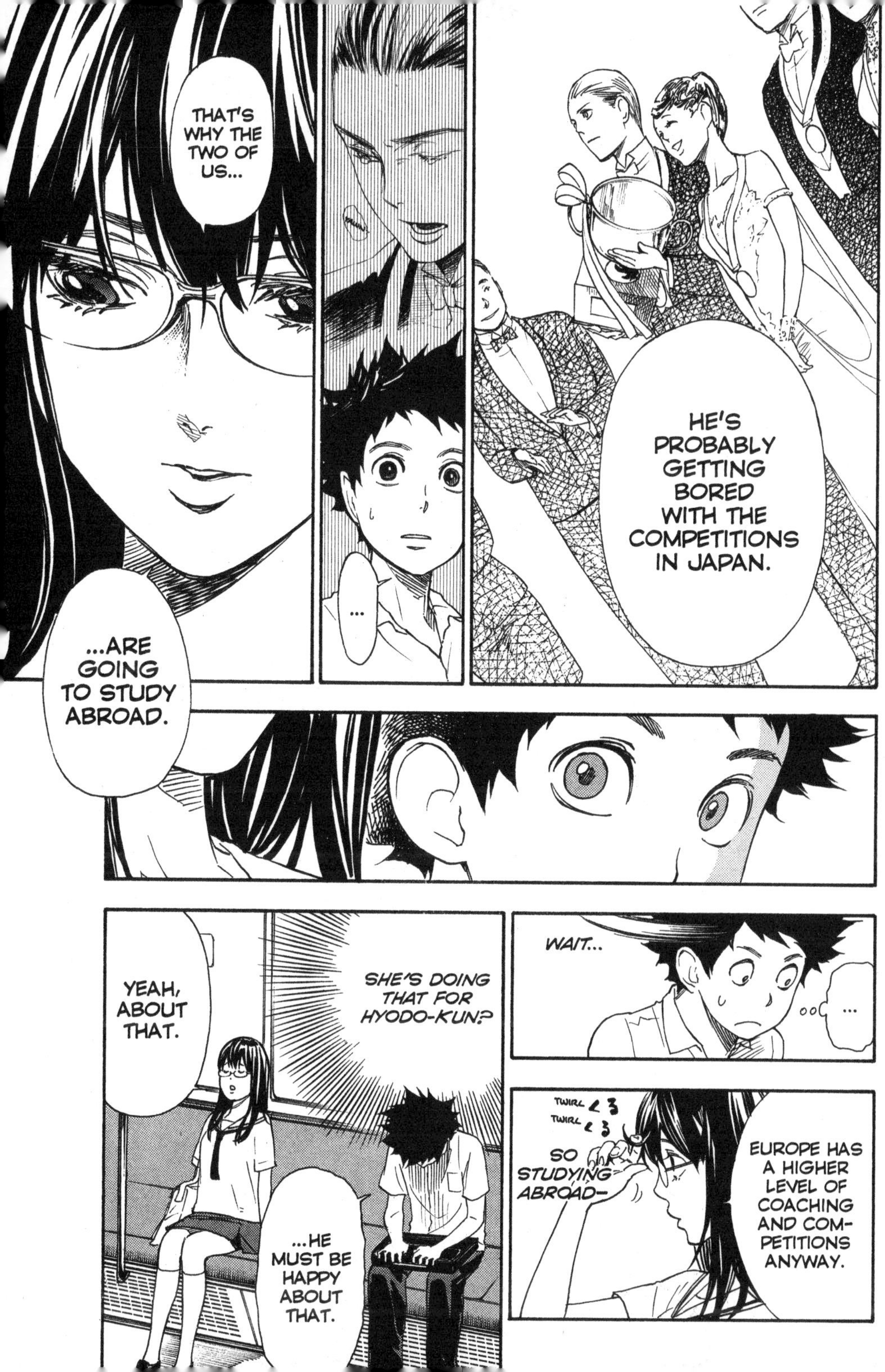
HE'S PROBABLY GETTING BORED WITH THE COMPETITIONS IN JAPAN.
...
THAT'S WHY THE TWO OF US...
...ARE GOING TO STUDY ABROAD.
WAIT...
...
EUROPE HAS A HIGHER LEVEL OF COACHING AND COMPETITIONS ANYWAY.
TWIRL TWIRL
SO STUDYING ABROAD—
SHE'S DOING THAT FOR HYODO-KUN?
YEAH, ABOUT THAT.
...HE MUST BE HAPPY ABOUT THAT.

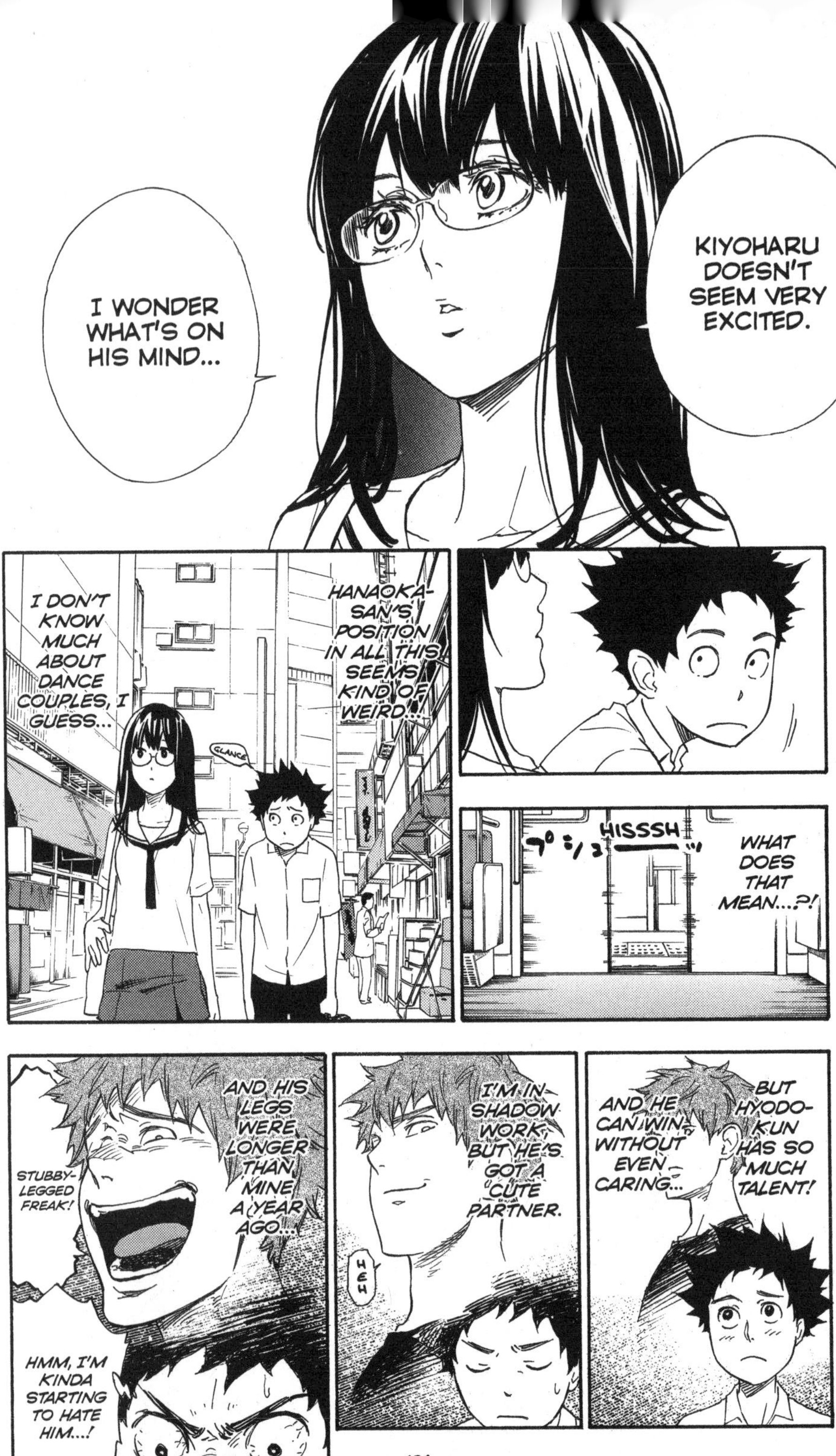
KIYOHARU DOESN'T SEEM VERY EXCITED.
I WONDER WHAT'S ON HIS MIND...
HISSSH
WHAT DOES THAT MEAN...?!
HANAOKA-SAN'S POSITION IN ALL THIS SEEMS KIND OF WEIRD...
GLANCE
I DON'T KNOW MUCH ABOUT DANCE COUPLES, I GUESS...
BUT HYODO-KUN HAS SO MUCH TALENT!
AND HE CAN WIN WITHOUT EVEN CARING...
I'M IN SHADOW WORK BUT HE'S GOT A CUTE PARTNER.
HEH
AND HIS LEGS WERE LONGER THAN MINE A YEAR AGO...
STUBBY-LEGGED FREAK!
HMM, I'M KINDA STARTING TO HATE HIM...!

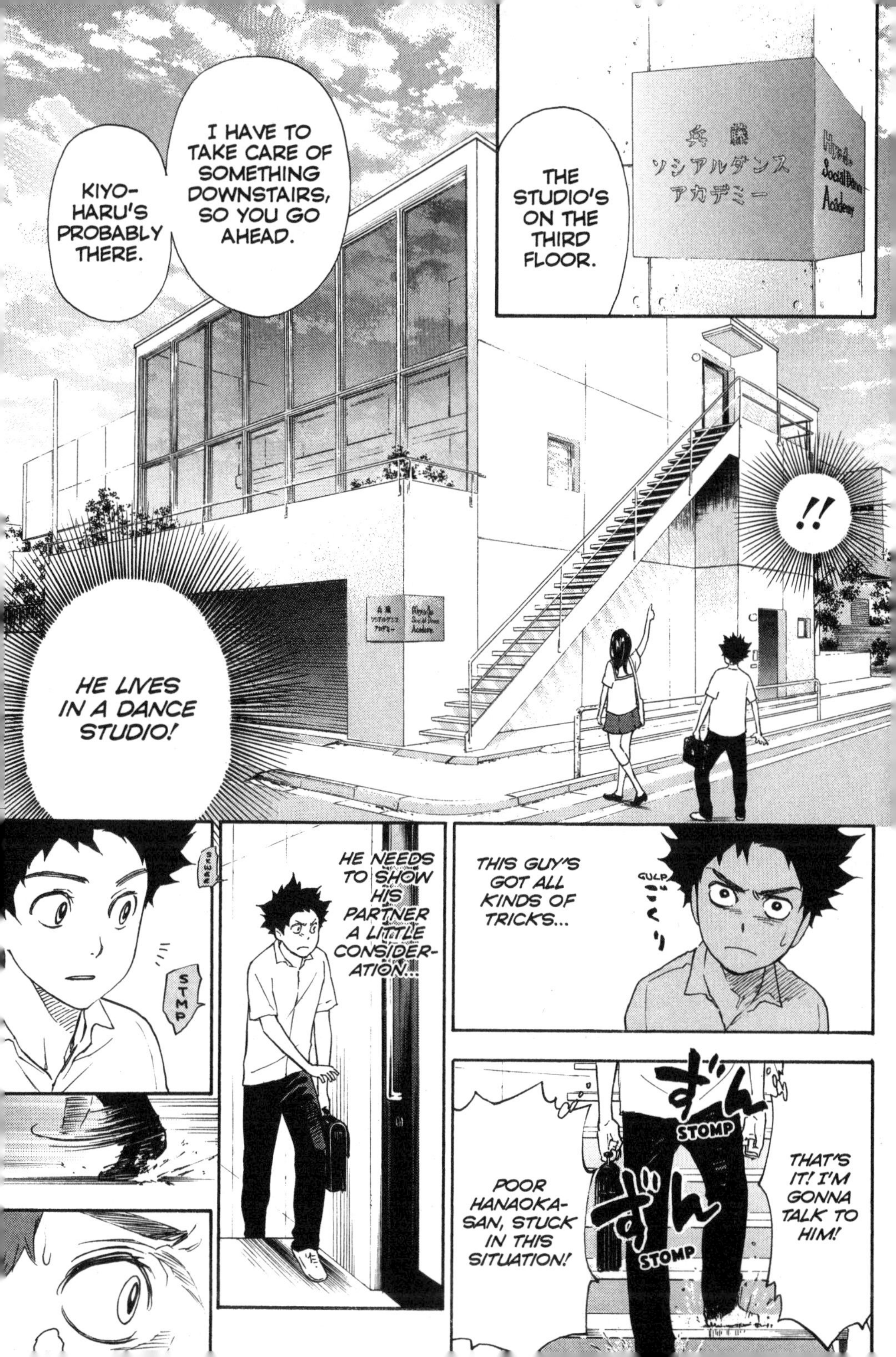
兵藤
ソシアルダンス
アカデミー
THE STUDIO'S ON THE THIRD FLOOR.
I HAVE TO TAKE CARE OF SOMETHING DOWNSTAIRS, SO YOU GO AHEAD.
KIYO-HARU'S PROBABLY THERE.
!!
HE LIVES IN A DANCE STUDIO!
THIS GUY'S GOT ALL KINDS OF TRICKS...
GULP
HE NEEDS TO SHOW HIS PARTNER A LITTLE CONSIDERATION...
STMP
ずん
STOMP
THAT'S IT! I'M GONNA TALK TO HIM!
POOR HANAOKA-SAN, STUCK IN THIS SITUATION!
ずん
STOMP

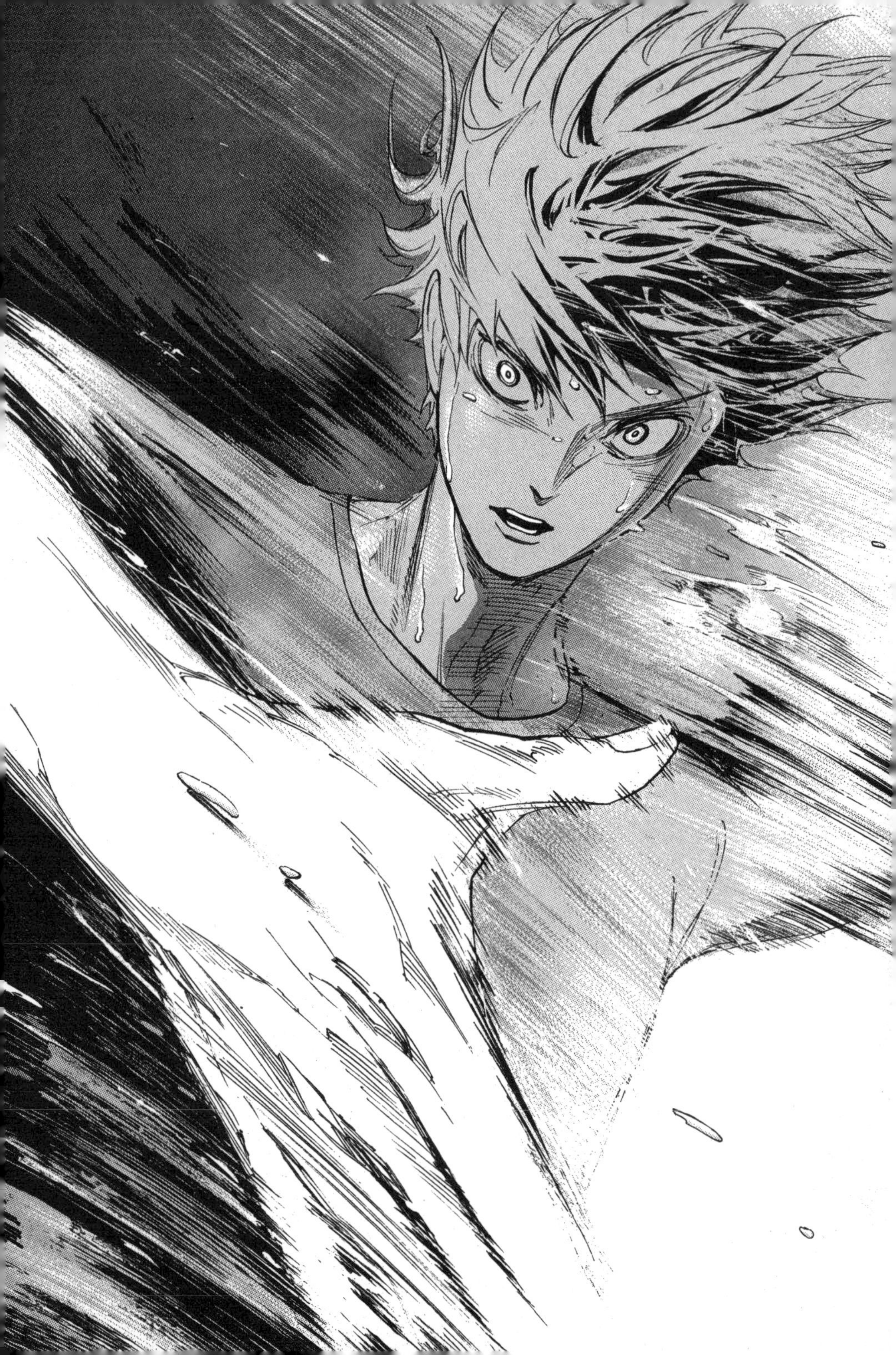

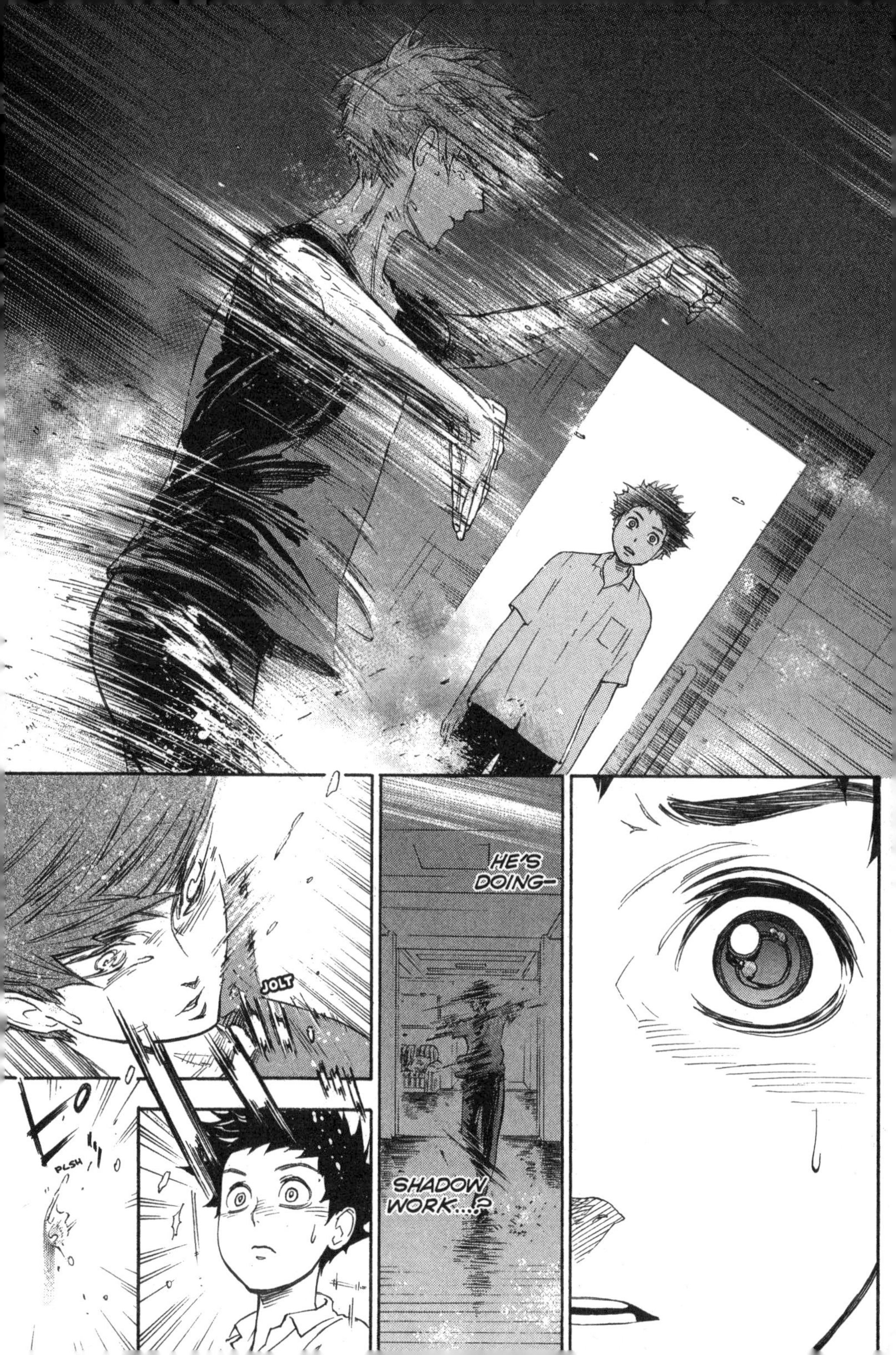
HE'S DOING—
SHADOW WORK...!?
JOLT
PLSH

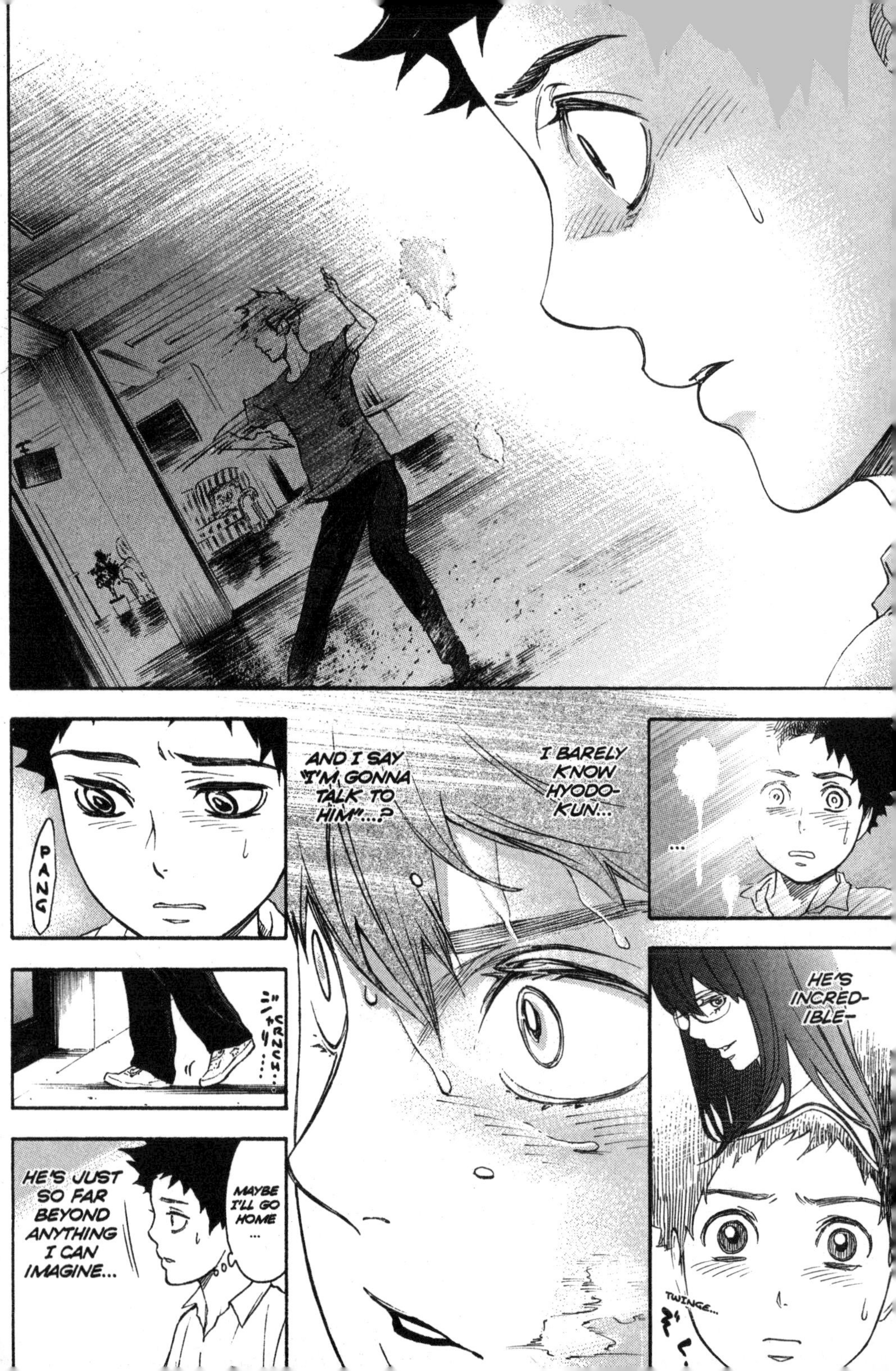
...
HE'S INCREDIBLE-
TWINGE...
I BARELY KNOW HYODO-KUN...
AND I SAY "I'M GONNA TALK TO HIM"...?
PANG
CRNCH...
MAYBE I'LL GO HOME...
HE'S JUST SO FAR BEYOND ANYTHING I CAN IMAGINE...

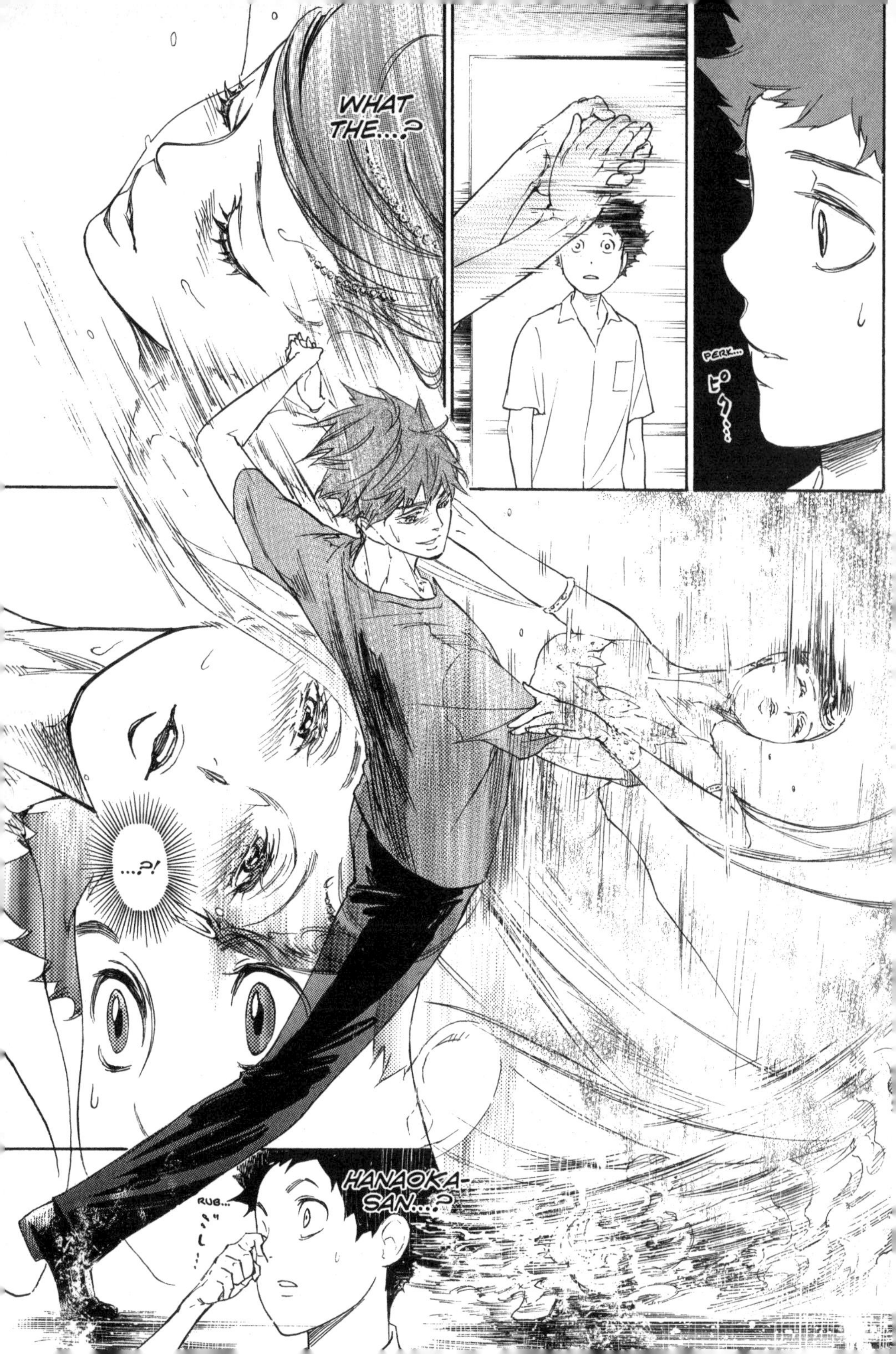
PERK...
ピク...
WHAT THE...?
...?!
HANAOKA-SAN...?
RUB...

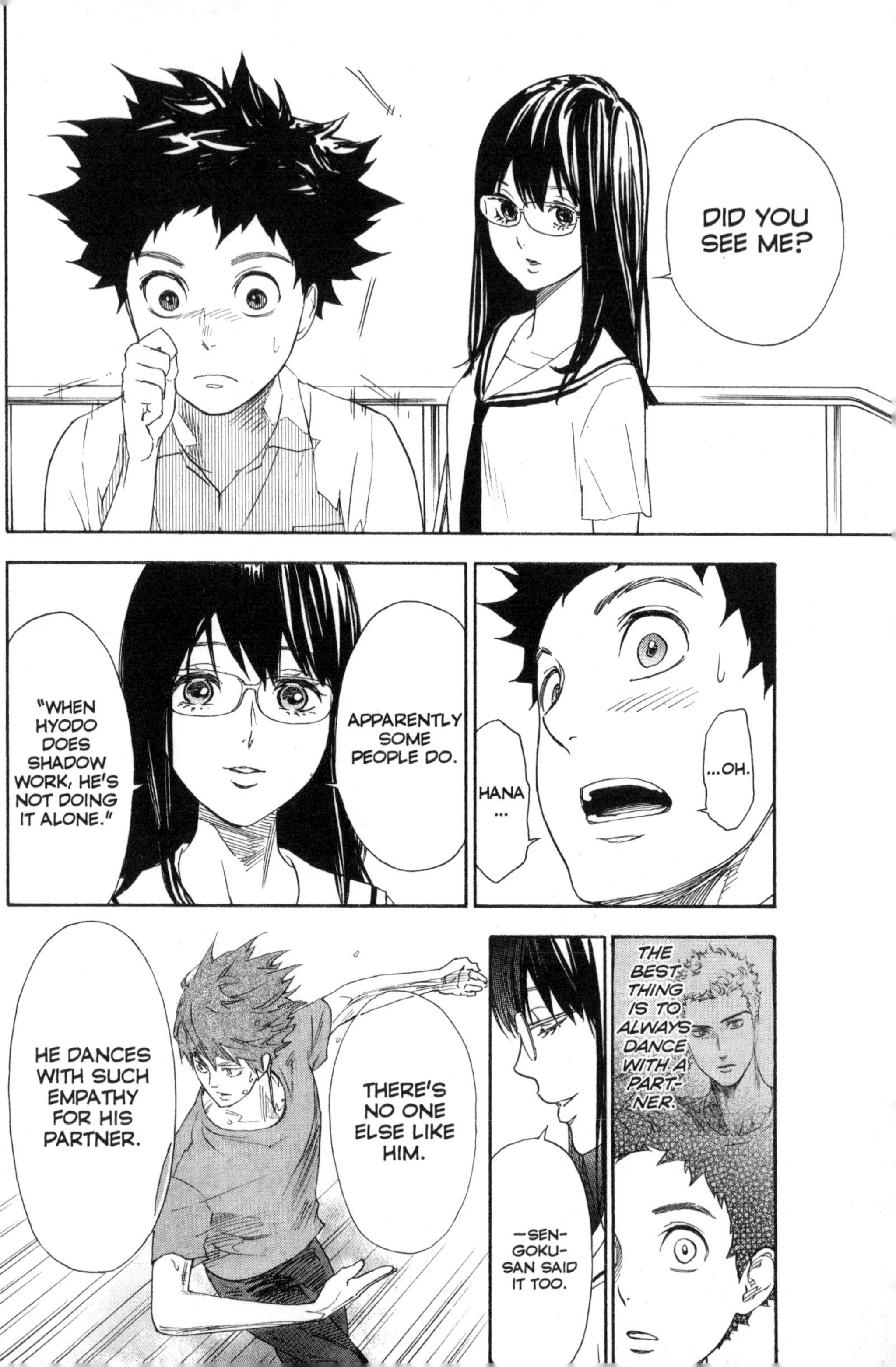
DID YOU SEE ME?
...OH.
HANA...
APPARENTLY SOME PEOPLE DO.
"WHEN HYODO DOES SHADOW WORK, HE'S NOT DOING IT ALONE."
THE BEST THING IS TO ALWAYS DANCE WITH A PART-NER.
—SEN-GOKU-SAN SAID IT TOO.
THERE'S NO ONE ELSE LIKE HIM.
HE DANCES WITH SUCH EMPATHY FOR HIS PARTNER.

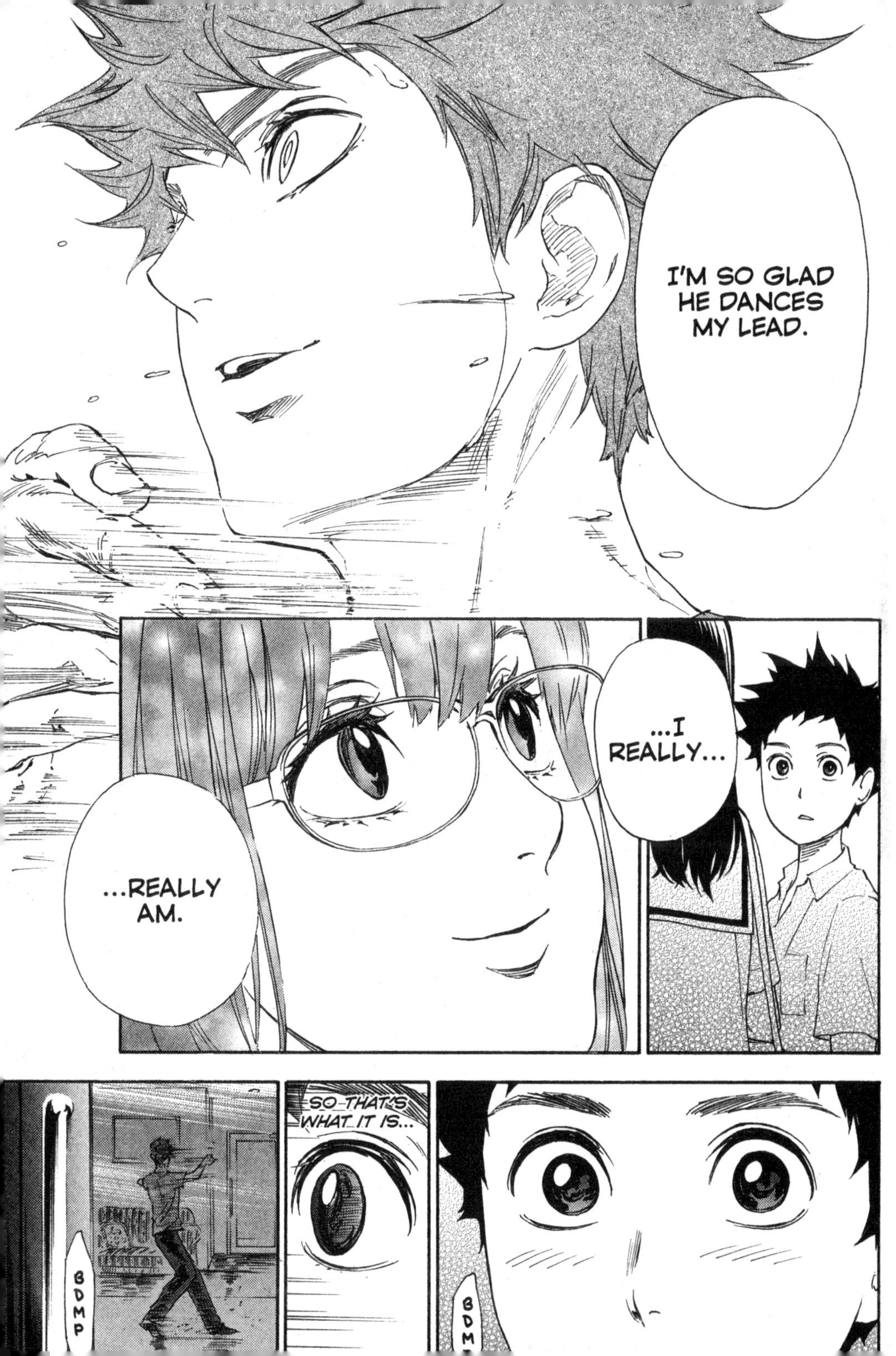
I'M SO GLAD HE DANCES MY LEAD.
...I REALLY...
...REALLY AM.
SO THAT'S WHAT IT IS...
BDMP
BDMP

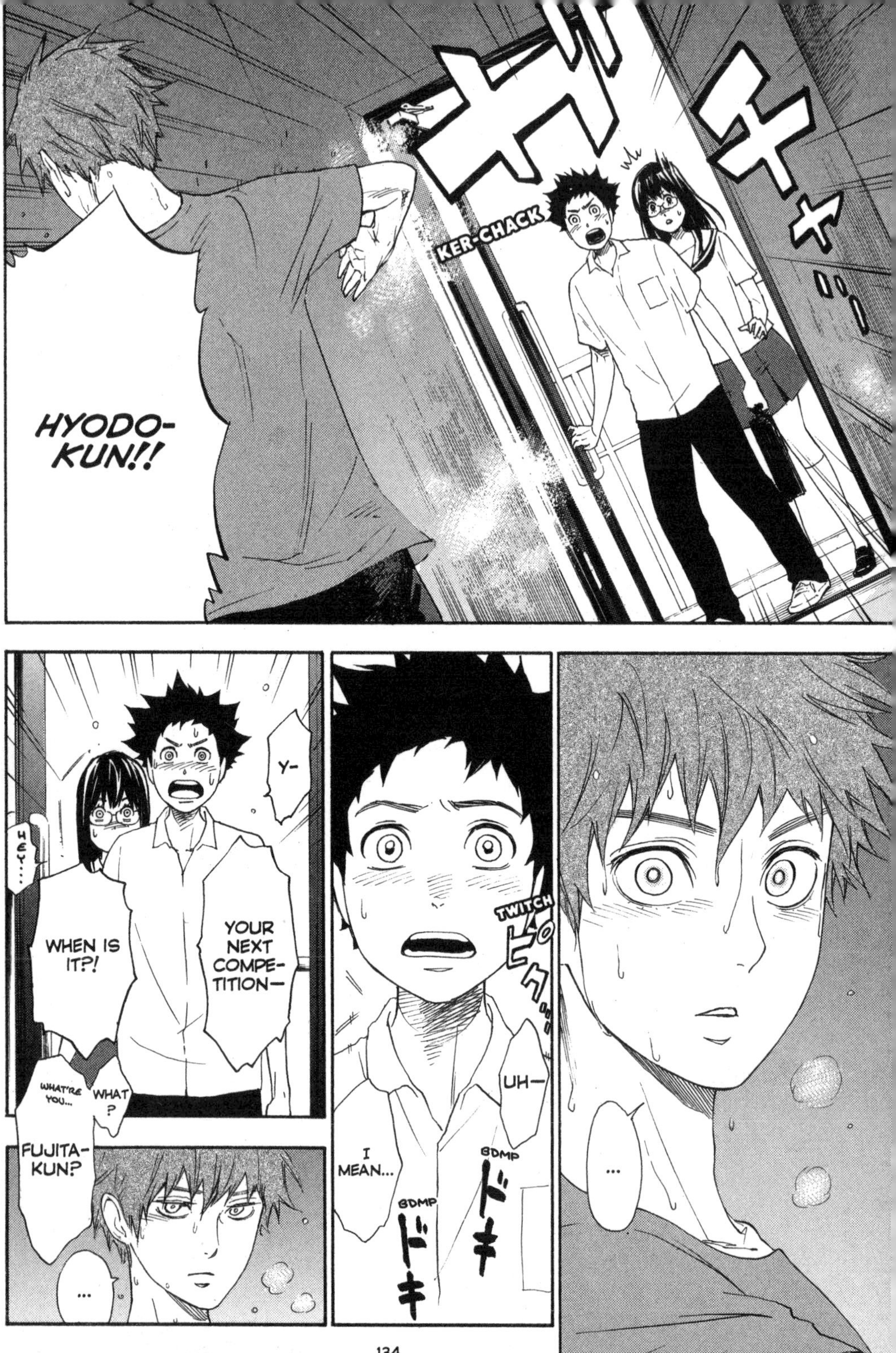
KER-CHACK
HYODO-KUN!!
...
TWITCH
UH—
I MEAN...
BDMP
BDMP
Y-
YOUR NEXT COMPETITION—
WHEN IS IT?!
HEY...
WHAT?
WHAT'RE YOU...
FUJITA-KUN?
...

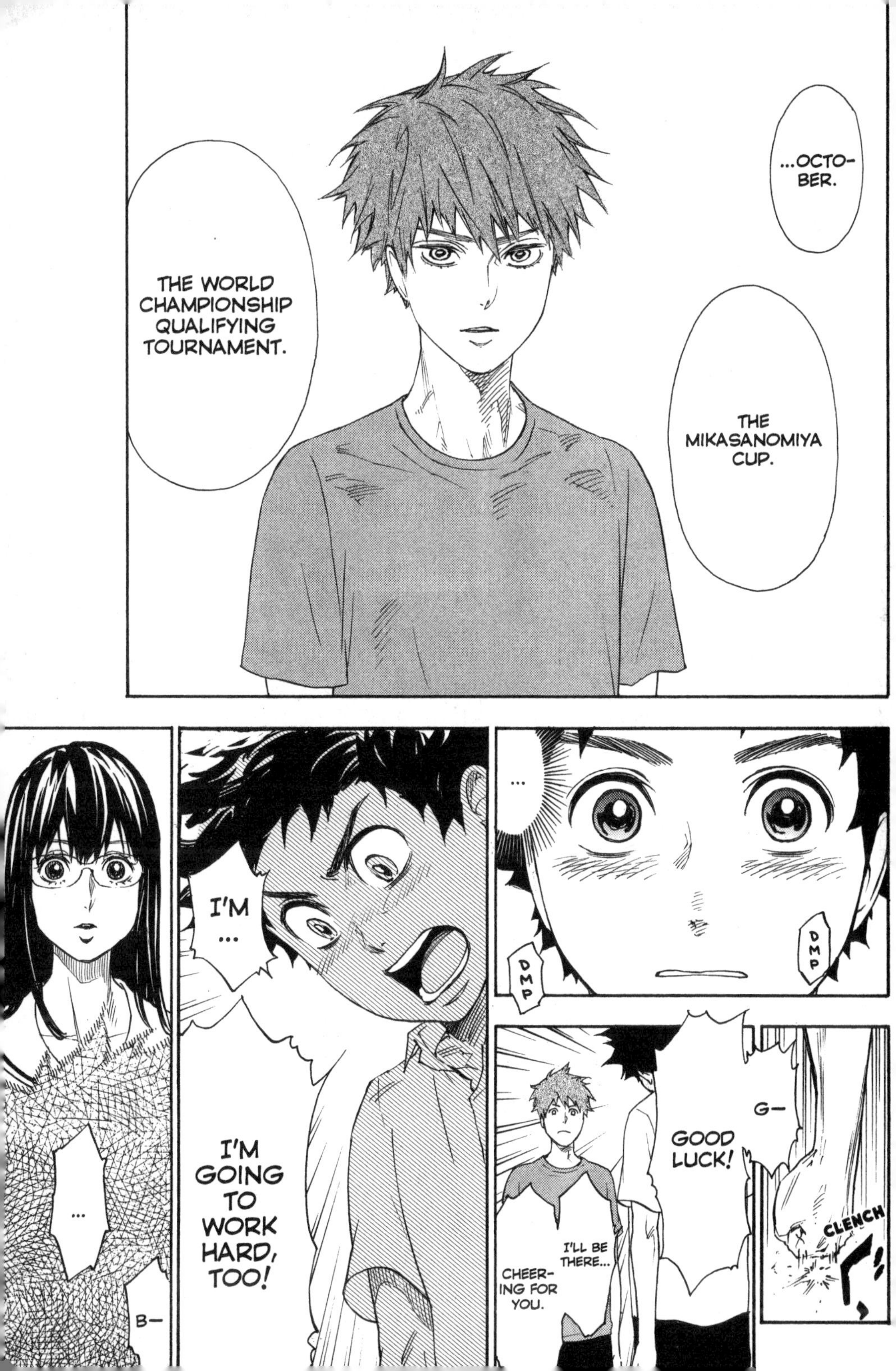
...OCTO-BER.
THE MIKASANOMIYA CUP.
THE WORLD CHAMPIONSHIP QUALIFYING TOURNAMENT.
...
DMP
DMP
G—
GOOD LUCK!
CLENCH
I'LL BE THERE...
CHEER-ING FOR YOU.
I'M ...
I'M GOING TO WORK HARD, TOO!
...
B—

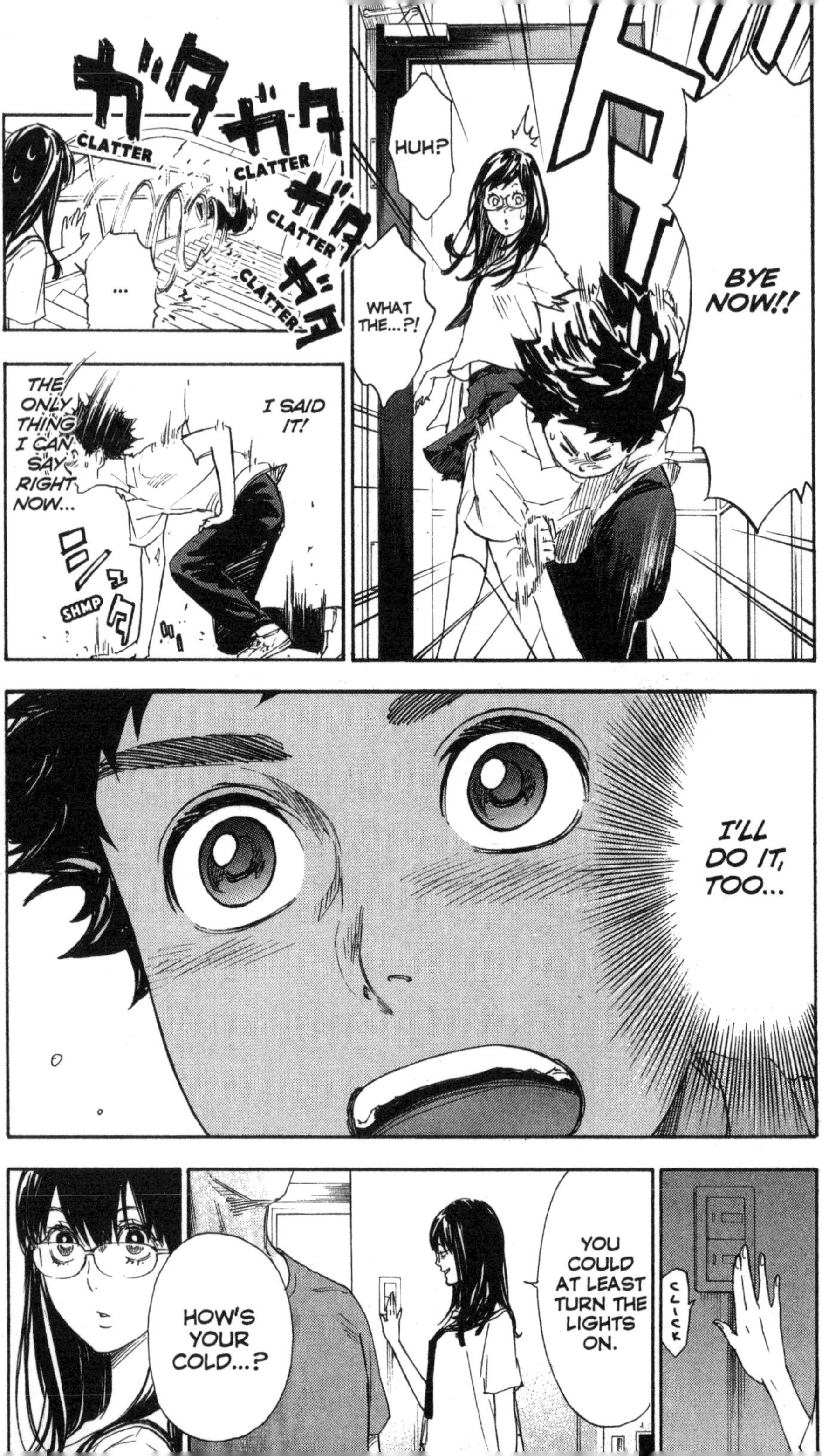
BYE NOW!!
HUH?
WHAT THE...?!
CLATTER
CLATTER
CLATTER
CLATTER
...
I SAID IT!
THE ONLY THING I CAN SAY RIGHT NOW...
SHMP
I'LL DO IT, TOO...
CLICK
YOU COULD AT LEAST TURN THE LIGHTS ON.
HOW'S YOUR COLD...?

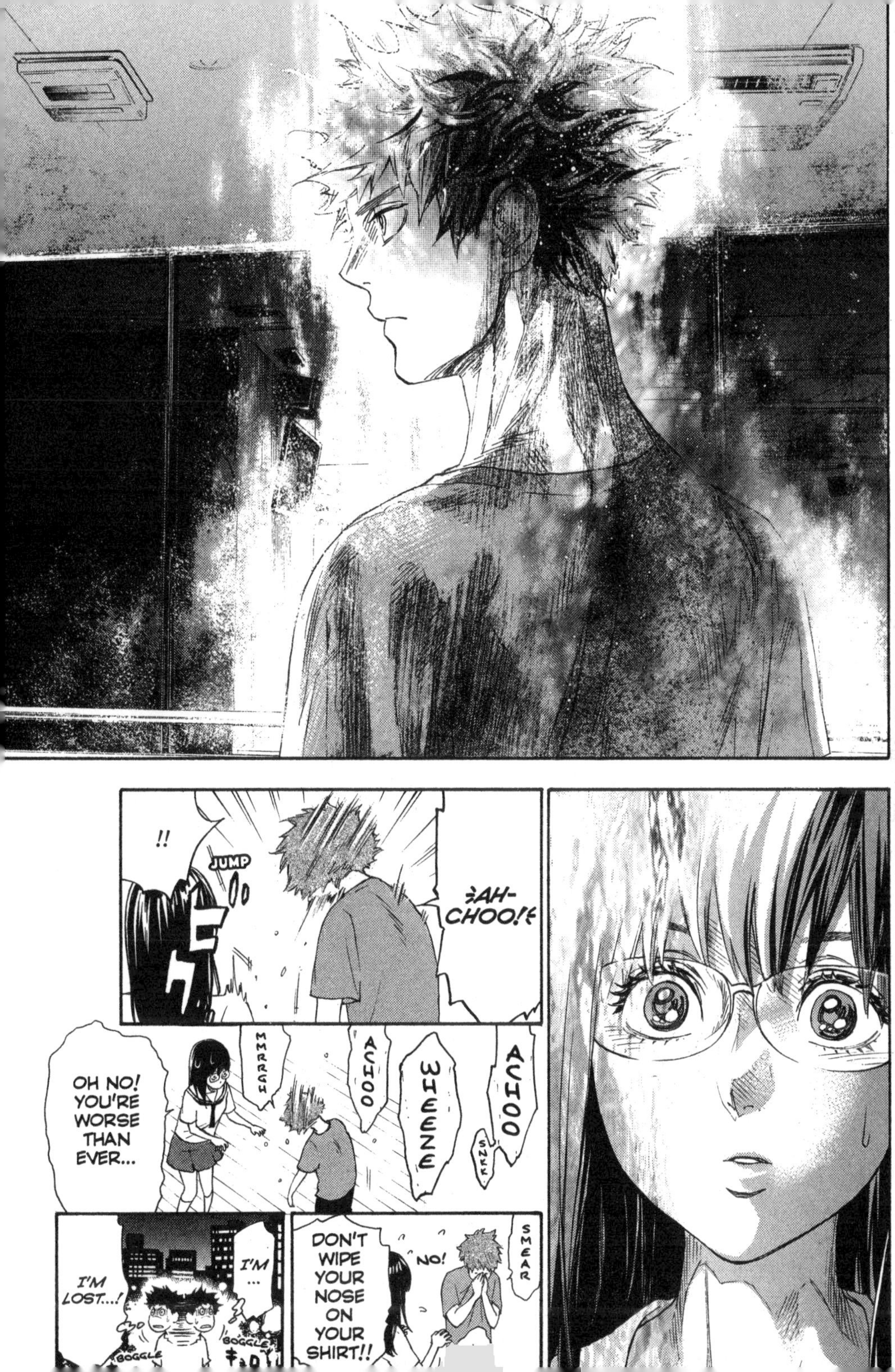
AH-CHOO!
JUMP
!!
ACHOO
SNKK
WHEEZE
ACHOO
MMRRGH
OH NO! YOU'RE WORSE THAN EVER...
SMEAR
NO!
DON'T WIPE YOUR NOSE ON YOUR SHIRT!!
I'M ...
I'M LOST...!
BOGGLE
BOGGLE

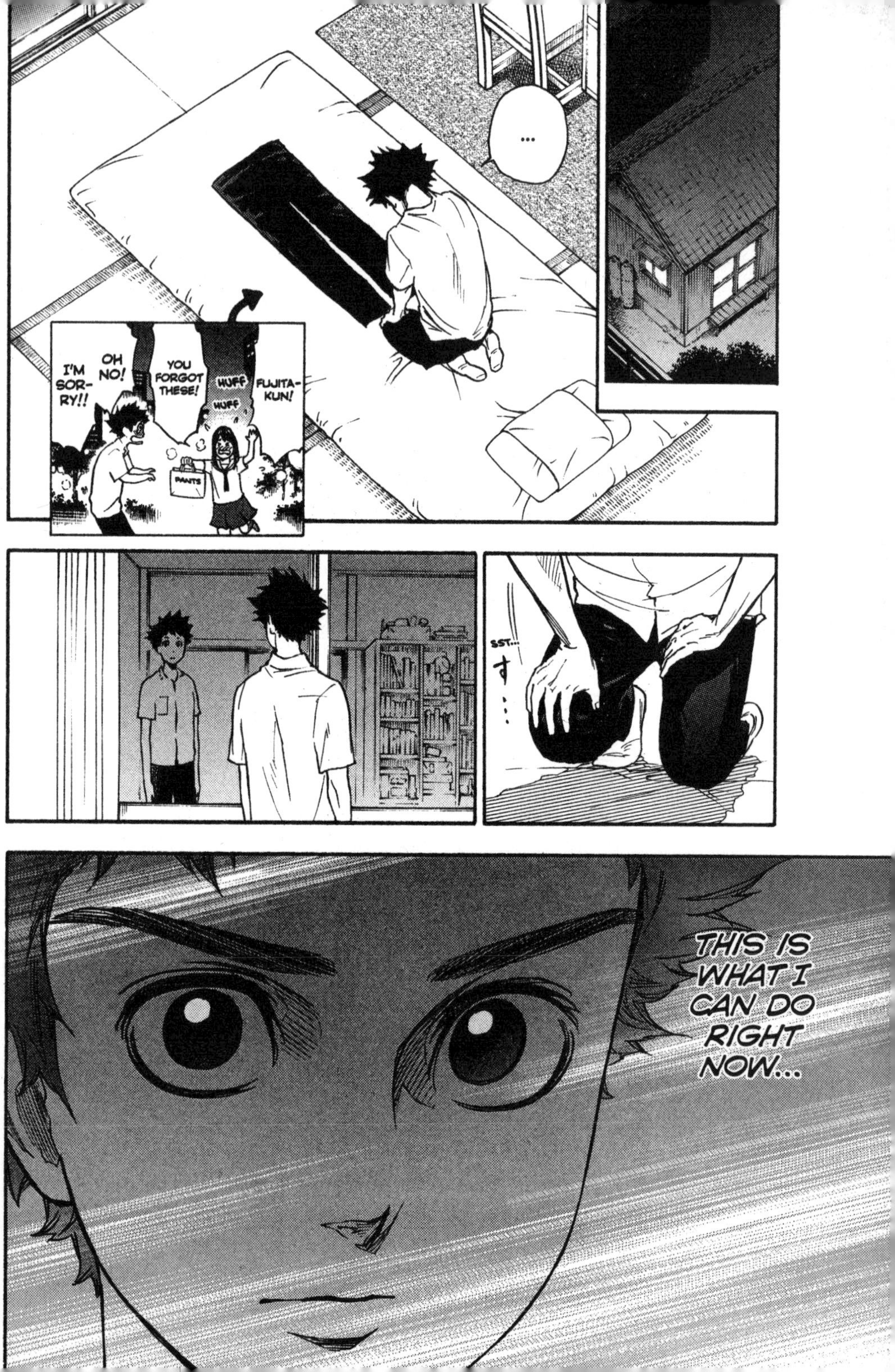
...
FUJITA-KUN!
HUFF
HUFF
YOU FORGOT THESE!
PANTS
OH NO!
I'M SOR-RY!!
SST...
す・・・
THIS IS WHAT I CAN DO RIGHT NOW...

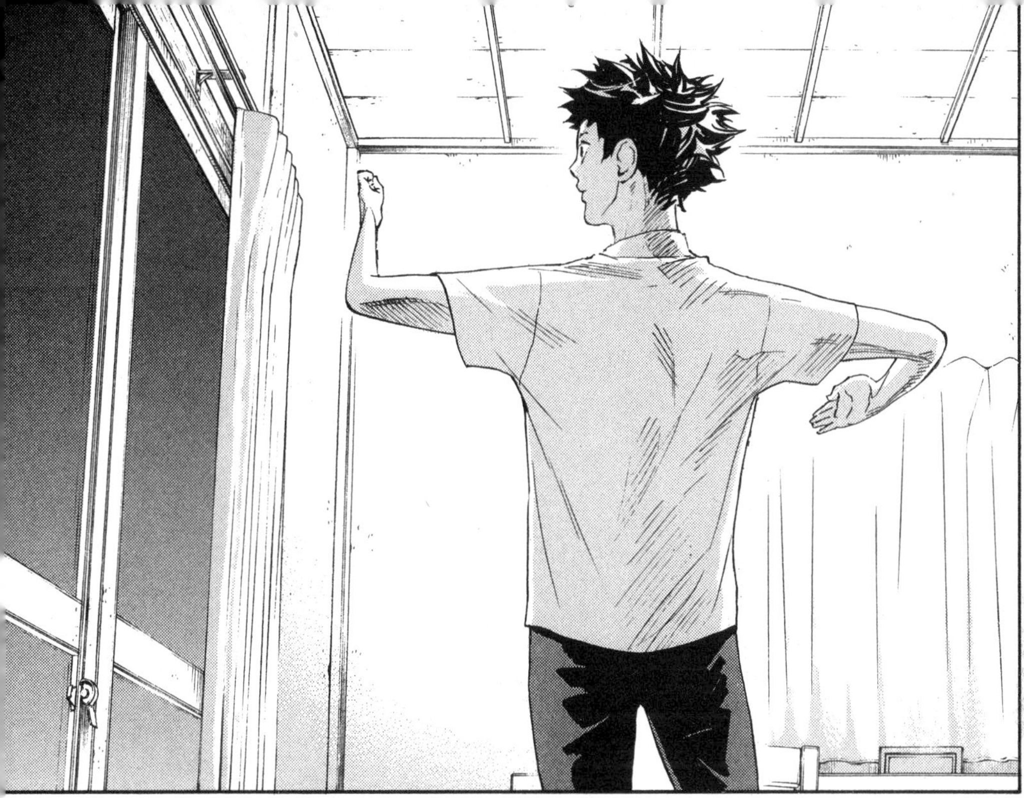

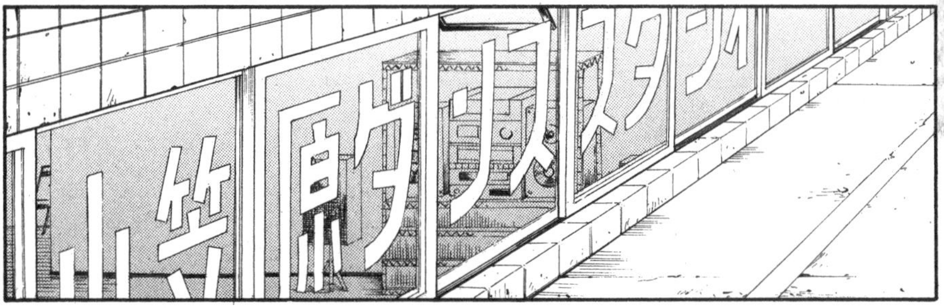

SIGN: OGASAWARA DANCE STUDIO

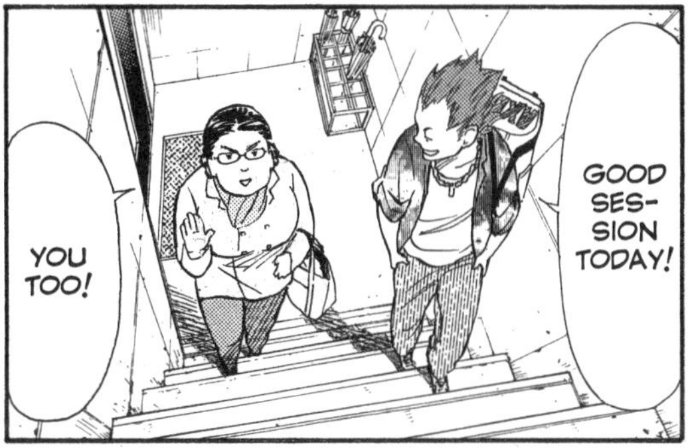
GOOD SES-SION TODAY!
YOU TOO!

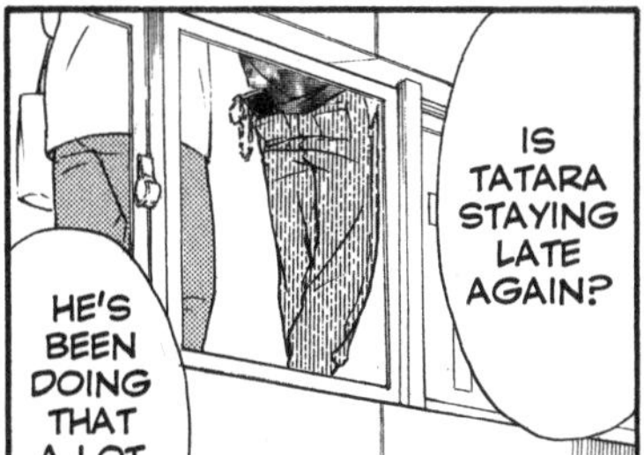
IS TATARA STAYING LATE AGAIN?
HE'S BEEN DOING THAT A LOT LATE-LY.

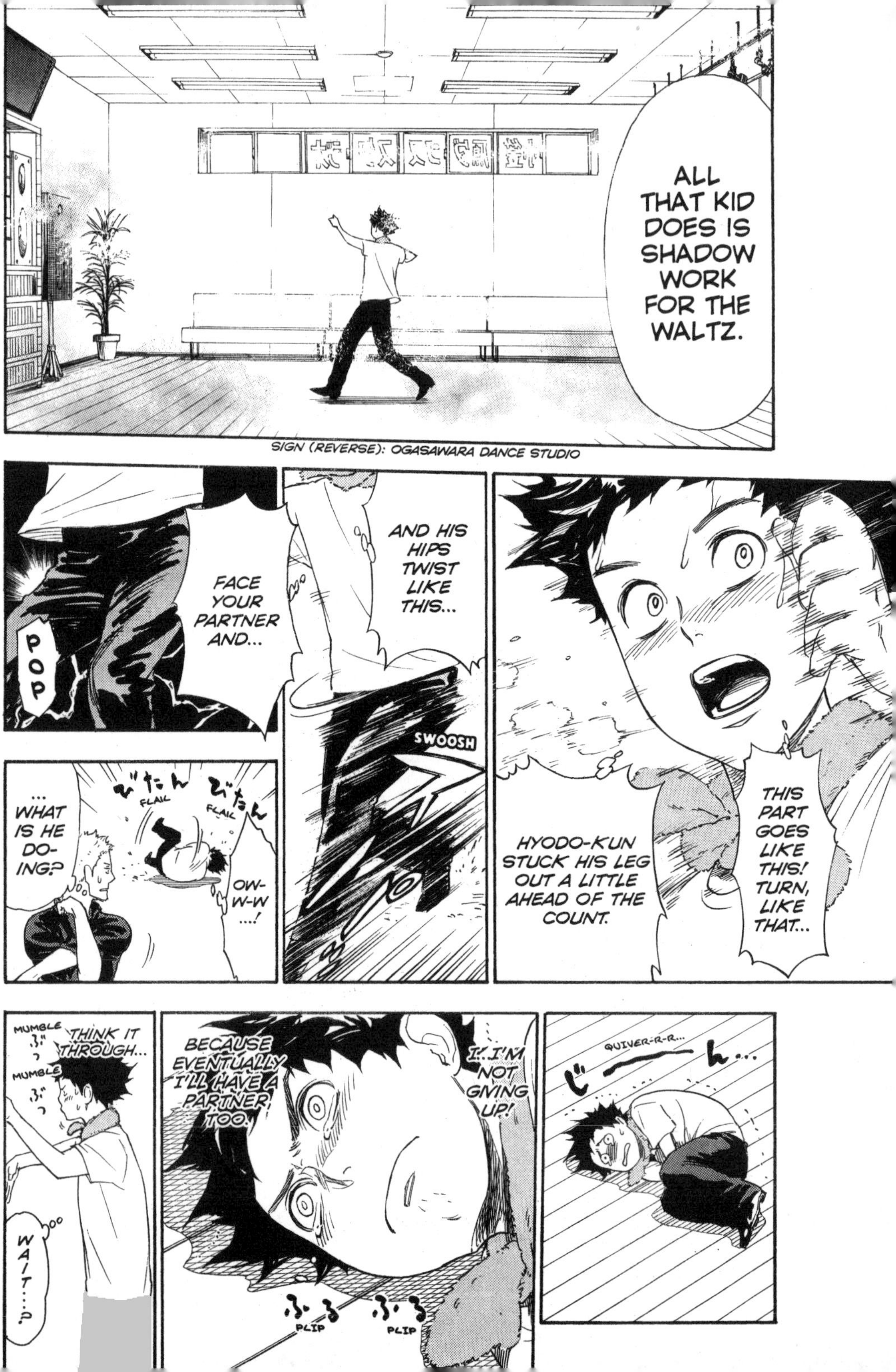
ALL THAT KID DOES IS SHADOW WORK FOR THE WALTZ.
SIGN (REVERSE): OGASAWARA DANCE STUDIO
THIS PART GOES LIKE THIS! TURN, LIKE THAT...
HYODO-KUN STUCK HIS LEG OUT A LITTLE AHEAD OF THE COUNT.
AND HIS HIPS TWIST LIKE THIS...
SWOOSH
FACE YOUR PARTNER AND...
POP
FLAIL
FLAIL
OW-W-W...!
... WHAT IS HE DOING?
QUIVER-R-R...
I..I'M NOT GIVING UP!
BECAUSE EVENTUALLY I'LL HAVE A PARTNER, TOO.
PLIP
PLIP
THINK IT THROUGH...
MUMBLE
MUMBLE
WAIT...?

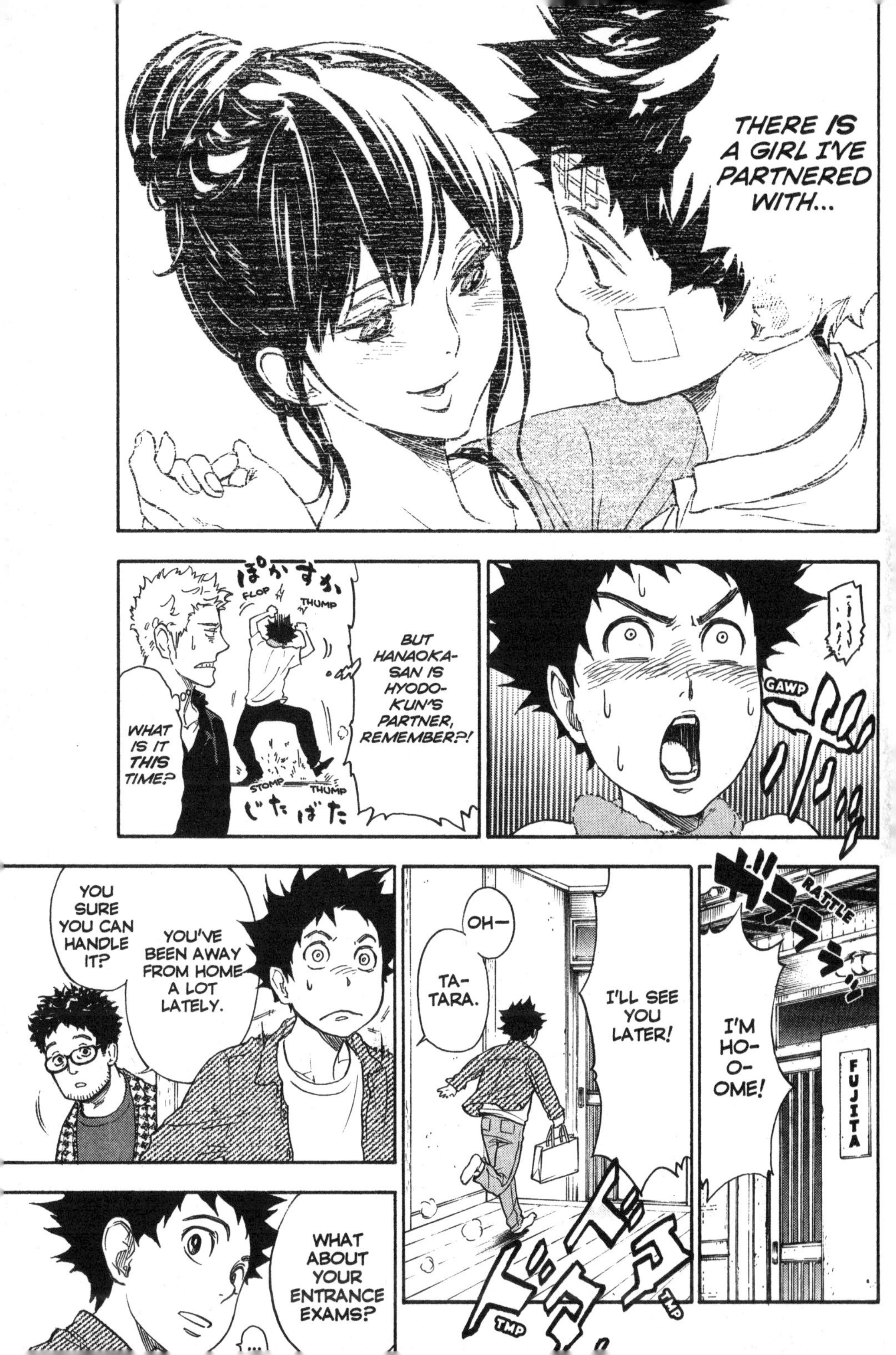
THERE IS A GIRL I'VE PARTNERED WITH...
GAWP
BUT HANAOKA-SAN IS HYODO-KUN'S PARTNER, REMEMBER?!
ぽかすか
FLOP
THUMP
WHAT IS IT THIS TIME?
STOMP
THUMP
じたばた
RATTLE
I'M HO-O-OME!
FUJITA
I'LL SEE YOU LATER!
OH—
TA-TARA.
TMP
TMP
YOU SURE YOU CAN HANDLE IT?
YOU'VE BEEN AWAY FROM HOME A LOT LATELY.
WHAT ABOUT YOUR ENTRANCE EXAMS?
...

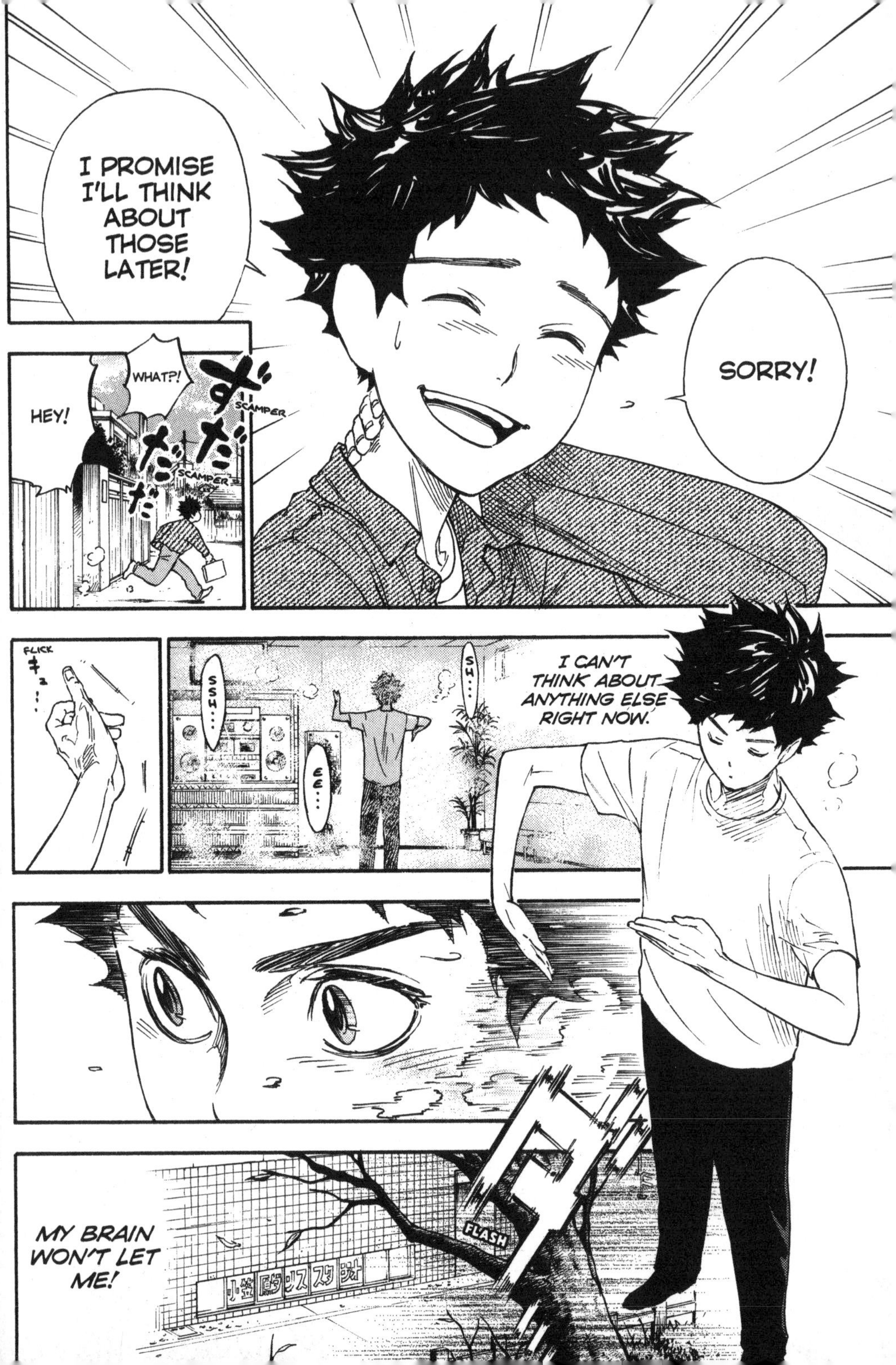
SORRY!
I PROMISE I'LL THINK ABOUT THOSE LATER!
ずだ
SCAMPER
だだ
SCAMPER
WHAT?!
HEY!
I CAN'T THINK ABOUT ANYTHING ELSE RIGHT NOW.
SH...
SSH...
EE...
FLICK
FLASH
MY BRAIN WON'T LET ME!

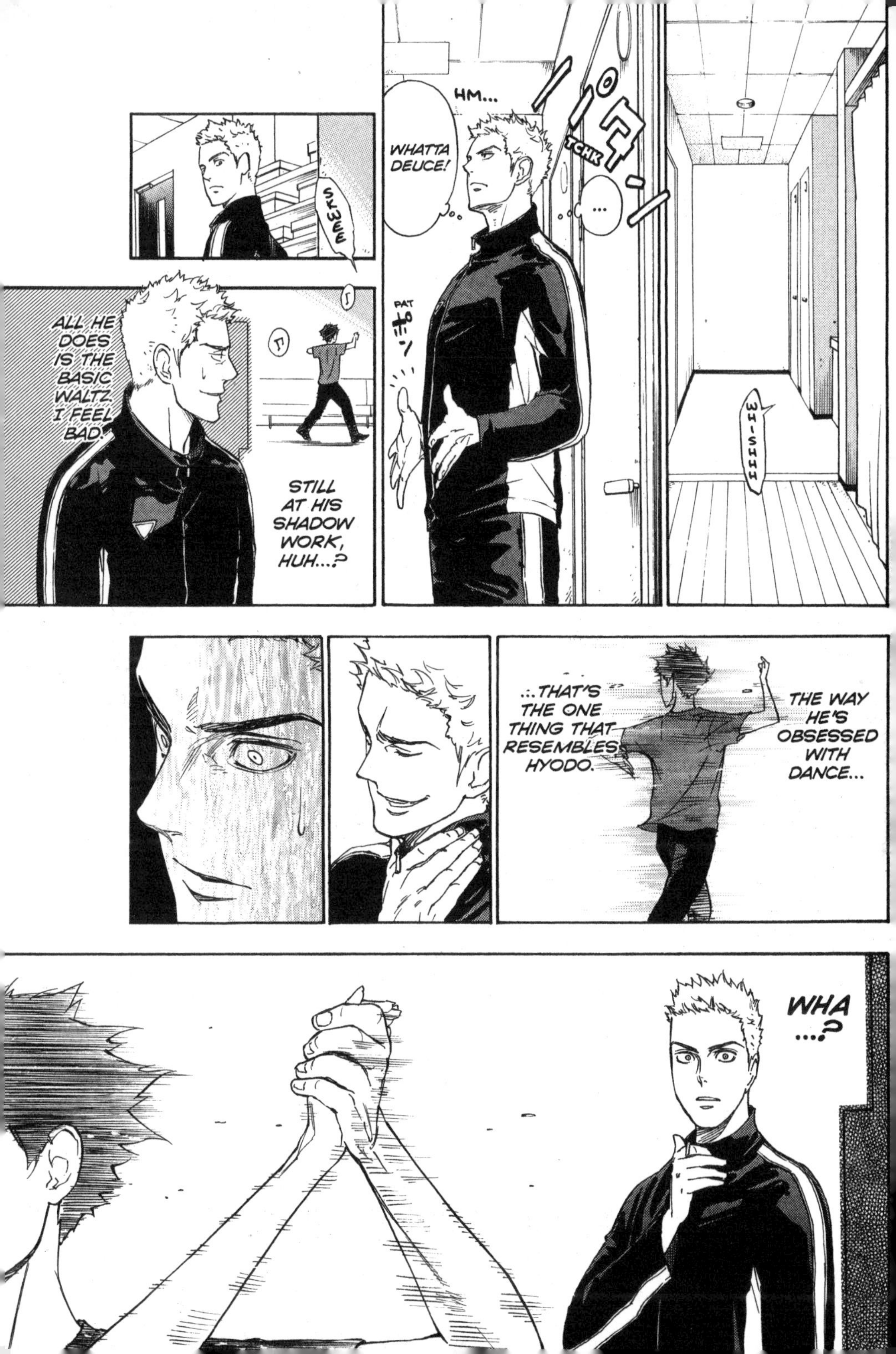
WHISHHH
HM...
WHATTA DEUCE!
TCHK
...
PAT
SKWEEE
STILL AT HIS SHADOW WORK, HUH...?
ALL HE DOES IS THE BASIC WALTZ. I FEEL BAD.
THE WAY HE'S OBSESSED WITH DANCE...
...THAT'S THE ONE THING THAT RESEMBLES HYODO.
WHA ...?

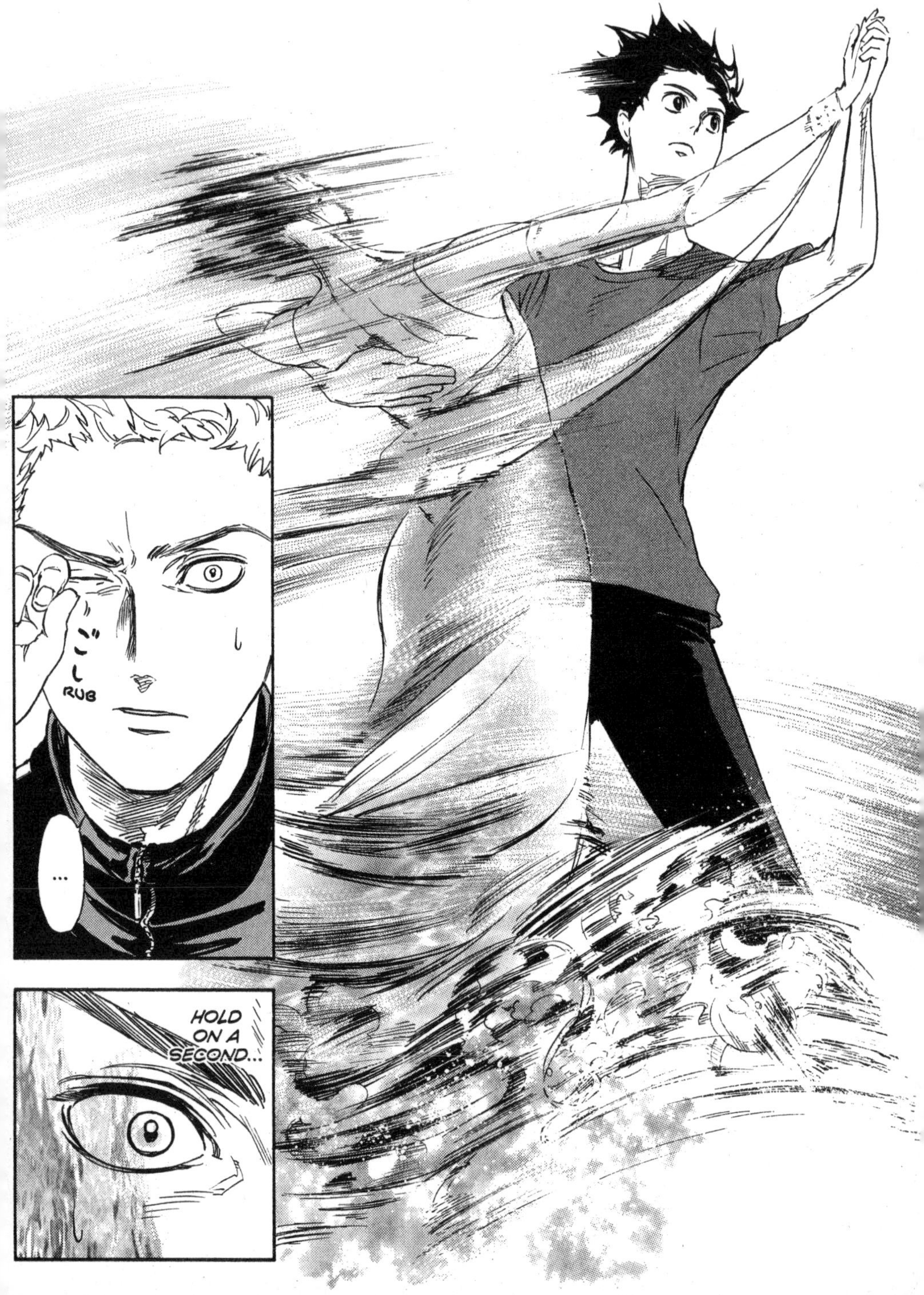
ごし
RUB
...
HOLD ON A SECOND...

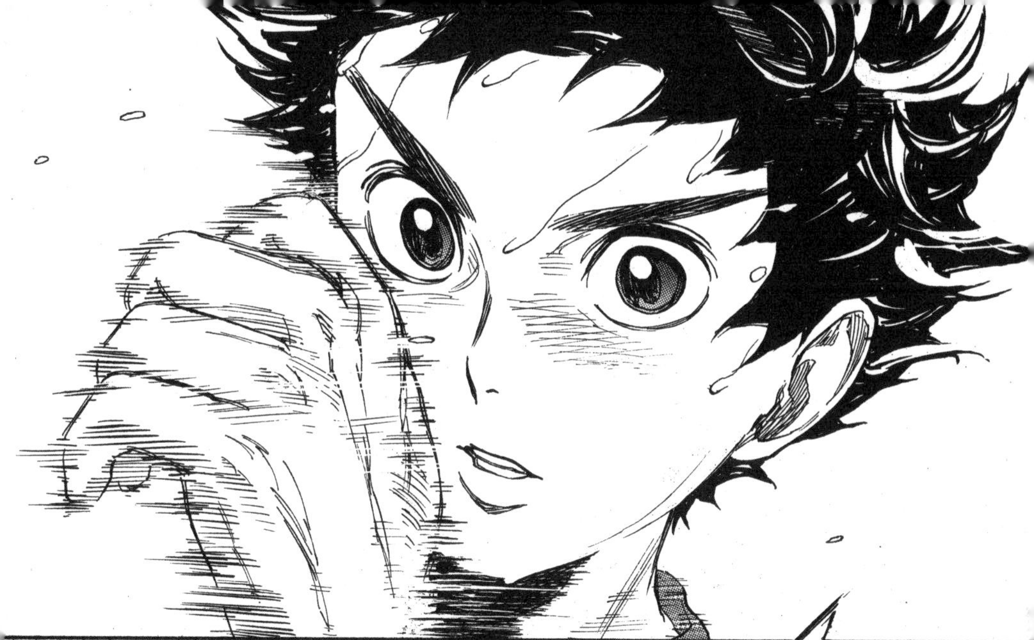

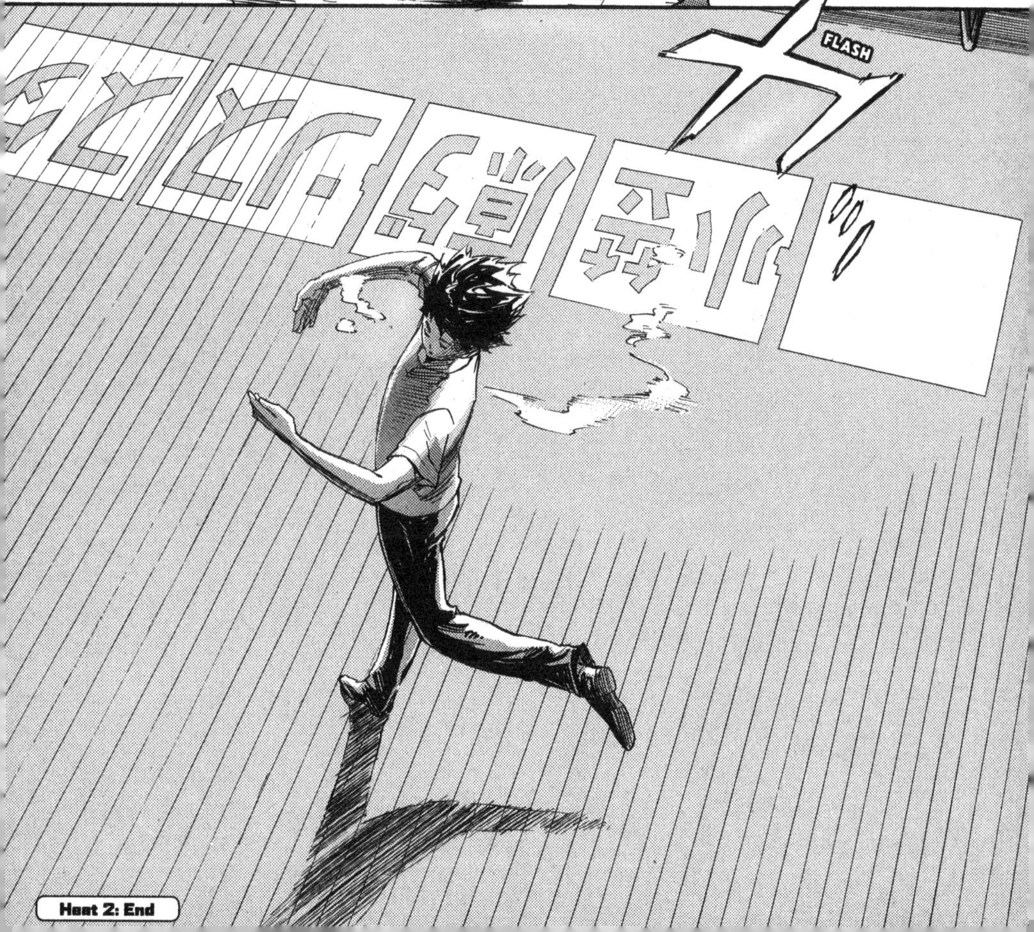
FLASH

Heat 2: End

Special Thanks

INTERVIEW ASSISTANCE
Masayuki Ishihara
Yumiya Kubota

BACKGROUND ASSISTANCE
Hanemura Dance Studio
Choice Dance Studio

RESEARCH ASSISTANCE
Dance Time Editorial Department

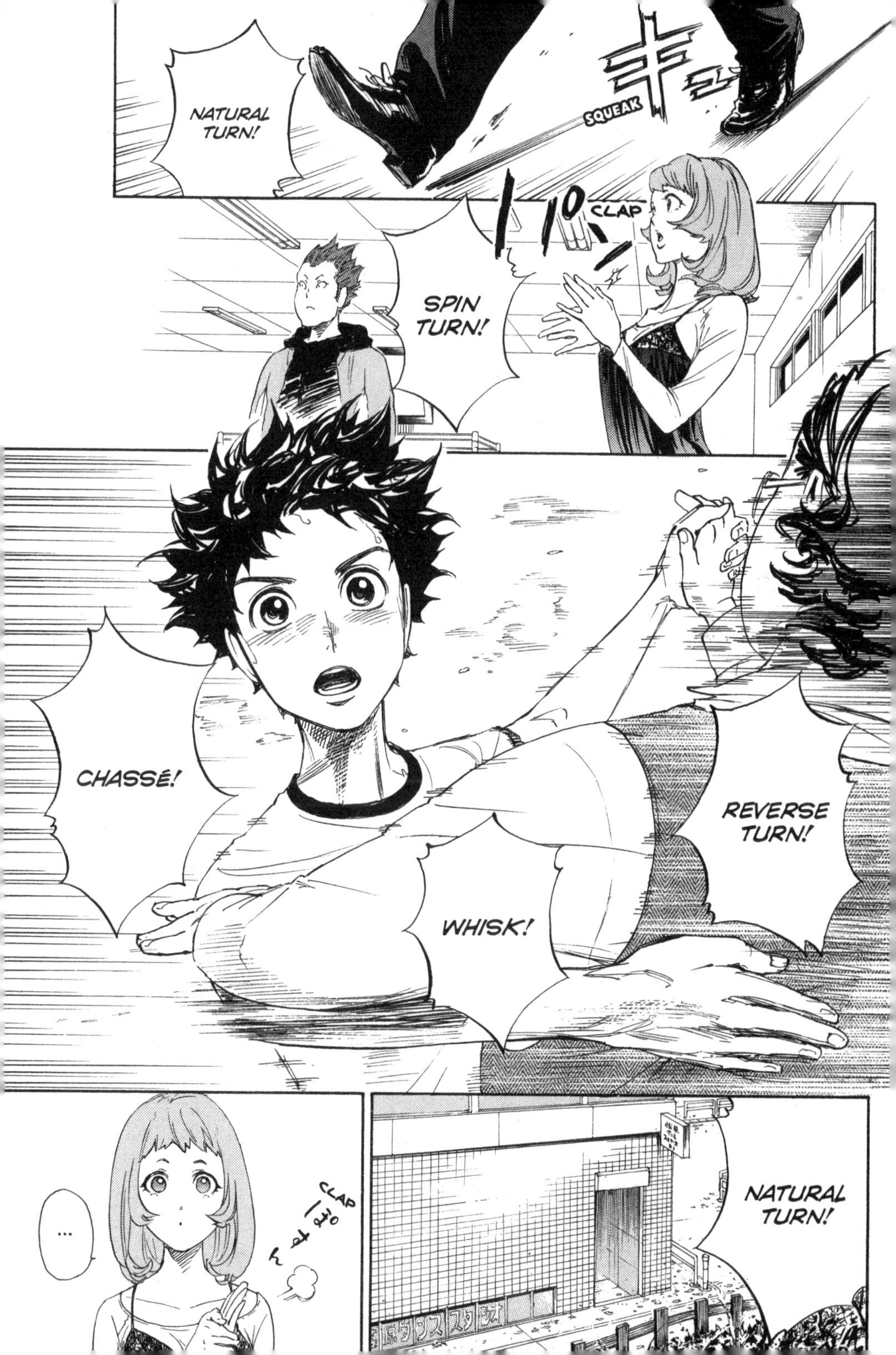
SQUEAK
NATURAL TURN!
CLAP
SPIN TURN!
REVERSE TURN!
WHISK!
CHASSÉ!
NATURAL TURN!
CLAP
...

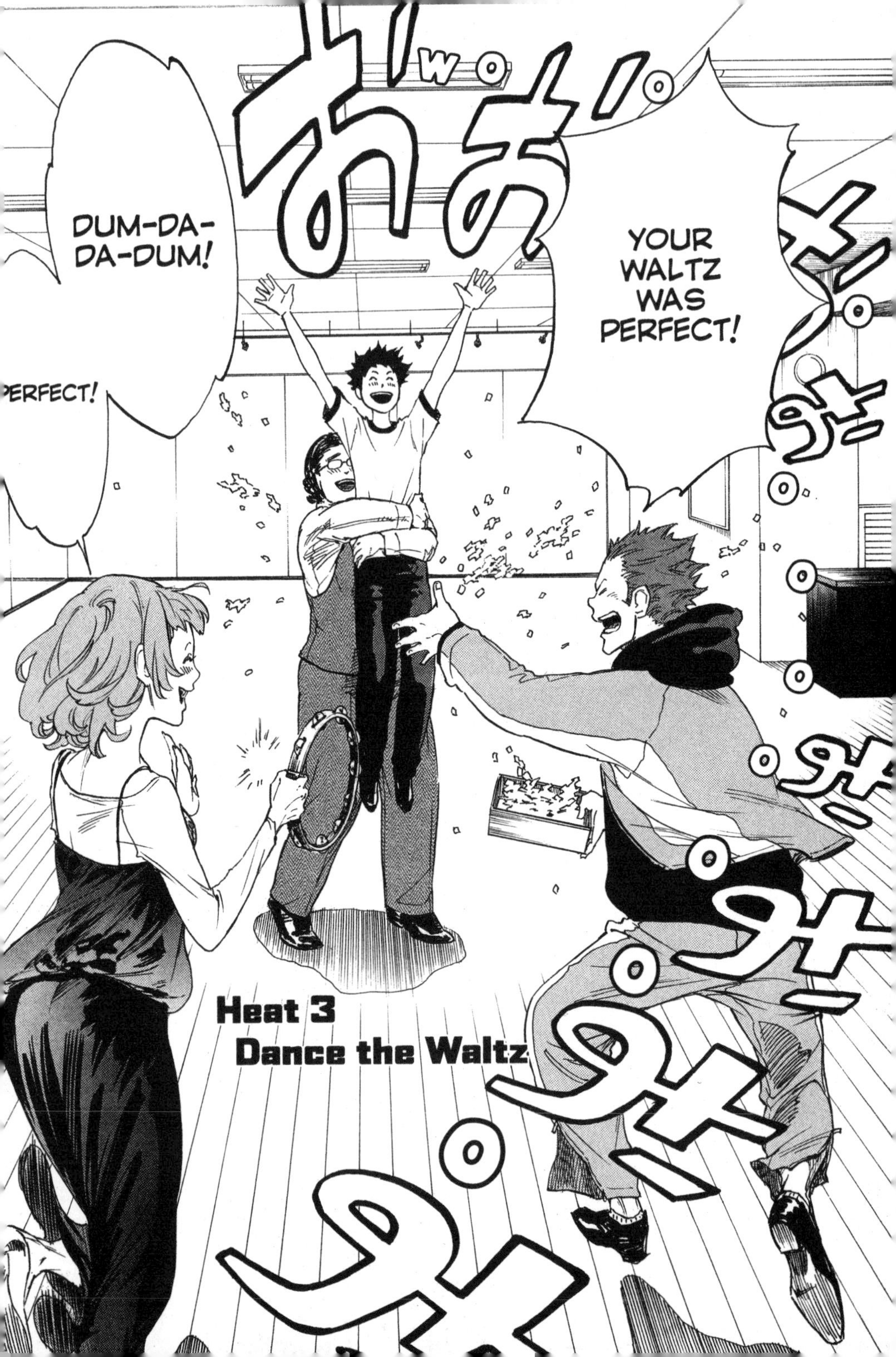
WOO
おお
YOUR WALTZ WAS PERFECT!
DUM-DA-DA-DUM!
ERFECT!
Heat 3
Dance the Waltz

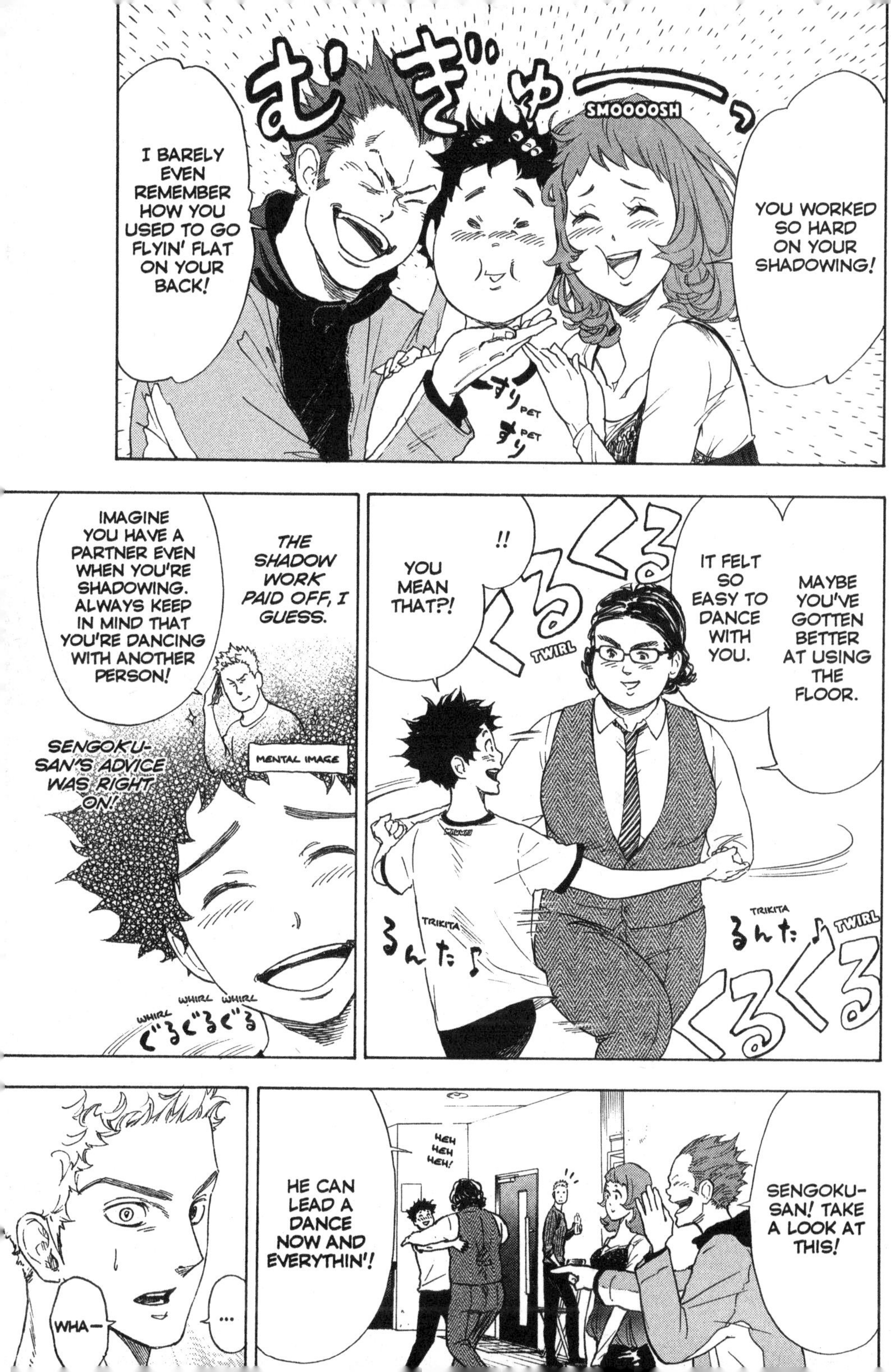
むぎゅーっ
SMOOOOSH
YOU WORKED SO HARD ON YOUR SHADOWING!
I BARELY EVEN REMEMBER HOW YOU USED TO GO FLYIN' FLAT ON YOUR BACK!
すり PET
すり PET
MAYBE YOU'VE GOTTEN BETTER AT USING THE FLOOR.
IT FELT SO EASY TO DANCE WITH YOU.
くるくる
TWIRL
!!
YOU MEAN THAT?!
るんた♪
TRIKITA
TWIRL
くるくる
るんた♪
TRIKITA
THE SHADOW WORK PAID OFF, I GUESS.
IMAGINE YOU HAVE A PARTNER EVEN WHEN YOU'RE SHADOWING. ALWAYS KEEP IN MIND THAT YOU'RE DANCING WITH ANOTHER PERSON!
MENTAL IMAGE
SENGOKU-SAN'S ADVICE WAS RIGHT ON!
WHIRL WHIRL WHIRL
ぐるぐるぐる
SENGOKU-SAN! TAKE A LOOK AT THIS!
HEH HEH HEH!
HE CAN LEAD A DANCE NOW AND EVERYTHIN'!
...
WHA—

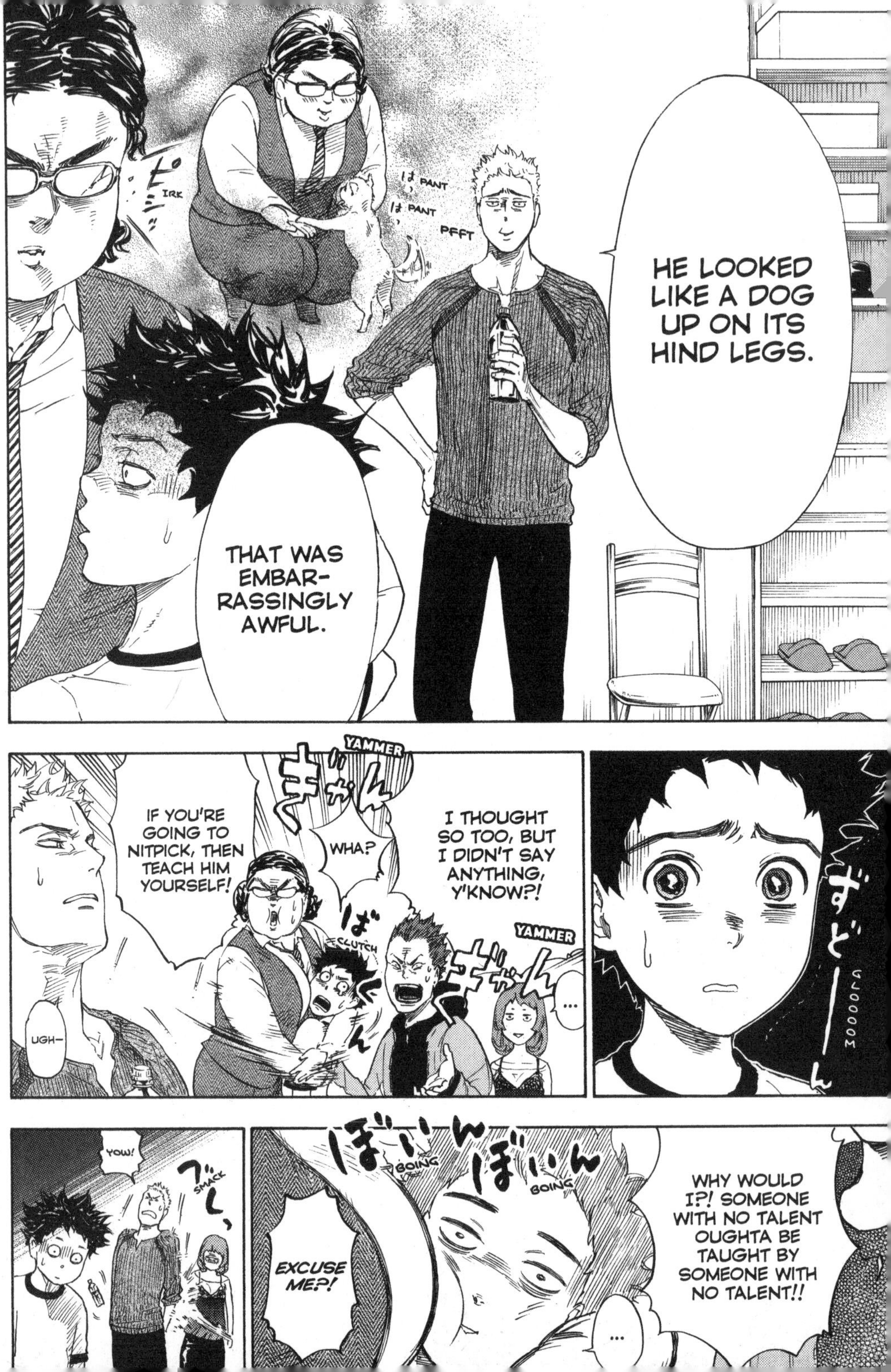
HE LOOKED LIKE A DOG UP ON ITS HIND LEGS.
PANT
PANT
PFFT
IRK
THAT WAS EMBARRASSINGLY AWFUL.
GLOOOOM
YAMMER
I THOUGHT SO TOO, BUT I DIDN'T SAY ANYTHING, Y'KNOW?!
WHA?
IF YOU'RE GOING TO NITPICK, THEN TEACH HIM YOURSELF!
CLUTCH
YAMMER
...
UGH–
WHY WOULD I?! SOMEONE WITH NO TALENT OUGHTA BE TAUGHT BY SOMEONE WITH NO TALENT!!
BOING
BOING
EXCUSE ME?!
...
SMACK
YOW!

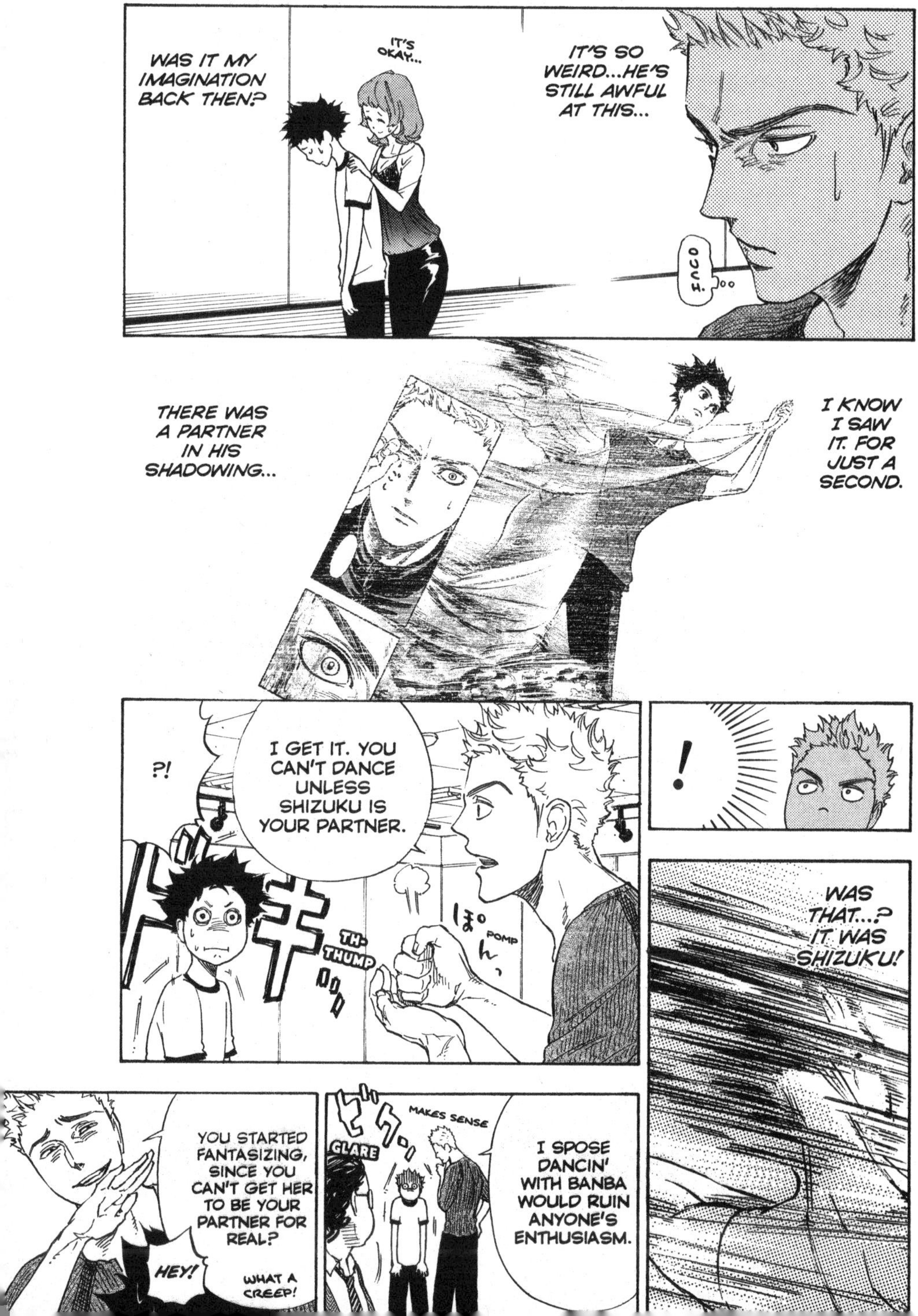
IT'S SO WEIRD...HE'S STILL AWFUL AT THIS...
OUCH.
IT'S OKAY...
WAS IT MY IMAGINATION BACK THEN?
I KNOW I SAW IT. FOR JUST A SECOND.
THERE WAS A PARTNER IN HIS SHADOWING...
!
WAS THAT...? IT WAS SHIZUKU!
I GET IT. YOU CAN'T DANCE UNLESS SHIZUKU IS YOUR PARTNER.
?!
POMP
TH-THUMP
I SPOSE DANCIN' WITH BANBA WOULD RUIN ANYONE'S ENTHUSIASM.
MAKES SENSE
GLARE
YOU STARTED FANTASIZING, SINCE YOU CAN'T GET HER TO BE YOUR PARTNER FOR REAL?
HEY!
WHAT A CREEP!

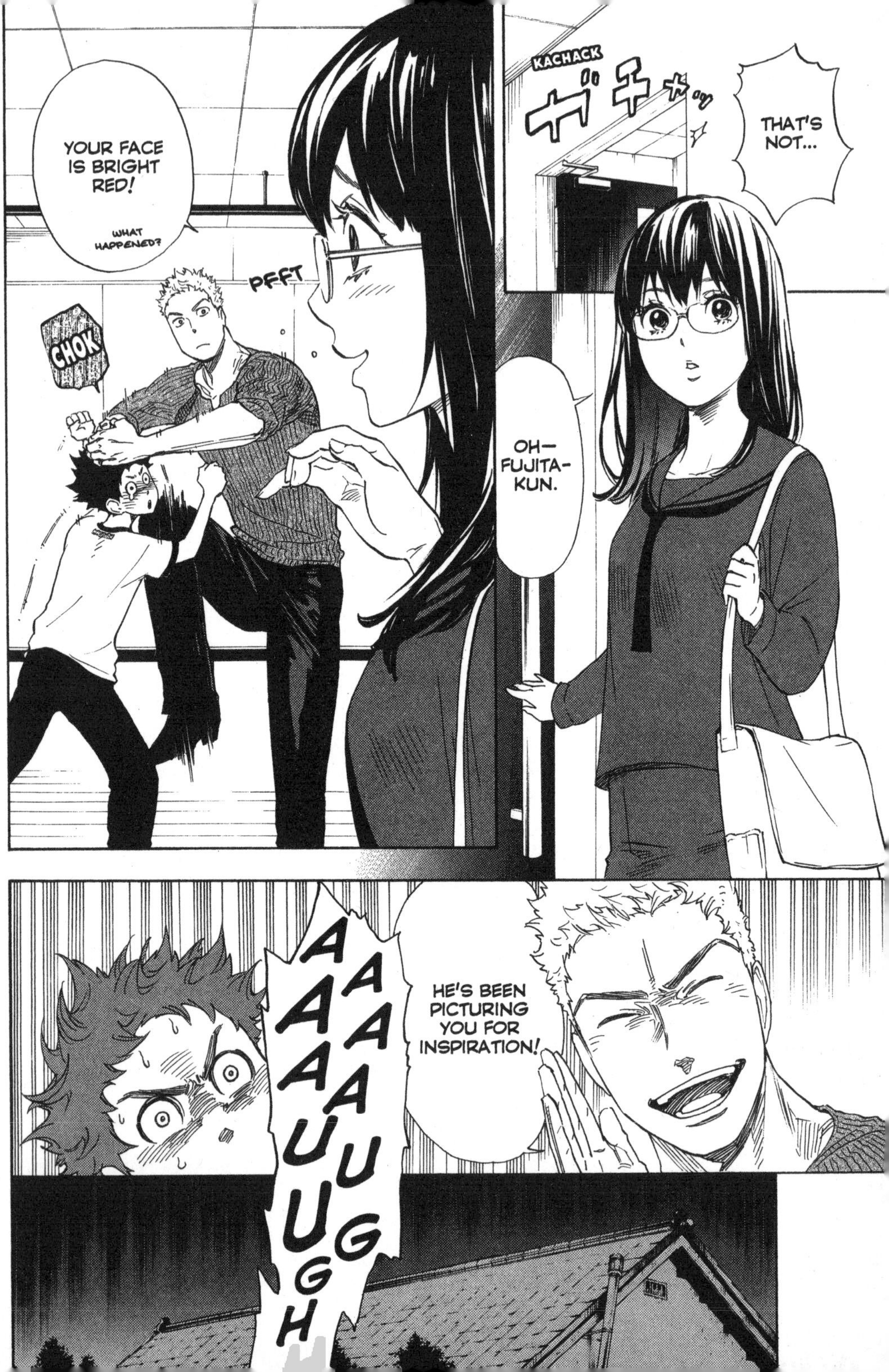
THAT'S NOT...
KACHACK
OH— FUJITA-KUN.
YOUR FACE IS BRIGHT RED!
WHAT HAPPENED?
PFFT
CHOK
HE'S BEEN PICTURING YOU FOR INSPIRATION!
AAAAAAAUUUUGGH

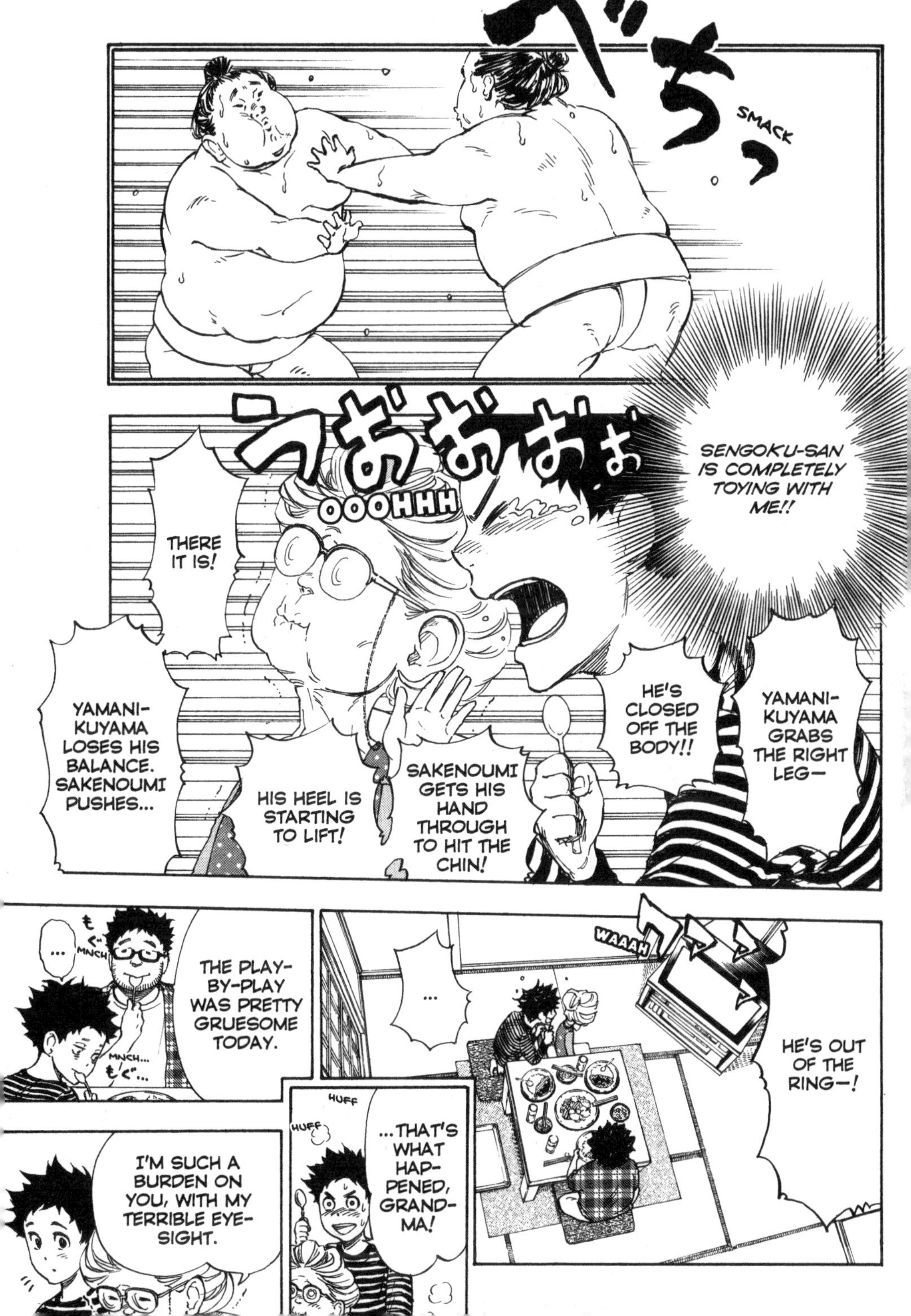
べちっ
SMACK
SENGOKU-SAN IS COMPLETELY TOYING WITH ME!!
うおおぉ
OOOHHH
YAMANI-KUYAMA GRABS THE RIGHT LEG—
HE'S CLOSED OFF THE BODY!!
SAKENOUMI GETS HIS HAND THROUGH TO HIT THE CHIN!
HIS HEEL IS STARTING TO LIFT!
THERE IT IS!
YAMANI-KUYAMA LOSES HIS BALANCE. SAKENOUMI PUSHES...
ワァァ
WAAAH
...
HE'S OUT OF THE RING—!
THE PLAY-BY-PLAY WAS PRETTY GRUESOME TODAY.
もぐ
MNCH
...
MNCH...
もぐ...
HUFF
HUFF
...THAT'S WHAT HAP-PENED, GRAND-MA!
I'M SUCH A BURDEN ON YOU, WITH MY TERRIBLE EYE-SIGHT.

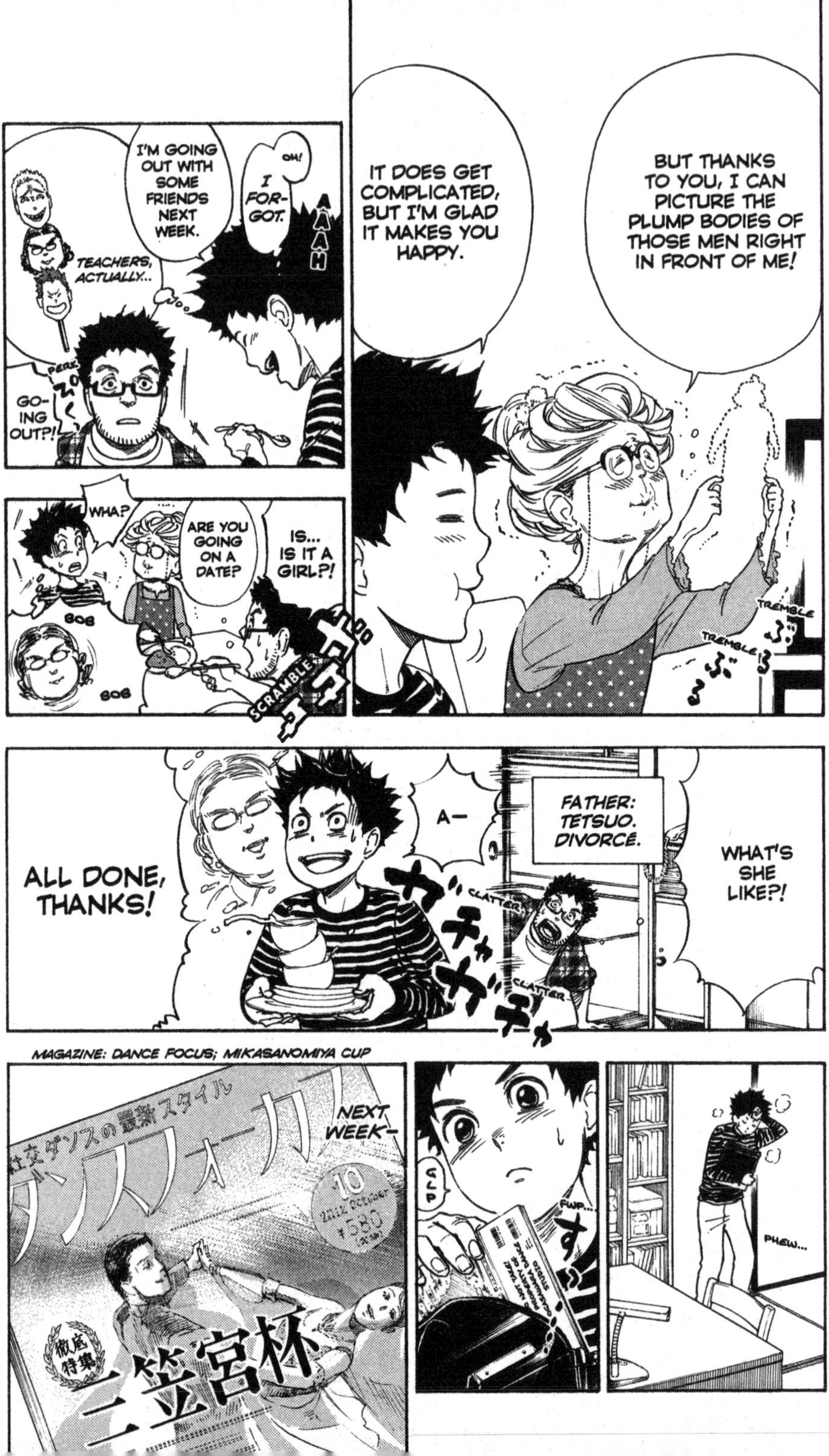

BUT THANKS TO YOU, I CAN PICTURE THE PLUMP BODIES OF THOSE MEN RIGHT IN FRONT OF ME!
IT DOES GET COMPLICATED, BUT I'M GLAD IT MAKES YOU HAPPY.
TREMBLE
TREMBLE
OH! I FORGOT.
AAAH
I'M GOING OUT WITH SOME FRIENDS NEXT WEEK.
TEACHERS, ACTUALLY...
PERK
GOING OUT?!
IS... IS IT A GIRL?!
ARE YOU GOING ON A DATE?
WHA?
BOB
BOB
SCRAMBLE
WHAT'S SHE LIKE?!
FATHER: TETSUO. DIVORCE.
A—
CLATTER
CLATTER
ALL DONE, THANKS!
MAGAZINE: DANCE FOCUS; MIKASANOMIYA CUP
PHEW...
GULP
FWP...
NEXT WEEK—
社交ダンスの最新スタイル
10
¥580
徹底特集
三笠宮杯

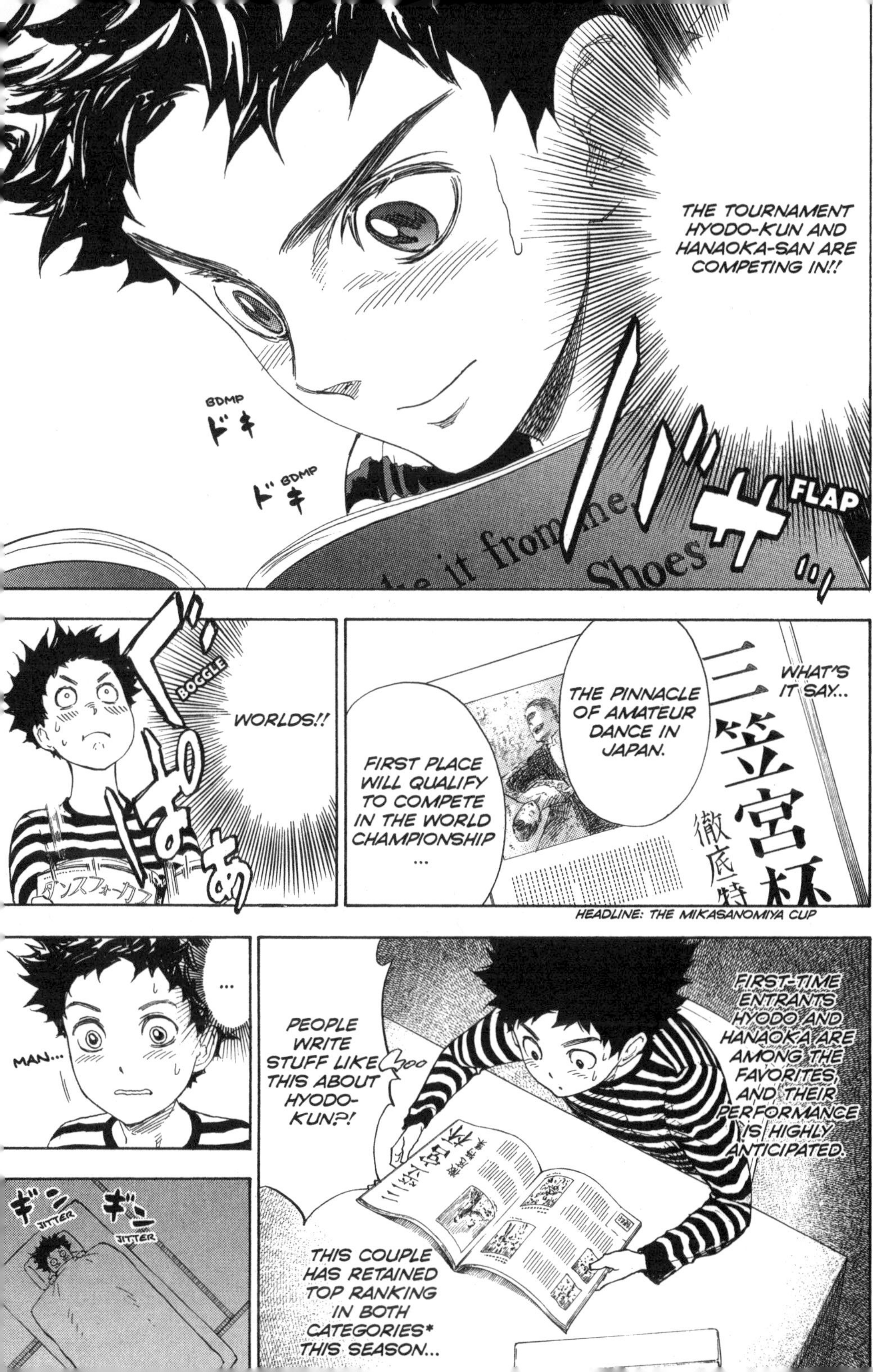
THE TOURNAMENT HYODO-KUN AND HANAOKA-SAN ARE COMPETING IN!!
FLAP
BDMP
BDMP
Shoes
ke it from me.
WHAT'S IT SAY...
THE PINNACLE OF AMATEUR DANCE IN JAPAN.
FIRST PLACE WILL QUALIFY TO COMPETE IN THE WORLD CHAMPIONSHIP ...
HEADLINE: THE MIKASANOMIYA CUP
BOGGLE
WORLDS!!
ダンスフォーカス
FIRST-TIME ENTRANTS HYODO AND HANAOKA ARE AMONG THE FAVORITES, AND THEIR PERFORMANCE IS HIGHLY ANTICIPATED.
PEOPLE WRITE STUFF LIKE THIS ABOUT HYODO-KUN?!
THIS COUPLE HAS RETAINED TOP RANKING IN BOTH CATEGORIES* THIS SEASON...
...
MAN...
JITTER
JITTER

*"STANDARD" AND "LATIN AMERICA

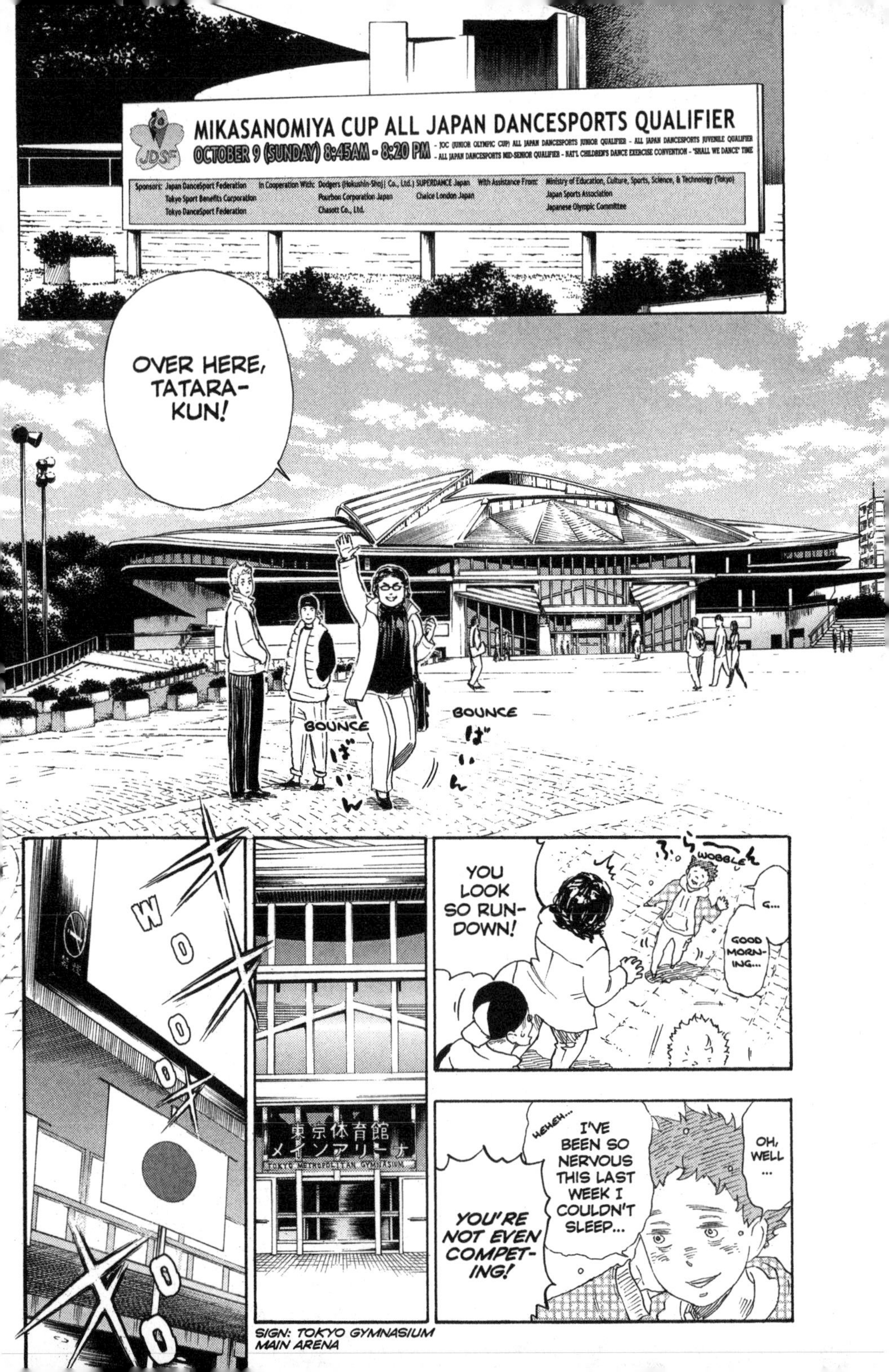
JDSF
MIKASANOMIYA CUP ALL JAPAN DANCESPORTS QUALIFIER
OCTOBER 9 (SUNDAY) 8:45AM - 8:20 PM
- JOC (JUNIOR OLYMPIC CUP) ALL JAPAN DANCESPORTS JUNIOR QUALIFIER - ALL JAPAN DANCESPORTS JUVENILE QUALIFIER
- ALL JAPAN DANCESPORTS MID-SENIOR QUALIFIER - NAT'L CHILDREN'S DANCE EXERCISE CONVENTION - "SHALL WE DANCE" TIME
Sponsors: Japan DanceSport Federation, Tokyo Sport Benefits Corporation, Tokyo DanceSport Federation
In Cooperation With: Dodgers (Hokushin-Shoji Co., Ltd.) SUPERDANCE Japan, Pourbon Corporation Japan, Chaice London Japan, Chasott Co., Ltd.
With Assistance From: Ministry of Education, Culture, Sports, Science, & Technology (Tokyo), Japan Sports Association, Japanese Olympic Committee
OVER HERE, TATARA-KUN!
BOUNCE
ばいん
BOUNCE
ばいん
YOU LOOK SO RUN-DOWN!
ふら〜ん WOBBLE
G...
GOOD MORNING...
OH, WELL...
I'VE BEEN SO NERVOUS THIS LAST WEEK I COULDN'T SLEEP...
HEHEH...
YOU'RE NOT EVEN COMPETING!
東京体育館
メインアリーナ
TOKYO METROPOLITAN GYMNASIUM
SIGN: TOKYO GYMNASIUM MAIN ARENA
WOOOOOO

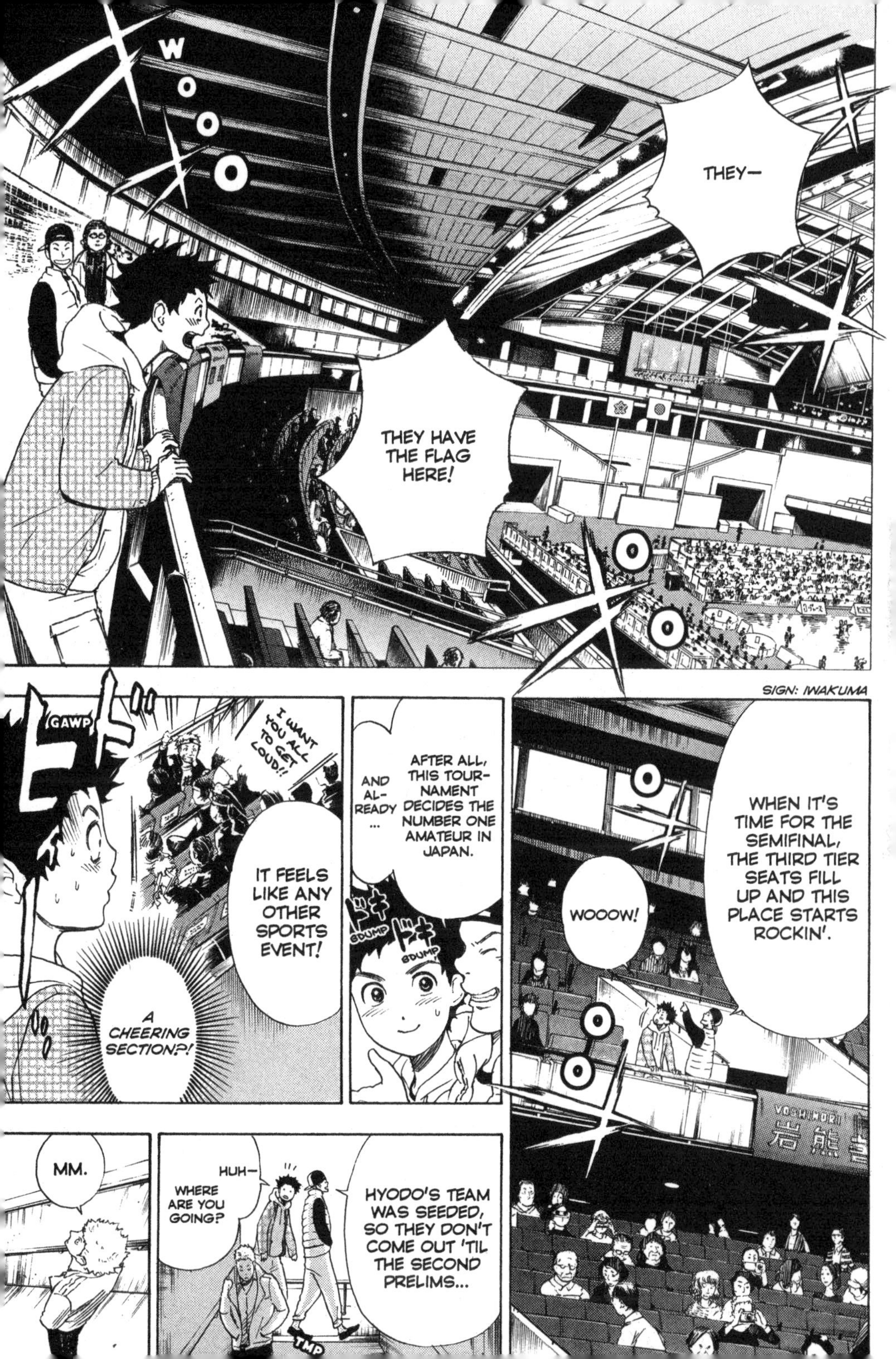
WOOOO
THEY—
THEY HAVE THE FLAG HERE!
SIGN: IWAKUMA
WHEN IT'S TIME FOR THE SEMIFINAL, THE THIRD TIER SEATS FILL UP AND THIS PLACE STARTS ROCKIN'.
WOOOW!
YOSHINORI
岩熊
AFTER ALL, THIS TOUR-NAMENT DECIDES THE NUMBER ONE AMATEUR IN JAPAN.
AND AL-READY ...
IT FEELS LIKE ANY OTHER SPORTS EVENT!
ドキ BDUMP
ドキ BDUMP
I WANT YOU ALL TO GET LOUD!!
GAWP
A CHEERING SECTION?!
HYODO'S TEAM WAS SEEDED, SO THEY DON'T COME OUT 'TIL THE SECOND PRELIMS...
HUH—
WHERE ARE YOU GOING?
TMP
MM.

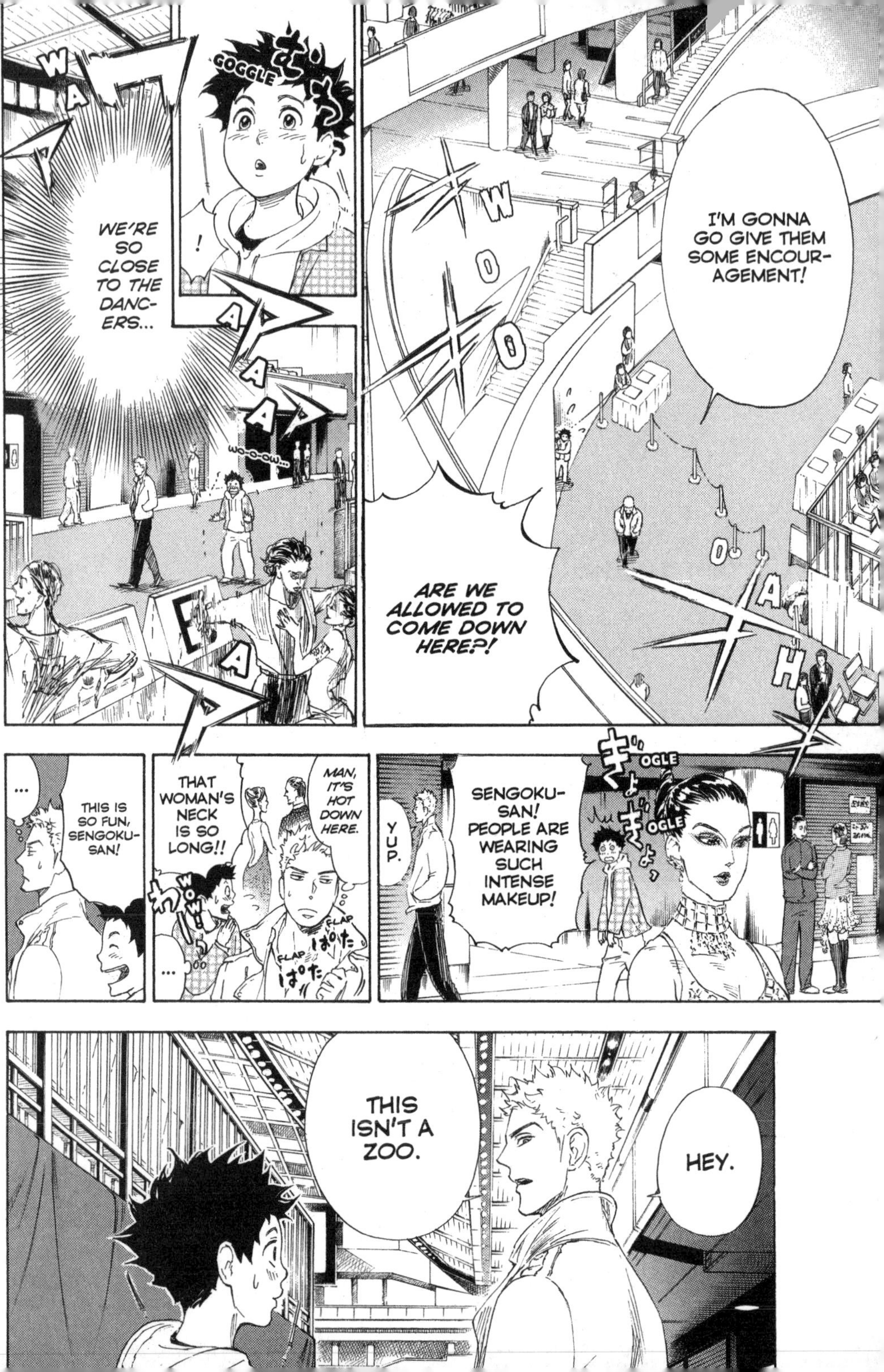
I'M GONNA GO GIVE THEM SOME ENCOURAGEMENT!
ARE WE ALLOWED TO COME DOWN HERE?!
WOOOAH
GOGGLE
!
WAAAAAAA
WE'RE SO CLOSE TO THE DANCERS...
WO-O-OW...
SENGOKU-SAN! PEOPLE ARE WEARING SUCH INTENSE MAKEUP!
OGLE
OGLE
YUP.
MAN, IT'S HOT DOWN HERE.
THAT WOMAN'S NECK IS SO LONG!!
WOW!
FLAP
FLAP
...
THIS IS SO FUN, SENGOKU-SAN!
...
HEY.
THIS ISN'T A ZOO.

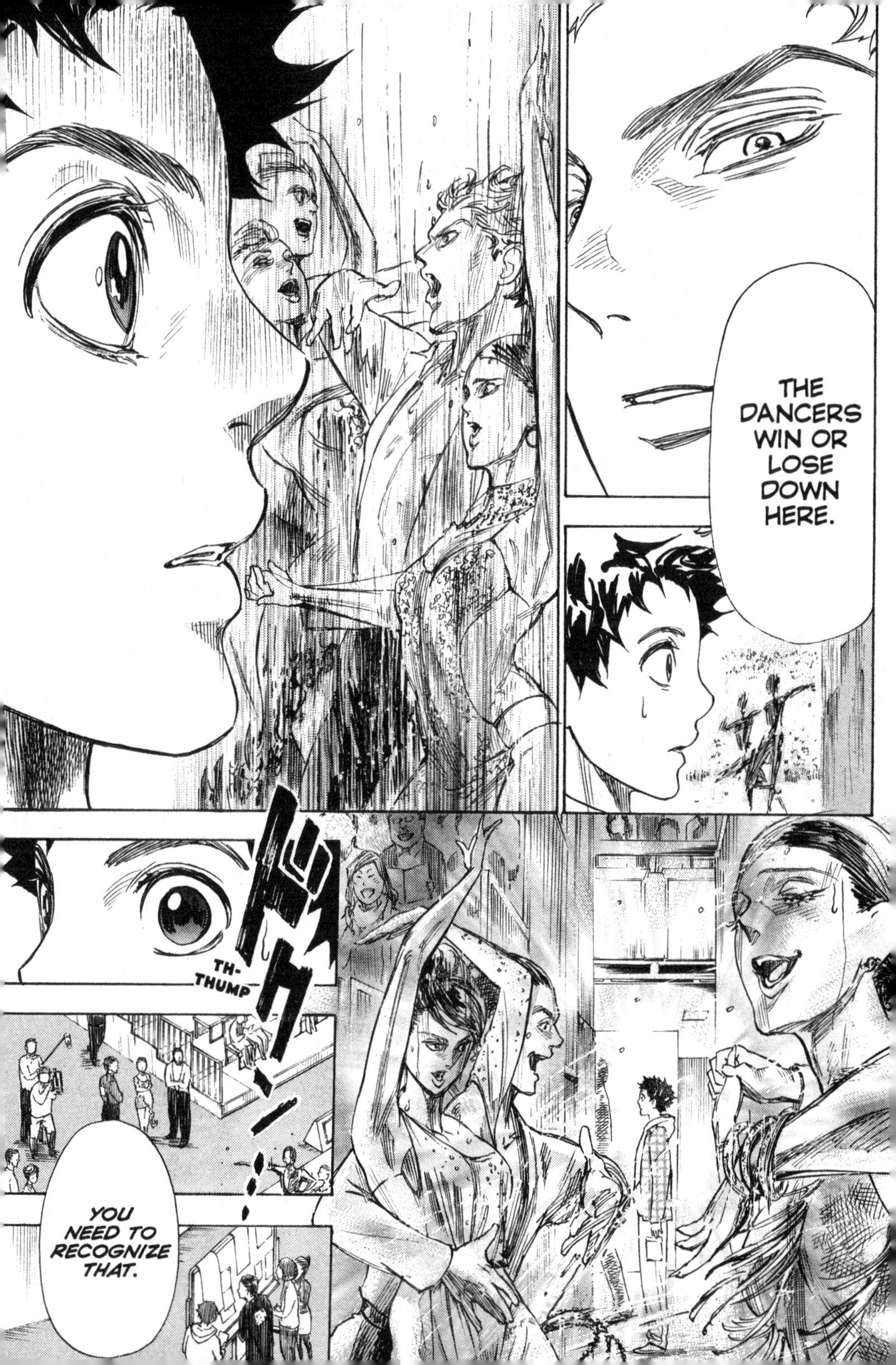
THE DANCERS WIN OR LOSE DOWN HERE.
TH-THUMP
YOU NEED TO RECOGNIZE THAT.

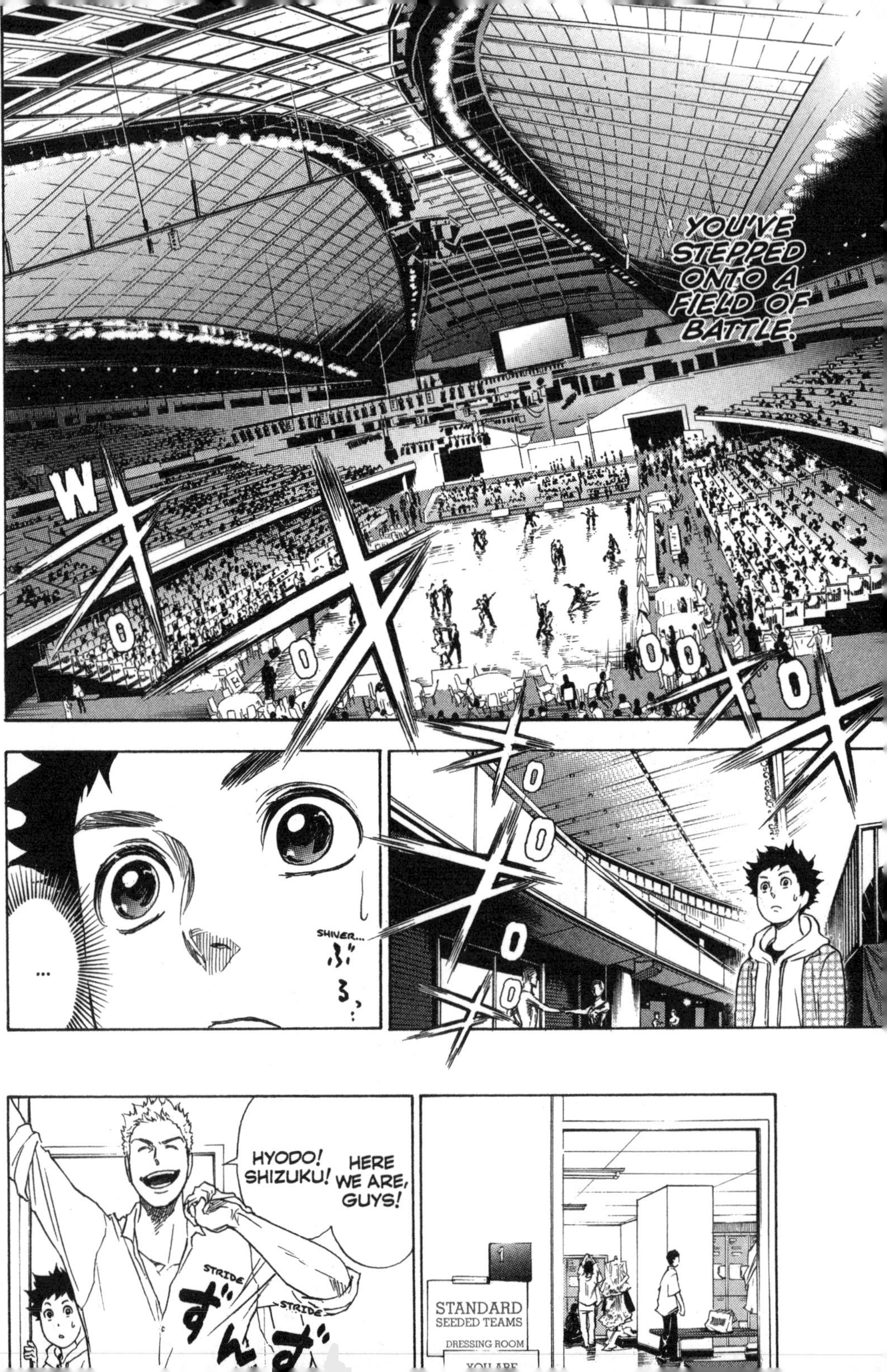
YOU'VE STEPPED ONTO A FIELD OF BATTLE.
WOOOOOOOO
OOOO
SHIVER...
ぶるっ
...
STANDARD
SEEDED TEAMS
DRESSING ROOM
HYODO! SHIZUKU! HERE WE ARE, GUYS!
STRIDE
STRIDE
ずんず

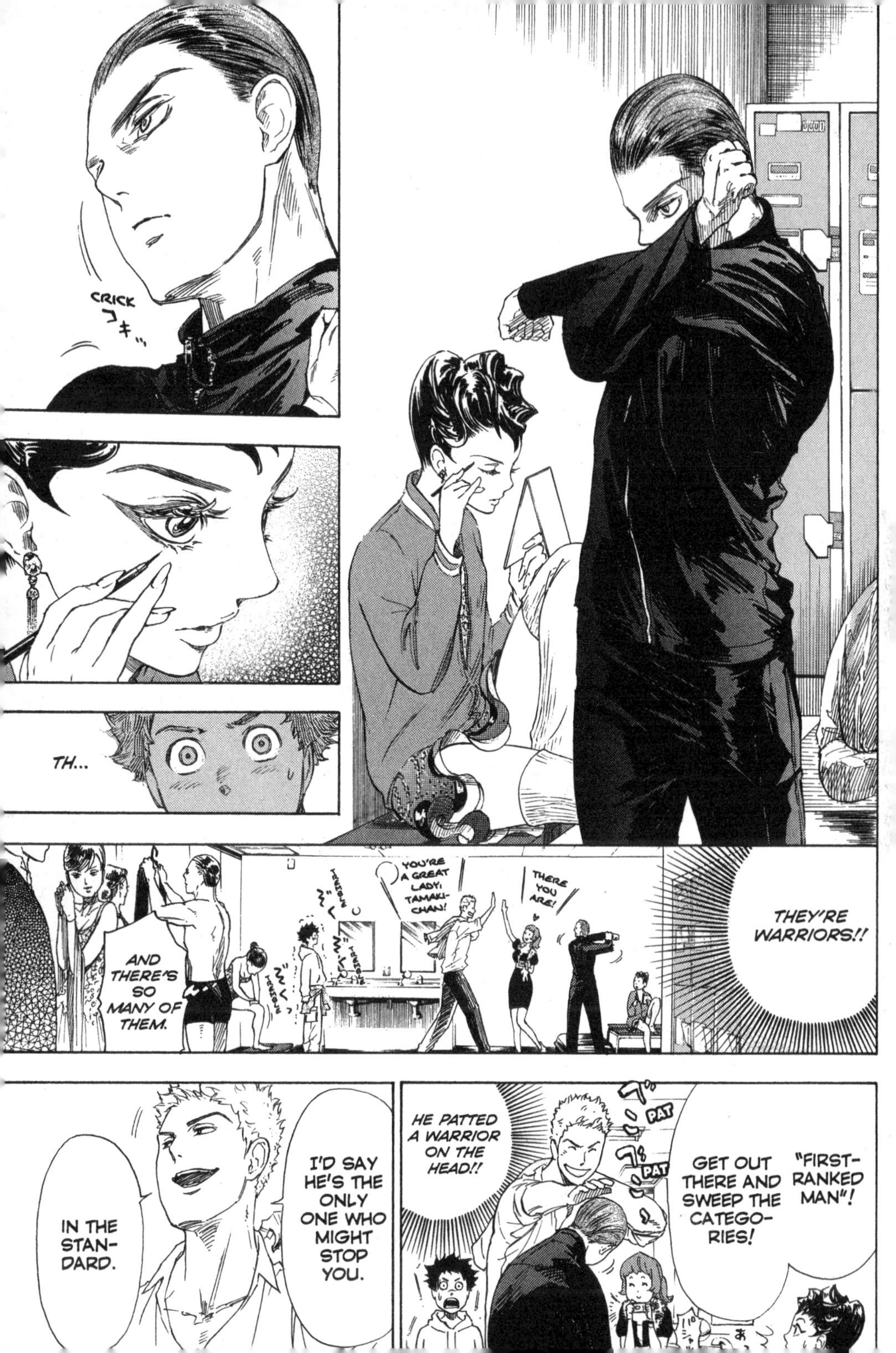
CRICK
コキッ
TH...
THEY'RE WARRIORS!!
THERE YOU ARE!
YOU'RE A GREAT LADY, TAMAKI-CHAN!
AND THERE'S SO MANY OF THEM.
"FIRST-RANKED MAN"!
GET OUT THERE AND SWEEP THE CATEGORIES!
PAT
PAT
HE PATTED A WARRIOR ON THE HEAD!!
I'D SAY HE'S THE ONLY ONE WHO MIGHT STOP YOU.
IN THE STANDARD.

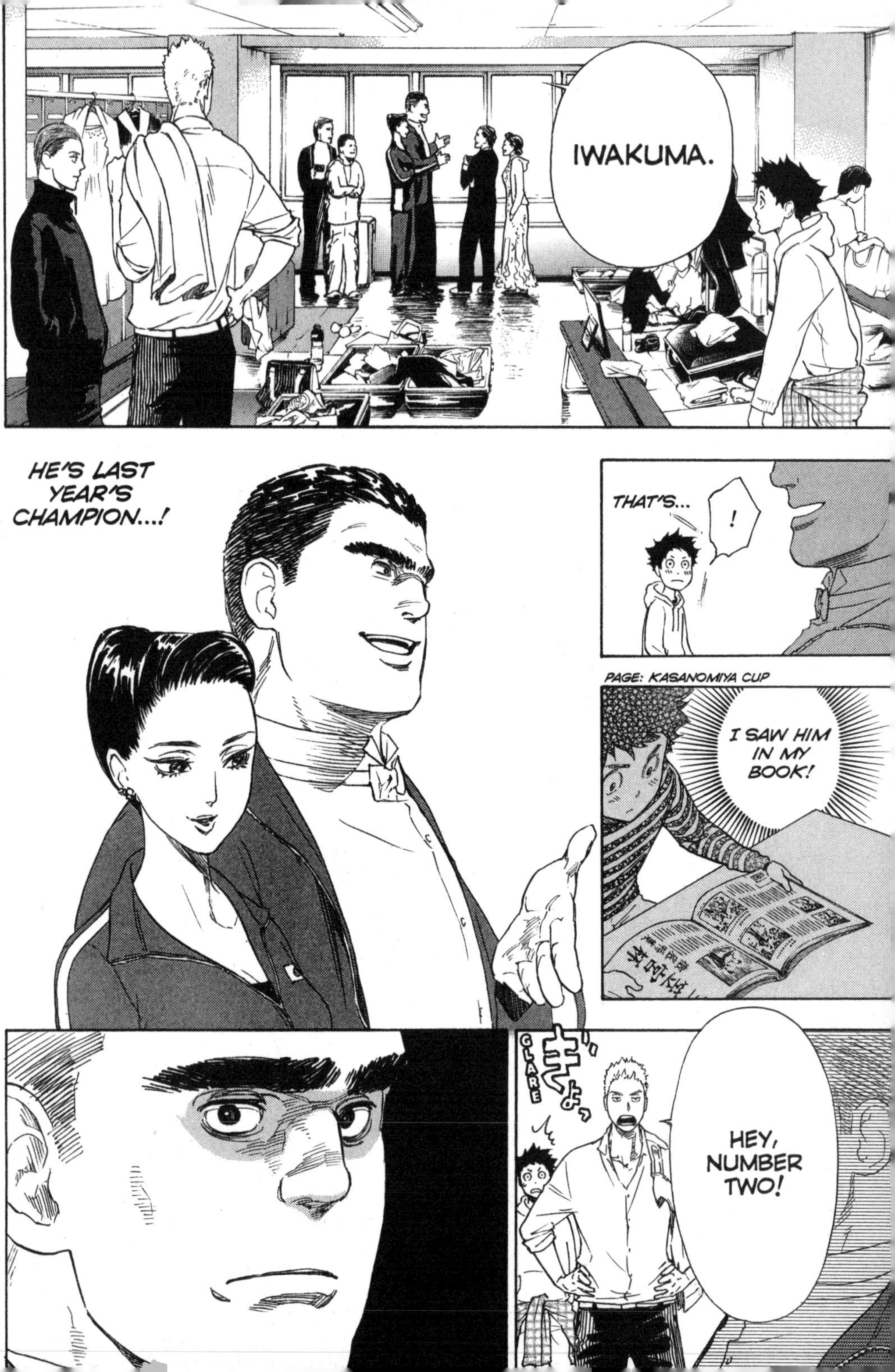
IWAKUMA.
THAT'S...
!
PAGE: KASANOMIYA CUP
I SAW HIM IN MY BOOK!
HE'S LAST YEAR'S CHAMPION...!
GLARE
HEY, NUMBER TWO!

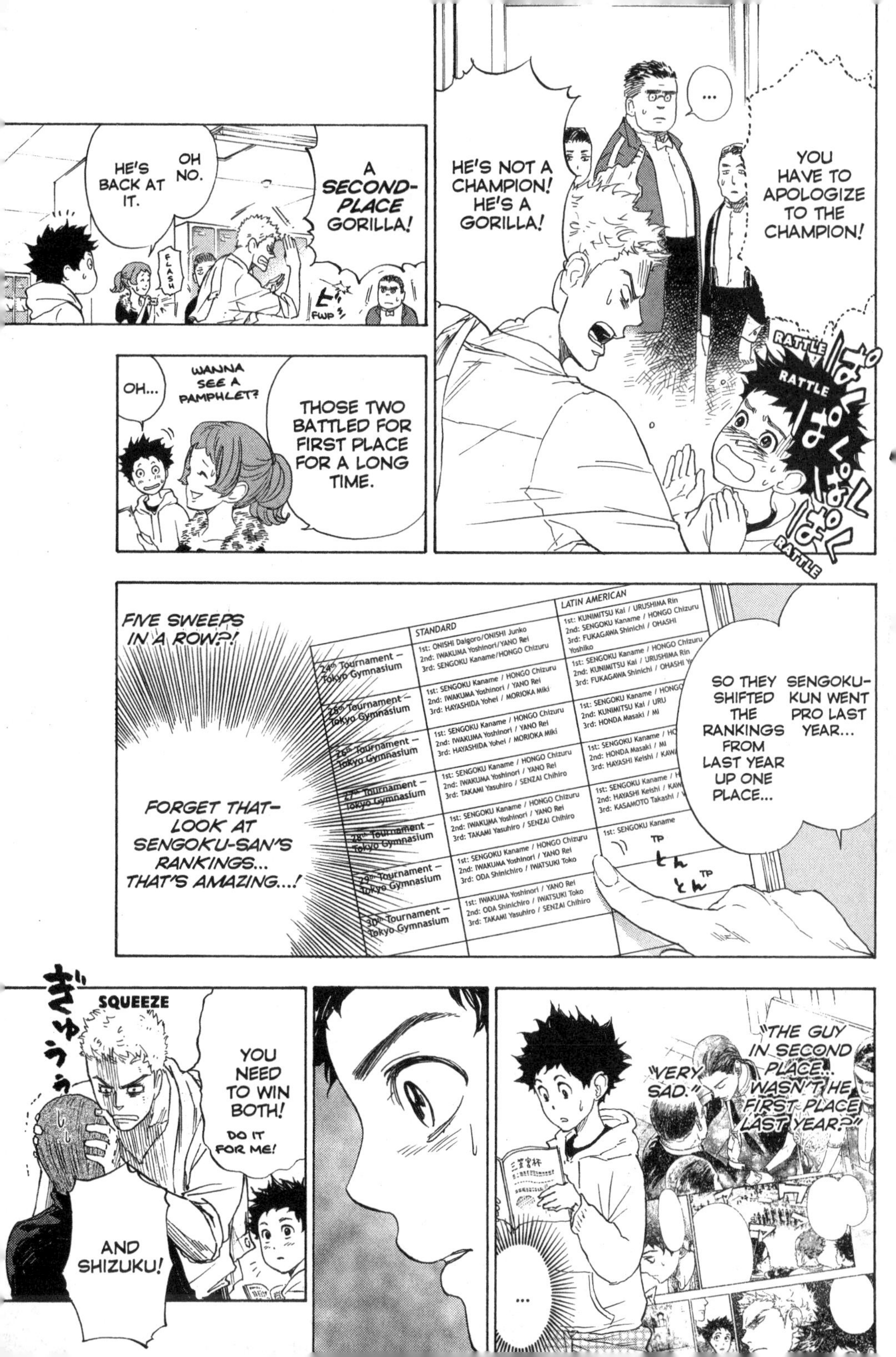
...
YOU HAVE TO APOLOGIZE TO THE CHAMPION!
HE'S NOT A CHAMPION! HE'S A GORILLA!
RATTLE
RATTLE
RATTLE
A SECOND-PLACE GORILLA!
OH NO.
HE'S BACK AT IT.
FLASH
FWP
THOSE TWO BATTLED FOR FIRST PLACE FOR A LONG TIME.
WANNA SEE A PAMPHLET?
OH...
SENGOKU-KUN WENT PRO LAST YEAR...
SO THEY SHIFTED THE RANKINGS FROM LAST YEAR UP ONE PLACE...
STANDARD
LATIN AMERICAN
24th Tournament – Tokyo Gymnasium
1st: ONISHI Daigoro/ONISHI Junko
2nd: IWAKUMA Yoshinori/YANO Rei
3rd: SENGOKU Kaname/HONGO Chizuru
1st: KUNIMITSU Kai / URUSHIMA Rin
2nd: SENGOKU Kaname / HONGO Chizuru
3rd: FUKAGAWA Shinichi / OHASHI Yoshiko
25th Tournament – Tokyo Gymnasium
1st: SENGOKU Kaname / HONGO Chizuru
2nd: IWAKUMA Yoshinori / YANO Rei
3rd: HAYASHIDA Yohei / MORIOKA Miki
1st: SENGOKU Kaname / HONGO Chizuru
2nd: KUNIMITSU Kai / URUSHIMA Rin
3rd: FUKAGAWA Shinichi / OHASHI Y
26th Tournament – Tokyo Gymnasium
1st: SENGOKU Kaname / HONGO Chizuru
2nd: IWAKUMA Yoshinori / YANO Rei
3rd: HAYASHIDA Yohei / MORIOKA Miki
1st: SENGOKU Kaname / HONGO
2nd: KUNIMITSU Kai / URU
3rd: HONDA Masaki / MI
27th Tournament – Tokyo Gymnasium
1st: SENGOKU Kaname / HONGO Chizuru
2nd: IWAKUMA Yoshinori / YANO Rei
3rd: TAKAMI Yasuhiro / SENZAI Chihiro
1st: SENGOKU Kaname / HO
2nd: HONDA Masaki / MI
3rd: HAYASHI Keishi / KAWA
28th Tournament – Tokyo Gymnasium
1st: SENGOKU Kaname / HONGO Chizuru
2nd: IWAKUMA Yoshinori / YANO Rei
3rd: TAKAMI Yasuhiro / SENZAI Chihiro
1st: SENGOKU Kaname / H
2nd: HAYASHI Keishi / KAW
3rd: KASAMOTO Takashi / V
29th Tournament – Tokyo Gymnasium
1st: SENGOKU Kaname / HONGO Chizuru
2nd: IWAKUMA Yoshinori / YANO Rei
3rd: ODA Shinichiro / IWATSUKI Toko
1st: SENGOKU Kaname
30th Tournament – Tokyo Gymnasium
1st: IWAKUMA Yoshinori / YANO Rei
2nd: ODA Shinichiro / IWATSUKI Toko
3rd: TAKAMI Yasuhiro / SENZAI Chihiro
TP
TP
FIVE SWEEPS IN A ROW?!
FORGET THAT—LOOK AT SENGOKU-SAN'S RANKINGS... THAT'S AMAZING...!
"THE GUY IN SECOND PLACE... WASN'T HE FIRST PLACE LAST YEAR?"
"VERY SAD."
...
SQUEEZE
YOU NEED TO WIN BOTH!
DO IT FOR ME!
AND SHIZUKU!

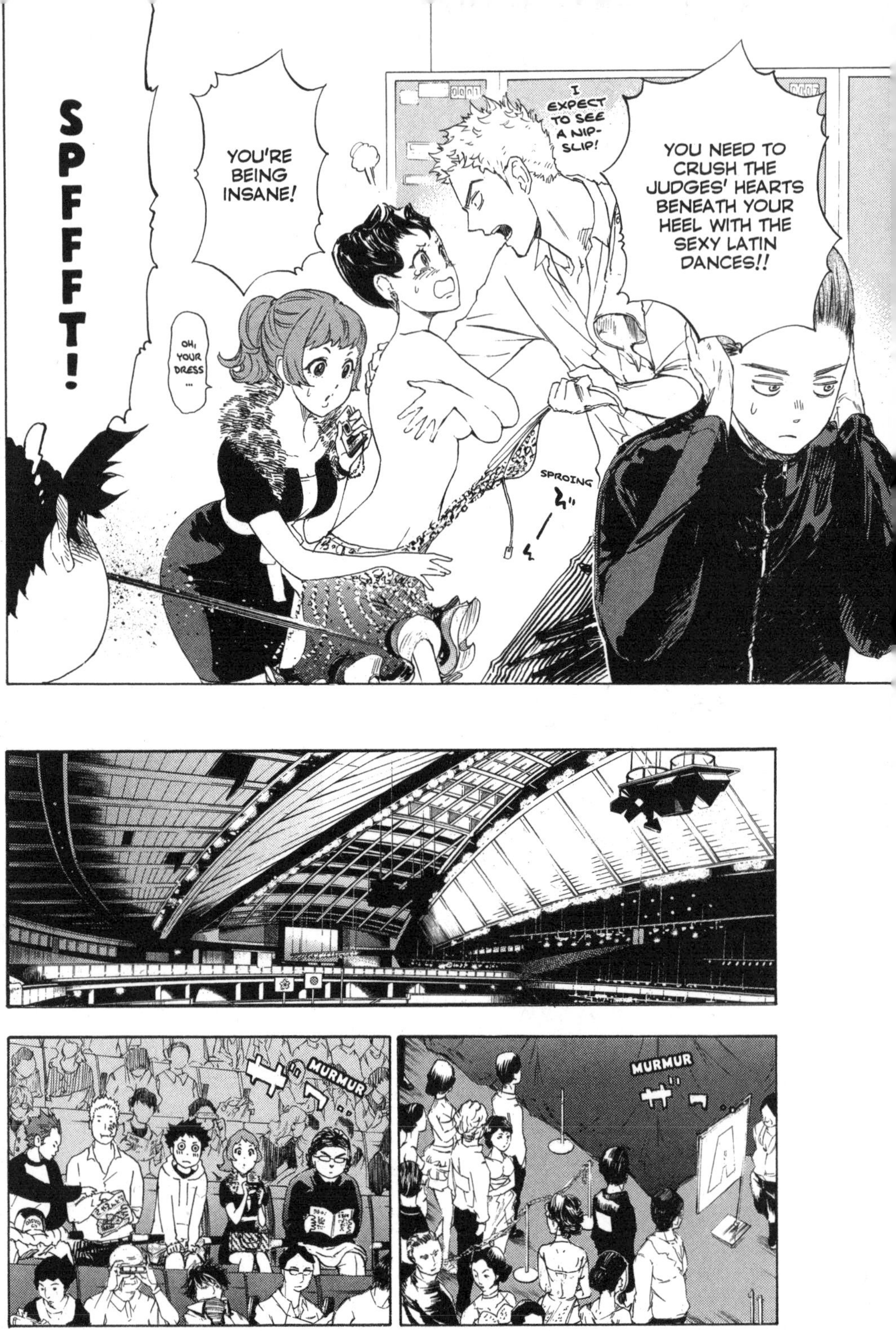
YOU NEED TO CRUSH THE JUDGES' HEARTS BENEATH YOUR HEEL WITH THE SEXY LATIN DANCES!!
I EXPECT TO SEE A NIP-SLIP!
YOU'RE BEING INSANE!
SPROING
OH, YOUR DRESS...
SPFFFT!
MURMUR
MURMUR

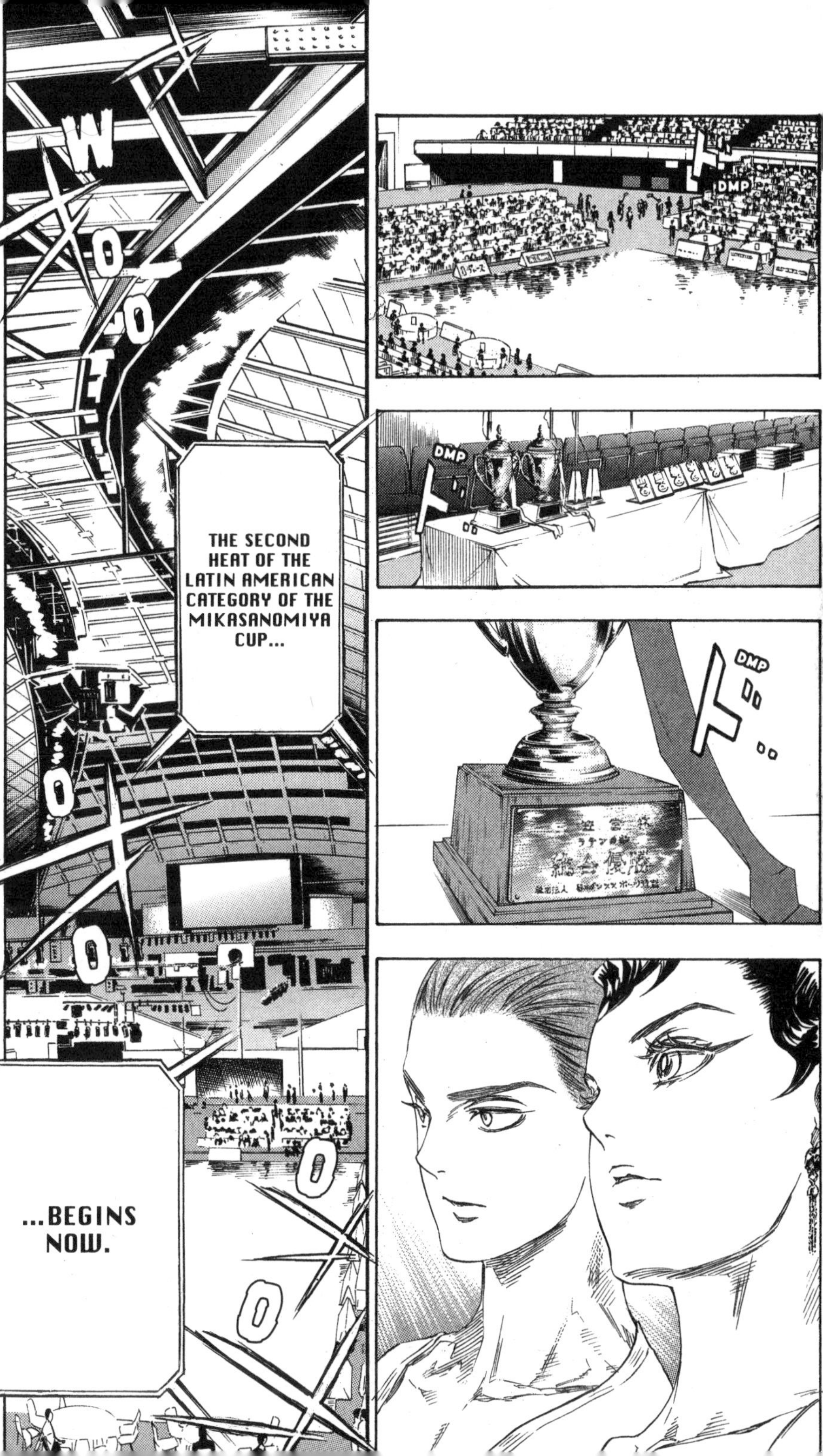
DMP
DMP
DMP
WOOOOOO
THE SECOND HEAT OF THE LATIN AMERICAN CATEGORY OF THE MIKASANOMIYA CUP...
...BEGINS NOW.

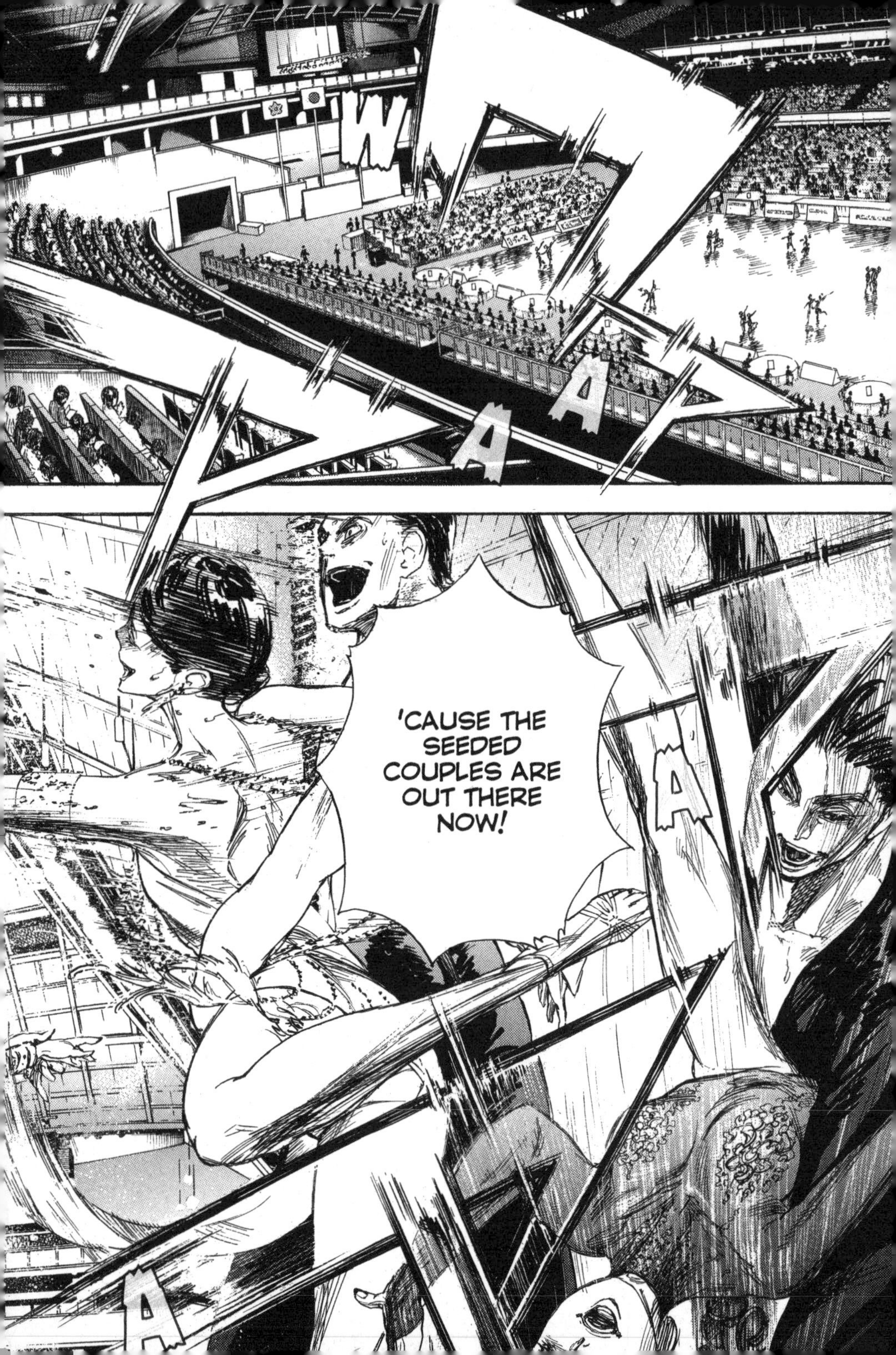
WAAAA
'CAUSE THE SEEDED COUPLES ARE OUT THERE NOW!

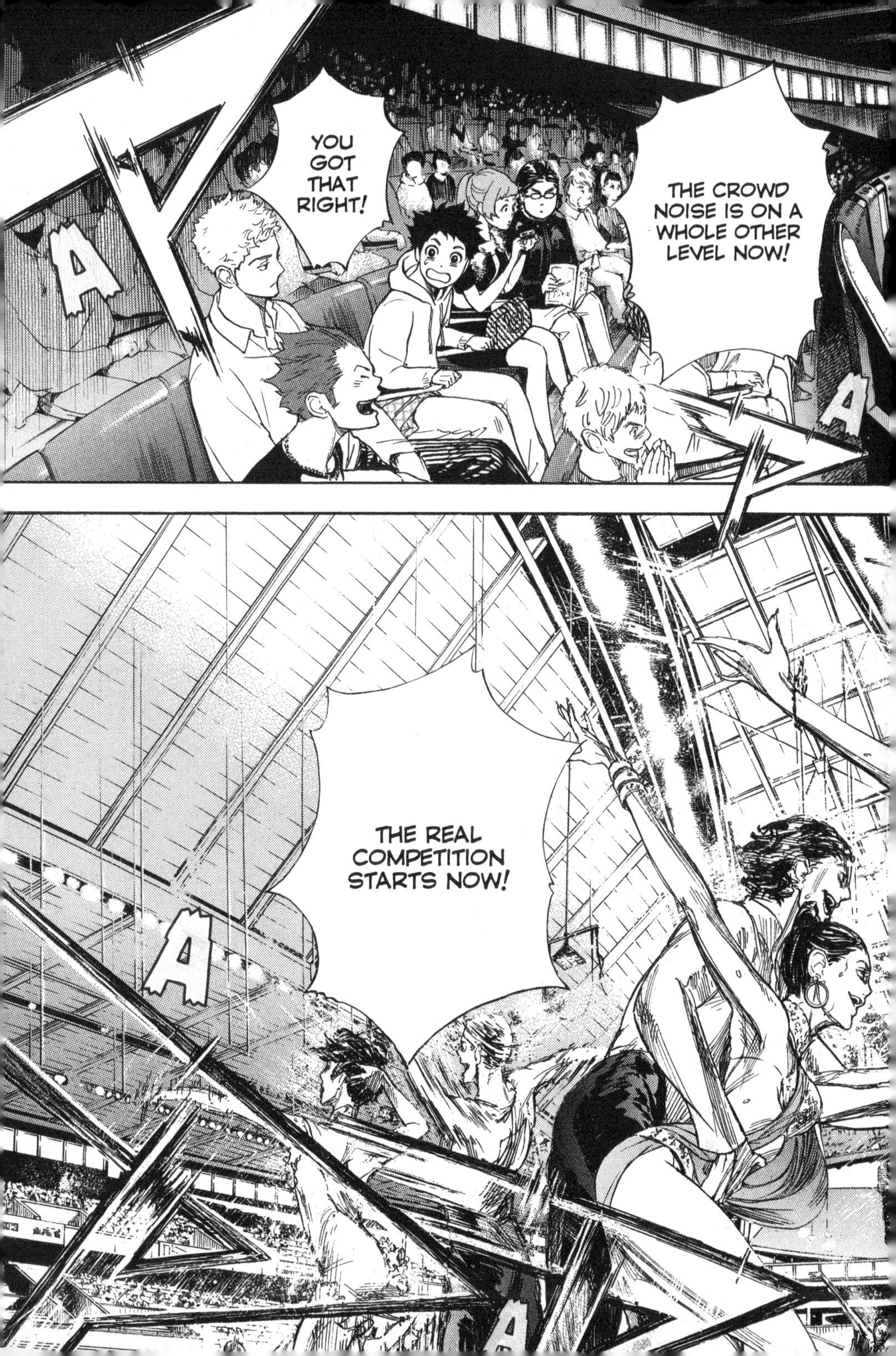
THE CROWD NOISE IS ON A WHOLE OTHER LEVEL NOW!
YOU GOT THAT RIGHT!
THE REAL COMPETITION STARTS NOW!

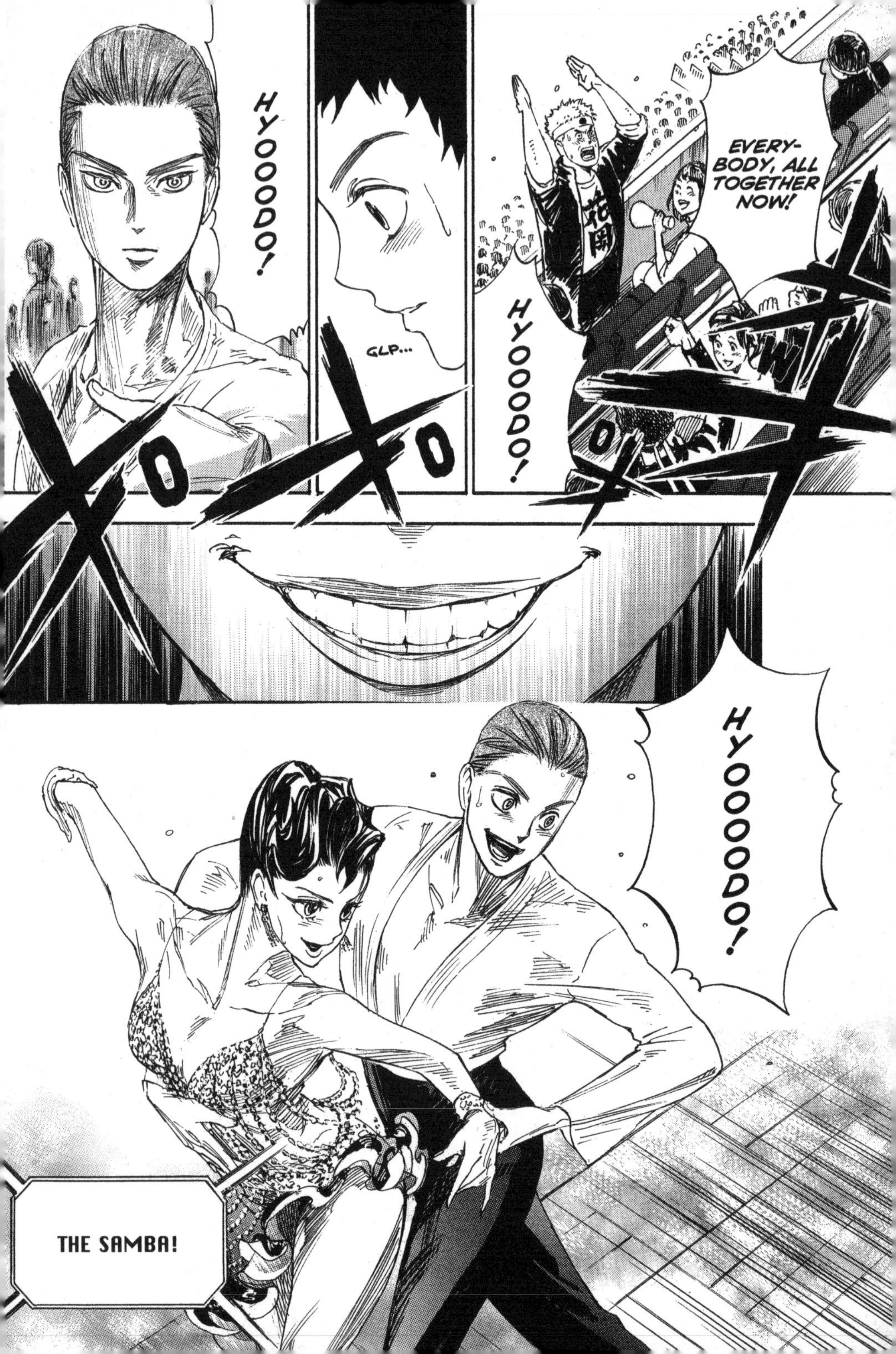
EVERY-BODY, ALL TOGETHER NOW!
HYOOOODO!
GLP...
HYOOOODO!
HYOOOOODO!
THE SAMBA!

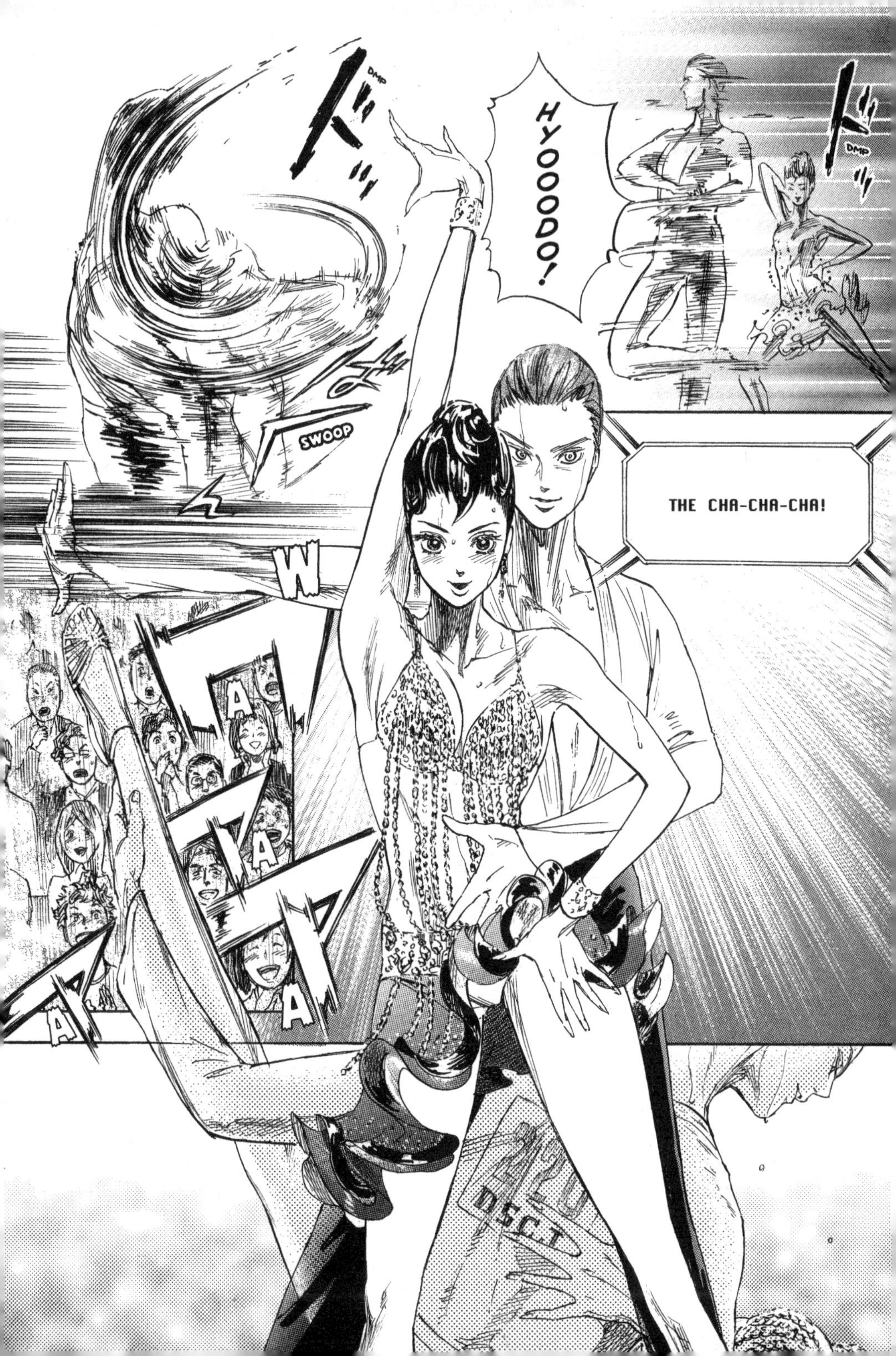
DMP
HYOOODO!
DMP
SWOOP
THE CHA-CHA-CHA!
WAAAAAA

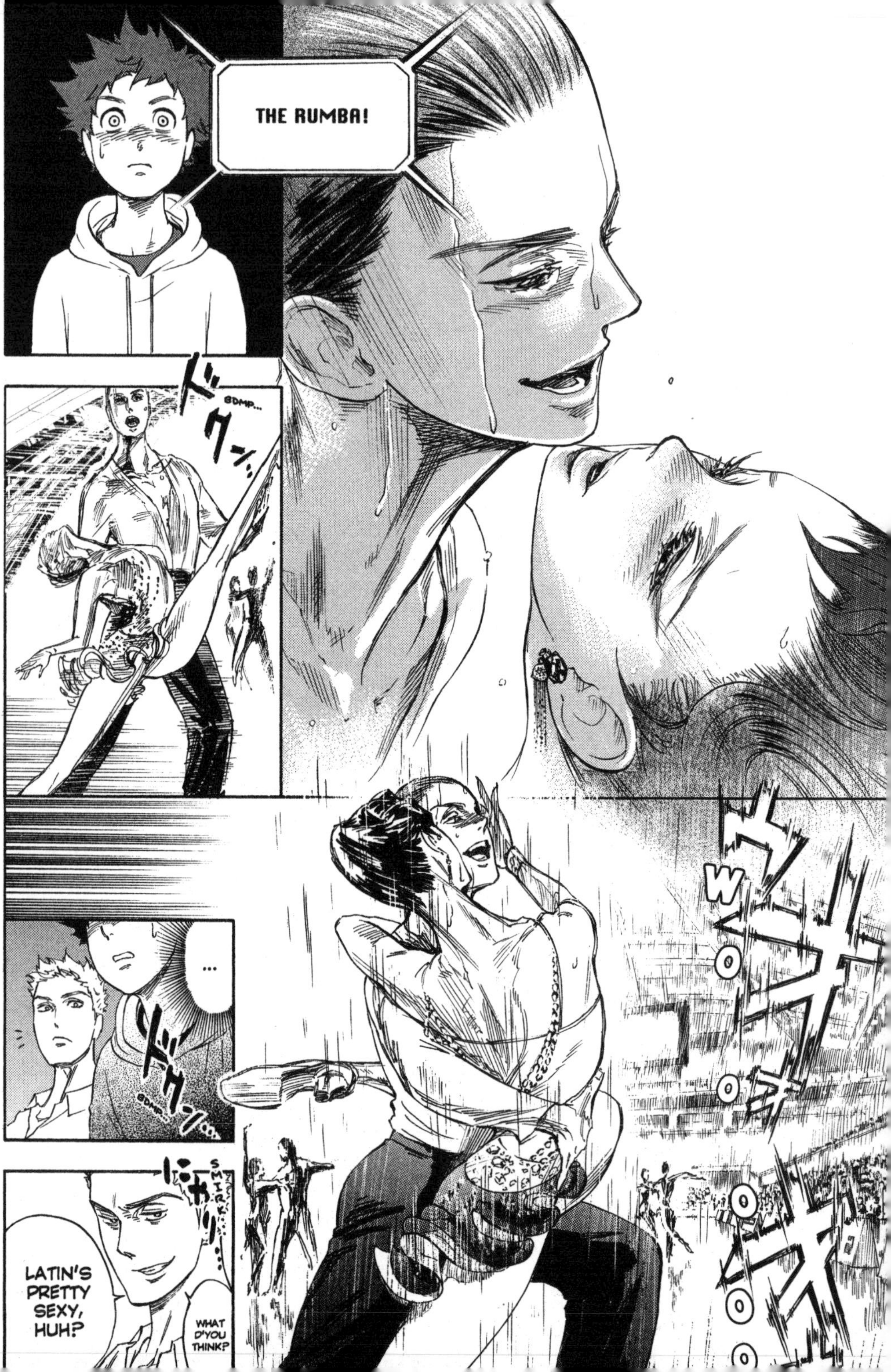
THE RUMBA!
SDMP...
WOOOOO
...
SDMP...
SMIRK
LATIN'S PRETTY SEXY, HUH?
WHAT D'YOU THINK?

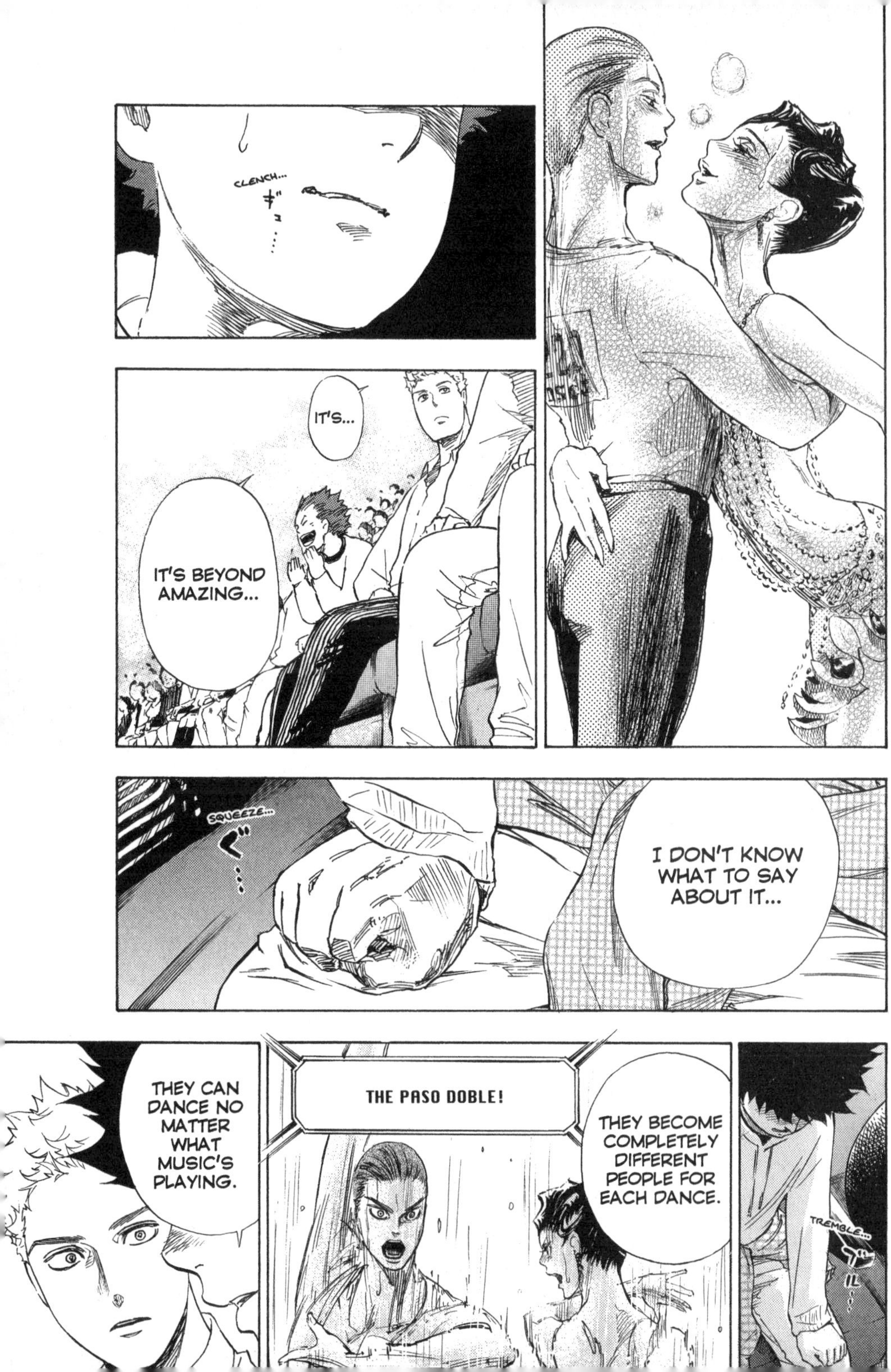
CLENCH...
IT'S...
IT'S BEYOND AMAZING...
I DON'T KNOW WHAT TO SAY ABOUT IT...
SQUEEZE...
TREMBLE...
THE PASO DOBLE!
THEY BECOME COMPLETELY DIFFERENT PEOPLE FOR EACH DANCE.
THEY CAN DANCE NO MATTER WHAT MUSIC'S PLAYING.

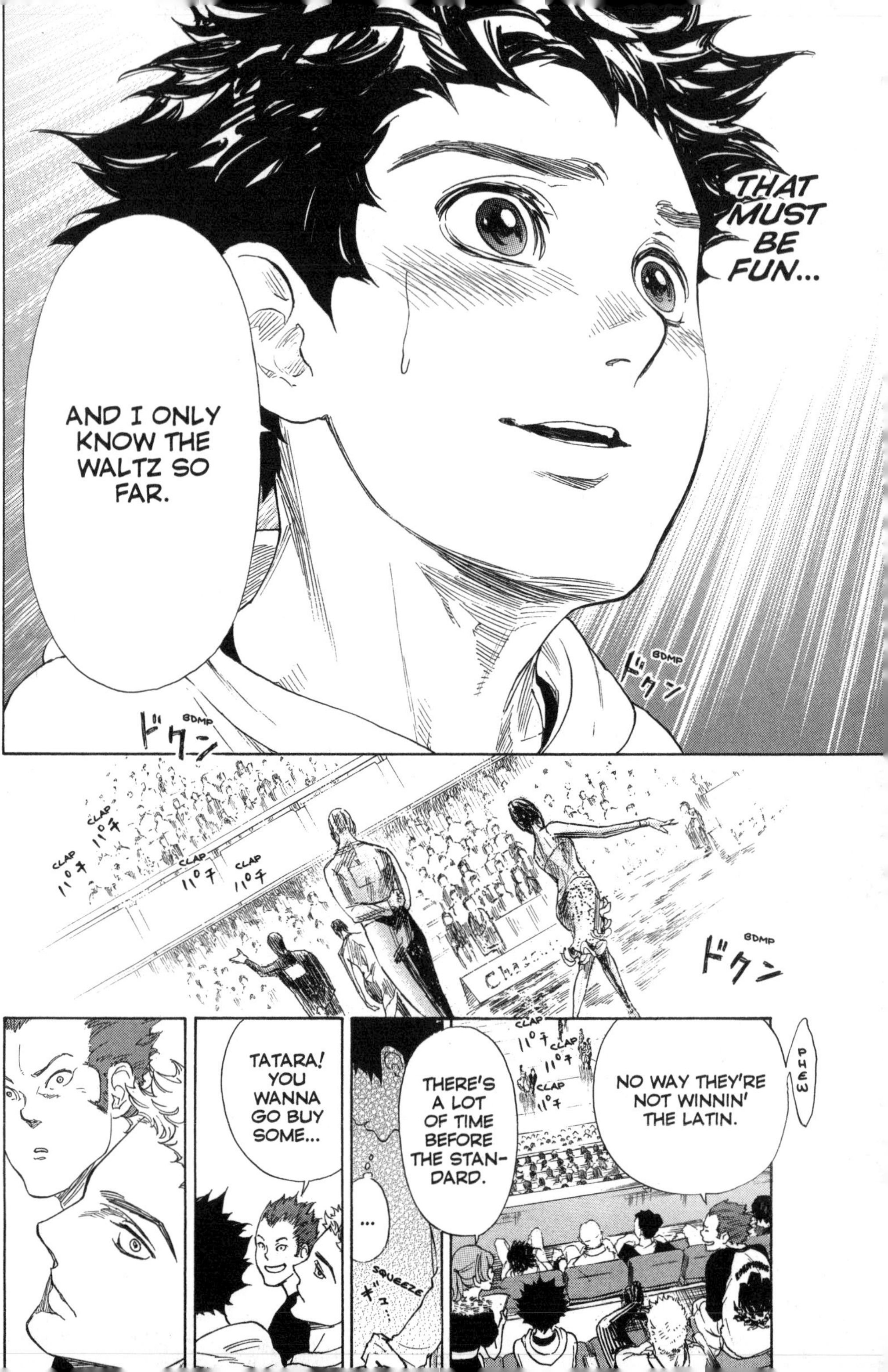
THAT MUST BE FUN...
BDMP
ドクン
AND I ONLY KNOW THE WALTZ SO FAR.
BDMP
ドクン
BDMP
ドクン
CLAP
パチ
CLAP
パチ
CLAP
パチ
CLAP
パチ
PHEW
NO WAY THEY'RE NOT WINNIN' THE LATIN.
CLAP
パチ
CLAP
パチ
CLAP
パチ
THERE'S A LOT OF TIME BEFORE THE STANDARD.
...
SQUEEZE
ギュ
TATARA! YOU WANNA GO BUY SOME...

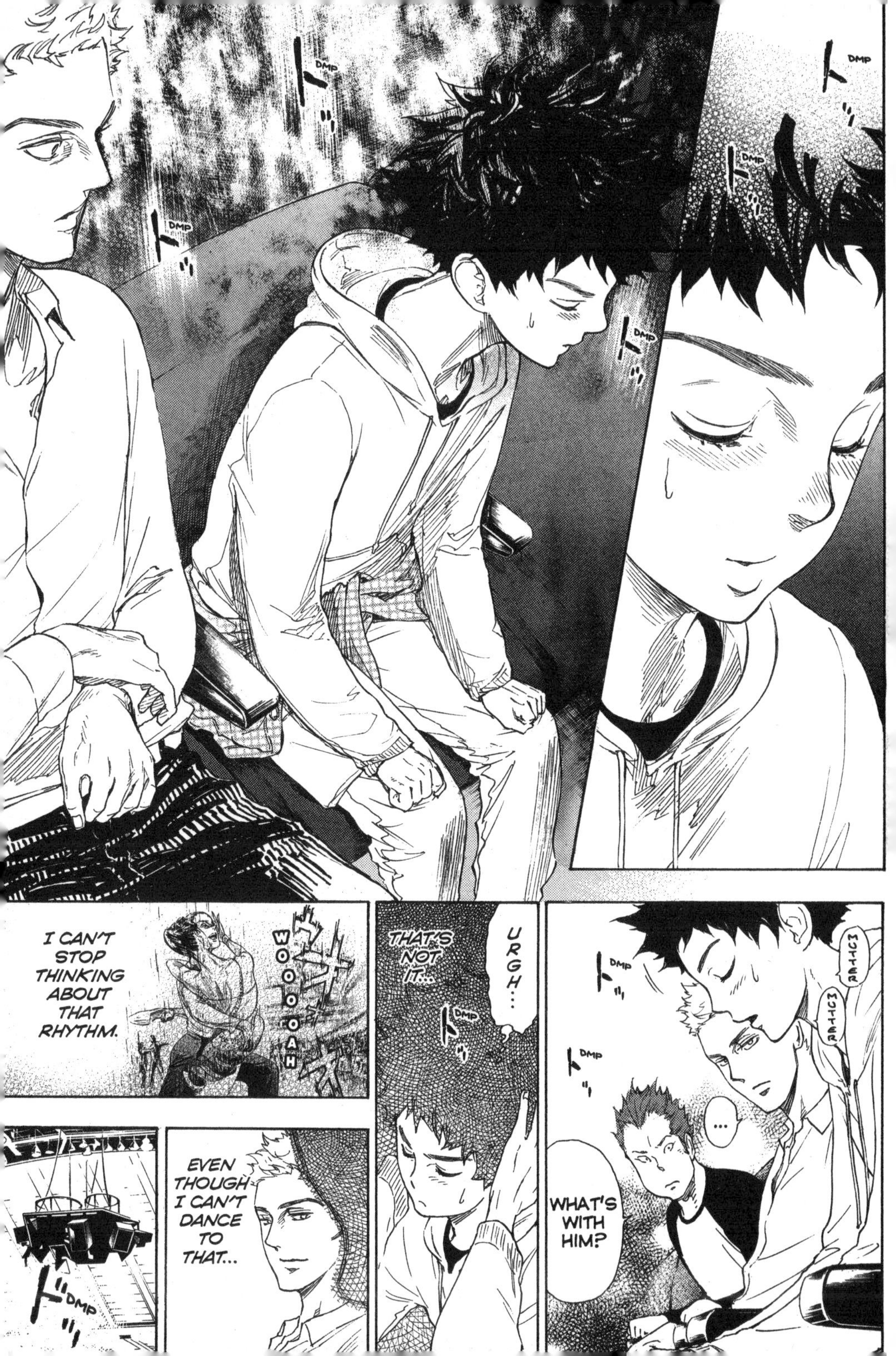
DMP
DMP
DMP
DMP
DMP
MUTTER
MUTTER
DMP
DMP
...
WHAT'S WITH HIM?
URGH...
THAT'S NOT IT...
DMP
WOOOOOAH
I CAN'T STOP THINKING ABOUT THAT RHYTHM.
EVEN THOUGH I CAN'T DANCE TO THAT...
DMP

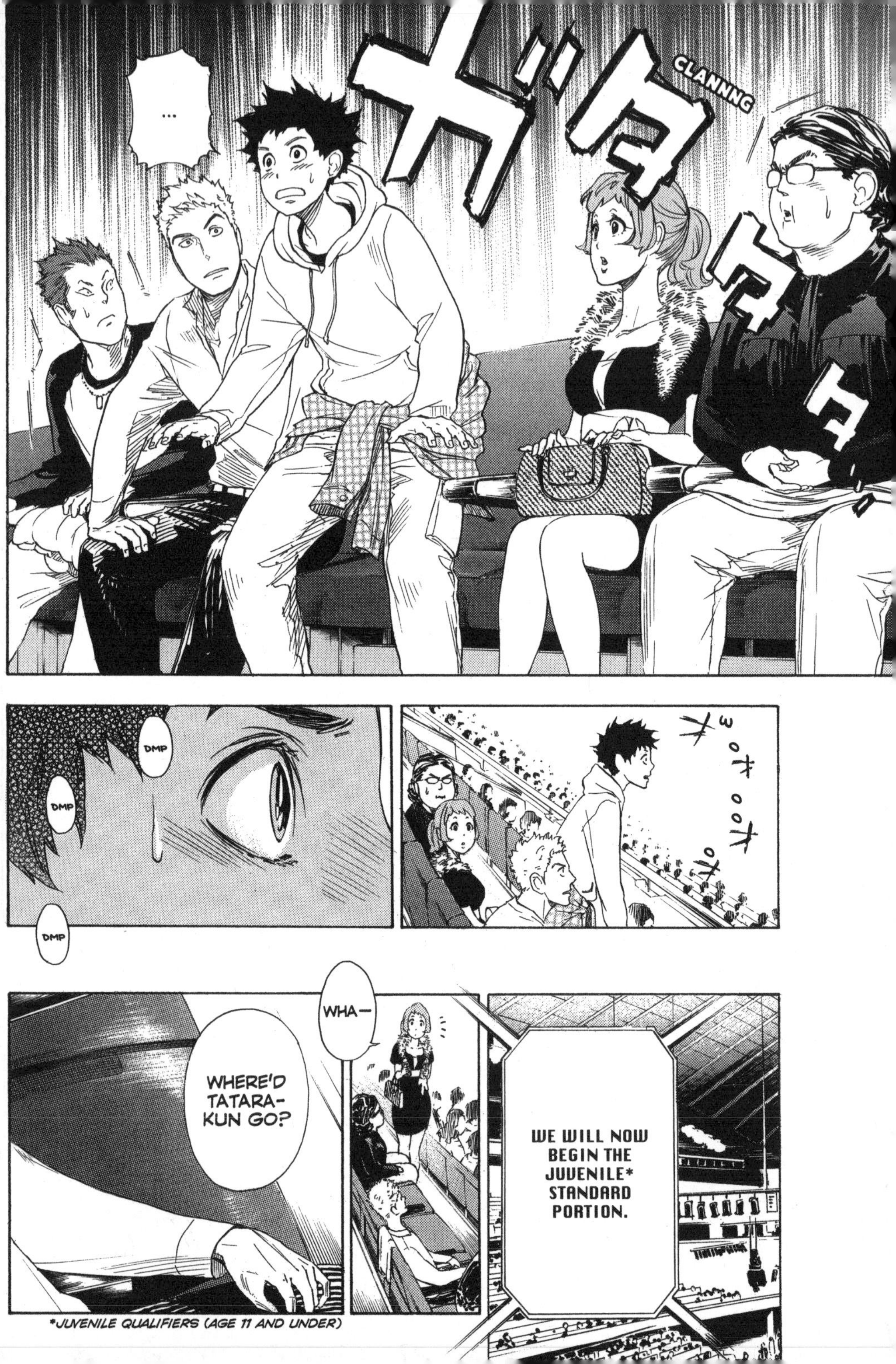
CLANNNG
...
DMP
DMP
DMP
WE WILL NOW BEGIN THE JUVENILE* STANDARD PORTION.
WHA—
WHERE'D TATARA-KUN GO?
*JUVENILE QUALIFIERS (AGE 11 AND UNDER)

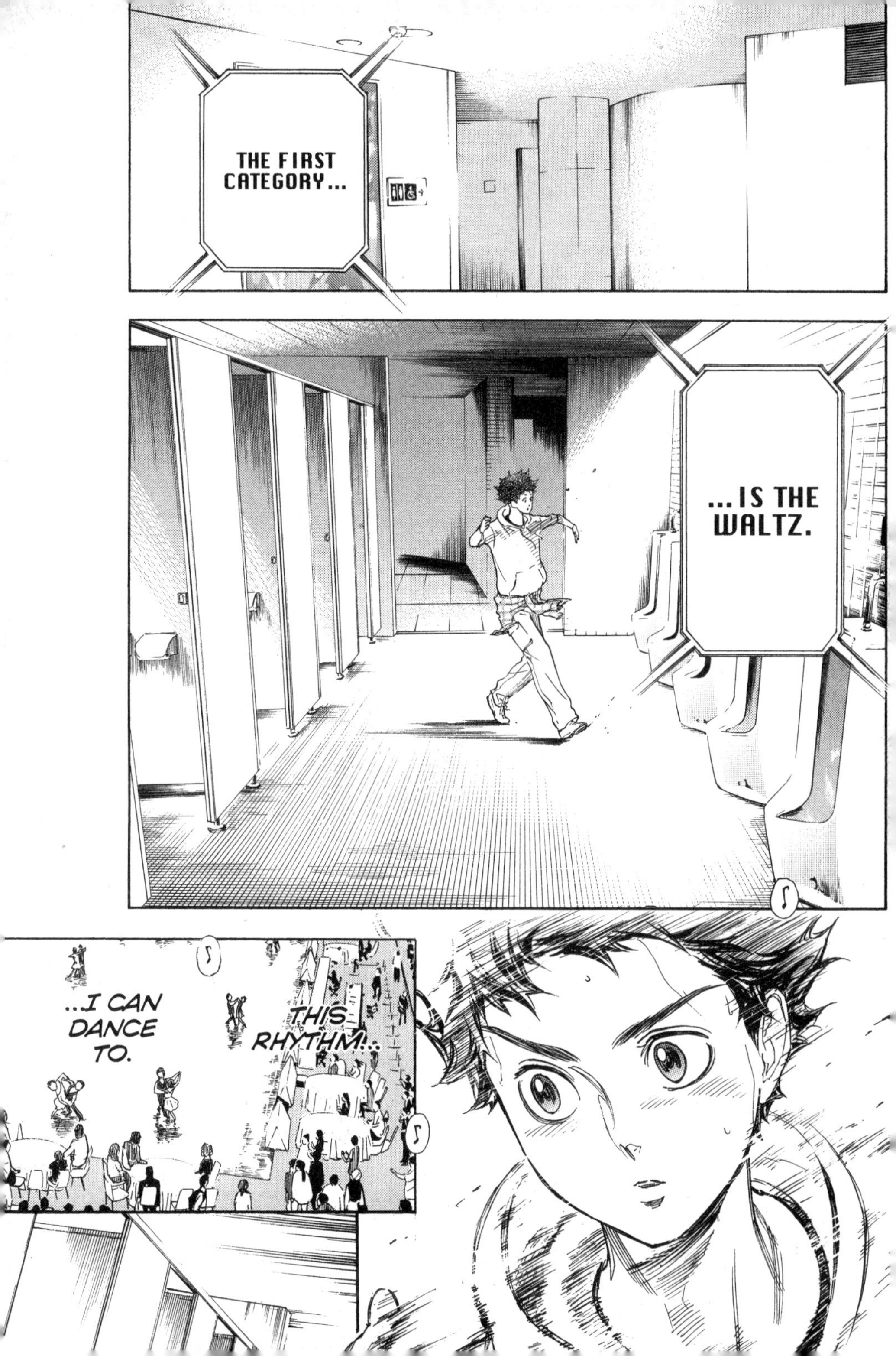
THE FIRST CATEGORY...
...IS THE WALTZ.
THIS RHYTHM...
...I CAN DANCE TO.

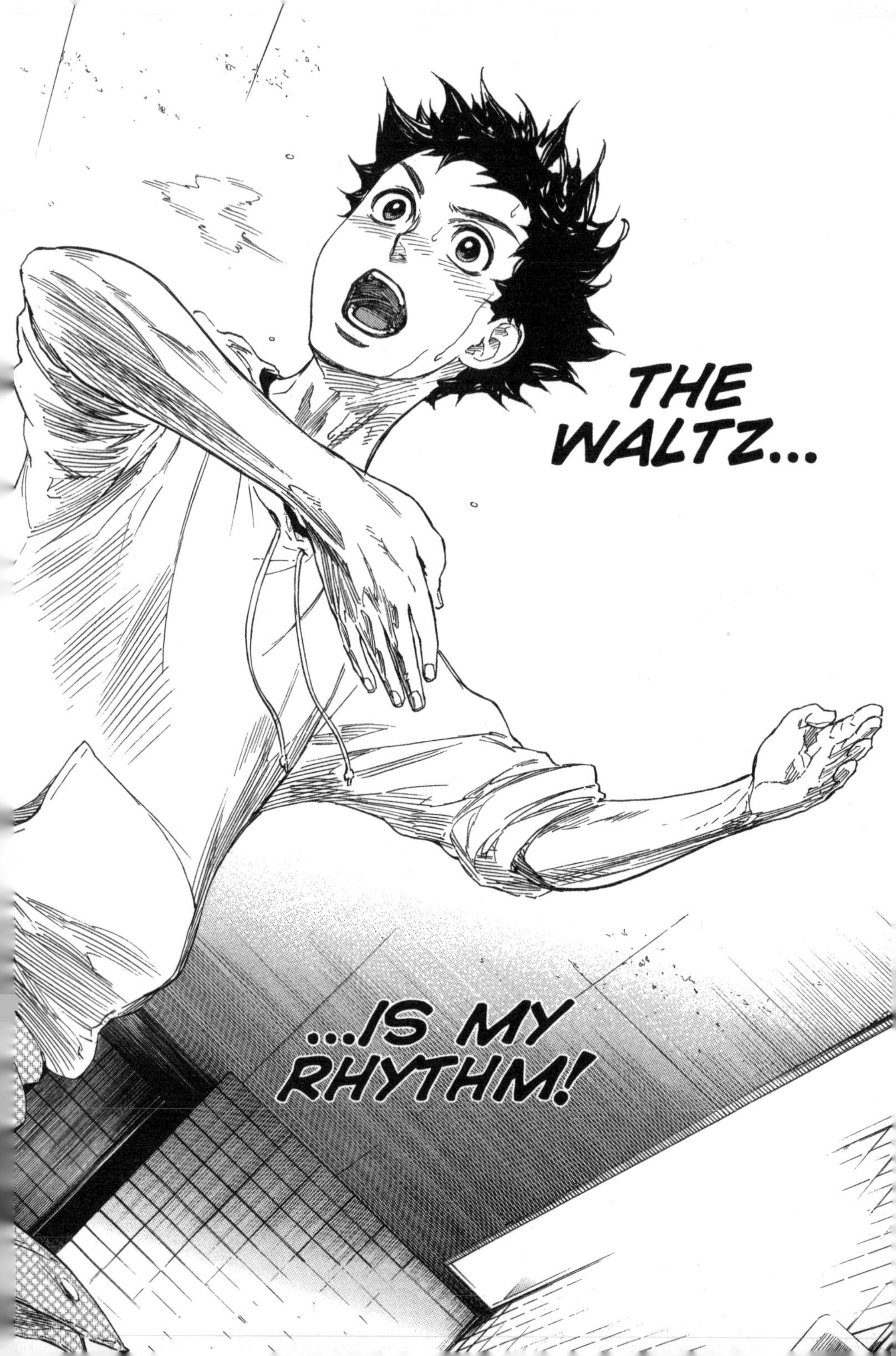
THE WALTZ...
...IS MY RHYTHM!

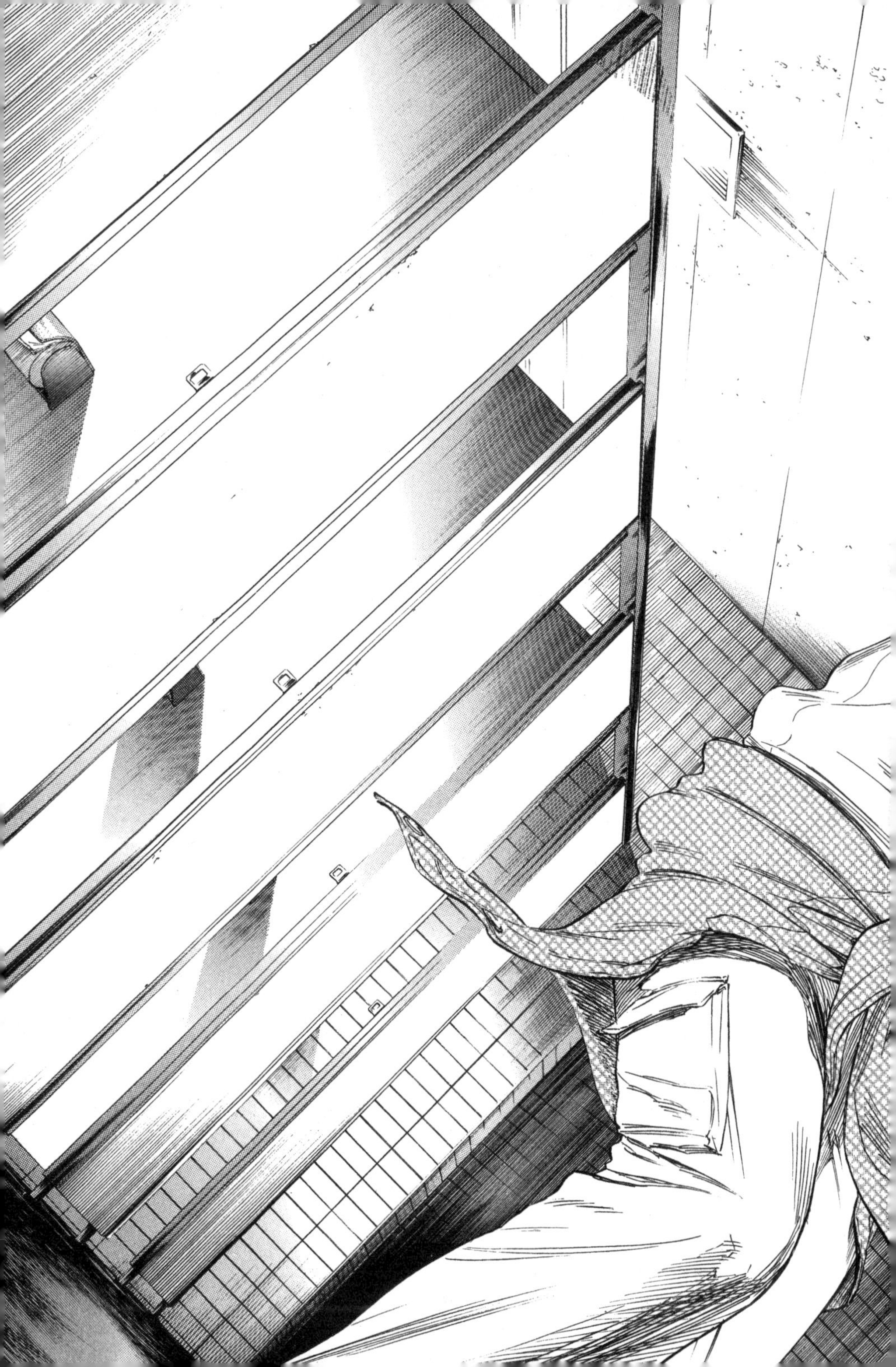

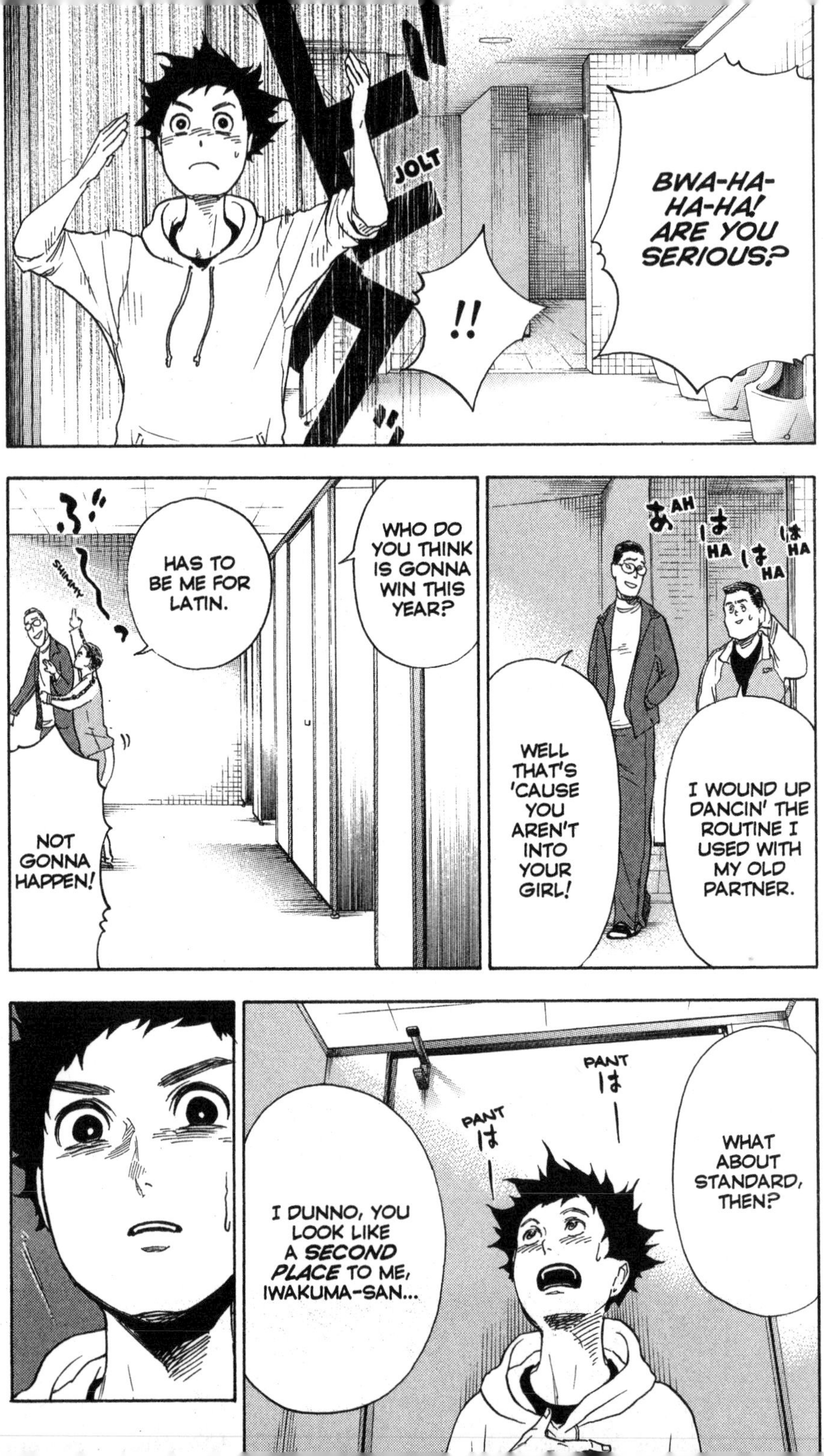

BWA-HA-HA-HA! ARE YOU SERIOUS?
JOLT
!!
あ AH
は HA
は HA
は HA
I WOUND UP DANCIN' THE ROUTINE I USED WITH MY OLD PARTNER.
WELL THAT'S 'CAUSE YOU AREN'T INTO YOUR GIRL!
WHO DO YOU THINK IS GONNA WIN THIS YEAR?
HAS TO BE ME FOR LATIN.
SHIMMY
NOT GONNA HAPPEN!
WHAT ABOUT STANDARD, THEN?
PANT
は ー
PANT
は ー
I DUNNO, YOU LOOK LIKE A *SECOND PLACE* TO ME, IWAKUMA-SAN...

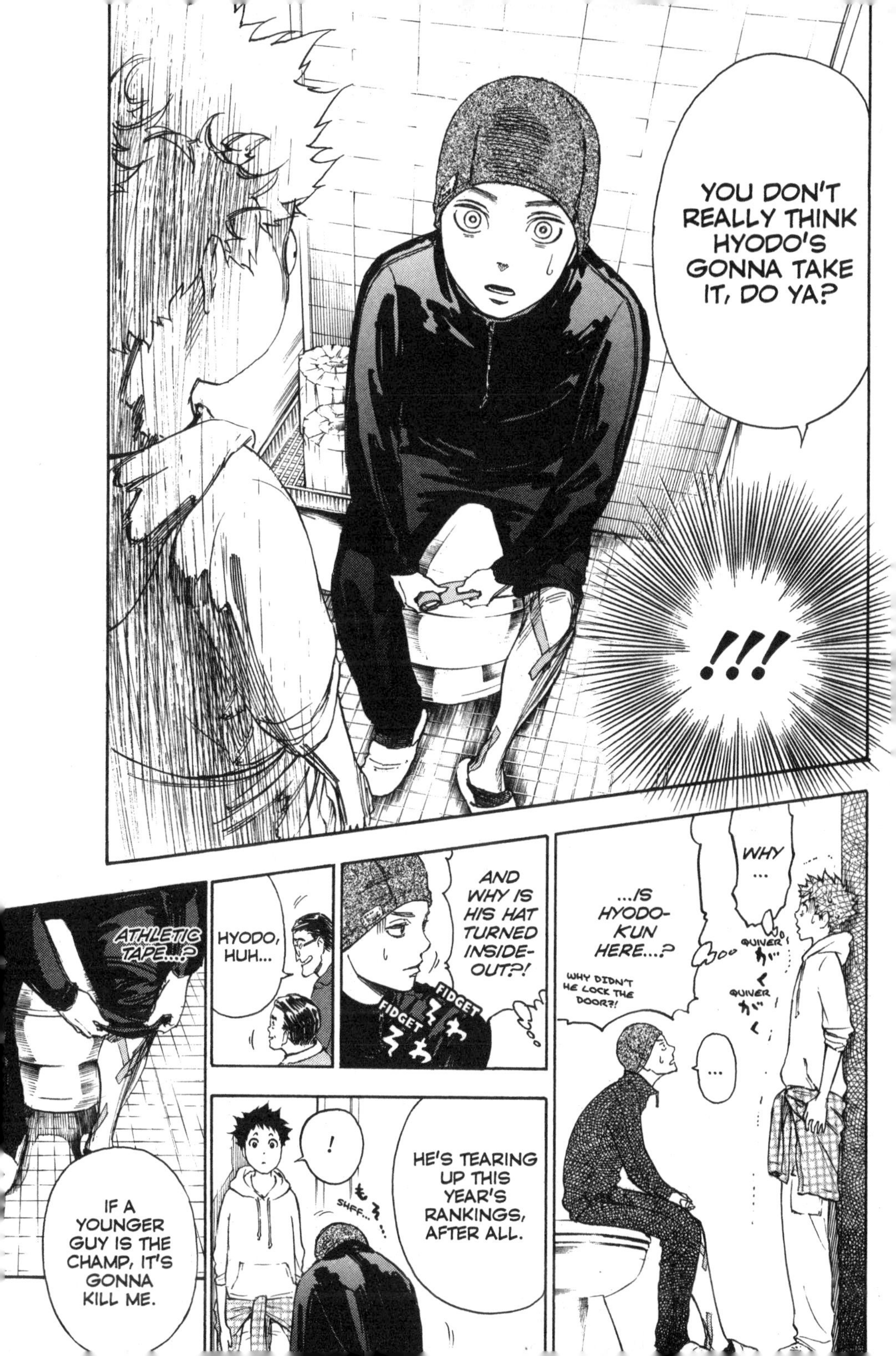
YOU DON'T REALLY THINK HYODO'S GONNA TAKE IT, DO YA?
!!!
WHY ...
...IS HYODO-KUN HERE...?
WHY DIDN'T HE LOCK THE DOOR?!
QUIVER
QUIVER
...
AND WHY IS HIS HAT TURNED INSIDE-OUT?!
FIDGET
FIDGET
HYODO, HUH...
ATHLETIC TAPE...?
!
SHFF...
HE'S TEARING UP THIS YEAR'S RANKINGS, AFTER ALL.
IF A YOUNGER GUY IS THE CHAMP, IT'S GONNA KILL ME.

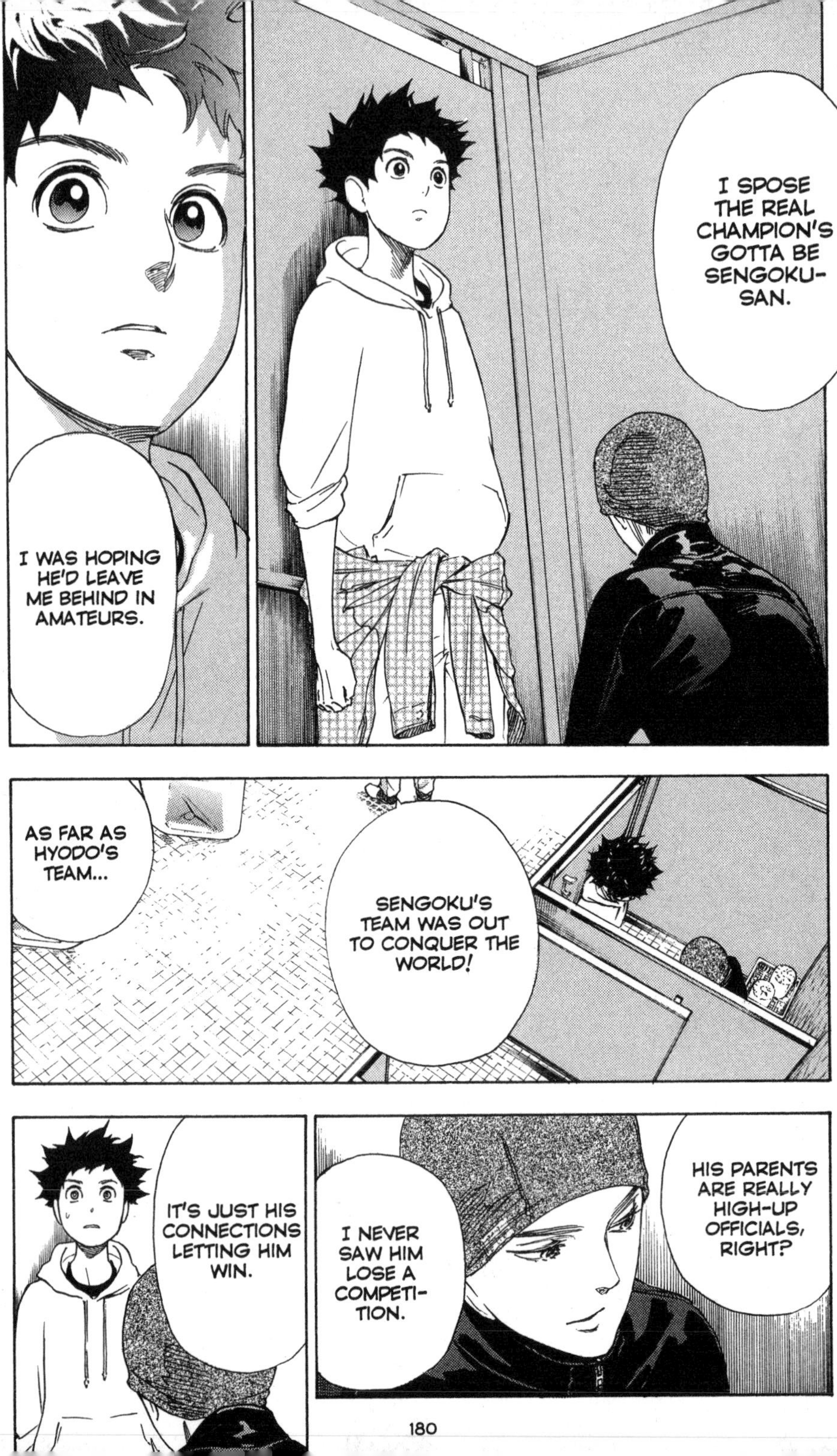
I SPOSE THE REAL CHAMPION'S GOTTA BE SENGOKU-SAN.
I WAS HOPING HE'D LEAVE ME BEHIND IN AMATEURS.
SENGOKU'S TEAM WAS OUT TO CONQUER THE WORLD!
AS FAR AS HYODO'S TEAM...
HIS PARENTS ARE REALLY HIGH-UP OFFICIALS, RIGHT?
I NEVER SAW HIM LOSE A COMPETITION.
IT'S JUST HIS CONNECTIONS LETTING HIM WIN.

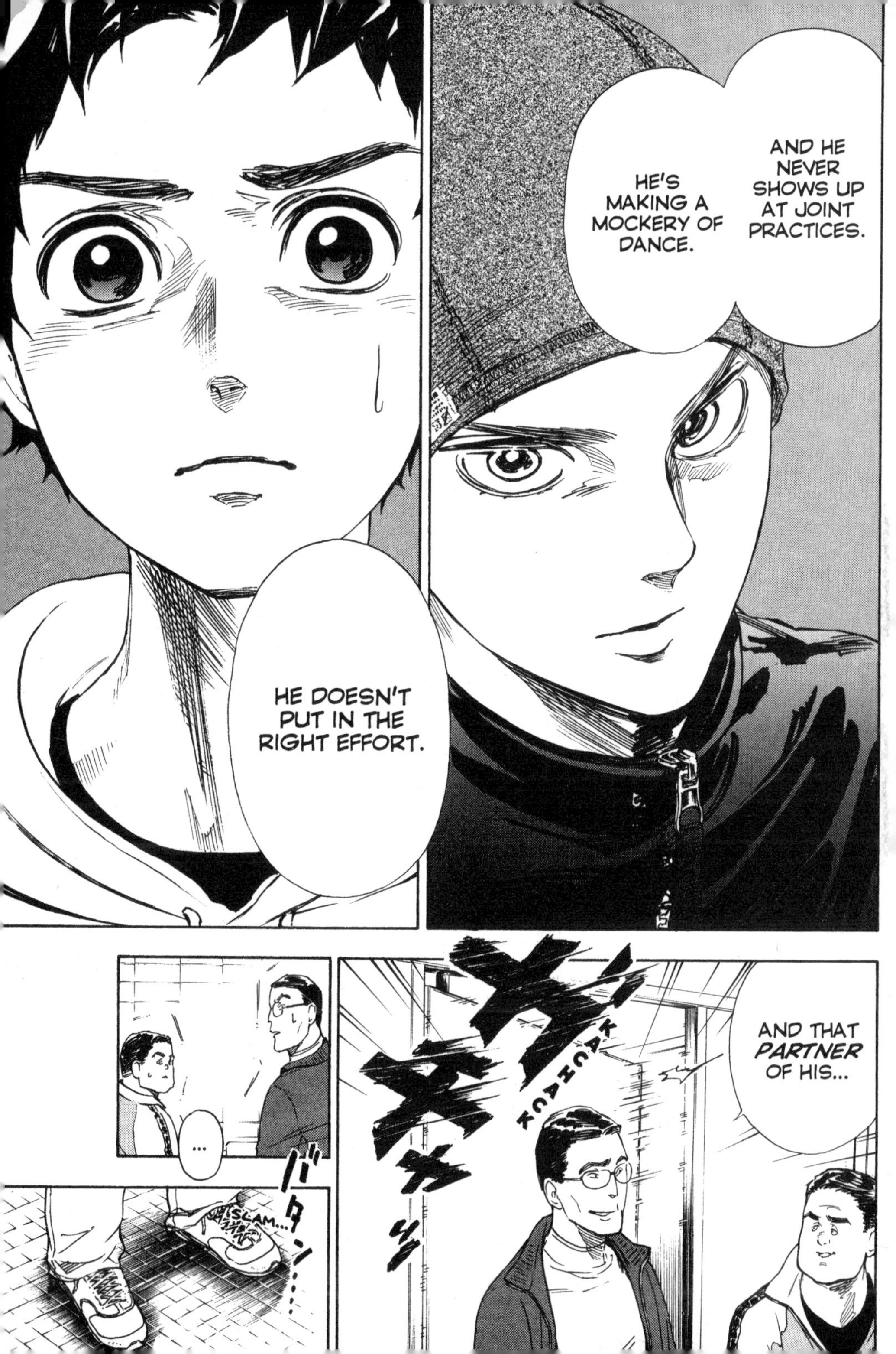
AND HE NEVER SHOWS UP AT JOINT PRACTICES.
HE'S MAKING A MOCKERY OF DANCE.
HE DOESN'T PUT IN THE RIGHT EFFORT.
AND THAT *PARTNER* OF HIS...
KACHACK
...
SLAM...

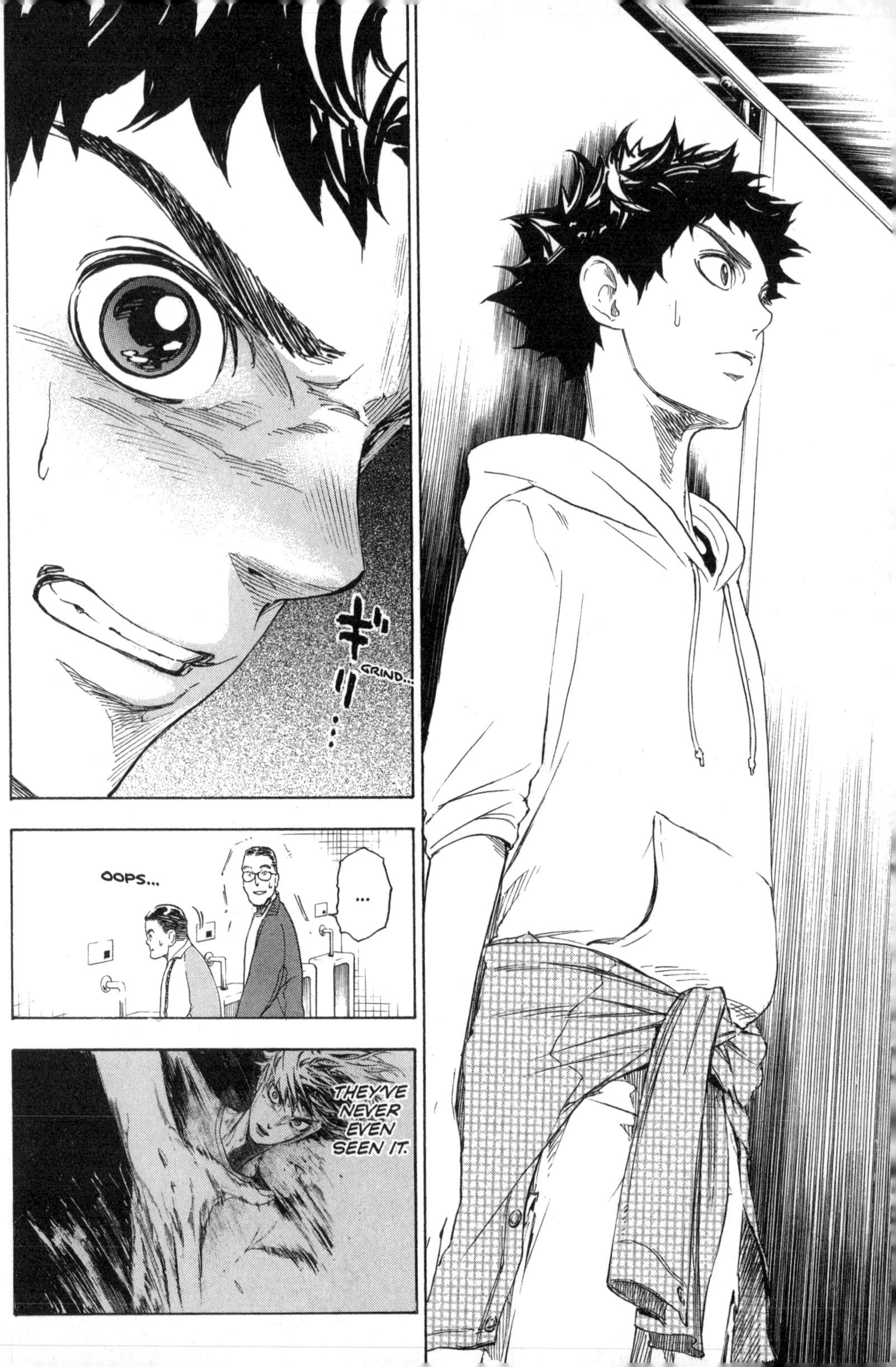
ギリ…
GRIND...
...
OOPS...
THEY'VE NEVER EVEN SEEN IT.

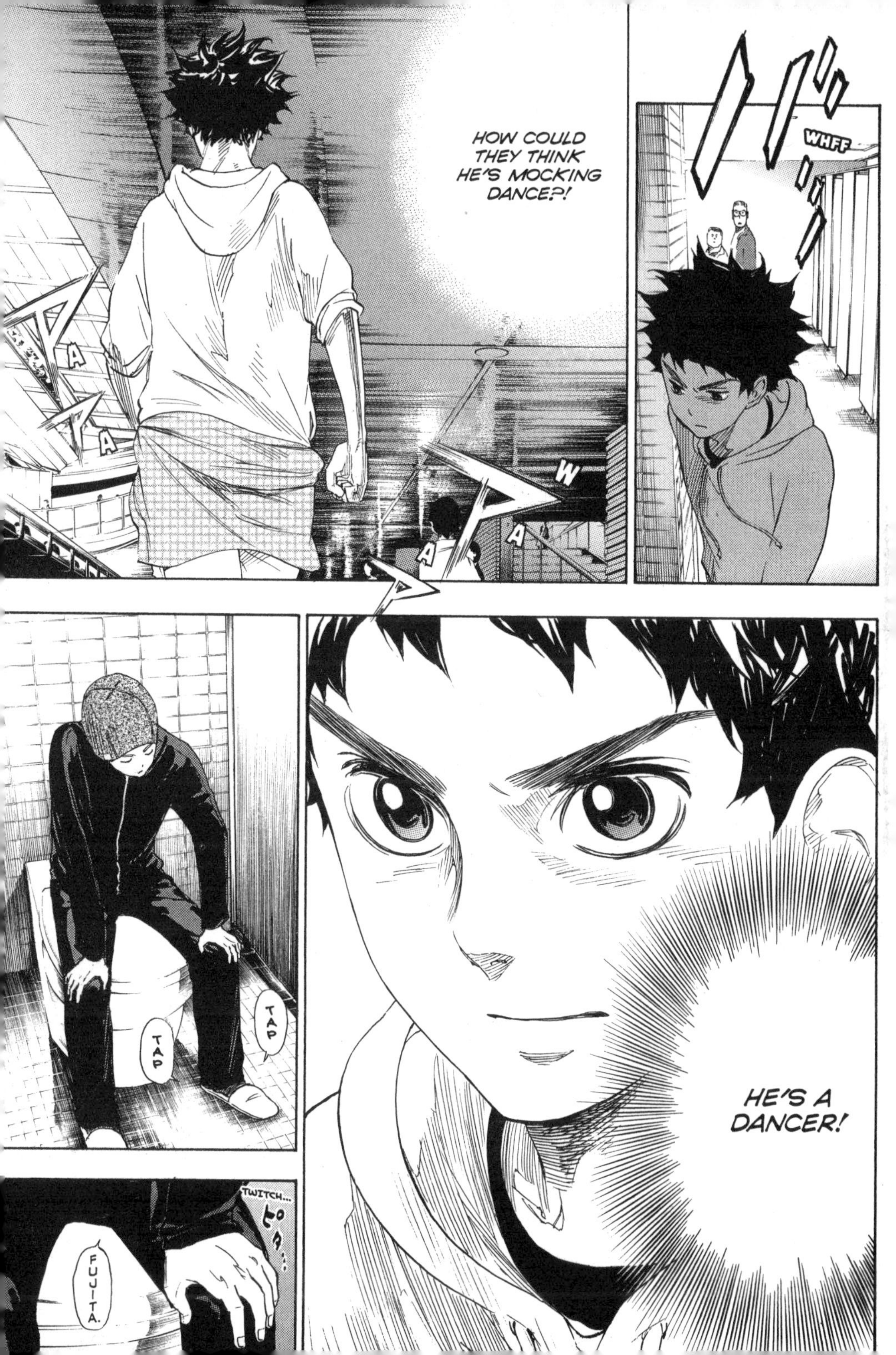
WHFF
HOW COULD THEY THINK HE'S MOCKING DANCE?!
A
A
W
A
A
HE'S A DANCER!
TAP
TAP
TWITCH...
FUJITA.

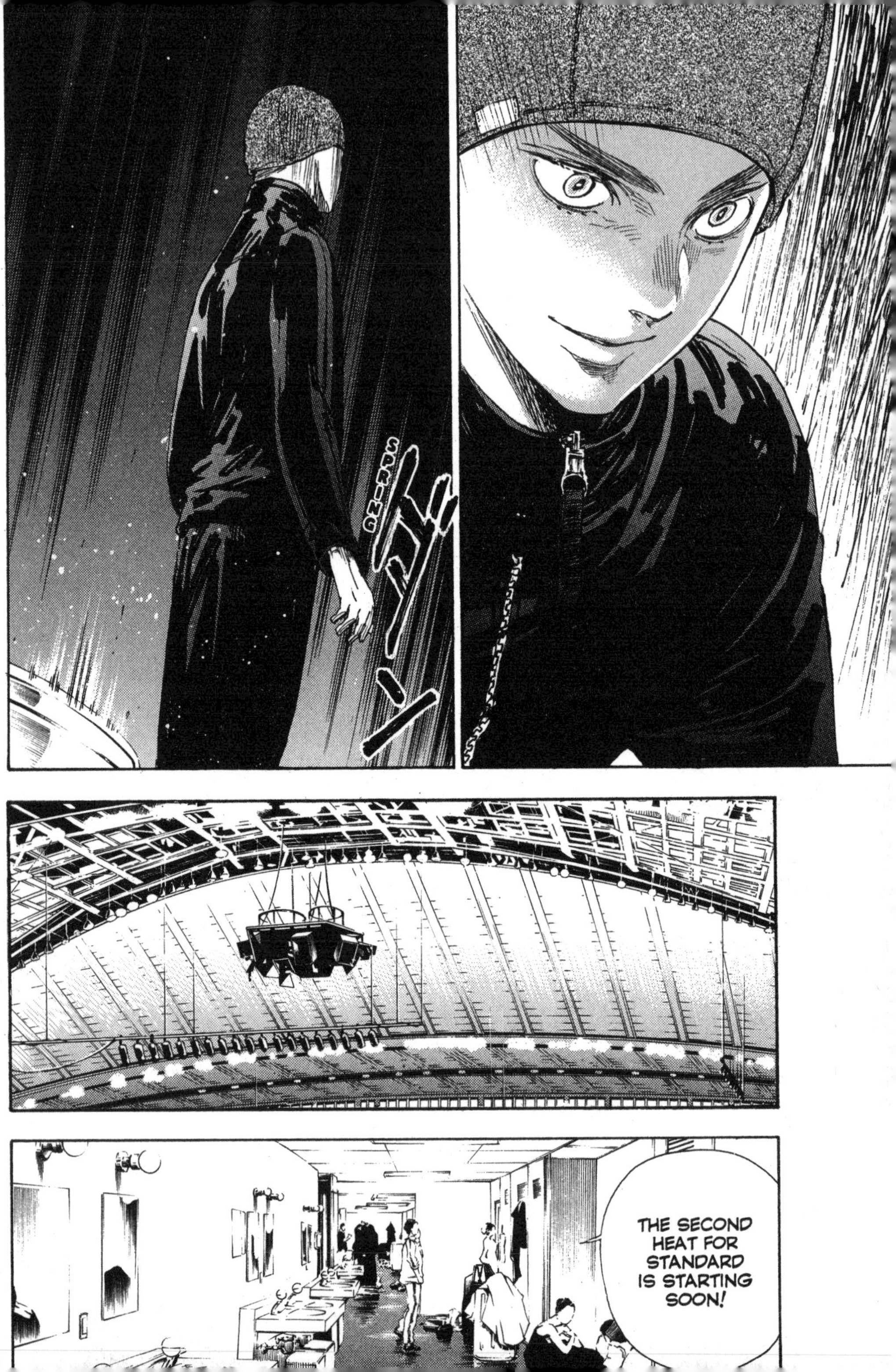
SPRING
THE SECOND HEAT FOR STANDARD IS STARTING SOON!

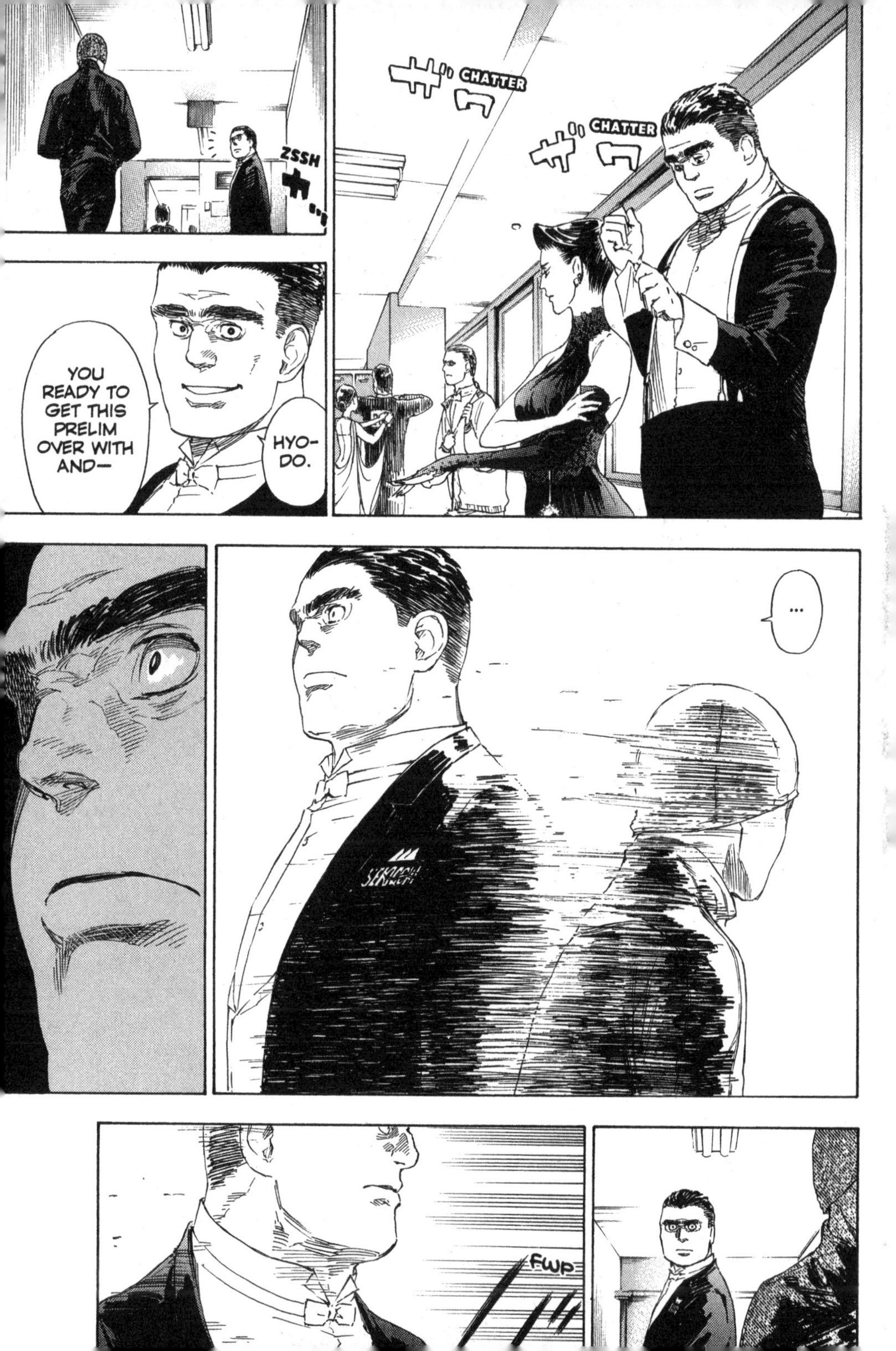
CHATTER
CHATTER
ZSSH
HYO-DO.
YOU READY TO GET THIS PRELIM OVER WITH AND—
...
FWP

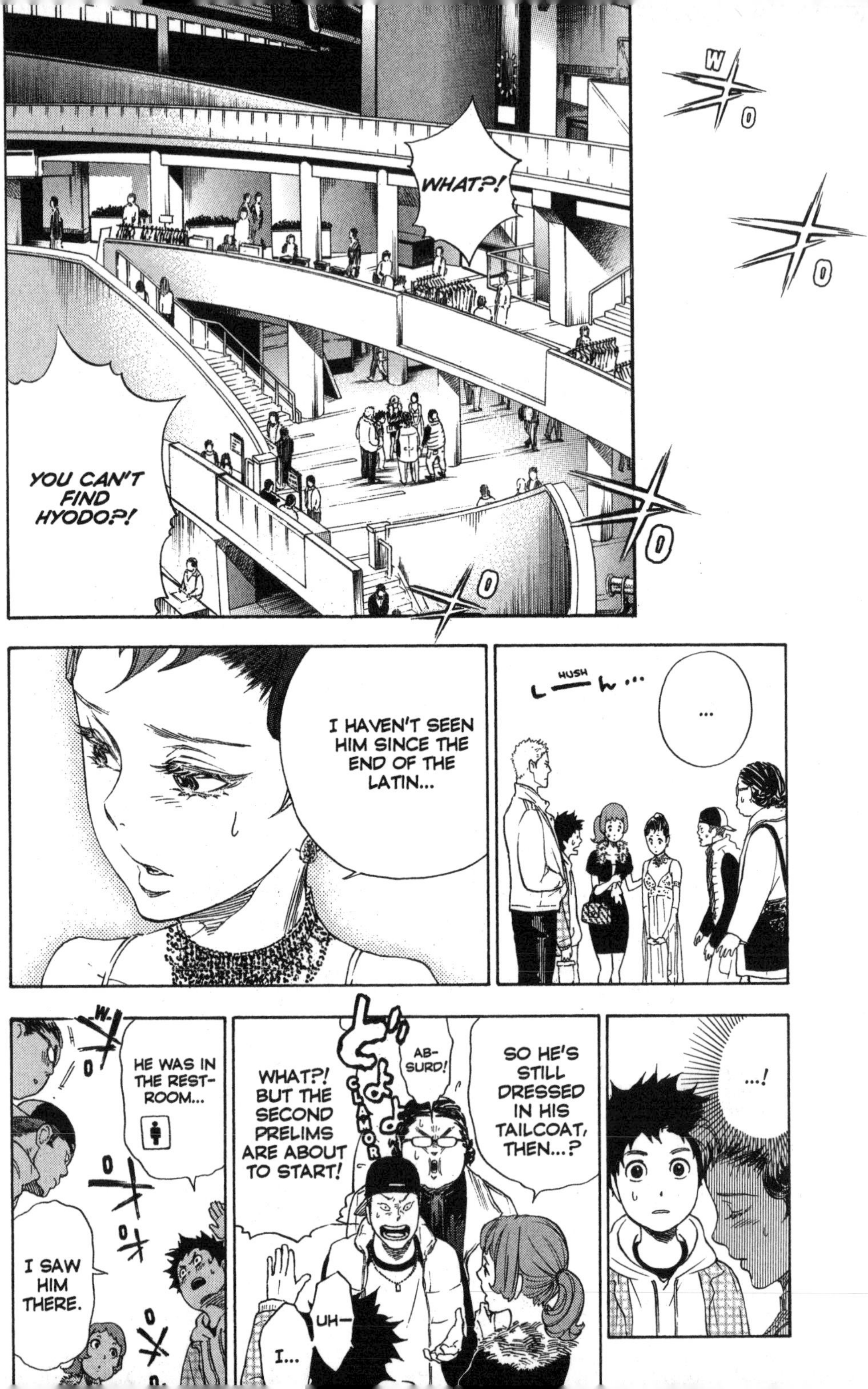
W
O
O
WHAT?!
O
O
YOU CAN'T FIND HYODO?!
HUSH
...
I HAVEN'T SEEN HIM SINCE THE END OF THE LATIN...
...!
SO HE'S STILL DRESSED IN HIS TAILCOAT, THEN...?
AB-SURD!
CLAMOR
WHAT?! BUT THE SECOND PRELIMS ARE ABOUT TO START!
UH—
I...
W-
HE WAS IN THE REST-ROOM...
O
I SAW HIM THERE.

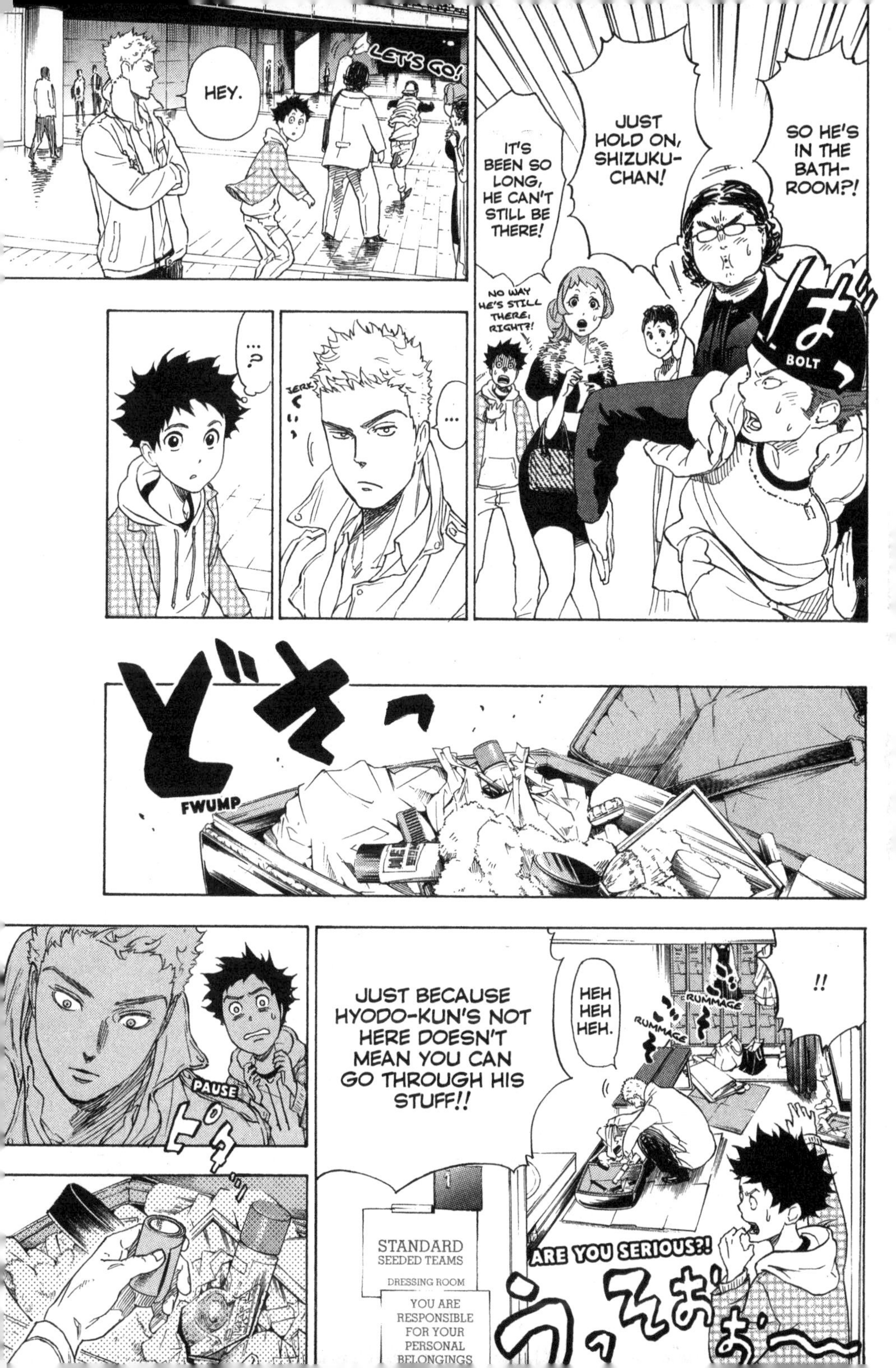
SO HE'S IN THE BATH-ROOM?!
JUST HOLD ON, SHIZUKU-CHAN!
IT'S BEEN SO LONG, HE CAN'T STILL BE THERE!
NO WAY HE'S STILL THERE, RIGHT?!
BOLT
LET'S GO!
HEY.
JERK
...
...?
FWUMP
JUST BECAUSE HYODO-KUN'S NOT HERE DOESN'T MEAN YOU CAN GO THROUGH HIS STUFF!!
!!
RUMMAGE
RUMMAGE
HEH HEH HEH.
STANDARD
SEEDED TEAMS
DRESSING ROOM
YOU ARE RESPONSIBLE FOR YOUR PERSONAL BELONGINGS
ARE YOU SERIOUS?!
PAUSE

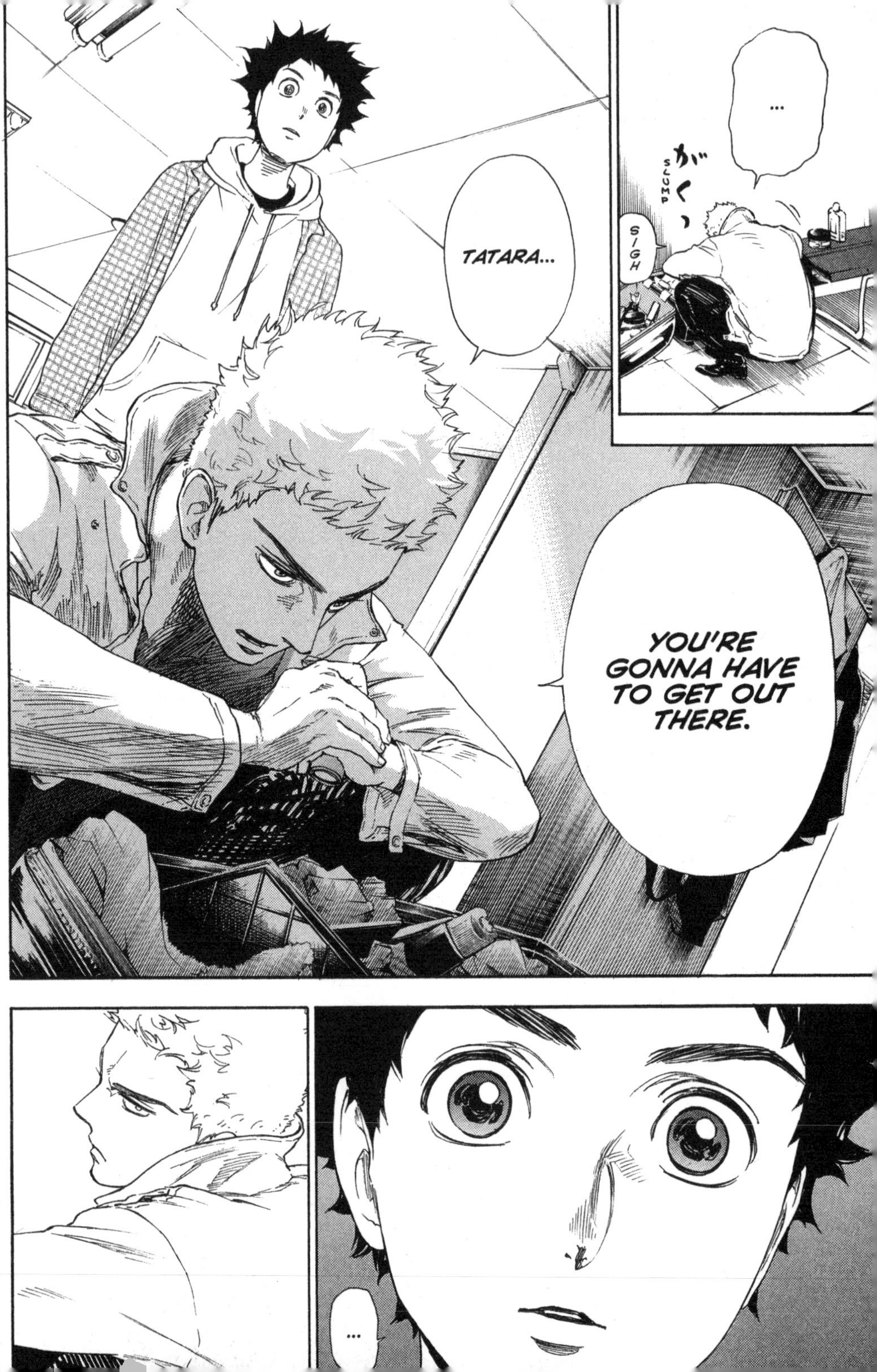
...
SLUMP
SIGH
TATARA...
YOU'RE GONNA HAVE TO GET OUT THERE.
...

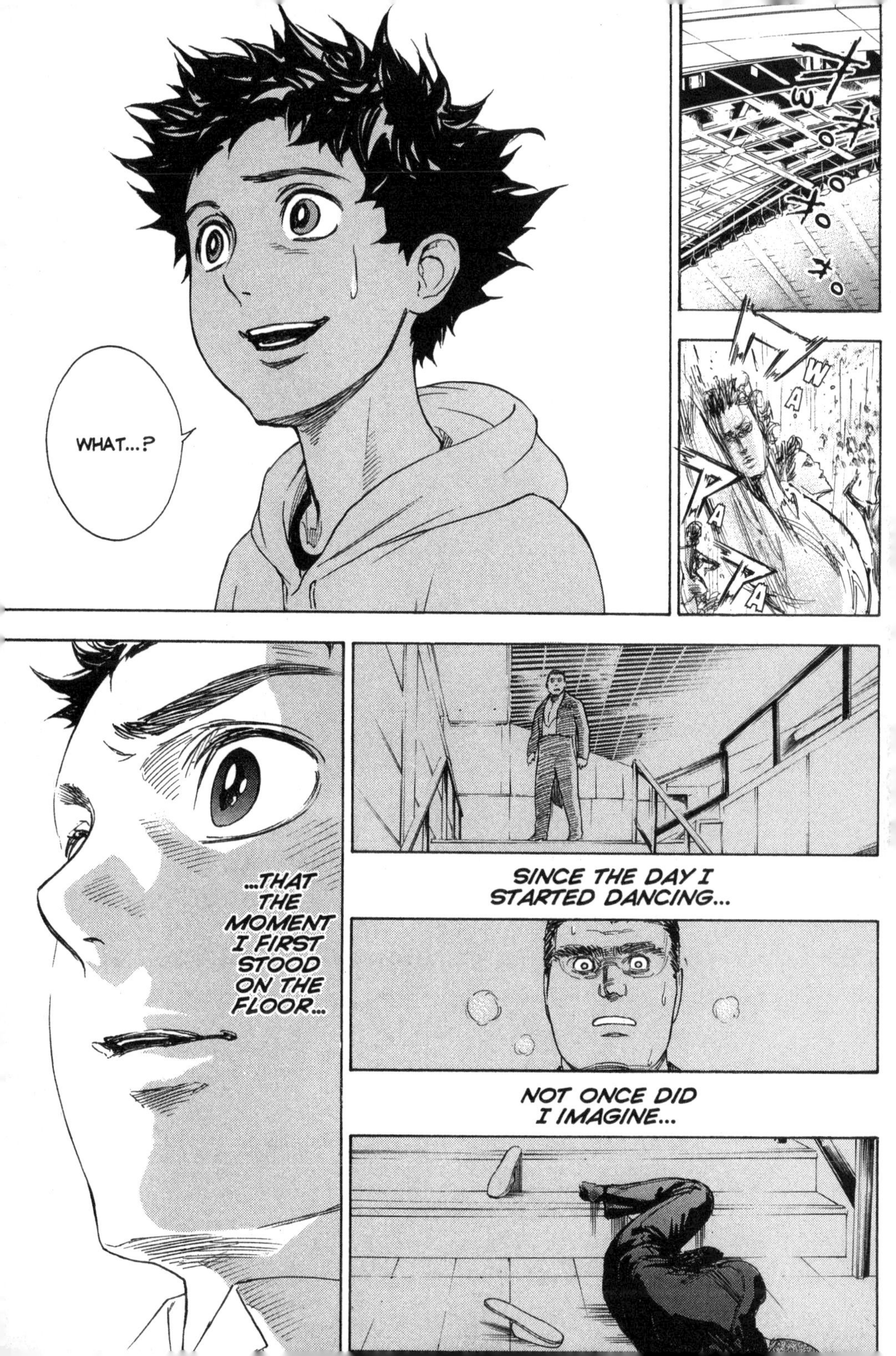
WA
WHAT...?
SINCE THE DAY I STARTED DANCING...
NOT ONCE DID I IMAGINE...
...THAT THE MOMENT I FIRST STOOD ON THE FLOOR...

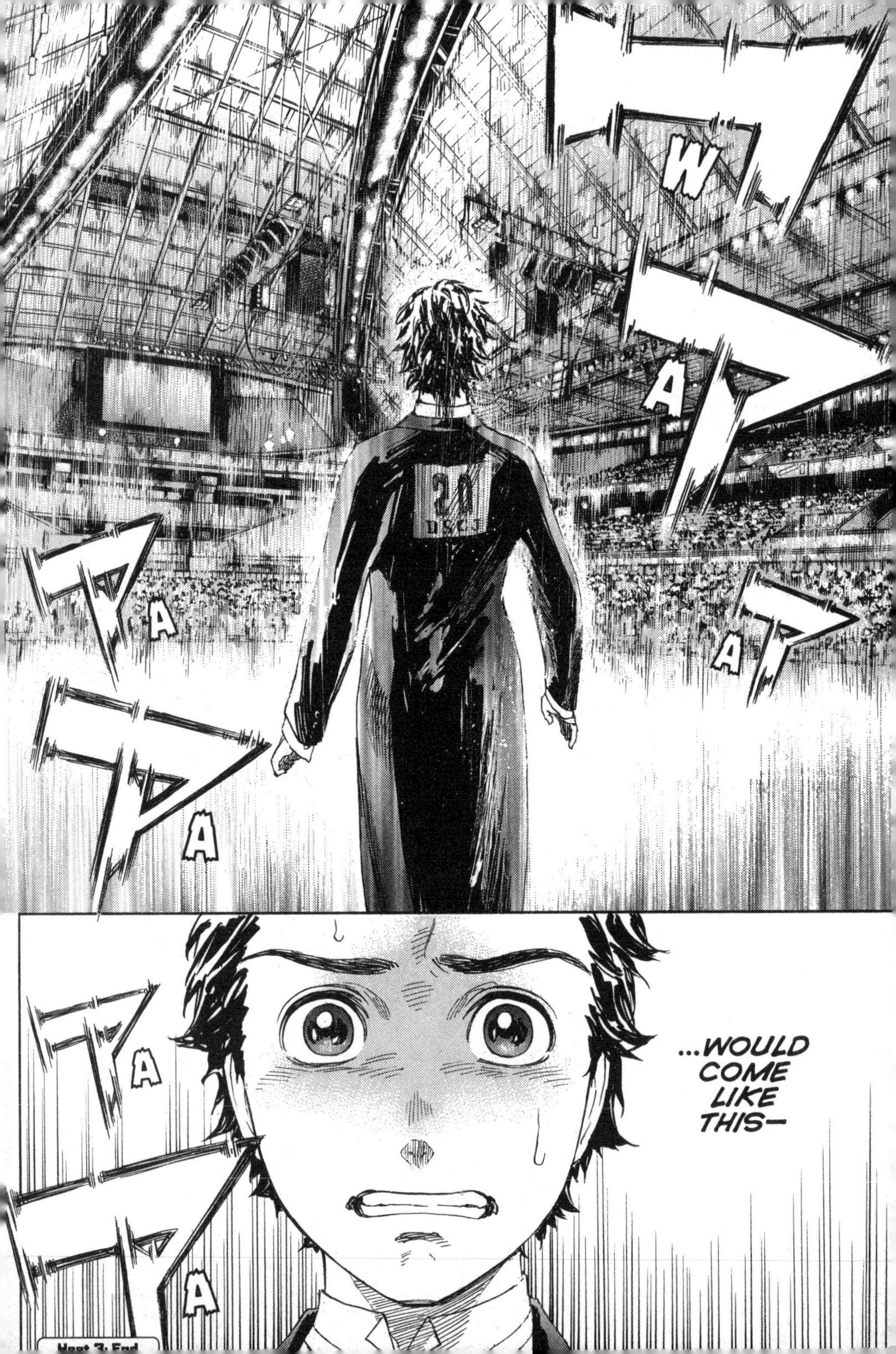
W
A
A
A
A
...WOULD COME LIKE THIS—
A
A
Heat 3: End

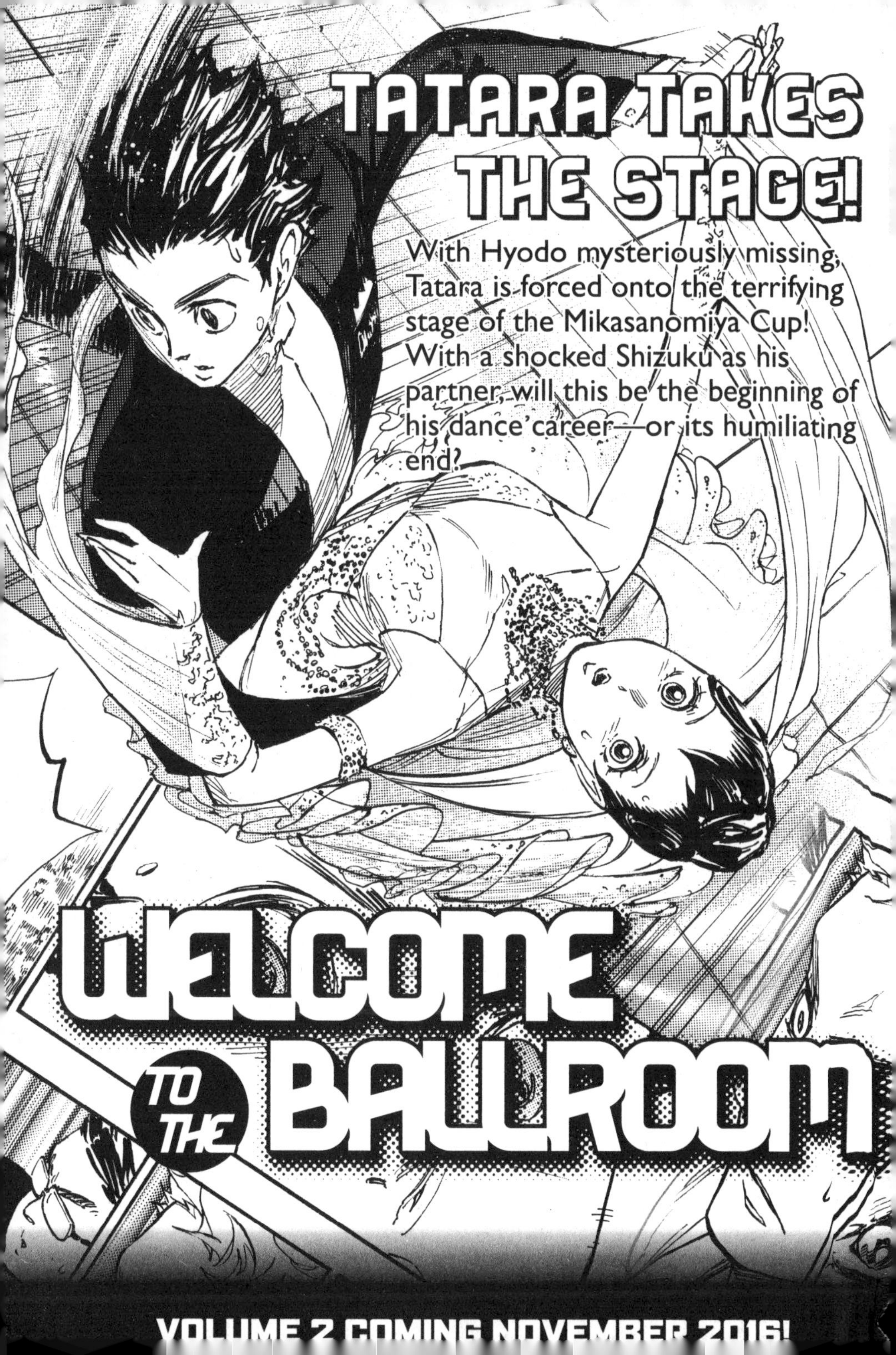
TATARA TAKES THE STAGE!
With Hyodo mysteriously missing, Tatara is forced onto the terrifying stage of the Mikasanomiya Cup! With a shocked Shizuku as his partner, will this be the beginning of his dance career—or its humiliating end?
WELCOME TO THE BALLROOM
VOLUME 2 COMING NOVEMBER 2016!

Welcome to the Ballroom volume 1 is a work of fiction. Names, characters, places, and incidents are the products of the author's imagination or are used fictitiously. Any resemblance to actual events, locales, or persons, living or dead, is entirely coincidental.

A Kodansha Comics Trade Paperback Original.

Welcome to the Ballroom volume 1 copyright © 2012 Tomo Takeuchi, English translation copyright ©2016 Tomo Takeuchi

All rights reserved.

Published in the United States by Kodansha Comics, an imprint of Kodansha USA Publishing, LLC, New York.

Publication rights for this English edition arranged through Kodansha Ltd., Tokyo.

First published in Japan in 2012 by Kodansha Ltd., Tokyo, as Ballroom e Yōkoso volume 1.

ISBN 978-1-63236-376-3

Printed in the United States of America.

www.kodanshacomics.com

9 8 7 6 5 4 3 2 1

Translation: Karen McGillicuddy
Lettering: Brndn Blakeslee
Editing: Paul Starr

Kodansha Comics edition cover design: Phil Balsman